Building Smart Home Automation Solutions with Home Assistant

Configure, integrate, and manage hardware and software systems to automate your home

Marco Carvalho

BIRMINGHAM—MUMBAI

Building Smart Home Automation Solutions
with Home Assistant

Group Product Manager: Preet Ahuja

Publishing Product Manager: Surbhi Suman

Senior Content Development Editor: Adrija Mitra

Technical Editor: Arjun Varma

Copy Editor: Safis Editing

Project Coordinator: Ashwin Kharwa

Proofreader: Safis Editing

Indexer: Pratik Shirodkar

Production Designer: Nilesh Mohite

Marketing Coordinator: Rohan Dobhal

First published: September 2023

Production reference: 1170823

Published by Packt Publishing Ltd.

Grosvenor House

11 St Paul's Square

Birmingham

B3 1RB, UK.

ISBN 978-1-80181-529-1

www.packtpub.com

Contributors

About the author

Marco Carvalho is an experienced home automation hobbyist engineer, electrical engineer, and technician. Pursuing his passion for electronics and embedded systems, he created an embedded home automation task scheduler using X10 Home Automation devices in 2006. Nowadays, he uses wireless electronic devices and the Home Assistant software to build different smart home automation applications.

As an MSc in Computer Science, Marco has worked with several well-known companies such as IBM, Jabil, Phillips, and Hexagon where he extended his support in development and manufacturing of electronic products. At the time of this publication, he is the Director of Engineering for Apex Microtechnology, where he is involved in the development of high power, high precision analog components.

I want to thank Paulus Schoutsen, who created Home Assistant, this amazing software used to automate my home. Also, thanks to Theo Arends, who created Tasmota, another great embedded IoT software.

Being a self-learning person, most of my recent knowledge about Home Assistant and related applications came mainly from YouTube videos. They mostly are very well produced by YouTubers such as Kiril Peyanski, who is one of the reviewers of this book. Being a digital content creator is not an easy task so I wish all my gratitude to the home automation YouTubers. Thank you.

Many thanks to the Home Assistant communities existent around the world. They have helped many hobbyists like me to solve their problems, share their points of view, and get advice. One special community for me is Home Assistant Brasil on Telegram. Thanks to all members of this nice community.

I'd like to thank Packt for this great opportunity to share my knowledge with the world through the publication of this book. I'm very grateful in particular for the Packt team who supported me along the writing process, including Nayana John, Surbhi Suman, Ashwin Kharwa, Adrija Mitra, and Arjun Verma.

I want to thank all those close to me that supported me during the process of writing this book, including some close friends and my family. Also, I'd like to thank other friends that indirectly supported me throughout my journey of learning the Home Automation base concepts. This includes my team at DIPV - Devex and my classmates (vagabundos-l) at UFMG. I'm also thankful to have had ETEFMC in my life. My personality and electronics knowledge were solidified there. Many thanks to all people at this school and friends from that time.

I would like to express a sincere tribute to my wife acknowledging her support and dedication to our family throughout the time I devoted to writing this book. Your love, understanding, and kindness have been instrumental in my journey, and I am forever grateful. I am sure that the future holds great promise and happiness for us. Thank you for always standing by my side, through every moment. Love you.

About the reviewers

Kiril Peyanski is an IT professional with over 20 years of experience in the technology industry. With a strong background in software development, cybersecurity, and system administration, Kiril has become a recognized figure in the field. He shares his expertise through his YouTube channel @ *KPeyanski* and his popular blog, where he provides insightful reviews, tutorials, and in-depth analyses of the latest smart home tech trends. Kiril's ability to break down complex concepts into accessible and engaging content has earned him a dedicated following of tech enthusiasts and professionals alike. His passion for technology and commitment to empowering others with knowledge make him an invaluable resource in the digital world.

I would like to express my heartfelt gratitude to my wife, my daughter, and my baby son for their support and understanding during the process of producing this book and my work. Their love and encouragement have been instrumental in keeping me motivated. I am also deeply grateful to my parents for instilling in me a curiosity for technology and nurturing my passion throughout my life.

Dheerendra Panwar is a seasoned professional in the field of IoT with over ten years of experience. He earned his master's degree in embedded electrical and computer systems from San Francisco State University, further fortifying his expertise in the domain. Throughout his career, he has contributed significantly to various IoT projects, ranging from manufacturing and smart cities to the retail and energy sectors. Having worked in both large organizations and startups, he possesses a comprehensive understanding of the intricacies of IoT/edge technologies and their practical applications.

Grateful for the unwavering support from my family, friends, and colleagues on my IoT journey. Their belief in my abilities inspires me. Collaborating with brilliant minds and passionate teams pushing IoT boundaries has been truly inspiring. Thanks to my mentors and industry experts for guiding my career in IoT and technology. Lastly, I appreciate all individuals advancing the field, shaping a connected world powered by IoT and AI technologies.

Table of Contents

Part 2: Install, Create, and Hack Sensors and Actuators

3

Hands-On Project 1 – Creating Your Own Sensor   59

4

Hacking a Commercial Actuator to Work with Home Assistant   89

Part 3: Automations, Customizations, and Integrations Using Home Assistant

5

Creating Automations Using Home Assistant   121

6

Doing More Using Integrations and Customizations   147

Part 4: Expanding Home Assistant's Capabilities

7

Extending Home Automation Capabilities Using Add-ons   185

8

Installing and Setting Up Home Assistant Container   211

Part 5: Learn by Doing and Future Trends

9

Hands-On Project 2 – Creating an LED Strip Controller and Adding It to Home Assistant   235

Preface

Home Automation has been a popular subject for numerous years and is progressively growing in fascination, primarily due to the active involvement and introduction of innovative product launchings by prominent market leaders. In the middle of the huge amount of solutions and products available, you, as a Home Automation enthusiast, will have multiple questions. How can I start to automate my home? Can I build my own system? How can I manage it?

This book will help you to answer this and many other questions you have related to Home Automation. The central piece of the Home Automation technology discussed in this book is Home Assistant. This customizable software will allow you to understand how to connect all the dots of Home Automation technology by creating and managing your own system. Depending on your level of knowledge and skills, you could even be able to create your own electronic hardware devices and develop automations to control your day-to-day tasks.

In this book, I share all my knowledge learned and consolidated over more than 20 years of experience in this area dealing with Home Automation as a hobby activity. All the examples in the book are real and implemented in my home, so you can imagine that writing this book was a very pleasant adventure for me. I tried to provide as practical a guide as possible so you can implement the examples in a very straightforward approach according to your needs and interest.

This book will support you in creating your own ecosystem to automate your home using Home Assistant software. It will explain the components of a Home Automation system and how to create, hack, and configure them to operate seamlessly. You'll learn how to set up Home Assistant on Raspberry Pi to work as a Home Automation server. Using practical examples and three hands-on projects, you'll create and install your own IoT sensors and actuators based on ESP32/ESP8266 and set up real-life automation use cases. Other software tools, such as Node-RED, InfluxDB, and Grafana, will help you to manage, present, and use data collected from your in-house devices. Finally, you'll gain insights into new technologies and trends in the Home Automation space to help you continue with your learning journey.

As the author of this book, I want to clarify that the content included within the pages of this book represents a careful selection of relevant information based on my personal experiences. It is important to note that not all content pertaining to the Home Automation and Home Assistant subject could be covered comprehensively. Nevertheless, I have striven to provide valuable insights and perspectives that I believe will be beneficial to you.

After reading this book, you'll be able to build your own creative Home Automation IoT- based system using different hardware and software technologies.

Who this book is for

This book was written for students and professionals in the electronics, systems engineering, computer software, and programming areas. This book is also for engineers, technicians, teachers, and others who want to be updated about the different systems and technologies that exist related to Home Automation. All these professionals and also including the **Do It Yourself** (**DIY**) community composed of addicted and enthusiastic people passionate about the Home Automation subject will find this a practical guide of real examples to implement in their homes.

Prior knowledge of installing and configuring software in hardware devices, working with Raspberry Pi, creating hardware prototypes, and software programming will be beneficial for using this book.

What this book covers

Chapter 1, Understanding Home Automation Systems, will introduce the Home Automation system concept, giving an overview of it along the years, including architectures and configurations. The parts of the system will be listed and explained. The benefits of an automated home will be briefly discussed and an example of a real Home Automation system will be provided.

Chapter 2, Getting Started with Home Assistant, will explain Home Assistant in detail and a Home Automation server will be created using Raspberry Pi. A step-by-step guide will be presented to create and set up this server, which will be the first part of our Home Automation system.

Chapter 3, Hands-on Project 1 – Creating Your Own Sensor, will be where we create our first project in the book, which is a double measurement sensor, including motion and temperature sensors. Electronic parts will be connected and we will install and set up the sensor software to communicate with Home Assistant. We will also provide instructions on how to enclose and physically install the sensor in your home.

Chapter 4, Hacking a Commercial Actuator to Work with Home Assistant, involves a lot of hands-on work as well, where we will see how to get a commercial actuator and change (hack) its factory software by Tasmota. This will give us more control of the configuration and will provide the feature to be handled by Home Assistant seamlessly. We will explore how to install and configure this and other devices in the chapter.

Chapter 5, Creating Automations Using Home Assistant, will explain what an automation in Home Assistant is by providing the main idea and steps to create it. Using the sensors and actuators from previous chapters, we will create and test useful automation examples. Scripts and scenes will also be explored here.

Chapter 6, Doing More Using Integrations and Customizations, is where we will learn how to add more devices to Home Assistant using integrations. With more devices included in our system, we will learn about and create dashboards and populate them using cards. We will customize the dashboards using different approaches. We will also understand what else we can customize in Home Assistant.

Chapter 7, Extending Home Automation Capabilities Using Add-ons, is where the main IoT software add-ons will be presented and installed using Home Assistant. Brief examples will be provided on how to set up and use these applications. You will learn other ways to program, store, and present data from the devices installed in your home.

Chapter 8, Installing and Setting Up Home Assistant Container, is where you will learn how to safely back up your Home Automation server before moving to a new type of installation. Then, we will understand, install, and configure a Home Automation stack where a new Home Assistant installation approach is included.

Chapter 9, Hands-On Project 2 – Creating an LED Strip Controller and Adding It to Home Assistant, is the second hands-on project, which will teach you how to create an LED strip controller using a Wi-Fi microcontroller module and an LED strip light. We will learn how to deploy the software to control this project and provide fun examples to incorporate it into your home. We will also learn how to integrate and control this project in Home Assistant.

Chapter 10, Hands-On Project 3 – Creating a Five-Zone Temperature Logger for Your Home part of the knowledge learned in *Chapter 7*. We will go deep into the creation of a 5(five)-zone temperature logger using Bluetooth thermometers connected to a Wi-Fi microcontroller module, which provides data to the Home Automation server. This data is acquired, stored, and presented using IoT software tools. You will learn how to build and set up this system in your home.

Chapter 11, The Road Ahead in Home Automation Technologies, will present the possible new technologies and trends in the Home Automation area. A frequently asked questions section for Home Automation and Home Assistant will be provided. The chapter will inform you how to get insights and project ideas to automate your home. Links to internet resources will be presented.

To get the most out of this book

To better follow the content of the book, you should have some prior basic knowledge of electronic systems, including soldering and hardware assembly skills. You also should be familiar with software deployment and programming logic. The configuration and other home Assistant files are provided in YAML code.

To build your own minimum automation system using Home Assistant, besides the sensor and actuators that you can buy off the shelf in the market, you will need a **Single-Board Computer** (**SBC**) at least. The book uses Raspberry Pi 4 with 4 GB of RAM. Please check in the book what other hardware resources can be used.

The Home Assistant version used in the book varies since it started to be written in November 2022 when was installed the available version which was the **9.3**. Along the book, I updated the Home Assistant and now in August 2023 it is in the **2023.8.0**. Also the Tasmota version used when the book started to be written was the **12.3.1.3**. As I'm writing this part of the book, Tasmota is in its **13.0.0** version. All these changes in versions and releases could imply in differences in the menus, command sequences, button names, and screen names, from what is presented in the book. I tried to overcome this issue by providing different options to access configurations in Home Assistant and also present screenshots to make easier the navigation in the examples provided across the book. If the example sequence in some chapter is different from what you have in your current Home Assistant installation try to get the idea of what is being introduced in the example and guide yourself in the available options or seek for help about the related subject issue using the resources area in *Chapter 11*.

Software/hardware covered in the book	Operating system requirements
Raspberry Pi 4	**Home Assistant Operating System (HAOS)**
ESP8266, ESP32	Raspberry Pi OS, Docker, Home Assistant Container
Home Assistant, Node-RED, InfluxDB, Grafana, TasmoAdmin, Duck DNS, Tasmota, WLED	

When making changes to the electronics and installing the software, make sure you know what you are doing and follow the instructions in the book. In some situations, you will need to install software in plugs. Do not install them while connected to the outlet. There is an electric shock hazard. Do not install Sonoff actuators in outlets if you've never done it before. Call an electrician instead.

Install Home Assistant, Tasmota, and any other software installation mentioned in this book at your own risk. The author will not take any responsibility for any lost factory software not previously backed up before the installation of the software in this book.

If you are using the digital version of this book, we advise you to type the code yourself or access the code from the book's GitHub repository (a link is available in the next section). Doing so will help you avoid any potential errors related to the copying and pasting of code.

Download the example code files

You can download the example code files for this book from GitHub at `https://github.com/PacktPublishing/Building-Smart-Home-Automation-Solutions-with-Home-Assistant`. If there's an update to the code, it will be updated in the GitHub repository.

We also have other code bundles from our rich catalog of books and videos available at `https://github.com/PacktPublishing/`. Check them out!

Code in Action

The Code in Action videos for this book can be viewed at `https://bit.ly/3QGbKc7`

Conventions used

There are a number of text conventions used throughout this book.

`Code in text`: Indicates code words in text, database table names, folder names, filenames, file extensions, pathnames, dummy URLs, user input, and Twitter handles. Here is an example: "You can configure some attributes of the entities, such as `friendly_name`, to better serve your needs."

A block of code is set as follows:

```
- id: '1676691530760'
  name: ALL OFF
  entities:
    switch.desk_outlet:
      friendly_name: Desk outlet
      state: 'off'
    light.garagelights:
      supported_color_modes:
      - onoff
      friendly_name: GarageLights
      supported_features: 0
      state: 'off'
  icon: mdi:home-off
  metadata:
    switch.desk_outlet:
      entity_only: true
    light.garagelights:
      entity_only: true
```

Any command-line input or output is written as follows:

```
Rule1 on Switch1#state=1 do publish sensor/%topic%/PIR1 ON
endon on Switch1#state=0 do Publish sensor/%topic%/PIR1 OFF
endon
```

Bold: Indicates a new term, an important word, or words that you see onscreen. For instance, words in menus or dialog boxes appear in **bold**. Here is an example: "After the **Write** bar completes loading, if everything goes well, another window will present the message **Process successful! Power cycle the device**."

> **Tips or important notes**
> Appear like this.

Get in touch

Feedback from our readers is always welcome.

General feedback: If you have questions about any aspect of this book, email us at customercare@packtpub.com and mention the book title in the subject of your message.

Errata: Although we have taken every care to ensure the accuracy of our content, mistakes do happen. If you have found a mistake in this book, we would be grateful if you would report this to us. Please visit www.packtpub.com/support/errata and fill in the form.

Piracy: If you come across any illegal copies of our works in any form on the internet, we would be grateful if you would provide us with the location address or website name. Please contact us at copyright@packt.com with a link to the material.

If you are interested in becoming an author: If there is a topic that you have expertise in and you are interested in either writing or contributing to a book, please visit authors.packtpub.com.

Share Your Thoughts

Once you've read *Building Smart Home Automation Solutions with Home Assistant*, we'd love to hear your thoughts! Scan the QR code below to go straight to the Amazon review page for this book and share your feedback.

https://packt.link/r/1801815291

Your review is important to us and the tech community and will help us make sure we're delivering excellent quality content.

Download a free PDF copy of this book

Thanks for purchasing this book!

Do you like to read on the go but are unable to carry your print books everywhere?

Is your eBook purchase not compatible with the device of your choice?

Don't worry, now with every Packt book you get a DRM-free PDF version of that book at no cost.

Read anywhere, any place, on any device. Search, copy, and paste code from your favorite technical books directly into your application.

The perks don't stop there, you can get exclusive access to discounts, newsletters, and great free content in your inbox daily

Follow these simple steps to get the benefits:

1.   Scan the QR code or visit the link below

https://packt.link/free-ebook/9781801815291

2.   Submit your proof of purchase

3.   That's it! We'll send your free PDF and other benefits to your email directly

Part 1:
Introduction to
Home Assistant – Installation
and Configuration

In this part, we will learn how a Home Automation system is structured. We will introduce Home Assistant by guiding you through the installation and configuration process. At the end of this part, we will have created a base environment to automate your home.

This part has the following chapters:

- *Chapter 1, Understanding Home Automation Systems*
- *Chapter 2, Getting Started with Home Assistant*

1

Understanding Home Automation Systems

The idea of this chapter is to present what a home automation system is by giving a brief history and background of how it started and how it evolved over the years. Here, we will highlight and discuss the benefits of having an automated home. We will also get an overview of the main components used in the system, and discuss the role of each one of them so that you can understand how a home automation system is structured.

Real examples of home automation will be provided in this chapter, and you will learn about my experiences over the years with different home automation systems and how they were implemented. I will conclude the chapter by detailing how my home is configured nowadays and ideas about the cost and materials used on it. This will help you to think about what you will need and how much it will cost to implement your system.

In this chapter, we will cover the following main topics:

- Overview of home automation systems
- Benefits of having an automated home
- Home automation structure
- Example of a real home automation system

Technical requirements

For this chapter, it is good to know about client-server architecture to understand how a home automation system is configured but don't worry if you don't, since we will cover this content in the next section. Also, you will be able to learn about **Message Queuing Telemetry Transport** (**MQTT**) more effectively if you have some understanding of communication protocols broadly speaking. Knowledge of some electronic components will help you to understand the sensors and actuators topics in more detail.

Overview of home automation systems

Home automation became available and accessible to people when the industry started to provide devices that allowed some kind of sensor and actuator to be applied at home. The first devices of this kind I heard about were the **X10 devices**.

The X10 technology was created in 1975 by a company called *Pico Electronics* and became commercially available around 1978. Essentially, it uses the power line available in every home to turn lamps and appliances on and off. Initially, with the limited availability of computers, these so-called home automation systems used architecture that provided limited use. Limited because the control was not centralized and didn't allow really smart automation to be created. Besides that, there was not much hierarchy in the system, meaning that controllers could communicate with actuators and sensors too. The diagram in *Figure 1.1* shows more about the possible configuration used at that time:

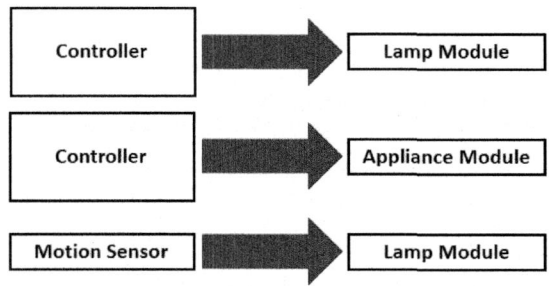

Figure 1.1: Early automation systems configuration

As can be seen in *Figure 1.1*, there was not much hierarchy in the system, which meant that controllers could communicate with actuators, but sensors could also communicate with them too.

When computers became more popular, software such as HomeSeer, Xtension, and Indigo were created to support the X10 technology. Some X10 computer translators were created so that the architecture allowed more intelligence to be added by using a centralized system, as can be seen in *Figure 1.2*:

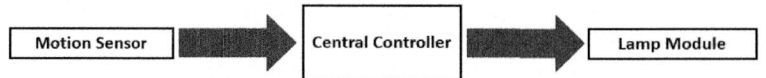

Figure 1.2: Recent configuration

Even with a computer, the X10 system was still limited because it was wire dependent, and the number of addresses was limited to 256 devices, meaning 16 houses or rooms, each one with 16 units or devices. Each address is configured manually in the module using two rotary switches, one from the module's house varying from A to P and the other for the unit varying from 1 to 16. As an example, a house or room in a home can have the letter A to designate it, and a unit such as a coffee maker is assigned the number 1, so the rotary switch for an X10 Appliance module will have the configuration A1. Other units in the same house A can have another number assigned to them, such as 4, so the rotary switch in another appliance or lamp module will have the configuration A4. If the house or room is configured as the letter P, we can have a rotary switch configured from P1 to P16 to represent 16 different units.

My first experience with the X10 protocol was around 2006 when I acquired a device set composed of two lamp modules (PLM03 and RLM20), an appliance module (PAM02), and a two-way power line interface (PSC05). At the same time, I saw an application note (AN-236 - X-10 Home Automation using the PIC16F877A) and decided to build a task controller using it, adding a temperature sensor and a local relay, and excluding the X10 controller/receiver which was replaced by the PSC05 module acquired. I was able to run my first home automation system, which just had actuators that were turned on and off based on pre-configured timer events embedded in the software application I created. The components of my first home automation system are presented in *Figure 1.3*:

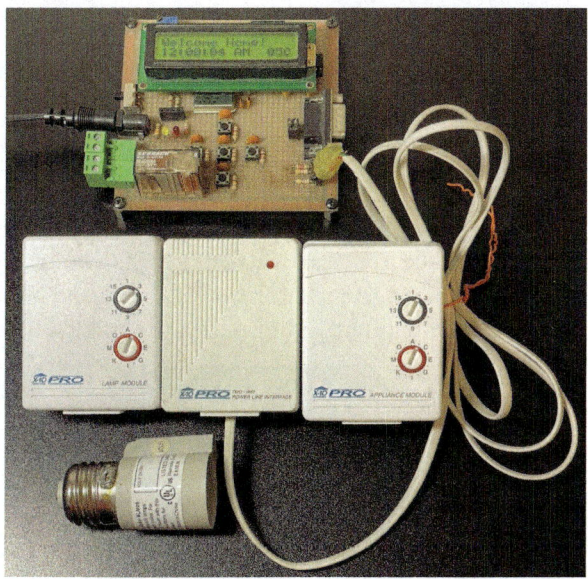

Figure 1.3: My first home automation system using X10 technology

Figure 1.3 presents the **X10 task controller** at the top showing a 16X2 LCD module, and underneath it (not shown in the picture) is the **Programmable Interface Controller** (**PIC**) microcontroller. The task controller connects to a **two-way power line interface module** (the white box in the middle) through the white cable, which is connected to a **power line**. This power line interface sends and receives commands to and from the **lamp module** (the white box on the left) or the **appliance module** (the white box on the right).

On top of this X10 task controller, I was able to hack a WRT-54G router from Linksys (seen in *Figure 1.4*) and add two serial ports to it. Later, I connected it to the X10 controller and turned it on, commanded by a **Google Android** application created specifically to do it:

Figure 1.4: Linksys router modified to be used as part of my home automation system

Figure 1.4 shows the router with the two DB-9 standard connectors for the RS-232 serial port. One of these serial ports was used to connect to the other DB-9 connector located in the X10 task controller and allow my system to be accessible using wireless communication.

In 2012, I bought my first Wi-Fi module from **Particle** (https://www.particle.io/), where I was able to replace my original PIC-based X10 controller with a small and powerful piece of hardware. Looking at *Figure 1.5*, my most up-to-date and optimized system using X10 technology is presented:

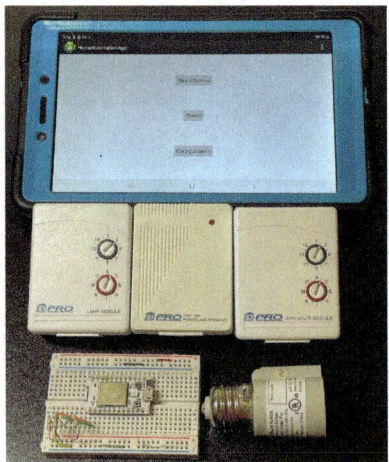

Figure 1.5: Latest configuration of my X10 home automation system

Figure 1.5 shows the tablet with my Google Android application (HomeAutomationApp) running, the X10 modules presented previously, and the Particle Wi-Fi module board (former Spark Core).

As can be seen over the years with my X10 system, I had to create my own hardware initially, hack a router, and create an embedded software for the task controller (PIC and Particle) and an Android application so the system could work as desired. Even then, my home automation system was very limited, wire dependent, and hard to maintain.

Based on the evolution of my home automation system over the years as mentioned in the previous examples, and lots of hardware and software programming developed, I felt something else was missing. In 2020, I was interested in learning more about current home automation systems. And it was at that time that I discovered a configuration that changed and made my life easier. This configuration was based on the **client-server architecture** and is introduced in *Figure 1.6*:

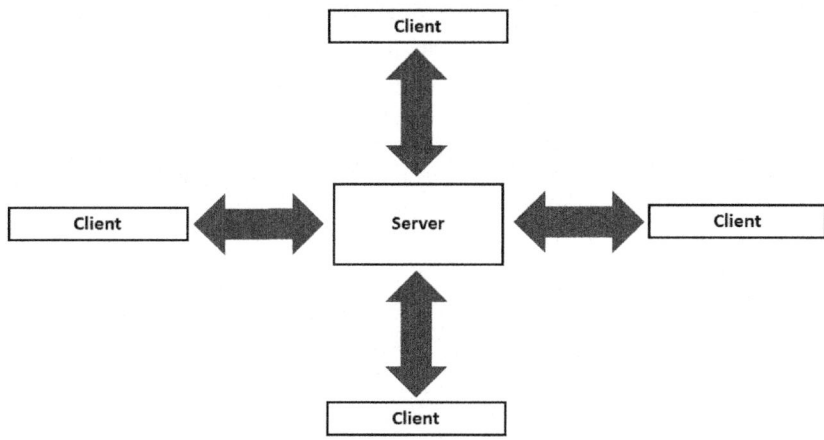

Figure 1.6: Client-server architecture

As demonstrated in *Figure 1.6*, the client-server architecture is configured as clients connect to a server via wireless communication, and the server manages the communication requests by taking some actions, including sending commands back to clients. This is the architecture that I will explore in the remainder of this chapter.

Now that we have an overview of home automation systems and its architecture, let's look at their benefits.

Benefits of having an automated home

Before we move on to the explanation of the architecture of a home automation system used nowadays and the one that is being used in my home, let's explore and highlight some of the benefits and advantages of having an automated home.

Saving time

The first benefit that can be highlighted is that an automated home will save you time. Think about a simple application; you can remotely turn on or off a lamp or an appliance using your cell phone or a voice assistant device, so you do not need to walk to the switch to do it. This can sound strange if the switch is close to you but think about the idea that you have to do this kind of thing many times a day. You can include, for example, an automation routine that can be triggered to turn a device on or off when a particular time of the day is reached. This can save you considerable time during your day if multiple similar routines are configured, and you do not need to go to each device and turn it on or off.

Feeling comfortable

Having an automated home will bring you some convenience. A good example of that is the automation routine I implemented in my home where the front lights turn on when at sunset, and after four hours, they turn off. This is very helpful for me because there is no public illumination in my street, so it is very dark at night. The lights help to illuminate my house numbers in case someone visits me for the first time at night.

Another example is when I wake up at night to take care of my youngest son, the movement sensor turns on a small light in the aisle so we can see where to go since the master bedroom is on the other side of the house.

Another good example is setting up a scene in your bedroom where you can dim the lights, and turn on the fan and TV automatically if it senses you are in your bedroom at a certain time of the night.

> **Important note**
>
> An automation routine is a resource used in a home automation system to automate certain actions using the devices installed in your home. These routines are configured to be triggered when certain events happen. An event can be different situations, such as sensor status or the time of the day, for instance. We will talk more about automation routines in *Chapter 5*.

Saving money

An automated home will save you money mainly by configuring some devices in your home to the savings or eco mode. You can configure these modes in the device or implement an automation routine that can emulate it. The example I gave in the last section, where the front lights are turned on and off at night, could save you some money on your electric bill rather than them staying on for the entire night and you having to turn them off in the morning. Another example, depending on the load and how much energy it consumes, is leaving a device turned off when it is not needed. This will be a more significant saving than the first example. A good example of this is the **Heating Ventilation and Air Conditioning (HVAC)** system that can be turned off when no one is at home.

Being safe

An automated home can help you to protect and make your house safer. Door sensors can be installed on the main doors of your house, and alarms can be configured to make sounds or announce people entering. This can prevent people from entering without your consent or the opposite, prevent people such as your kids from leaving the house without your awareness. Sensors can also be installed on windows to improve protection against burglars or thieves. Cameras can also be activated when door sensors are triggered, offering remote monitoring if you are not at home.

These are just a few benefits of having a home automation system in your home. You will probably find others during or after reading this book.

In the next section, we will review in more detail the structure of a home automation system when you will be able to understand the components that can be grouped to create it.

Home automation structure

After some background information about different architectures used for home automation and also aspects to motivate you to build your home automation system, it is now time to detail each component. The architecture that I will focus on in this book is the one that I have implemented in my home, so it is proven that it works. This architecture has the same idea of the client-server presented previously in *Figure 1.6*, but here, I have added the proper names and identifications of each part of the system. This architecture is presented in *Figure 1.7*:

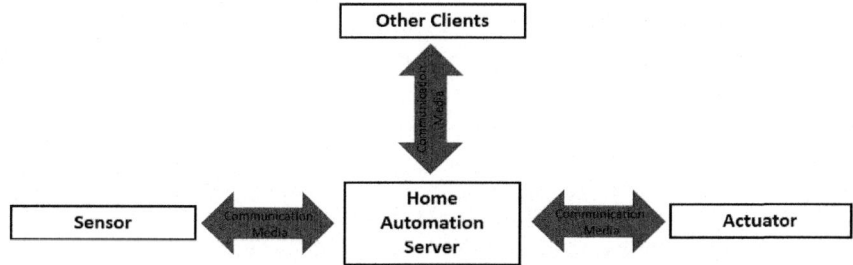

Figure 1.7: Home automation system architecture explored in this book

This architecture assumes you have a Wi-Fi 802.11g or above router in your home, but this router does not necessarily need to be connected to the internet unless you want to access your home automation system remotely.

In the following subsections, each part of the system presented in *Figure 1.7* is discussed in detail.

Home automation server

The **home automation server** is the central connection or the *heart* of a home automation system. It centralizes all the communication received from the sensors and transmits them to the actuators. It contains all the logic of the automation created by the user and also allows the configuration of new devices to be added to the system. The server also manages other connections to the system, such as applications that can be connected to it using a cell phone running Google Android or Apple **iPhone Operating System (iOS)**.

The home automation server is composed of two distinct parts: hardware and software. Depending on the level the user wants to go in the system, the hardware can vary from a desktop or notebook to their own design. It will all depend on the cost and time invested in creating or building the server. Due to the availability of open source hardware, I recommend that the system is implemented using an off-the-shelf device. I strongly recommend that a board such as a **Raspberry Pi 4** is used, but if you already have an old computer or any other hardware that can run Linux, it could be used. Another commonly used hardware option is the **Intel NUC** platform.

The home automation server should be able to run Linux or some other popular operating system such as Windows or macOS. Another requirement is that the server should support Wi-Fi 802.11n wireless protocol or above. Currently, I'm using a Raspberry Pi 4 Model B 2019 with 4 GB of RAM in my home automation system. This hardware will be the focus of the home automation server used in this book.

Speaking about the software component of the home automation server, you can try to build your own software to manage the role of the automation server. The only advantage of this method is the learning process that you will go through by creating it. I must confess that I learned a lot when I implemented the X10 task controller. The original software from the microchip application was written in Assembly and I migrated it to the C programming language. Later, I migrated the C application to the Arduino-like format used in the Particle Wi-Fi board. This learning process was useful for me in other aspects of my job and career, but nothing compares to the variety of home automation software available today.

As the name of the book somehow anticipates, **Home Assistant** (https://www.home-assistant. io/) is the software used in the home automation server adopted in this book. The reasons I chose Home Assistant to use at my home were because of the documentation, support, integrations, and add-ons it gives to the users. Home Assistant is one of the most used open source software for home automation projects and supports Linux, Windows, and macOS operating systems. It supports lots of add-ons that allow the system to be expanded, as will be explained in *Chapter 7*. Another open source software that can be used in home automation systems is **openHAB** (https://github.com/openhab).

One paradigm followed by this book is that you are free to choose your sensors and actuators to be integrated into your system, which is one of the reasons for using Home Assistant. In this case, the home automation server software should allow easy integration of sensors off the shelf and even sensors you decide to create. There are some home automation software and systems that interlock the hardware and software in their architecture, not allowing other types of devices to be used in your home automation system different from the architecture they offer. In my opinion, this kind of approach prevents the user from being free and flexible in the choice of sensors and actuators. The most popular systems of this nature are **Insteon**, **Lutron**, and **SmartThings**, owned by Samsung Electronics. In this regard, Home Assistant supports different ways of integrating the different sensors and actuators so it will not hold you to some particular platform or architecture. This free choice will certainly contribute to lowering the cost of your system since you will have more options of devices to select.

In general, I recommend that you choose compact hardware so it can easily be installed in any place in your home, preferably somewhere hidden, and then eventually, you have to be physically connected to it using a computer video screen. Once the home automation server is installed and initially configured, you will not need to access it physically anymore unless it presents some issue or if you want to install some other software on it that is not able to be installed remotely. If the idea is to use the hardware only as a home automation server, all configuration, automation, and any other new setup can be done remotely via a web browser. It is worth mentioning that the location for the installation should not be too far from the main source of the Wi-Fi router used in your home. If you need more reliability in your home automation server connectivity, it is recommended that you use a wired connection such as Ethernet (IEEE 802.3) connected to your Wi-Fi router.

In my home, the home automation server is installed at the back of my computer video screen using 3M VHB Scotch SJ3550 Dual Lock adhesive tape. *Figure 1.8* shows this installation:

Figure 1.8: My home automation server

Figure 1.8 shows the home automation server using Raspberry Pi on the left and also an **ESP32** Wi-Fi/ Bluetooth module (upside down) on the right used in the five-zone temperature logger explained in *Chapter 10*. In the next chapter, we will introduce Home Assistant as the software for the home automation server and will guide you to install it on a Raspberry Pi 4 as the hardware used for this server and used in this book.

Sensors

The sensors and actuators are what bring life to your home automation system and allow you to create automation, configuration, and integration using Home Assistant.

Sensors are electronic devices that contain certain electronic components able to measure or detect some measurement or status of what or where they are installed. They always provide an output signal that is used as an input signal to the home automation server to inform it about what the sensor is detecting.

The sensors can be generically classified into two types: **analog** and **digital**. Analog sensors are the ones that can provide discrete values of output signals. In other words, these sensors can have multiple values to express the information being measured. A temperature sensor, for example, is an analog sensor that can express in its output different measurements about each temperature value captured or sensed by it.

A digital sensor provides binary information in its output, meaning two states which can vary depending on the sensor. The common states associated with these sensors are *turned on*, *turned off*, *open*, and *closed*. These sensors can also inform about two values in reference to a threshold. In this case, one state will be above the threshold, and the other state will be below the threshold. One good example of a digital sensor used in home automation systems is a door sensor. It is basically composed of an electronic component called a reed switch, which works as a magnetic switch to provide two states: closed, to inform the door is closed, and opened, to inform the door is opened.

Table 1.1 lists some examples of sensors commonly used in home automation systems, including type and measurement sense:

Sensor	Type	Measurement	Typical values
Door sensor	Digital	Door status	Open, closed
Motion sensor	Digital	Motion status	Motion detected, Motion not detected
Temperature/humidity sensor	Analog	Temperature/humidity	Various, depending on the temperature or humidity range measured by the sensor
Light sensor	Analog/digital	Light intensity	Light on, light off. Light intensity values, depending on the range measured by the sensor
Energy meter sensor	Analog	Power consumption	Power values according to the sensor range

Sensor	Type	Measurement	Typical values
Gas sensor	Analog/digital	Gas status/value	Gas on, gas off. Gas intensity values, depending on the range measured by the sensor
Smoke sensor	Digital	Smoke status	Smoke/fire on, Smoke/fire off

Table 1.1: Examples of sensors used in home automation systems

A general block diagram of a sensor for home automation is demonstrated in *Figure 1.9*:

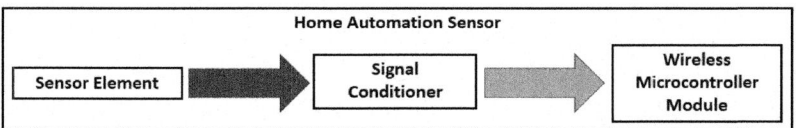

Figure 1.9: Home automation sensor block diagram

It is important to understand each one of the blocks discussed, to help you put together the parts and components to build your own sensor, which is discussed in *Chapter 3* of this book.

The first component part of a sensor, as seen on the left of *Figure 1.9*, is usually an electronic component able to capture some measurements related to the environment where it is installed. We called it the **sensor element**. Within the electronic components used, some of the following examples can be found:

- **Reed switches/magnetic switches**: These are electromechanical components composed of two ferromagnetic metallic plates hermetically sealed by a glass enclosure. These plates move up to contact one to the other when a magnetic field is applied. They provide two statuses, open and closed, and are commonly used in door sensors.

- **Passive Infrared (PIR) sensors**: These are electronic components that are able to detect the changes in infrared radiation when something crosses their field of view. The sensor converts these variations in voltage changes to be formatted as motion changes. Despite the voltage variation being an analog value, the application (motion sensors) where these sensors are used only considers the digital variation of it. They are used in motion sensors.

- **Light Dependent Resistor (LDR) sensors**: These are electronic components that vary their resistance when light is applied. They provide an analog value according to the light intensity variation. They are used in light sensors.

- **Thermal Resistors (thermistors) and temperature measurement Integrated Circuits (ICs):** These temperature sensors are electronic components built with different technologies to provide an analog value associated with the temperature to which the sensor is submitted. In the past, resistors were made with the purpose of changing their values with the temperature, or thermistors were used, but today different electronic components manufacturers are using ICs as sensors, which provide much more reliability and measurement range. As the name suggests, they are used in temperature sensors.

The next block part of the sensor, as seen in the middle block of *Figure 1.9*, is the **signal conditioner**. These circuits are usually required to modify the signal generated by the sensor. This signal from the sensor could require some voltage level conversion, or in a lot of situations, the signal coming from the sensor has small voltage or current variations, so it needs to be amplified. Also, this same signal could be generated with a lot of noise and needs to be filtered. Signal conditioner circuits can perform the filtering process to make sure the signal will be cleaned and well-interpreted by the upstream circuit.

In summary, signal conditioner circuits translate the information from the electronic sensor components into something understandable by the next part of the sensor, the wireless microcontroller module. The signal could be conditioned to be read by the microcontroller as a digital binary or analog input. In some cases, as we will see in *Chapter 3*, the signal conditioner could encode the signal to generate some digital communication standard to interface to the microcontroller. These standards can be in different formats, but the most popular are serial communication interfaces such as **Inter-Integrated Circuit (I2C)** and **Serial Peripheral Interface (SPI)**.

The last block of a home automation sensor (the right block in *Figure 1.9*) is the wireless microcontroller module. This module receives the information translated or converted from the sensor by the signal conditioner circuit and sends it via wireless to be managed by the home automation server.

If you are curious enough to open one of the home automation sensors, you may find a shield in the format of a metallic box where this wireless microcontroller electronic component is located. In some cases, to reduce the circuit footprint and cost, these microcontrollers are found without the metallic shield box. Actually, in most cases, these electronic components are called **System on Chip (SoC)**. They are large-scale integrated circuits that combine a microcontroller and wireless radio in one single chip. Due to this large-scale integration, few external electronic components are required, keeping the size of the entire circuit small, which is highly desirable when it comes to a home automation sensor.

These SoCs are commonly used by many hobbyists to implement various kinds of **Internet of Things (IoT)** projects. The most popular of these components are from a Chinese component manufacturer called **Espressif Systems**. Espressif manufactures the ESP8265, ESP8266, and ESP32 SoCs. The main reasons for the mass utilization of these SoCs are, in my opinion, the easy availability of them in the market, affordable cost, and an active community of developers. You can easily find wireless communication modules based on the ESP8266 and ESP32 from the biggest world-famous dealers costing around $10 or less. You can also develop and deploy software programs using Arduino sketches via the Arduino **Integrated Development Environment (IDE)**. This means if you know how to develop a program for Arduino using the different software libraries available, you should be able to develop applications using ESP8266 and ESP32.

In the next chapters, we will build some projects for sensors, and we will use the ESP8266 and ESP32 Wi-Fi-based modules to do it.

Actuators

The actuators receive the information from the home automation server and provide a type of output, such as turning on or off a switch connected to an appliance, for example. It can also receive information to send a command to simply turn a lamp on or off or change its color or brightness.

Likewise as the sensors, the signal sent to an actuator output can be digital or analog. Turning a switch on or off is a good example of digital binary information sent to an actuator. Other examples of actuators can be given according to *Table 1.2*:

Actuator name	Type	Status
Switch	Digital	On, off, and other intermediate states
Lamp	Digital/analog	On, off (digital) light intensity, light color (analog)
Alarm sound	Digital/analog	Sound on/sound off (digital) sound levels, sound tones (analog)

Table 1.2: Examples of actuators

The block diagram of an actuator follows the opposite sequence found in a sensor and is configured according to *Figure 1.10*:

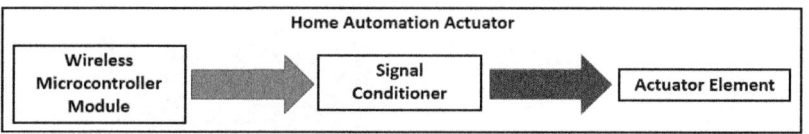

Figure 1.10: Home automation actuator block diagram

The wireless microcontroller module referenced in *Figure 1.10* in the left block is usually the same found in the sensors and, again, mostly the ones manufactured by Espressif Systems, ESP8266, and ESP32. It receives information from the home automation server and translates it into an output command that will ultimately control the actuator element. This command could be a voltage level representing a binary signal, an analog signal, or even a serial digital communication protocol such as I2C or SPI.

The wireless microcontroller module becomes very versatile since it provides different input/output pins, serial interfaces, and other features and peripherals, allowing multiple combinations of electronic components and circuits. These can lead to sensors and actuators or more than one sensor element being used in the same enclosure. You can build a sensor that can be used for temperature and motion detection at the same time using just one wireless microcontroller, as can be seen in *Chapter 3*.

The signal conditioner circuit (the middle block in *Figure 1.10*) has the same idea used in the sensors, but in this case, it is conditioning the output signal sent by the wireless microcontroller module. It could be a voltage or current level converter, for example. This circuit is required in most cases due to a wireless microcontroller module limitation preventing the end actuator element from working properly.

The actuator element presented in *Figure 1.10* on the right is what promotes the final effect when the home automation actuator is triggered. It is an electronic component or circuit. The simplest example of an actuator element is represented by an electronic component called an electromechanical relay. Combined with a conditional circuit, it allows direct control from a wireless microcontroller module. The relay converts an electronic binary signal into a mechanical switch command. So, the relay is an electronically controlled switch. This switch attached to an outlet can connect or disconnect the voltage from it, allowing it to turn an appliance on or off, for instance. *Figure 1.11* shows a typical circuit used in a relay-based actuator and also a photo of a commercial actuator where each block of it is represented:

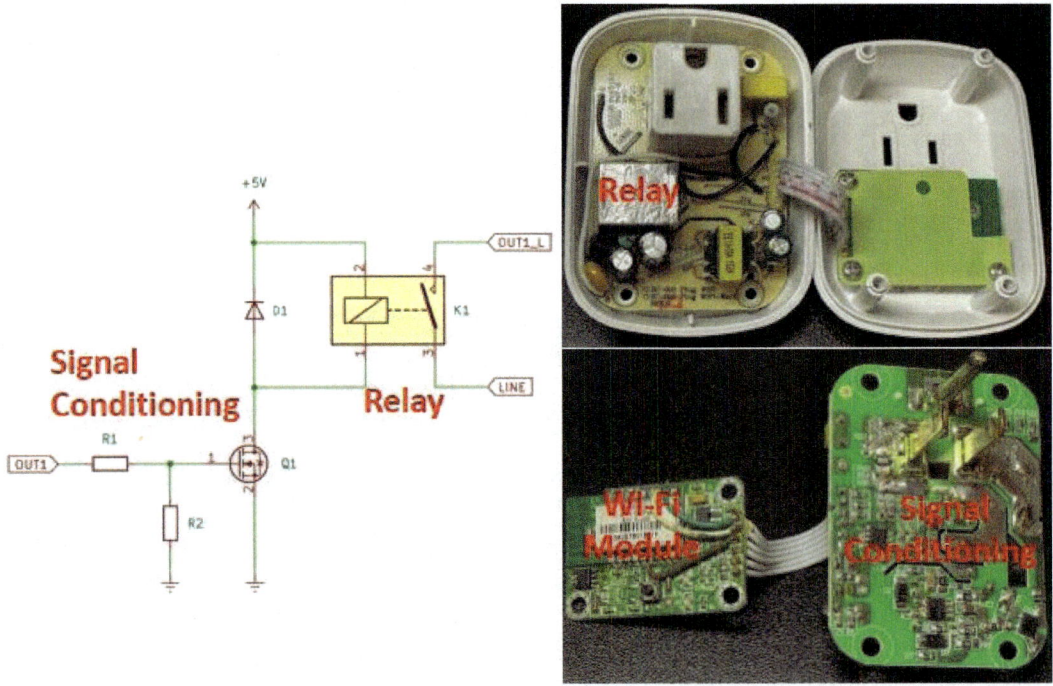

Figure 1.11: Circuits found in a home automation actuator

Communication media

Communication media is the environment or infrastructure where the home automation server talks to sensors, actuators, and other applications or devices that will connect to your system. It is important to understand how the communication media is structured and works so you can choose the proper media to implement your system and configure it by knowing which parameters to set up.

Wired systems

Commercial home automation systems can use wired media to communicate. These systems came in different formats, such as structured cabling using **Unshielded Twisted Pair** (**UTP**), coaxial, and fiber optic cables. Usually, they attend to some specific types of systems such as phones, cable TV, multimedia, and computers. As a disadvantage, this media type somehow limited the expansion of the systems and was not designed to automate a home, just to allow some type of devices to share or communicate using the same media. It is also not flexible since the communication node is available where a cable is present. Among the advantages of wired systems is the reliability and communication speed that some technologies can offer such as fiber optic cables.

As highlighted previously, one good example of wired systems targeting a home automation system was the X10 technology. The X10 uses the power line available in each home to encode binary information, and devices attached to the power line can decode this information and process it accordingly.

Wireless systems

Wireless systems are much more commonly used for home automation systems. The most common wireless protocols used are Wi-Fi and Zigbee. Wi-Fi (IEEE 802.11) is well-known, supported, and available. It works under the 2.4 and 5 GHz operating frequencies. When implemented in the sensors and actuators, it allows direct communication to the Raspberry Pi automation server, which also implements this protocol. The issue with the Wi-Fi wireless protocol is that it was not developed exactly for home automation and IoT systems. The power consumption in the Wi-Fi protocol is high, which in some situations prevents it from being extensively used in battery-powered sensors, for example.

The Zigbee wireless protocol (IEEE 802.15.4) is more applicable for home automation systems in some circumstances. It operates under the 2.4 GHz **Industrial, Scientific, and Medical** (**ISM**) band. It was created with a low overhead in the communication layer (low bandwidth), allowing efficiency when it comes to small-scale projects. It also has low-power radios compared to Wi-Fi, so it is more suitable for battery-powered applications. Due to the simplified communication stack, the Zigbee protocol can wake up from low power modes much quicker compared to the Wi-Fi protocol, so some sensors, such as door sensors, can react faster to events. The drawback of using the Zigbee protocol is that it is not as available as Wi-Fi, and when using commercial sensors, usually a specific router is required to add another layer of communication or device to the communication infrastructure, which adds costs and more configuration to be done in your home automation system. To date, I have not felt the need to add any infrastructure related to the Zigbee protocol in my home automation system. You have to evaluate your applications, and if you need to use lots of battery-powered sensors, it is worth considering Zigbee wireless communication in your system.

Another wireless protocol used for home automation systems is **Z-Wave**. It is a proprietary technology owned by the **Silicon Labs** company. It uses a **mesh** network arrangement, allowing devices to communicate among themselves. The mesh network can expand the range of the network and become stronger since it will continue to work if one node or the main node fails. Another advantage of Z-Wave wireless is that it operates under the sub-1 GHz frequency range band, which is less congested than 2.4 GHz, so it allows it to be low power, long range, and with less **Radio Frequency** (**RF**) interference.

Finally, I would like to mention the **Bluetooth Low Energy** (**BLE**) wireless communication protocol. This Bluetooth variation has many advantages related to home automation systems. Some of them are power consumption, security features, interoperability, ease of use, and low cost. These features, combined with Wi-Fi, can create other powerful communication protocols such as the recently launched **Matter**, which we will cover in *Chapter 11*.

With regards to wireless systems, it is worth commenting that the communication range is one aspect that should be considered. The range of these wireless devices can communicate is up to 50–100 meters inside a home, so it is good to evaluate where your wireless router will be installed so the Wi-Fi signal can cover your entire house. Depending on the configuration, you may need to use repeaters spread throughout your house. Another aspect to consider is that the wireless signal can be attenuated differently depending on the material your house is built. It means that a wall made of bricks and cement can attenuate more the signal compared to a wall made of wood. Make sure your entire house has enough wireless signal coverage; otherwise, your system will not work properly.

> **Important note**
>
> The wireless communication range of sensors and actuators is limited by the small size of the internal circuits, including the antenna, which is usually made as part of the **Printed Circuit Boards** (**PCBs**).

The communication media used in this entire book is the wireless Wi-Fi network. As mentioned, it is not required that this Wi-Fi network be connected to the internet unless you need to access your home automation system remotely.

Protocols and brokers (MQTT)

Protocols and brokers define the entire home automation structure and what language the devices in the system use to talk to each other. A protocol implements a set of commands, configurations, and communication schemes that allow one device to exchange information better with another. It can implement some sophisticated mechanisms to improve reliability, such as error correction, package retransmission, and so on.

In the sequence, I will provide details about a wired (X10 protocol) and wireless communication protocol (MQTT). MQTT will be very important to understand because it will be used in most of the future chapters of this book.

The X10 protocol

The X10 wired protocol works as follows. In the USA, the AC typically has a 60 Hz frequency and is represented by a sine wave crossing zero with a peak of 120 V. Each time that the current crosses the zero, a binary representation is encoded to the sine wave to represent ones and zeros. The binary **1** is represented by a 120 KHz burst with a *1-millisecond* duration, and a binary **0** is represented by an absence of the 120 KHz burst after the crossing. In the three AC phase distribution systems, these bursts should be transmitted in each phase spaced 2.778 ms from each other.

One basic message encoded in the X10 format has 11 cycles of a power line. The first two cycles represent a **Start Code** (b1110), the following four cycles are the **House Code** (1…16), and the last five are a **Number Code** (1…16) or a **Function Code** (on, off, and so on). This complete block, including the Start Code, House Code, and Key Code, should always be transmitted twice spaced by three power line cycles between them. In order to improve reliability, the X10 protocol also states that the House Code and Key Code should be decoded as a complement form on alternate half cycles of the power line. This means, for example, if no signal is transmitted in the first half cycle (binary 0) then a 1 millisecond 120 KHz burst of the signal should be transmitted in the next half cycle (binary 1). *Figure 1.12* explains how it works and also includes a table with the House Codes and Key Codes:

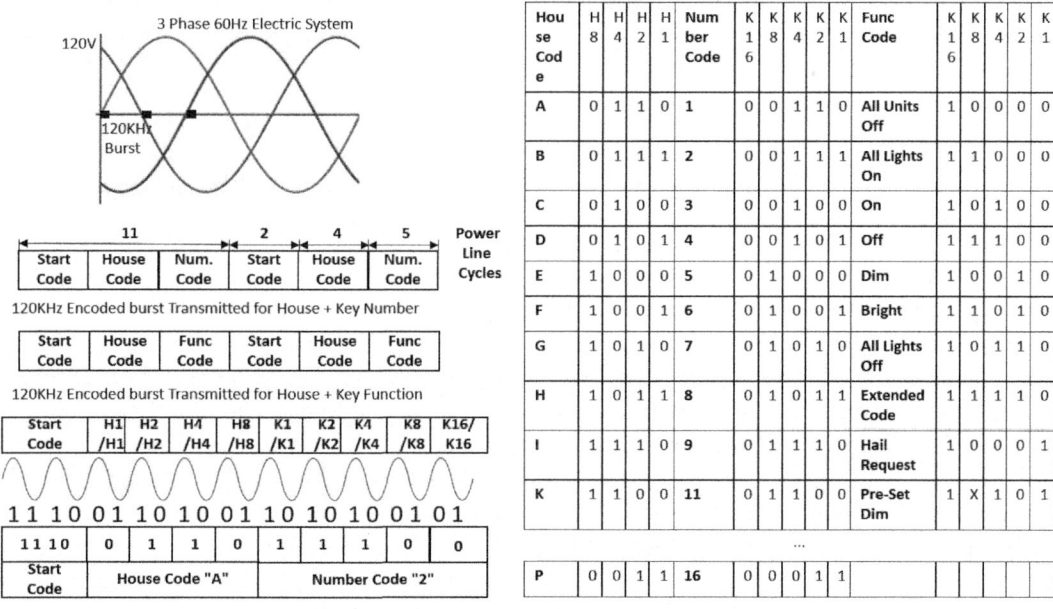

House Code	H8	H4	H2	H1	Number Code	K16	K8	K4	K2	K1	Func Code	K16	K8	K4	K2	K1
A	0	1	1	0	1	0	0	1	1	0	All Units Off	1	0	0	0	0
B	0	1	1	1	2	0	0	1	1	1	All Lights On	1	1	0	0	0
C	0	1	0	0	3	0	0	1	0	0	On	1	0	1	0	0
D	0	1	0	1	4	0	0	1	0	1	Off	1	1	1	0	0
E	1	0	0	0	5	0	1	0	0	0	Dim	1	0	0	1	0
F	1	0	0	1	6	0	1	0	0	1	Bright	1	1	0	1	0
G	1	0	1	0	7	0	1	0	1	0	All Lights Off	1	0	1	1	0
H	1	0	1	1	8	0	1	0	1	1	Extended Code	1	1	1	1	0
I	1	1	1	0	9	0	1	1	1	0	Hail Request	1	0	0	0	1
K	1	1	0	0	11	0	1	1	0	0	Pre-Set Dim	1	X	1	0	1
											…					
P	0	0	1	1	16	0	0	0	1	1						

Figure 1.12: Information about the X10 protocol

Figure 1.12 at the very top on the left presents how the 120 KHz is encoded in the three-phase power line system. Actually, this is just a representation since the 120 KHz burst is superimposed on the 60 Hz sinusoidal signal. On the left, in the middle of *Figure 1.12*, the protocol fields for the House Code/Key Code and House Code/Function Code are presented. An example of how the house address *A2* is coded is presented in the bottom left of *Figure 1.12*. The table on the right of *Figure 1.12* presents the numbers used by House Code, Number Code, and Function Code representations.

As you may note, per the protocol specifications, X10 was developed to use in home automation systems, which can address 256 devices minimum with some possibility of extension using an **Extended Code**. It is relatively easy to implement the software code that implements the protocol. I implemented an X10 task controller using a PIC16F877 microcontroller, which was able to store 16 different events associated with the day and time. It was based on the **Application Note (AN)** 236 from Microchip (`https://www.microchip.com/en-us/application-notes/an236`). I used an X10 modem (PSC05) to interface the PIC microcontroller and encode the X10 signals to be transmitted to the power line.

The MQTT protocol

Before going into detail about the MQTT protocol, it is worth mentioning that wireless communication media has different layers. Each layer is responsible for a different level of abstraction of the communication, from how the data received or transmitted will interface to the medium to how the frames or datagrams are organized. It is not the goal of this book to detail these layers since you will not need to implement anything related to the level of the common wireless protocol. The only thing you will need to know for now is how to configure or connect to the Wi-Fi **Service Set Identifier (SSID)** and password of the router used in your home.

The MQTT message protocol is designed to run above the Wi-Fi or Zigbee communication layers. It was developed to run on IoT devices, meaning lightweight code that perfectly fits small microcontrollers. Besides that, it requires minimal network bandwidth and implements **Quality of Service (QoS)**, improving the reliability of the message delivery.

MQTT is very suitable for home automation systems because it follows the client-server approach discussed previously. It implements an MQTT broker located in the home automation server, and the sensors are the MQTT clients. These MQTT clients are configured as publishers and publish or send information to MQTT brokers. This information is published by the MQTT clients under a specific topic. This topic is commonly the main information that the MQTT client wants to inform all interested parties. The MQTT broker holds the information from the MQTT clients and makes them available. If another MQTT client wants access to the information published by some other client, it subscribes to the topic of interest by sending a request to the MQTT broker. Once the MQTT client is subscribed to the topic of interest, the MQTT broker starts to publish the information under the topic subscribed to the MQTT client that requests the information. *Figure 1.13* illustrates how the MQTT communication message protocol works:

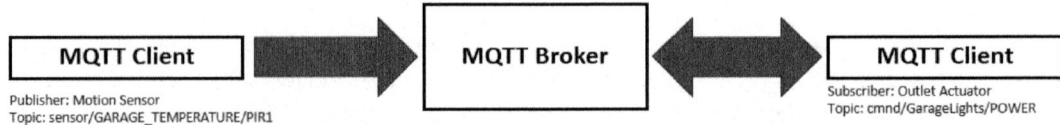

Figure 1.13: MQTT protocol example for garage motion detection

Figure 1.13 shows a simplified example of a **garage light motion sensor** I implemented at my home. The motion sensor is installed at the top of my garage, and when a motion is detected, it sends a message via MQTT to the broker, which depending on the hour of the day, sends a message to an outlet actuator installed in my garage lights and turns on the lights. It keeps the lights on for 90 seconds, and if no other motion is detected after this time, the MQTT broker sends a message to the outlet actuator to turn it off. We will build this motion sensor together in *Chapter 3* and we will see the automation I described using the garage lights actuator in *Chapter 5* and *Chapter 7* implemented in different ways.

By using the Arduino `pubsubclient` library (`https://github.com/knolleary/pubsubclient`), it is possible to implement a software code for an MQTT client. We will use another approach in this book by using software installed in the sensors so you will not need to create your own software to implement an MQTT client. Regarding the MQTT broker, Home Assistant has an integration that allows it to be configured and implemented.

For now, the only important information about MQTT you should know besides the basic information provided previously is some parameters that need to be configured on the MQTT client or server:

- **MQTT Host IP**: This is the IP address used to set up the MQTT broker.
- **MQTT Port**: This is the port used to connect the MQTT service. A typical value is `1883`.
- **Topic**: This is the name used to identify the topic.
- **Full Topic**: This is the full name used with the topic to identify certain classes of devices.

More information about the MQTT protocol can be found on the project's web page (`https://mqtt.org`).

User interface and other clients

The user interface is a component part of the home automation server, which allows the end user to interact with and configure the home automation system. In the case of this book, the user interface is implemented by Home Assistant.

The other clients are external devices that are not necessarily a direct part of the home automation system but can be used to access the automation server and use the Home Assistant user interface to control or configure different devices in your home. Some examples of these clients are other computers or your smartphone connected to your home wireless network.

> **Note**
> Your smartphone can be used to access the system remotely and as a sensor to indicate you are at home.

In this section, we were able to understand what the components of a home automation system are. We also explained how these components work and how they can be connected and used as intended.

In the next section, I will provide you with an idea of how my home automation system is distributed in terms of sensors and actuators. You will learn about how many devices I have, where they are located, associated costs, and so on. I hope that this motivates you to create your own.

Example of a real home automation system

In this section, the idea is to give you an overview of what a real home automation system looks like. I will do this by providing details about my own system.

History

I started to build my current system in 2017 when I first purchased my first four Wi-Fi actuator plugs. At that time, I didn't have any idea how the system evolve. I just wanted to try to control them remotely and use the phone application to be able to turn them on or off remotely or program them to turn on or off based on a schedule. In 2019, I purchased the Raspberry Pi 4, again, with no idea of how to install any specific software to it, only a regular Linux distribution. I was living in a small, rented apartment with my family and had no plans to implement any automation.

In 2020, I finally decided to invest time in learning about Home Assistant and the ecosystem related to it. I installed Home Assistant on Raspberry Pi, and then I hacked the four actuator plugs by installing **Tasmota** on them. In the same year, I also purchased my first ESP8266 module and BME280 temperature sensor. I was able to create my own temperature sensor and integrate it into Home Assistant.

We purchased a house in 2021, and I became motivated to really automate it. In less than 1 year, I was able to grow the number of devices from 4 actuator plugs to 23 different devices, including commercial and homemade sensors and actuators.

> **Note**
> Tasmota (`https://tasmota.github.io/`) is the software system that will be installed on the sensors and actuators to work with the home automation system. It will be explained in *Chapter 3*.

Current configuration

The following tables list all devices I have at home, separated by device type. At the time of writing, besides the home automation server, there are 11 sensors and 11 actuators.

Home automation server

The home automation server is just one device, and *Table 1.3* provide more details about it:

ID	Device name	Location	System installed	Specifications	Function
1	HomeCamino	Office	Home Assistant	Raspberry Pi 4	Home Automation Server

Table 1.3: Details about the home automation server

As mentioned previously, the home automation server I have at home is shown in *Figure 1.8*, and its creation and configuration will be covered in the next chapter.

Sensors

Table 1.4 presents the current sensors I have in my home automation system:

ID	Device name	Location	System installed	Specifications	Function
2	MB_Thermo	Master bedroom	ATC_ MiThermometer	Xiaomi Mi thermometer	Measure the master bedroom temperature
3	MB_backyard_ door	Master bedroom	Tuya	Door sensor	Detect the master bedroom to backyard door open
4	Front_door	Dining room	Tuya	Door sensor	Detect the front door open
5	LivingRoom_ Thermo	Living room	ATC_ MiThermometer	Xiaomi Mi thermometer	Measure the living room temperature
6	Kitchen_backyard _door	Kitchen	Tuya	Door sensor	Detect the kitchen to backyard door open
7	Backyard_Thermo	Backyard	ATC_ MiThermometer	Xiaomi Mi thermometer	Measure the backyard temperature
8	Kid1_Thermo	Kid1 bedroom	ATC_ MiThermometer	Xiaomi Mi thermometer	Measure kid1 bedroom temperature

ID	Device name	Location	System installed	Specifications	Function
9	Kid2_Thermo	Kid2 bedroom	ATC_MiThermometer	Xiaomi Mi thermometer	Measure kid2 bedroom temperature
10	Garage_door	Laundry	Tuya	Door sensor	Detect the laundry to garage door open
11	Garage_Thermo_Motion	Garage	Tasmota	ESP8266 own sensor	Measure the temperature and detect motion in the garage
12	ESP32_Thermo	Office	Tasmota	ESP32 own sensor	Five-zone BlueTooth temperature Hub

Table 1.4: Sensors in my home automation system

In regards to the sensors, it is worth commenting on the IDs *11* and *12*, which are homemade sensors. In this book, we will cover them using hands-on projects in *Chapter 3* and *Chapter 10*, respectively. In *Chapter 10*, the process of hacking the thermometer IDs *3*, *5*, *7*, *8*, and *9* will also be explained.

Actuators

Table 1.5 presents the current actuators in my home automation system:

ID	Device name	Location	System installed	Specifications	Function
13	MB_TV	Master bedroom	Tasmota	CT-065W plug	Turn on/off the master bedroom TV
14	MB_Fan	Master bedroom	Tasmota	SONOFF Basic R2 r	Turn on/off the master bedroom fan
15	DiningRoomLamp1	Dining room	Tasmota	CT-065W plug	Turn on/off one of the dining room lamps

ID	Device name	Location	System installed	Specifications	Function
16	Front Lights	Dining room	Tasmota	SONOFF Basic R2	Turn on/off master front lights
17	Kid1_Fan	Kid1 bedroom	Tasmota	SONOFF Basic R2 Mini	Turn on/off the master bedroom fan
18	Corridor_Lights	Corridor	Tasmota	SONOFF Basic R2 Mini	Turn on/off corridor lights
19	Laundry Lights	Laundry	Tasmota	SONOFF Basic R2 Mini	Turn on/off laundry lights
20	WLed_SW	Garage	Tasmota	CT-065W plug	Turn on/off front yard decoration lights
21	Coffeemaker	Anywhere	Tasmota	CT-065W plug	Turn on/off different lights at home
22	Wled	Front yard	WLED	WS2812 strip **Light Emitting Diode (LED)** lights	Control front yard decoration lights
23	Wled_tree	Dining room	WLED	WS2811 LED lights	Control Christmas tree LED lights

Table 1.5: Actuators in my home automation system

Most of my actuators are commercial based. Most of them are from SONOFF, which is known to be based on the ESP8265/8266 chip from Espressif Systems. In *Chapter 4*, I will tell you how I hacked two actuator models used at my home. *Chapter 9* in this book will be another hands-on project to explain how actuators *22* and *23* were created.

Bill of materials and costs

I captured in *Table 1.6* all the information you need to know about the cost and material used in my home automation system. Some items I purchased as kits with more than one unit, so I'm just including the items I need. I'm also including some tools and accessories I purchased for the installation. All costs are final costs after taxes.

More information and details about specific parts will be provided later in each of the hands-on project chapters:

Item	Function	Unit Cost (USD)	Qty	Total (USD)
Raspberry Pi 4 + power supply + case + 32 GB SD card	Home automation server	86	1	86
ESP32 module	Five-zone BT temperature collector	9	1	9
ESP8266 + BME280 (temperature sensor)	Part of a homemade temperature sensor	14	1	14
WS2811 LED lights	Christmas tree lights	15.50	1	15.50
ESP8266	Christmas light and front yard lights controller	3	2	6
Power Supply + WS2812 LED strip lights	Front yard LED strip lights	50	1	50
SONOFF basic R2	Various actuators	6.60	4	26.41
HC-SR501 PIR sensor	Part of a homemade motion sensor	2.50	1	2.50
Crimping tool + wire connector	Actuators installation	34	1	34
Universal Serial Bus (USB) wall charger	Homemade sensor	2.50	1	2.50
USB to Serial converter	Hack commercial sensors	6.50	1	6.50
SONOFF Mini R2 Basic	Various actuators	6.84	3	20.54
Tuya Smart Wi-Fi door sensor	Door sensors	5.80	4	23.2

Item	Function	Unit Cost (USD)	Qty	Total (USD)
Bluetooth Xiaomi thermometer	Five-zone Bluetooth temperature sensor	4.42	5	22.12
Total Cost				**318.27**

Table 1.6: Bill of materials and cost of my home automation system

I hope this section inspires and supports you to see how your home automation system could be if you don't have one yet. If you do have one, I still believe it could inspire you to include new and different devices in your home. You will see that it is not difficult to create your home automation system. We will start to do this in the next chapter. Therefore we can conclude this section and this chapter with the following summary.

Summary

In this chapter, we briefly reviewed the history of home automation systems and how they have evolved. I took you through some practical examples based on my experience with home automation.

We also looked at some key benefits of having a home automation system.

We learned about the components of a home automation system and how they are interconnected. The role of each component was explained in some detail.

Then we explored a real example of a home automation system by evaluating how its components are configured and distributed.

I also provided some insights into the materials and costs associated with building my own home automation system.

In the next chapter, we will start to build our home automation system by creating a home automation server using a Raspberry Pi 4 as the base hardware and Home Assistant as the main software. We will also get our first exposure to Home Assistant by learning more about its main features and its basic configuration.

2
Getting Started with Home Assistant

This chapter will introduce you to the Home Assistant software. You will learn how it was created and maintained. You will also learn about the different Home Assistant resources available at present and ways you can access and contribute to the community of developers and makers.

Besides this, this chapter will also cover a brief introduction to **YAML Ain't Markup Language (YAML)** so you will be familiar with how Home Assistant handles configurations and customizations using an interpreted language. We will see how to create a **home automation server** by guiding you to install Home Assistant on **Raspberry Pi**. Next, we will do some menu navigation to give you an overview of the resources available in Home Assistant. I will also guide you through the basic configurations, applications, and integrations required to set up the Home Assistant server to interact with **sensors** and **actuators**.

We will cover the following main topics in this chapter:

- Learning about Home Assistant
- YAML
- Raspberry Pi and Home Assistant
- Installing Home Assistant on Raspberry Pi
- Exploring a Home Assistant installation
- Home Assistant basic configuration

By the end of this chapter, you will understand how Home Assistant works and have a server based on Home Assistant able to manage your home automation system.

Technical requirements

In this chapter, you will need some familiarity with software installation done using a **Secure Digital (SD) card**. You will understand more about Home Assistant configurations if you have already configured some other kind of software before. Also, it will be easier for you to understand the **YAML pseudo-code language** if you have previously been exposed to some interpreted programming language.

You will understand the Raspberry Pi hardware specifications better if you know how a basic computer is configured, including its parts.

Learning about Home Assistant

In this section, the idea is to provide some background information about Home Assistant. This information will be useful in the next section when we talk more about the software installation.

Introduction and evolution

The Home Assistant is a software developed to be used as a home automation server. It was first released in 2013 and developed using the **Python** programming language by **Paulus Schoutsen**. It is free and open source software licensed under the **Apache 2.0** license.

In 2017, in order to ease the installation in some compacted devices, an operating system called **Hass.io** was introduced allowing users to manage, back up, update the local installation, and add some extra functionality by including **add-ons**. Also in 2017, an optional subscription service was introduced to address questions related to secured remote access and extend Home Assistant access to work with Amazon Alexa and Google Home Assistant. A company called **Nabu Casa** was created to manage this subscription service.

In 2020, some changes were made to handle the Home Assistant installation types better. The main part of the software was renamed **Home Assistant Core**, and the operating system Hass.io was renamed **Home Assistant** or **Home Assistant Operating System** (HAOS).

Since it was created, Home Assistant has *190,590* active home installations and is the second largest open source project by contributors in **GitHub** with *13,500* people, according to data shared in November 2022. It supports over *2,285* integrations, allowing it to be connected to different devices from different manufacturers. For more up-to-date statistics about Home Assistant, visit https://analytics.home-assistant.io/.

Home Assistant features and resources

Among the features and resources provided by Home Assistant, the following can be highlighted:

- It was developed to be used with a focus on **local control** and **privacy**. As mentioned in *Chapter 1*, there is no need to be connected to the internet to have your home automated using Home

Assistant.

- It supports the **client-server architecture** mentioned in *Chapter 1*, allowing the control of the wireless sensors and actuators installed in your home.

- Every device that is visible to Home Assistant can be managed by it using automation triggered by events, template routines (**blueprints**), or simply controlling them directly via the **dashboard**.

- The configuration of different devices is done seamlessly with the different integrations provided by Home Assistant.

- Depending on the installation type used, add-on software can be accessed directly through the Home Assistant interface.

- The default dashboard (formerly called **Lovelace**) provides a graphic interface access to users allowing different **cards** to be displayed. These cards inform the user about the status of the devices, also allowing some to be controlled directly using them. Other dashboards can be created according to your preference.

Important Home Assistant definitions

Home Assistant has some definitions that are important to understand before starting to use the system. These include the following terms:

- **Device**: This is any type of hardware or software that can be connected to or configured by Home Assistant.

- **Entity**: These are parameters, properties, or features that can be monitored or controlled by Home Assistant. We will explore these in more detail in *Chapter 5*.

- **Service**: This is the method used by Home Assistant to control some device or entity output. We will also learn more about this in *Chapter 5*.

- **Integration**: These are software packages that allow devices to be integrated or configured using Home Assistant. Integrations will be discussed in *Chapter 6*.

- **Add-on or application**: This is official or third-party software that can be used with or without Home Assistant. Add-ons will be explored in *Chapter 7*.

Home Assistant availability

Home Assistant can be available in different ways, allowing the users to choose the type of installation for the operating system according to their preference. It is available for the most popular clients operating systems enabling it to be used in phones, tablets, and other compact devices.

In the sequence, the Home Assistant software availability will be discussed by installation type, hardware, server operating system, and client operating system.

Availability – server installation types

Home Assistant can be installed in four ways:

- **HAOS**: This installation will be covered in this chapter. It provides access to all Home Assistant features, including automation, dashboard, integrations, blueprints, supervisor, add-ons, and backups.

- **Home Assistant Container**: This installation will be covered as part of the **IOTstack** in *Chapter 8*. It provides a container-based installation for the Home Assistant core. It contains all Home Assistant features except the ability to install add-ons directly to the Home Assistant interface.

- **Home Assistant Supervised** and **Home Assistant Core**: These two installations are recommended for experienced users and will not be covered in this book.

It is good to comment that the first installation I used for Home Assistant in my home was the Home Assistant Container. The main reason to use it was that I wanted to try Home Assistant and use the Raspberry Pi operational system at the same time. If Home Assistant was not what I was looking for, it could be easily removed by deleting the container and continuing to use the Raspberry Pi operational system.

Availability – hardware and server operating system types

Home Assistant can be installed on different hardware types and depending on the hardware type, the different options for installation (mentioned in the previous subsection) are available.

As already mentioned, this book will be focused on Raspberry Pi, which supports HAOS, Home Assistant Container, and Home Assistant Core.

The other hardware devices supported by Home Assistant are **Odroid**, **Asus Tinker Board**, **Intel NUC**, **Home Assistant Blue**, and **Home Assistant Yellow**. Home Assistant Blue and Yellow are devices developed specifically to run Home Assistant and are based on **Odroid-N2+** and **Raspberry Pi Compute Module 4**. Home Assistant Blue is currently discontinued.

Regarding operating systems, Home Assistant is available to install on Windows, macOS, and Linux. Among these, only Linux supports all four installation types mentioned in the previous subsection.

Availability – client operating system installations

Besides the installation types, devices, and server operating systems, Home Assistant can also provide client application software compatible with the main operating systems used in cell phones and smartwatches. It is available for Android and iOS. You can download them using the following links:

- **Android**: https://play.google.com/store/apps/details?id=io.homeassistant.companion.android

- **iOS**: https://apps.apple.com/us/app/home-assistant/id1099568401

The Home Assistant installation for cell phones not only allows the user to access Home Assistant through it but also register and integrate it as a device that can be used as a presence sensor in your home. This will be discussed later in this chapter when we talk about basic configuration.

Community and support

Home Assistant has a highly active official community. This community provides support using the following channels:

- **Forums**: `https://community.home-assistant.io/`
- **Discord**: `https://discord.com/invite/home-assistant`
- **Youtube**: `https://www.youtube.com/@home_assistant`
- **Twitter**: `https://twitter.com/home_assistant`
- **Reddit**: `https://www.reddit.com/r/homeassistant/`
- **Facebook**: `https://www.facebook.com/homeassistantio`

There are other local communities that use **Telegram**, for example. In this case, it is worth mentioning **Home Assistant Brasil** (`https://t.me/HomeAssistantbrasil`) and **Home Assistant BR** (`https://t.me/HomeAssistant_Brasil`) Telegram channels.

You can participate in the community by accessing these channels and posting questions, commenting, or answering somebody else. In the forums, there are up to 16 topics where you can interact with other users.

In the next section, we will review the configuration language used by Home Assistant to define several aspects of the system.

YAML

YAML (`www.yaml.org`) is a data serialization language created to be used for programming languages. It is used to configure parameters for those who prefer to work with Home Assistant in a programming language style. You do not need to use YAML to do basic configuration, but if you need more complex configuration or if you like programming languages, it is good to know more about it.

The `automations.yaml` file is one of the most important files in Home Assistant. It is used to store the automation configured in the system. I will use this file so you can gain an understanding of what the YAML language looks like.

> **Important note**
> The `automations.yaml` file is managed by the user interface and should not be edited manually. If you want to manually create automation, the `configuration.yaml` file should be used instead.

The following YAML code is what is implemented in my home for my homemade motion sensor installed in my garage:

```yaml
- id: '1634873959087'
  alias: Garage Lights On - Motion Detected
  description: Turn On Garage Lights when Motion is Detected
  trigger:
  - platform: state
    entity_id: binary_sensor.garage_pir
    from: 'OFF'
    to: 'ON'
  condition:
  - condition: sun
    before: sunrise
    after: sunset
  action:
  - type: turn_on
    device_id: 14a825059d81043431cf317bce918c5c
    entity_id: light.garagelights
    domain: light
  - wait_template: ''
    timeout: '120'
  - type: turn_off
    device_id: 14a825059d81043431cf317bce918c5c
    entity_id: light.garagelights
    domain: light
  mode: single
```

The YAML pseudo code has a condition that if the sun entity is after the sunset entity and before the sunrise entity when the state platform of the binary_sensor.garage_pir entity changes from 'OFF' to 'ON', it triggers an action throught the action parameter to turn_ on the light.garagelights entity. In the sequence, a timeout of 120 seconds is created as indicated by the timeout parameter. After this timeout expires, the action continues by turning off the light.garagelights entity_id entity. This automation is configured to be executed in single mode, meaning that if the motion sensor is triggered again while the automation is being executed, there will be no effect.

An aspect to observe while using YAML is that the indentation is particularly important. Everything indented belongs to the upper-level variable, and the comments started with #.

It is worth mentioning that the main configuration user file maintained by Home Assistant is the configuration.yaml file. This file defines various aspects of Home Assistant, such as integrations, devices, and automations. The content of this file varies depending on your specific setup and utilization. *Figure 2.1* shows a screenshot of the configuration.yaml file, accessed using a file editor inside a Home Assistant installation:

Figure 2.1: Example of the configuration.yaml file

The file in *Figure 2.1* shows comments and indented text, as discussed previously. It also has configurations related to the mqtt protocol and the sensor configuration. We will see the content of this and other items in *Chapter 5* and *Chapter 6*. Some content of configuration.yaml is added automatically by Home Assistant, such as the automation:, script:, and scene: lines, which are added once an automation, script, and scene is created.

For more information about using YAML with Home Assistant, visit this link: `https://www.home-assistant.io/docs/configuration/yaml`.

After learning about the Home Assistant software and getting a brief overview of YAML, it's time for us to move to the next section where we will discuss the hardware we will use to install Home Assistant.

Raspberry Pi as a home automation server

In this section, we will explore some aspects of Raspberry Pi, and in the next section, install Home Assistant on it. The idea here is to focus on important aspects required for a hardware device when installing a home automation server software such as Home Assistant. We will not explain details about the Raspberry Pi hardware. For more information about Raspberry Pi, including all models currently available, please visit `https://www.raspberrypi.org`.

Hardware architecture

One of the popular hardware devices used for Home Assistant software installations is Raspberry Pi. This particular **Single Board Computer** (**SBC**) is the one chosen for the examples given in this book. The model I recommend is the Raspberry Pi Model B with 4 GB of **RAM** or above. I've been running this installation for my home automation system since mid-2021 without any problem. It has all the resources and peripherals needed for the home automation server, including the following specifications:

- **Advanced RISC Machines** (**ARM**) **Cortex A-72** quad-core processor with 1.5 GHz clock speed and 64-bit address/data bus. This processor is embedded in a **System on Chip** (**SoC**) from **Broadcom**.

- 4 GB of RAM.

- **Wi-Fi 802.11ac**.

- 1x **Ethernet port**

- SD card slot support.

- Input voltage: **5V@2.5A**.

- Size, including enclosure: **9 x 6 x 3 cm**.

The hardware already includes Bluetooth 5, four USB ports (two USB 3.0/two USB 2.0), a dual screen monitor via micro **High-Definition Multimedia Interface** (**HDMI**) ports, and different **Input/ Output** (**IO**) pins for generic use, but these features will not be used by the home automation server implemented in this book.

Figure 2.2 shows the main components of the Raspberry Pi so you can be familiar with the hardware:

Figure 2.2: The main components of the Raspberry Pi

Figure 2.2 shows some of the hardware features to be used by the home automation server that are explained in the next section. It is important to mention that the **SD card** slot is not represented in the picture since it is located underneath the board on the opposite side.

Main Raspberry Pi features used by the home automation system

The ARM processor architecture is powerful and allows Raspberry Pi to run operating systems such as Linux and Hass.io, which was developed to be a standalone variation to use just Home Assistant on it.

As previously discussed, the Wi-Fi support on the Raspberry Pi enables wireless communication to be used in our home automation system. If preferred, access to a wireless network can be obtained by connecting the Raspberry Pi directly to a router via the Ethernet port. The router will always provide wireless connectivity between the Raspberry Pi and the sensors and actuators.

The Ethernet port can be used initially to configure the Home Assistant installation connected to a router directly connected to the internet. After the installation, you can choose to keep it connected to the Ethernet network via cable, which improves reliability, or connect using Wi-Fi wireless communication.

The USB ports can be used as external ports to connect a keyboard and mouse to monitor the Raspberry Pi installation if required. A USB dongle can provide access to a Bluetooth keyboard or mouse for Raspberry Pi. After the installation, the system can be used remotely, so the USB ports could be used to provide power to other devices, as I am doing today, using it to feed an **ESP32** module.

The dual-screen monitor ports can be useful during the initial installation of the system. Just one monitor port is enough for the Home Assistant installation. After the installation, the system can be accessed remotely after the boot, so it is no longer required.

The SD card slot support allows SD cards to install the operating system, including Home Assistant. A 32 GB SD card is recommended to install all the software required to run your home automation system.

The **power supply** for the Raspberry Pi is a key factor to consider and a critical part of the system. Depending on the power supply used, the power range could not be enough to supply the energy required causing undesirable instabilities such as the system rebooting and even crashing. For a Raspberry Pi 4, the minimum power range required is **15 W** or **5 V at 3 A of current**.

The Raspberry Pi size is just something to consider because it allows the home automation server to be physically located in small places in your home.

The Raspberry Pi 4 is certainly a good hardware for the Home Assistant installation since it is a compact device with plenty of suitable features. This will be proved in the next section when we will install Home Assistant on a Raspberry Pi.

Installing Home Assistant on a Raspberry Pi

To install Home Assistant on a Raspberry Pi, you will need the following material:

- The hardware required to prepare the Home Assistant software in the SD card

  - An SD card reader used to prepare the SD card for installation using a computer

  - A desktop or laptop computer

- Home automation server:

  - Raspberry Pi 4 Model B 4 GB (recommended, but others can be used)

  - A Raspberry Pi case

  - Raspberry Pi power supply (15 W minimum)

  - 32 GB SD card minimum

- Peripherals used just for installation with the Raspberry Pi:

  - A router connected to the internet

  - An Ethernet cable

Preparing the SD card for Home Assistant installation

The installation type used in this chapter and in the first, second, and third parts of this book (up to *Chapter 7*) will be the recommended installation method, the HAOS. This includes the Supervisor software to manage the Home Assistant Core and to install the add-ons.

To prepare the SD card with the image software required to install Home Assistant on Raspberry Pi, follow these steps:

1. Download and install the **balena Etcher** software (https://www.balena.io/etcher/) on your computer. Make sure the SD card is connected to the SD card reader.

2. Start the software in admin mode and select **Flash from URL**, as shown in *Figure 2.3*:

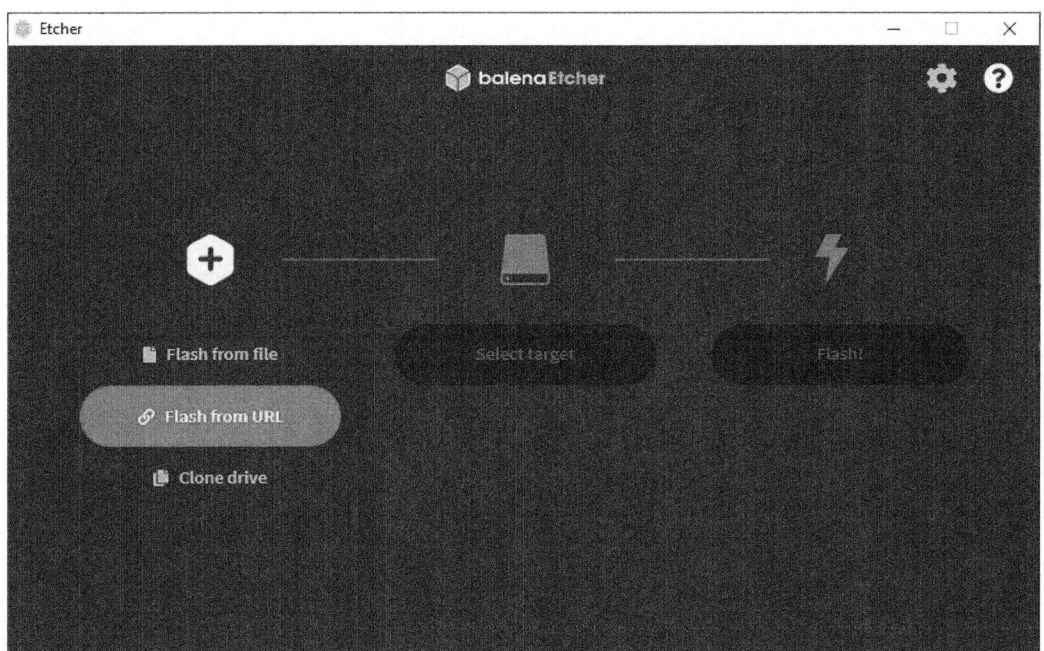

Figure 2.3: balena Etcher software – the Flash from URL option

3. You should look for the most recent release version for the Raspberry Pi operating system in this Home Assistant repository: https://github.com/home-assistant/operating-system/releases. The file name should usually be in the haos_rpiX-YY-ZZ.img.xz format, where the following is true:

    *   X is the **Raspberry Pi model**. In the case of this installation, X=4.

    *   YY is the address/data bus size. In our case YY=64.

    *   ZZ is the release version. The latest version for Raspberry Pi at the time of writing is 9.3.

4. The complete URL for the installation will be `https://github.com/home-assistant/operating-system/releases/download/9.3/haos_rpi4-64-9.3.img.xz`. Type or copy and paste the URL into the **Use Image URL** field and click **OK**.

5. On the next screen, click on the **Select target** button, and then on the other screen that will be shown, select the target SD card you want to flash the software image onto and click the **Select** button.

6. Flash the Home Assistant image by clicking on the **Flash!** button.

    The image will be flashed and validated on the SD card. After five to eight minutes, if everything goes well, you should get a screen with the **Flash Complete!** message, indicating the SD image was installed successfully. *Figure 2.4* shows two points of the installation progress:

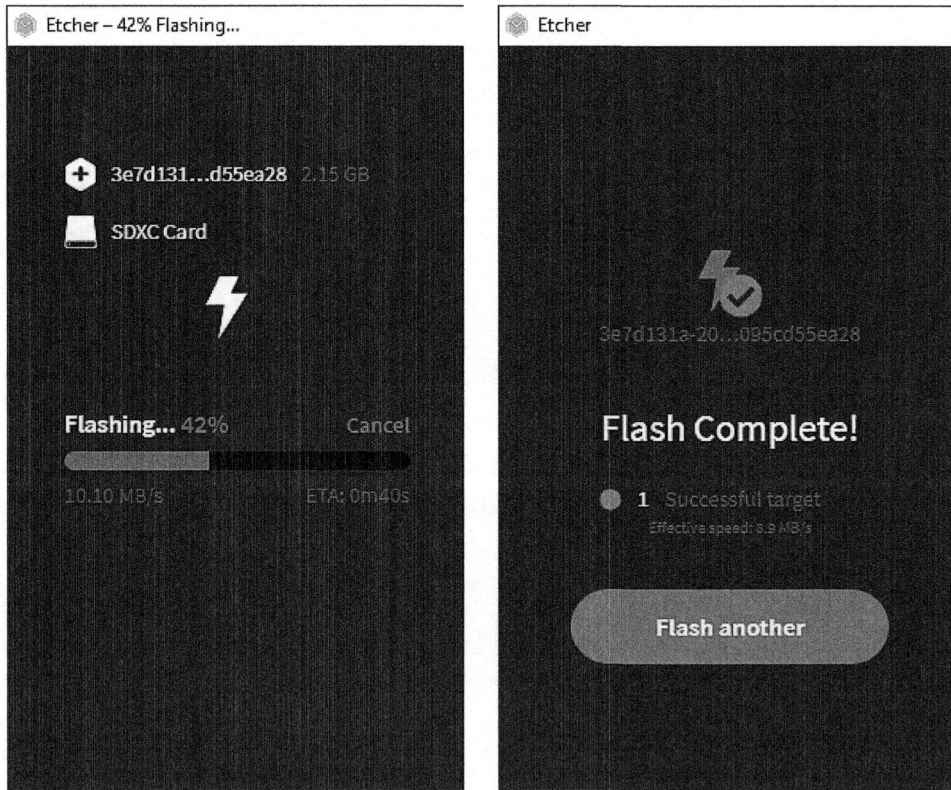

Figure 2.4: SD card installation progress

The left side of *Figure 2.4* shows the SD card being flashed at 42%, and on the right, the completed flash process.

After the Home Assistant image installation in the SD card, the next step is to remove it from the computer and use it on Raspberry Pi, which will be covered in the next section.

> **Important note**
>
> If preferred, the option of installing from a file could be easier in case of slow internet speeds. You can download the file to the computer and install it using the **Flash from File** option instead of **Flash from URL**.

Home Assistant installation verification of Raspberry Pi

The router, the Ethernet cable, and the Raspberry Pi should be connected, as shown in *Figure 2.5*, to verify the Home Assistant operating system installation on the SD card. The Raspberry Pi should be installed in its case for the best protection and connected to its power supply. The SD card configured in the last section should now be inserted into the Raspberry Pi. These parts will compose the home automation server. Besides these parts, the other peripherals should be connected to the Raspberry Pi to complete the verification:

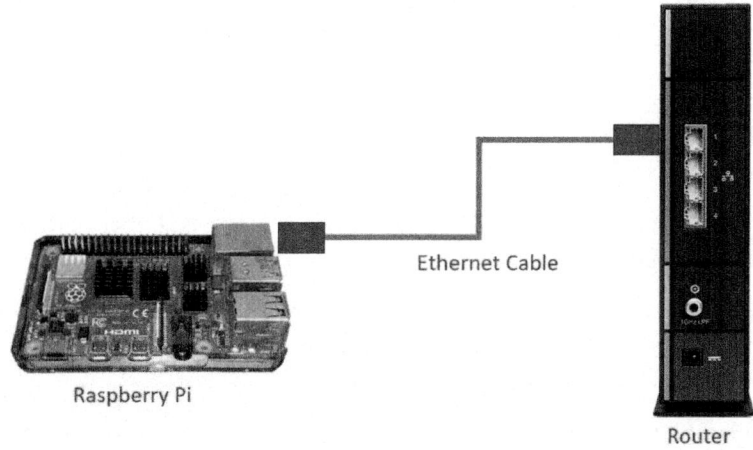

Figure 2.5: The Raspberry Pi interconnection for Home Assistant installation verification

After connecting all the parts shown in *Figure 2.5*, turn on the Raspberry Pi. If you are using a monitor, it will be possible to see the Raspberry Pi boot process of the Home Assistant **Command Line Interface** (**CLI**). If not, after turning on the Raspberry Pi, you will need to wait for at least two to three minutes until the Raspberry Pi boot completes. After completing the boot process, you can access the `http://homeassistant.local:4357/` URL using a web browser to check whether the system is connected and installed correctly. The web browser should return the information presented in *Figure 2.6*:

Home Assistant observer

Supervisor: Connected
Supported: Supported
Healthy: Healthy

Figure 2.6: Home Assistant installation status

The three indicators, **Supervisor**, **Supported**, and **Healthy** should be green and with the messages **Connected**, **Supported**, and **Healthy**, respectively, as presented in *Figure 2.6*.

Now that you verified the Home Assistant system was installed correctly, you will configure it so you can start to use it. This will be the topic for the next section.

> **Important note**
> If for some reason you got different information from the previous screenshot required in the web browser, review the SD card preparation process steps and try to create it again. Also, make sure you have working Raspberry Pi hardware. You can also follow the boot process by using the monitor to check whether everything is being initiated correctly.

Home Assistant initial configuration

In this section, we will do the initial configuration so you can start using the system. Currently, there will just be the configuration related to the home automation server. Other types of configurations will be presented later in this section or in the next chapters.

As you will have noticed, all the access and configuration of Home Assistant are done using a web browser. You just need to have the Raspberry Pi turned on and connected to your home network to be able to use your Home Assistant installation.

The initial configuration required to use the home automation server includes the following steps:

1.   Create a user account to use with Home Assistant.

2.   Create a house name and do the general setup.

3.   Configure initial integrations.

Creating a user account to use with Home Assistant

The account creation will allow you and your family to use the home automation server using a web browser from a computer or other electronic devices in your home, such as tablets or cell phones.

These are the steps to create a user account to be used in Home Assistant:

1. With the Raspberry Pi turned on and connected to the router, point your browser to `http://homeassistant.local:8123`. The following message will be presented: **Preparing Home Assistant**.

2. After some minutes, the user account creation screen will be presented. Fill the **Name** field with your house name and the **Username** value you want for you. Type your password and confirm it. I'm using `your_name_and_family_name` for both the **Name** and **Username** fields for educational purposes. These field details are presented in *Figure 2.7*:

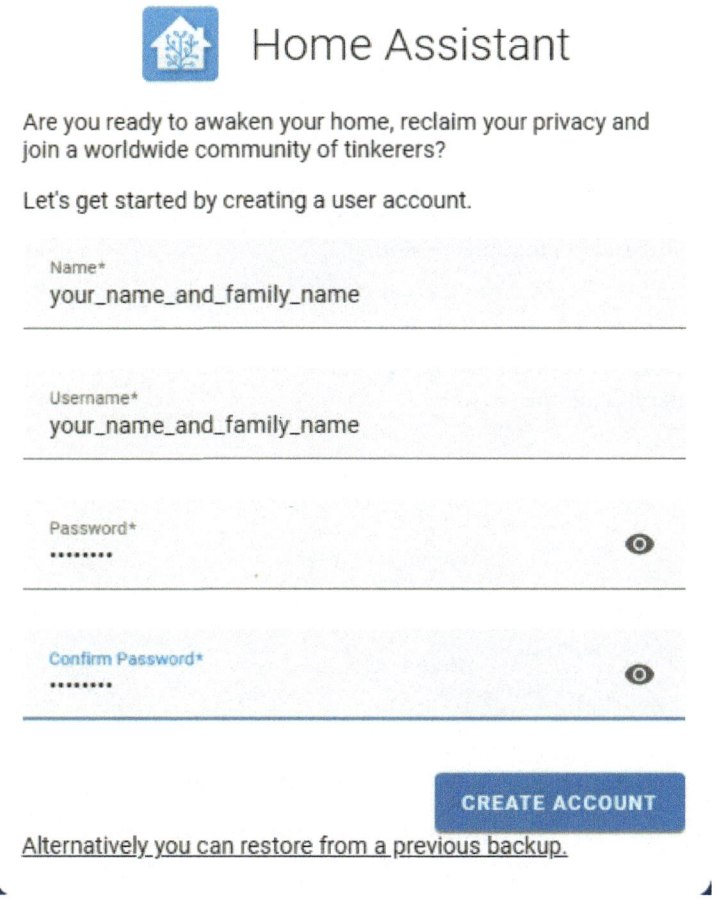

Figure 2.7: The Home Assistant create account screen

3. Click on the **CREATE ACCOUNT** button. Your Home Assistant account will be created.

Creating a house name and general setup

After creating the user account, it is time to configure the name of your home and other information, including the following:

- **Location**: This is where the home automation server will be installed
- **Country**
- **Timezone**
- **Language**
- **Elevation**
- **Measurement Unit System**
- **Currency**

> **Important note**
> Your location will be important for displaying information and will be helpful when setting automation events based on the sun's position.

A screen, as shown in *Figure 2.8*, will present the previously defined fields, so complete them according to your location and preference and click **NEXT**. You do not need to fill in all the information because you can change it later if required:

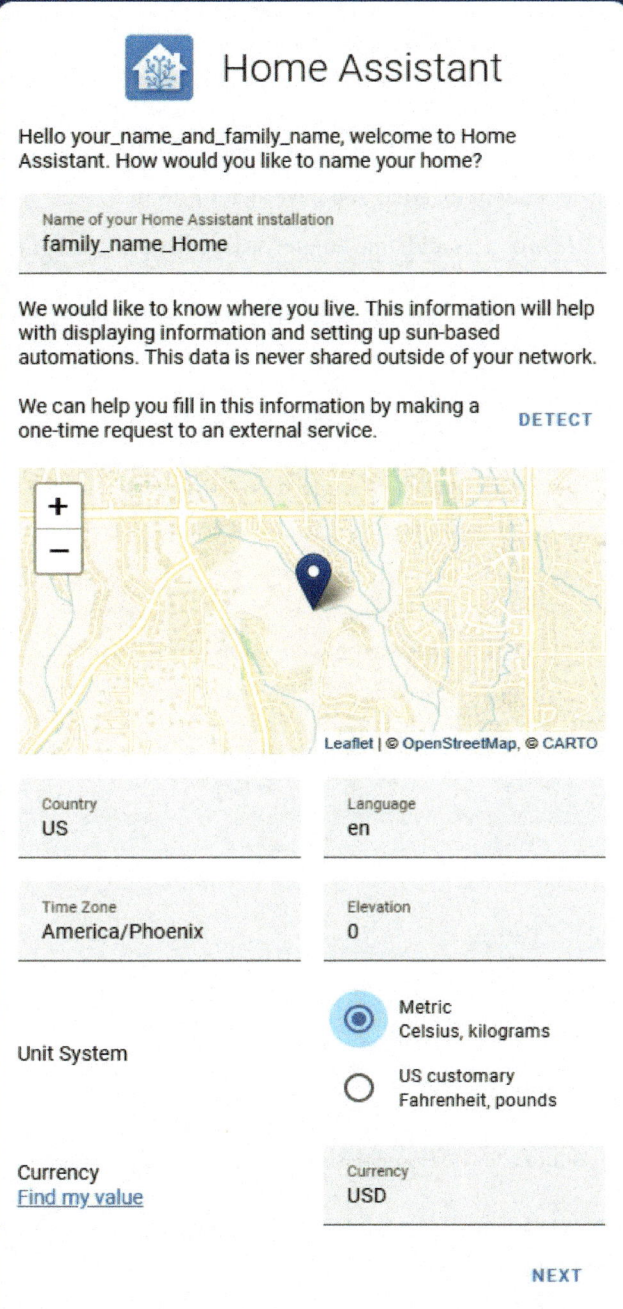

Figure 2.8: The Home Assistant initial configuration screen

Another screen could be presented in the sequence asking to share information data. I used to turn all the options on so the system could be improved in several ways.

Configuring initial integrations

After performing the general and data-sharing configuration, it is time to configure some integrations if required. This will be dependent on what you have at your home.

A screen like the one in *Figure 2.9* will be presented, asking you to configure different devices. For example, using the devices I have at my home without any configuration, Home Assistant detected eight of them. You can select as many devices as you want to be automatically integrated into Home Assistant:

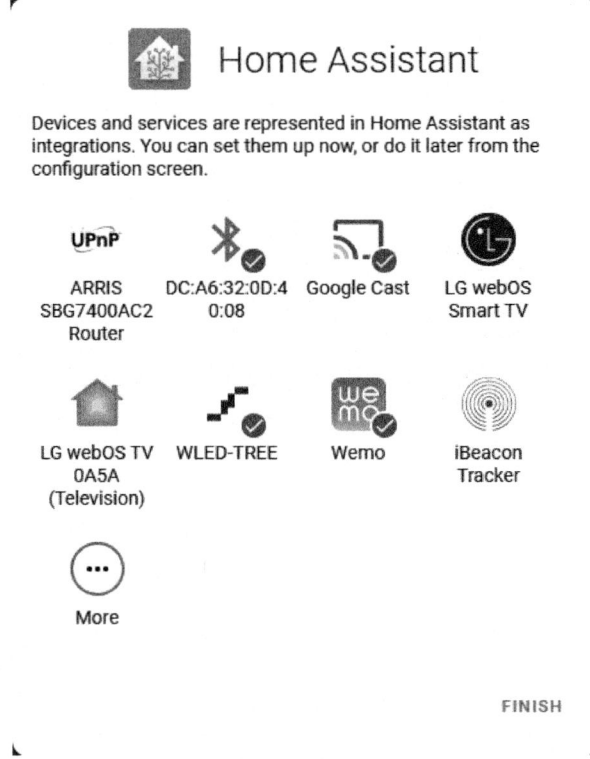

Figure 2.9: The Home Assistant initial integrations screen

As you click on the **FINISH** button, your initial configuration is done, and you can now start to use Home Assistant installed on your Raspberry Pi.

In this section, we covered the installation process of Home Assistant on a Raspberry Pi, from the SD card setup on the computer to the healthy verification process. We also learned how to create a user account to use with Home Assistant and configure the initial parameters. In the next section, we will explore and continue to configure your Home Assistant installation.

Exploring a Home Assistant installation

In this section, we will explore the Home Assistant installation performed in the last sections by explaining the screen and menu disposal and then navigating through the menus explaining notable features, system functions, and options. This will help you to understand how Home Assistant is organized and where to find the resources and features to be used and configured.

Home Assistant default screen and menu disposition

If you just configured the system and are following this book sequence, you will not need to proceed with the initial login to the system. It will automatically access the system.

If you have not logged in to the system yet, logged out, or are logging in from your tablet or cell phone for the first time, you will need to fill in some information to initiate Home Assistant. The login process is straightforward: just input your username and password in the fields provided when accessing the `http://homeassistant.local:8123` URL. After filling in these fields, click on the **LOGIN** button to access Home Assistant.

After the initial logging, the default screen presented is the dashboard, as can be seen in *Figure 2.10*. We will present dashboard in more detail in *Chapter 6*; for now, we will limit ourselves to introducing how the Home Assistant screen is organized so you can navigate and find what you need:

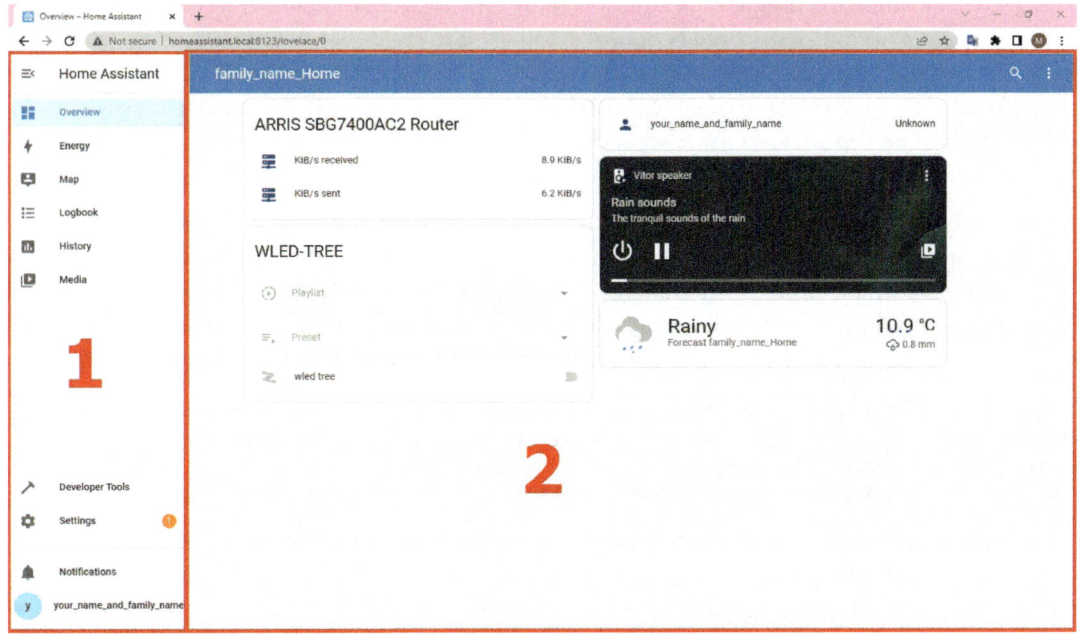

Figure 2.10: The Home Assistant default screen disposition

On the left side of *Figure 2.10*, marked as **1**, the Home Assistant sidebar is presented. Using it, you can access different information in Home Assistant and submenus that will guide you to different configurations and user options. On the right side, marked as **2**, the Home Assistant sidebar choice is presented.

Home Assistant sidebar navigation

In this section, we will explore all options in the sidebar, and briefly explain all the content that is accessible using those options. In some cases, such as the **Developer Tools** option, we will provide more detail that will be explained later in this or in *Chapters 5*, *6*, and *7*.

The sidebar options are as follows:

- **Overview**: This will present the dashboard. More details on this are provided in *Chapter 6*.

- **Energy**: This allows you to configure and monitor the energy consumption/generation in your home. More details can be found at `https://www.home-assistant.io/docs/energy/electricity-grid/`.

- **Map**: This helps you to map **zones** and **areas** in your home. Accessing this option using the sidebar allows you to create mapped zones based on latitude, longitude, and radius. The zone of your house is created during the initial configuration if you allow Home Assistant to do it. You can adjust/reconfigure the zones of your house if required. Other zones can be created using this option. That could be useful if you want to create automation based on where you are located. You can also create areas in your home using the **Map** option. Areas are rooms you have or want to create in your home. Examples of areas are bedrooms, the kitchen, or the garage. You can group sensors and actuators located or based in areas and take some action based on them at the same time by referring to an area, for instance.

- **Logbook**: This allows you to present and track all events generated by sensors, actuators, and other devices that are detected or connected to Home Assistant. You can filter by **Start date**, **End date**, and by **Entity**. An example of events that can be found on this tab is the changes in the state or property of some entity. When the event happens, the **event logger** will list details, including **entity name**, **event type**, **event time**, and **time elapsed** since the event occurred.

- **History**: This allows you to track what happened in a certain period of time in your home. You can use different filters to extract information by area, device, or by device entity.

- **Media**: Media management includes local images, videos, radio stations, and so on.

- **Developer Tools**: Different **Developer Tools** are used to check and change the states of entities, enable **services**, generate and listen to events, and present **statistics**. These options will be explored in *Chapter 5*, when we will test and debug automation.

- **Settings**: This is where all configuration is done. 10 submenus can be accessed using this option in release 9.3, as seen in *Figure 2.11*. We will cover the content of **Settings** in some of the configurations done in this and other chapters:

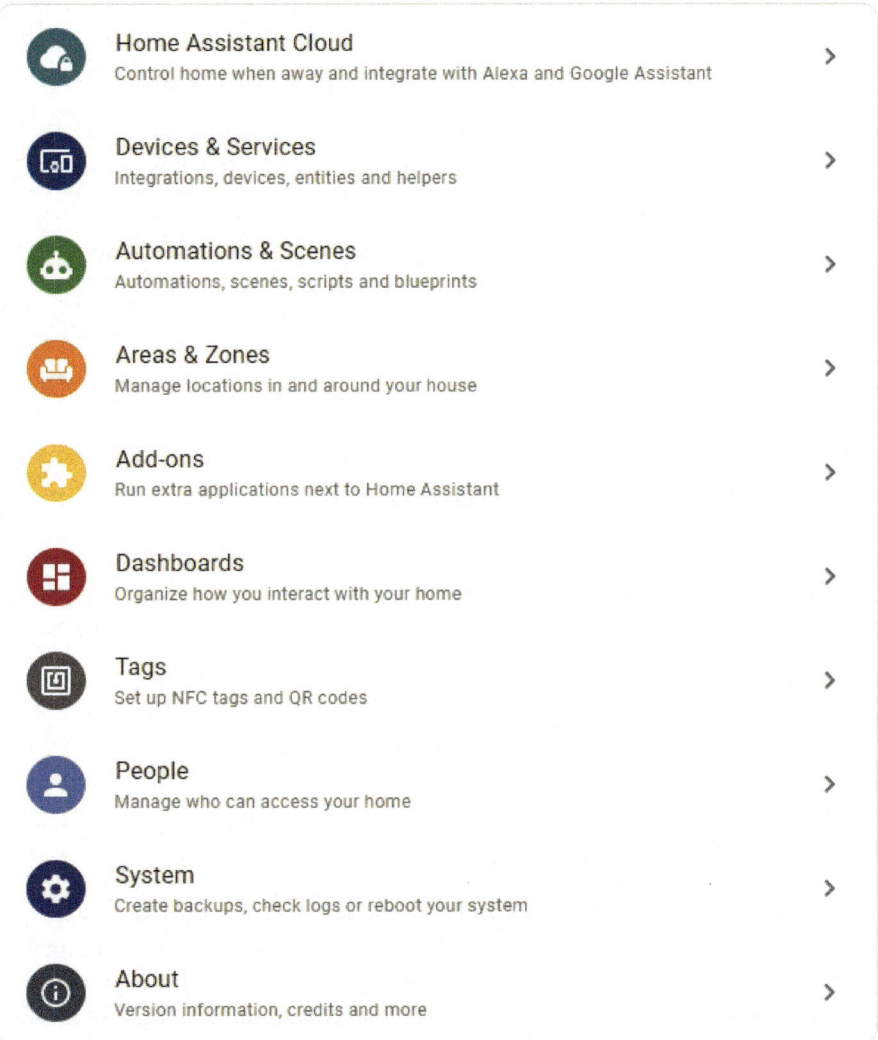

Figure 2.11: Configuration options available in the Settings menu

- **Notifications**: Clicking on this option on the sidebar allows you to check for notifications from Home Assistant. It can alert you that new devices were discovered by Home Assistant, for example.

- **Username**: The **Username** option accessed via the sidebar enables you to do basic configurations in your system related to user preference. The most important configurations will be explored later in this chapter.

Another way to navigate to Home Assistant is by using some keyboard hotkeys to look for specific parameters. You can type these hotkeys in any Home Assistant screen at the frontend. The following hotkeys are available:

- Entity filter – hotkey *E*: Allows you to quickly search for an entity configured in Home Assistant. It is similar to going through the following menus: **Settings** | **Devices & Services** | **Entities**.

- Command palette – hotkey *C*: This runs commands without having to change to another screen or view. It currently supports the **Navigate**, **Reload**, and **Server** commands.

In this section, we have seen how the Home Assistant screen is organized and how the configuration options can be found. We also reviewed the options provided by Home Assistant to automate your home. In the next section, we will perform some basic configurations in Home Assistant to prepare it to work with the sensors and actuators.

Home Assistant basic configurations

In this section, we will explore some of the basic configurations to be done in Home Assistant to prepare it for use as our home automation server. We will learn about some other basic configurations to be done in the system so you can better manage and handle it. We will clean up the dashboard so that we can add sensors and actuators in the coming chapters.

These configurations are supposed to be done initially when you start to use the system, and you will not have to change them regularly unless you need to change your home location, change some personal configuration, or other major changes occur.

User preference configuration

User preference configurations are optional and help you to interact better with the system. They can be found by clicking on the last option presented in the sidebar, located at the bottom-left corner of the screen, which has the **Username** value configured when Home Assistant was installed. Here, the username is **your_name_and_family_name**. These main configurations available in this option are as follows:

- **Language**: This allows language configuration to be used by Home Assistant. More than 60 different languages are supported.

- **Number Format**: This allows configuration for the number format.

- **Time Format**: This allows configuration for the time format.

- **First day of the week**: This allows you to choose the start day of the week.

- **Theme**: This allows you to change the colors in the user interface. More advanced configuration can be performed by adding data to the `configuration.yaml` file. Check out `https://www.home-assistant.io/integrations/frontend/#defining-themes` for more information.

- **Change Password**: This allows you to change the password to access Home Assistant.

General configuration

The **General** configuration option handles information initially created when the system is first configured. You can modify the **General** configuration by accessing **Settings | System | General**. The options that can be changed through this menu are house **Name**, **Time Zone**, **Elevation**, temperature **Unit System**, **Currency**, **Country**, and **Language**. An extra feature to edit the location of your home, using the **Edit location** option is also available. If you change any of these configurations, you will be required to click on the **UPDATE** button to confirm the changes.

People configuration

The **People** configuration option allows you to view what people are using Home Assistant and how these people can interact with it. It is helpful to configure people in your home because you can use the **presence** status of these people to include them in your automation. The **presence** status monitors whether a device such as the cell phone of a person is connected to the same Home Assistant network. If the cell phone associated with the person can be found in the Home Assistant network, it is declared **at home**; otherwise, it is assumed the person is **not at home**.

The **People** configuration option is accessible through **Settings | People**. You can edit the current configuration of the main user (here, it is **your_name_and_family_name**) or create a new person by clicking on the **ADD PERSON** button in the right corner. The screenshot in *Figure 2.12* appears after you click on the button:

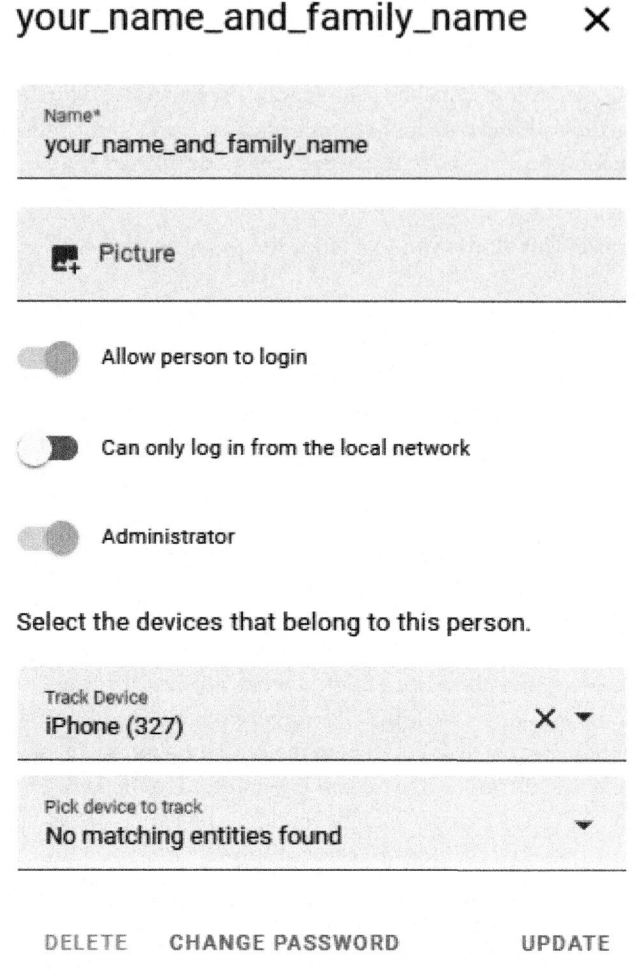

Figure 2.12: Configuring a person in your home

To associate a cell phone with a person, the easiest way to do it is to download the Home Assistant application on your cell phone using the links provided in the *Availability – client operating system installations* section in this chapter. After the application installation, log in to the system using the cell phone, providing the login name and password. After doing that, your cell phone will automatically be integrated with Home Assistant. Click on **Settings** | **People** | **your_name_and_family_name** and associate the cell phone integrated with Home Assistant to the person you desire by selecting it in the **Track Device** field, as shown in *Figure 2.11*. You can see what the configuration screen looks like. You should click on **UPDATE** so the configurations take effect.

> **Important note**
>
> For a person's home presence to work properly you will have to make sure your home location is set up correctly. You can verify it using the **Map** option located in the Home Assistant sidebar.

MQTT configuration

The **Message Queuing Telemetry Transport (MQTT)** configuration is an essential part of the system to work with the **Internet Of Things (IoT) devices** in Home Assistant. It is important to configure it now in Home Assistant so when we start to add sensors and actuators in *Chapters 3* and *4*, we will not need to configure Home Assistant, just these devices.

We need to install and configure an **MQTT broker** to use with Home Assistant. We will do it by installing an add-on called **Mosquitto** (`https://mosquitto.org/`). Click in the following sequence to install Mosquitto: **Settings | Add-ons | ADD-ON STORE** (lower right corner). Select **Mosquitto broker** under **Official add-ons** and then click **INSTALL**. After less than a minute, Mosquitto will be installed on your Home Assistant server, and the screen shown in *Figure 2.13* will be presented. Make sure to toggle the **Start on boot** option to on. Click on the **START** button to start the Mosquitto MQTT broker:

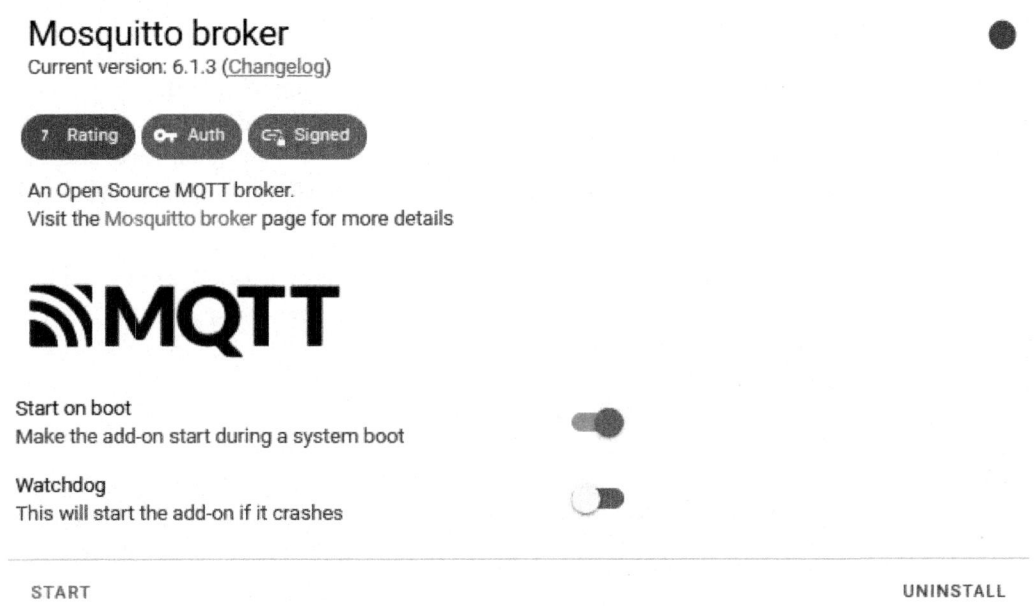

Figure 2.13: MQTT broker add-on installation and configuration

If everything goes well, a green circle will be presented at the top right of the **Mosquito Broker** window.

We have to authorize logins that will be able to use the Mosquitto MQTT broker. We can do this by clicking on **Settings | Mosquitto broker | Configuration** (tab). In the **Options | Logins** window, add the following:

```
- username: your_name
  password: your_password
```

You can choose the username and password of your choice. In this case, I chose your_name and your_password. After doing that, click on **Save**. A window will be presented asking you to restart the Mosquitto broker. Click on **Restart**. The Mosquitto broker will be restarted.

We now have to configure the **MQTT integration**. We will do this by assessing **Settings | Devices & Services**. Under the **Integrations** tab, you will notice an integration labeled **Discovered** with the **MQTT** name. Click on the **Configure** button inside the MQTT integration. A popup window will be presented with the **MQTT Broker via Home Assistant add-on** title. Click on the **Submit** button. Another window will be presented saying **Success in the creation of a configuration for Mosquito broker**. Click **Finish**.

For now, these configurations will be enough to be connected to the sensors and actuators.

Wi-Fi network configuration

Wi-Fi configuration can be done by accessing **Settings | System | Network**. On the screen that will be displayed, click on **WLAN0 | Wi-Fi | Scan for Access Points**. The name of the Wi-Fi networks will be displayed. Select the Wi-Fi network you want to connect to, and below that, select the security protocol of the network and include the password. Click **SAVE**. You will also need to set up the **IPV4** option. Click on **IPV4** and check the **DHCP** radio button and click on **Save**.

Now, if required, you can disconnect your Raspberry Pi from the Ethernet cable connected to your router and install it anywhere in your home with sufficient Wi-Fi signal coverage.

Dashboard cleanup

After learning some basic configurations that need to be done in the system, we are almost done with the chapter. All that's remaining is just a cleanup of the dashboard to leave the minimal information that will be used in the next chapters. To do the dashboard clean-up or cards deletion, follow these steps:

1. Access the **Overview** tab in the Home Assistant sidebar.

2. Click on the three vertical dots in the upper right corner and then click the **Edit Dashboard** option.

3. For each card, click on the three vertical dots in its lower right corner and then select **Delete card** to delete the card.

4. Delete all cards except the one related to your presence at home and the one related to the forecast for your home.

5.   After the cleanup, click on the **DONE** button in the upper right corner. After cleanup, the dashboard should present the following cards or something similar to what is shown in *Figure 2.14*:

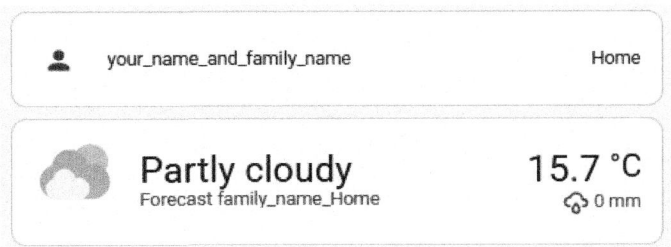

Figure 2.14: The dashboard configuration after cleanup

In this section, we performed some setup involving user preferences, general, people, and Wi-Fi configurations. We also did an important configuration involving the MQTT communication protocol enabling Home Assistant to integrate sensors and actuators. We finalized the section by cleaning the dashboard in preparation for future configurations to be done in *Chapter 6*.

Summary

In this chapter, we started the journey to create a home automation system using Home Assistant. We learned more about the Home Assistant software by reviewing its history, development purposes, availability, and resources. We prepared an SD card and installed Home Assistant on a Raspberry Pi. We learned how to navigate the Home Assistant menus, submenus, and tabs and identified where to find different options available for configuring the system. Talking about configuration, we learned how to configure the basics of the system to prepare it to integrate the first sensors and actuators.

This chapter also gave you an idea about YAML and how to use it to do some configurations in Home Assistant.

Your home automation system now has the first component: the home automation server.

In *Chapters 3* and *4*, you will learn how to create your own sensor and hack a commercial actuator to be used with Home Assistant. Let's continue the journey and add more devices to your system!

Part 2:
Install, Create, and Hack Sensors and Actuators

In this part, you will learn everything needed about sensors and actuators to integrate them into your Home Automation system. We will create our own sensor and hack an actuator to work with Home Assistant. By the end of this part, you will be able to view and configure sensor statuses and control actuators using Home Assistant.

This part has the following chapters:

- *Chapter 3, Hands-On Project 1 – Creating Your Own Sensor*
- *Chapter 4, Hacking a Commercial Actuator to Work with Home Assistant*

3
Hands-On Project 1 – Creating Your Own Sensor

This chapter will perhaps be one of the most interesting in this book as it contains lots of hands-on exercises. In this chapter, you will learn how to create a combined **sensor** with two different element inputs: a **temperature sensor** and a **motion sensor**. I will refer to it as a **double measurement sensor**. First, I will explain each electronic part that can be integrated with the **sensor** and teach you how to interconnect the parts using an electronic circuit. I will also show you how to deploy the **MQTT software client** that's been customized for the **sensor** and show you how the MQTT software client works so that you can use not only this **sensor** but also other devices that you can customize and integrate in the future. Following this, I will provide detailed coverage of how to set up the MQTT software client so that it works with **Home Assistant**. Finally, you will learn how to enclose and install the sensor in your home.

We will cover the following main topics in this chapter:

- Knowing the parts and tools to build your sensor
- Understanding Tasmota and how to install it in our sensor
- Integrating the sensor data into Home Assistant
- Enclosing, calibrating, and installing the sensor

After reading this chapter, you will be able to identify the different parts of a sensor, as described in *Chapter 1*. You will also be able to create a sensor and manage the data provided by it using the **sensor software interface**, as well as Home Assistant. Finally, you will know how to build an infrastructure of devices that are required to automate your home.

Technical requirements

You will understand the content of this chapter better if you are familiar with electronic components and circuits. To integrate and assemble the sensor parts, you will need to be able to follow an electronic diagram and know how to solder electronic components. You will also need to know how to deploy software to electronic devices. If you have already deployed software on **Arduino**, then this process will be similar. The **Tasmota** software configuration file, which I deployed in the sensor used in this chapter, can be found at `https://github.com/PacktPublishing/Building-Smart-Home-Automation-Solutions-with-Home-Assistant/tree/main/Chapter%2003`. Check out the following video to view the Code in Action: `https://bit.ly/47CkINl`

Knowing the parts and tools to build your sensor

In this section, we will look at each part you can use to build your double measurement sensor. You will understand the purpose of each so that you can integrate them using a provided electronic circuit, something that we'll do later in this chapter. We will frequently reference the *Sensors* section in *Chapter 1* and the block diagram shown in *Figure 1.9* of that chapter.

Each description isn't meant to provide deep details about how each part works but just the information required so that you can build a sensor or make some important adjustments or configurations so that the final circuit can work according to its intended use.

To build the double measurement sensor, you will need the following electronic parts and components:

- **HC-SR501 motion sensor**
- **BMP280 environmental sensor module**
- **ESP8266 Wi-Fi module**
- **USB cable (USB Type A to USB Type B micro)**
- **USB adapter (IN: AC 100 ~ 240V/OUT: 5V @ 1A)**
- **Arduino wire jumpers**

These parts for building the **sensor** can be purchased from many electronic suppliers around the world.

You will also need some other tools and accessories:

- A small screwdriver to adjust the motion sensor module's potentiometer
- Solder
- Solder iron
- Cutting plier

- Tweezers

- **Tasmotizer** software

- A computer with a USB port available

In the following subsections, we will describe these electronic parts and tools. Later in this chapter, we will see how the parts can be integrated using the tools required.

Element sensor and signal conditioner 1 – the motion sensor

The first component we will look at for building the double measurement sensor is the **motion sensor**. The **sensor module** we will use in this project is the **HC-SR501**. It can be purchased from major retailers around the world, including **Amazon** and **AliExpress**. *Figure 3.1* shows some details of this sensor module:

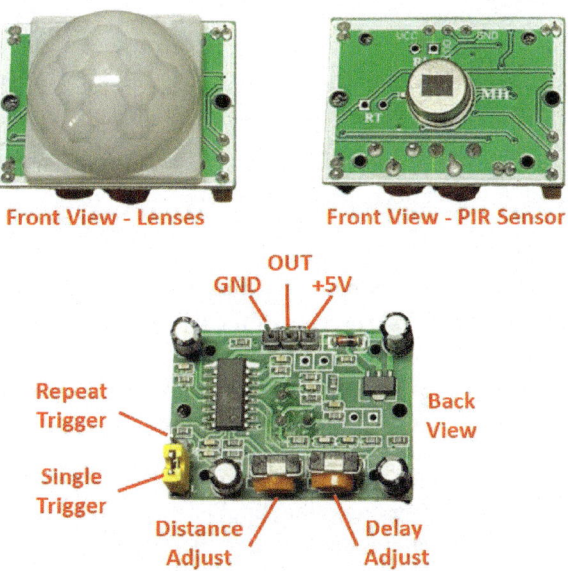

Figure 3.1 – HC-SR501 sensor details

This sensor module is based on the **passive infrared** (**PIR**) sensor element. This can be seen on the right-hand side of *Figure 3.1* with the cover lenses removed. What you need to know is that it works based on the infrared radiation that's reflected or emitted by objects. This sensor has a **signal conditioner circuit** attached to it; this circuit can be seen in the middle of *Figure 3.1*. This signal conditioner circuit translates the movement detected by the PIR sensor element into a binary or digital signal-level change. When a movement is detected, for example, the signal level changes from low to high or from 3.3V to 0V. The behavior of the change in the states will depend on some jumper configurations and adjustments, all of which can be done in the HC-SR501 sensor, as we will see later in this section.

As can be seen in *Figure 3.1*, a jumper is used to configure how the sensor should be triggered according to the detected movement. The following modes can be configured:

- **Single trigger**: When a movement is detected, the sensor's output will go from low to high. After the preconfigured time delay, it will go from high to low.

- **Repeat trigger**: When a movement is detected, the sensor's output will go from low to high. If a movement continues to be detected while the preconfigured delay time is still going, the movement is triggered again. This results in the sensor's output keeping the signal level high, even if the preconfigured delay is over. The output signal will be changed from high to low after the preconfigured delay if the **sensor** doesn't detect a new movement.

The jumper configuration for our sensor will be a single trigger.

We can also make configuration changes using the potentiometers (variable resistors) shown in *Figure 3.1* indicated by **Distance Adjust** and **Delay Adjust**. They allow the following configurations to be made:

- **Distance Adjust**: When using a small screwdriver and moving in a clockwise rotation, the sensing distance increases; moving it anti-clockwise results in the sensing distance being reduced. The distance range can vary from 3 to 7 meters.

- **Delay Adjust**: When moving the potentiometer in a clockwise rotation, the delay will increase; moving it anti-clockwise will decrease the delay. The delay range can be configured from 5 to 300 seconds.

We will have to calibrate the **Distance Adjust** of our **motion sensor module** when we install it in the *Enclosing, calibrating, and installing the sensor* section later in this chapter. With regard to the **Delay Adjust**, we will keep it to the minimum since we only want to capture when we have a movement and as soon as possible. We will need to calibrate the distance and delay to avoid the sensor triggering false positives. This happens when the sensor detects motion when there is no motion to detect.

The sensor module has three interface pins, two of which are used for the power supply and one of which is used for digital output. With regard to the supplied voltage, we will use 5V from a USB adapter to power it up. The sensor module's output has an inverted logic, which means that when a movement is detected, the output changes its state from a *high digital logic level* to a *low digital logic level*.

According to the **sensor module's specifications**, it needs at least 1 minute to initialize. During initialization, the sensor can change its output states from zero to three times. After initializing, the sensor will reach the standby state if no movement is detected.

Element sensor and signal conditioner 2 – environmental/temperature sensor

The second electronic component is a module that includes the **sensor element** and the signal conditioner circuit. We will be using the **BMP280** sensor module from **Bosch/Sensortec**. You can also use the **BME280** sensor module from the same supplier. **BME280** is more complete and expensive. It has all the features of the **BMP280**, plus an integrated **humidity sensor**. The **BMP280** is a versatile **environmental sensor** that can not only measure **temperature** but also **barometric pressure**. *Figure 3.2* shows this sensor module:

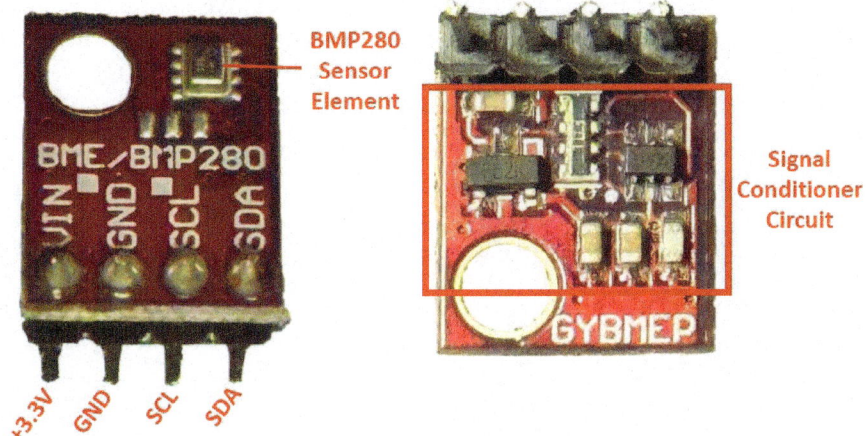

Figure 3.2 – BMP280 sensor details

The sensor element is highlighted in *Figure 3.2*; the rest of the electronic components are part of the signal conditioner circuit. The sensor element has the following specifications related to the measurement ranges:

- **Temperature**: `-40oC (-40F)` to `+85oC (185F)`
- **Air pressure**: `300hPa` to `1100hPa`

It has four interface pins – two for voltage supply (+3.3V and GND) and two for digital serial communication, which can be **I2C** or **SPI**. We will use 3.3V as the voltage supply and I2C as the serial communication interface. The SCL and SDA pins are used for the I2C serial interface, as shown on the left of *Figure 3.2*.

Wireless communication module – ESP8266

As mentioned in *Chapter 1*, **ESP8266** is a **system-on-chip** (**SOC**) made by **Expressif Systems**. This chip manufacturer provides **ESP8266** in two ways: **integrated circuit** (**IC**) and **module**. The IC is the chip itself, while the module is the chip plus all the minimal components needed so that the chip can work properly.

Using an ESP8266 module is very convenient because it can deal with critical component placement issues, which is required for **radio frequency** (**RF**) circuits. It also provides an embedded **printed**

circuit board (**PCB**) antenna, minimizing its footprint. Besides all these features, the ESP8266 module is protected by a metallic shield that protects it from **electromagnetic interference** (**EMI**). It also has some regulatory certifications, such as the **Federal Communications Commission** (**FCC**) in the USA, which can be helpful if you want to develop a mass-production Wi-Fi product.

Some companies use these ESP8266 modules and create electronic development boards, which makes these chips and modules very popular. This is similar to what **Arduino** did. We will be using one of these development boards as our **wireless microcontroller module** (detailed in *Chapter 1*). *Figure 3.3* shows the ESP8266 electronic development board we will be using, as well as its pinout:

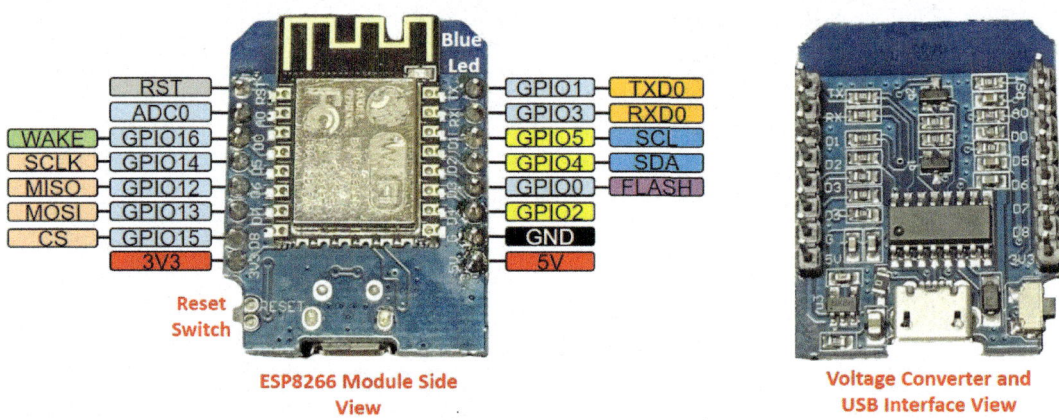

Figure 3.3 – ESP8266 electronic development board and pinout

The ESP8266 electronic board shown in *Figure 3.3* is known as **Wemos D1 mini**. We will use the following features of this board to build our sensor:

- **Wi-Fi 802.11b/g/n**: Used to communicate to our **Raspberry Pi**-based **home automation server**

- **11x GPIO pins exposed**: These GPIO2 pins will be used to communicate to the **HC-SR501 motion sensor**

- **1x I2C serial port**: To communicate to the **BMP280 environmental sensor**

- **5V supply input**: Input power for the module and the **HC-SR501 motion sensor**

- **3V3 power output**: Supply voltage to the **BMP280 environmental sensor**

- **USB communication and programming port**: Used to program the **sensor**

- **Reset switch**: To restart the module after programming or when needed

- **Blue indicator LED** (**D4 - GPIO2**): To check the programming status and calibrate the motion sensor

We will be using the GPIO2, GPIO4, and GPIO5 I/O pins in our project. These can be seen in *Figure 3.3*.

The **Wemos D1 mini** can be purchased from most global electronics suppliers around the world at a price of around 4 USD.

Power supply and cabling

Now that we've looked at the main electronic parts, let's look at the **power supply** and **cabling**. These are the final materials we will need to build our **double measurement sensor**.

The power supply can be of any type but must be able to provide a voltage of **5V** and a current of at least **1A**. A compact and handy power supply that you can use for internal sensors at home is a **power adapter** that's used to charge cell phone batteries.

With regard to cabling, we will be using two kinds of cables. The first kind of cable we'll need is a power cable to connect the **USB power supply adapter** to the **wireless microcontroller module**. This USB power cable must be a **USB Type A** on one side and an **USB Type B micro** on the other side. The other type of cable we'll need is one to connect the sensors to the **wireless microcontroller module**. These types of cables are popularly known as **Arduino jumper wires** because they are widely used in different **Arduino** prototype projects around the world. The USB power adapter and all the cables we will use to build our sensor can be seen in *Figure 3.4*:

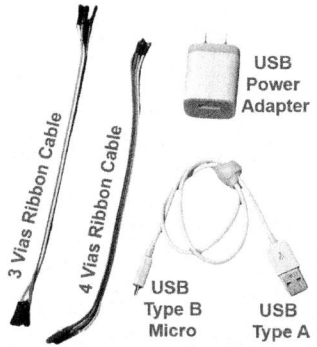

Figure 3.4 – USB power adapter and cables that will be used in our sensor

The power adapter shown in *Figure 3.4* has a **USB Type A** female connector, but a **USB Type C** type connector can also be used.

The Arduino jumper wires are ribbon cables and are commonly used in electronic prototype projects via breadboards. They come in different gender types: **male-to-male**, **female-to-female**, and **female-to-male**. We will be using the **female-to-female** gender type to connect the parts.

The Arduino jumper wires can be split according to the number of vias you wish to use. We will use three vias to connect the motion sensor and four vias to connect the environmental sensor.

In the next section, we will learn how the parts we've covered so far can be grouped to create the electronic hardware that's required to build our double measurement sensor.

Connecting the electronic parts and cables

The following is a diagram of the double measurement sensor circuit:

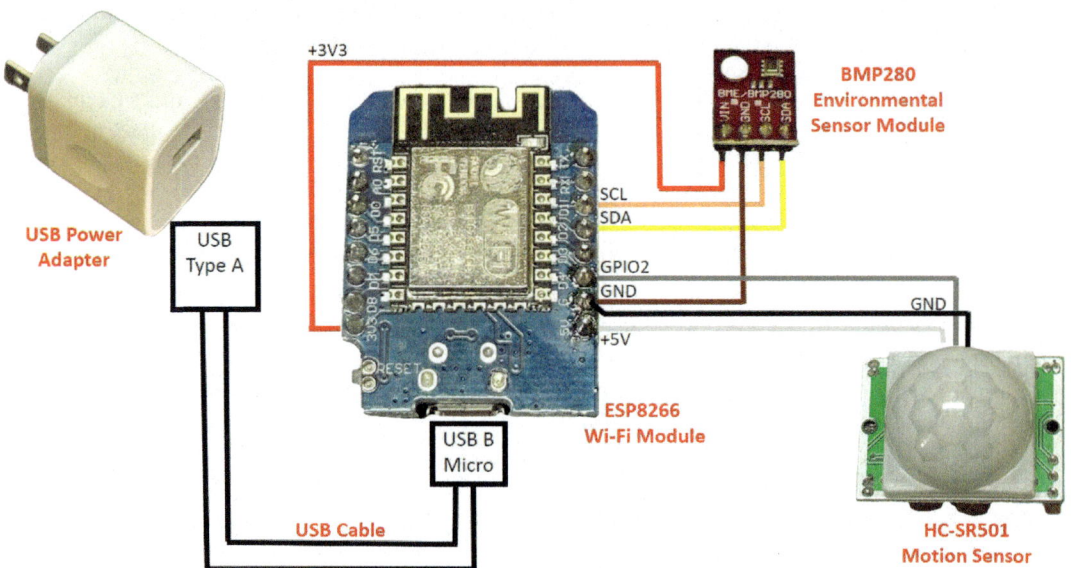

Figure 3.5 – Double measurement sensor circuit diagram

The complete **bill of materials** (**BOM**) for the **sensor** is listed in *Table 3.1*:

ID	Quantity	Description
1	1	ESP8266 Wi-Fi module
2	1	HC-SR501 motion sensor
3	1	BMP280 environmental sensor module
4	1	USB cable
5	1	USB power adapter
6	1	Arduino jumper female-to-female – three vias
7	1	Arduino jumper female-to-female – four vias

Table 3.1 – Double measurement sensor BOM

The following sequence is suggested for connecting all the electronic parts of our sensor:

1. Separate items **1**, **2**, and **6** from the preceding list (*Table 3.1*). Interconnect item **1** (**ESP8266 Wi-Fi module**) to item **2** (**HC-SR501 motion sensor**) using item **6** (**Arduino jumper female-to-female – three vias**). The connection should match the diagram shown in *Figure 3.5*. The **ESP8266 Wi-Fi module** pinout can be seen in *Figure 3.3*, while the **HC-SR501 motion sensor** pinout can be seen in *Figure 3.1*.

2. The **ESP8266 Wi-Fi module** doesn't have two **ground** (**GND**) pins available but you will need to somehow attach this connection to the GND pin in the module. Regarding item **6**, we will need to remove the female connector from the GND pin on the side so that it's connected to the **ESP8266 Wi-Fi module** and solder it directly to the module. You will need a soldering iron and a piece of solder to do this. `video ch3-1` details how to do this. With this, we have integrated the **motion sensor** into the **ESP8266 Wi-Fi module**.

3. Get the block you assembled in *Step 2* and use it with items **3** and **7** from *Table 3.1*. Connect the block with the **ESP8266 Wi-Fi module** to the **BMP280 environmental sensor module** (item **3**) using the **Arduino jumper female-to-female – four vias** (item **7**) while following the diagram in *Figure 3.5*. Again, the pinout should match what's shown in *Figure 3.1*. Besides the **ESP8266 Wi-Fi module**, which can be seen in *Figure 3.3*, the pinout for the **BMP280 environmental sensor module** can be seen in *Figure 3.2*. With that, we have integrated the **environmental sensor** into the **ESP8266 Wi-Fi module**.

4. The last part we need to assemble is the **power circuit**. To connect these parts, get the block you assembled in *Step 3* and items **4** and **5**. Connect item **4**, the **USB cable**, the **USB Type B micro** side, to the USB micro connector of the **ESP8266 Wi-Fi module**, as shown in *Figure 3.5*. Connect the other side of the USB cable on the **USB Type A** side to item **5**, the **USB adapter**. With that, we have finished assembling all our sensor parts.

Important note

While performing these steps, make sure the connections are not loose; otherwise, the sensor will not work properly. Just in case, review the assembly sequence to check that all the connections were made correctly.

Figure 3.6 shows what our **sensor** assembly should look like:

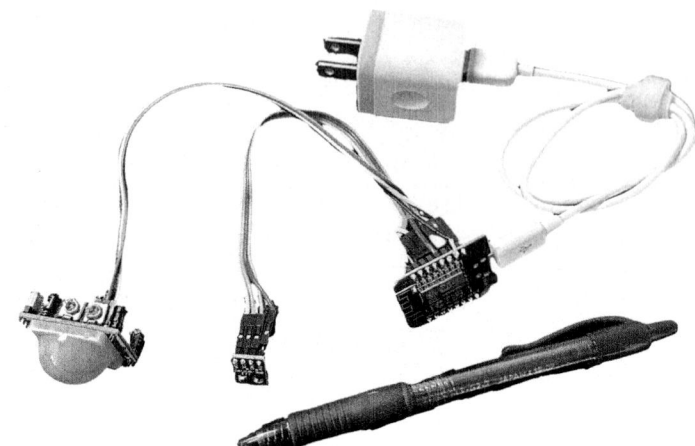

Figure 3.6 – Double measurement sensor parts connected

The pen in *Figure 3.6* is just to provide a scale so that you have a better idea of the sensor's size.

Now that all the parts have been integrated, I will explain the MQTT software, which will control the sensor and install it. After installing the software, I will explain how to configure the software so that it works with MQTT and Home Assistant.

Understanding Tasmota and how to install it in our sensor

In this section, we will learn what **Tasmota** is and how to install it in our sensor.

What is Tasmota?

As this book's main intention is to build a **home automation system** using **Home Assistant**, we will not spend time developing a piece of software to handle the sensor's data. The key secret to easily building your system is to know how to integrate and configure the different parts of it, including the **sensor**. I learned this lesson after spending a long time learning how to program the **ESP8266 Wi-Fi module**. After learning how to make basic software programs using tutorials on the internet, I discovered Tasmota (`https://tasmota.github.io/`). I found Tasmota to be a very useful software tool with plenty of resources for integrating different kinds of sensors and actuators. It can not just be used with Home Assistant but also with other IoT types of ecosystems. I hope you can also enjoy this software.

Tasmota is an **open source firmware** developed and maintained by *Theo Arendst* and is meant to be used with the family of devices and modules from **Espressif Systems**, meaning the ones based on **ESP8266** and **ESP32**. It was created in January 2016 with the purpose to be an alternate firmware for the popular **Sonoff** devices made by **ITEAD** (`https://itead.cc`). The Sonoff devices are based on **ESP8266**.

Tasmota implements an **MQTT software client**, as explained and detailed in *Chapter 1* and *Chapter 2*, so it will fit our needs and can be used with our **double measurement sensor** project.

> **Important note**
>
> There is another piece of software called **ESPHome** (`https://esphome.io/`) that can also be used as an alternative form of **ESP MQTT client** software for sensors and actuators. Since ESPHome does the same things as Tasmota and I'm more familiar with Tasmota, this software will not be covered in this book.

In the next subsection, we will explain how to install Tasmota in our assembled sensor so we can configure it.

Installing Tasmota in our sensor

There are several ways to install Tasmota in our sensor. The option that worked well for me was using a software called **Tasmotizer**, which can be used not only for Tasmota but also for other binary files you want to program for the **ESP8266** module. You will also need to download the **Tasmota binary file** to your computer, which you can install using **Tasmotizer**.

Follow these steps to install **Tasmota** in our sensor:

1. Download the latest executable software version of **Tasmotizer** at `https://github.com/tasmota/tasmotizer/releases`. I'm using `version 1.2` in this book.

2. Download the latest `tasmota-sensors.bin` file from `http://ota.tasmota.com/tasmota/release/`. The current release I'm using is `12.3.1 - Percy`.

3. Connect the double measurement sensor to your computer using a USB Type A connector. At this point, the blue LED in the **ESP8266 Wi-Fi module** will flash. If the module connects to the computer, you will hear a USB-adding device sound if you are on the Windows operating system.

4. Use **Windows Device Manager** and check for the **COM** and **LPT** ports. Check whether a device such as **USB-SERIAL CH340 device (COMX)** was added. Take note of the **COMX** port. This will be the **COM port number** you will need to use in Tasmotizer.

5. Open the `Tasmotizer.exe` file. Make sure you are using the admin mode by right-clicking the **Run as administrator** option.

6. Select the COMX port you found in *Step 4*. Click the **Open** button under **Select image**. Choose the `tasmota-sensors.bin` file you downloaded in *Step 2*. Check the **Erase before flashing** box to erase the module before programming it. Your screen will look like the one shown in *Figure 3.7*:

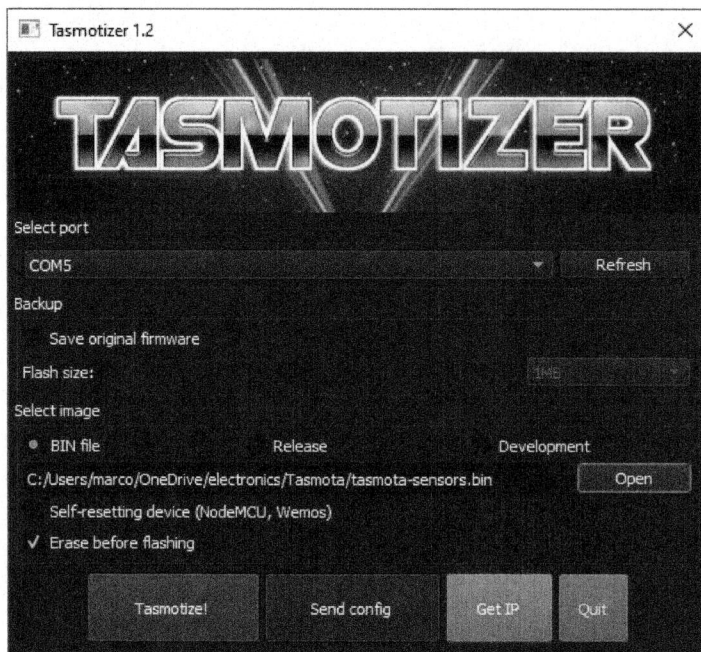

Figure 3.7 – Tasmotizer software screen ready to program our sensor

7. Click on the **Tasmotize!** button shown in *Figure 3.7*. Another screen will open. After erasing the **ESP8266 Wi-Fi module**, the **Tasmotizer** software will start to program our sensor with the `tasmota-sensors.bin` file. *Figure 3.8* shows the programming progress of a computer connecting and programming the **ESP8266 Wi-Fi module**:

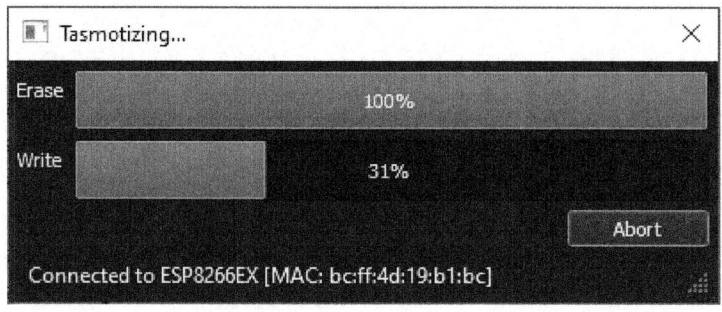

Figure 3.8 – The Tasmota file being programmed in our sensor

8. If communication between your computer and the **ESP8266 Wi-Fi module** could not be established, you will see a message stating a failure. In this case, click on the **OK** button and restart from *Step 7* by clicking the **Tasmotize!** button; press and release the **reset switch** after doing this.

9. Once the **Write** bar has finished loading, if everything goes well, another window will present a message stating **Process successful! Power cycle the device**. Click the **OK** button in this new window.

10. Press the reset switch in the **ESP8266 Wi-Fi module** to restart it. The blue LED will be turned on while you press the reset switch. Click on the **Send config** button shown in *Figure 3.7*. The **Send configuration to device** window will appear, as shown in *Figure 3.9*:

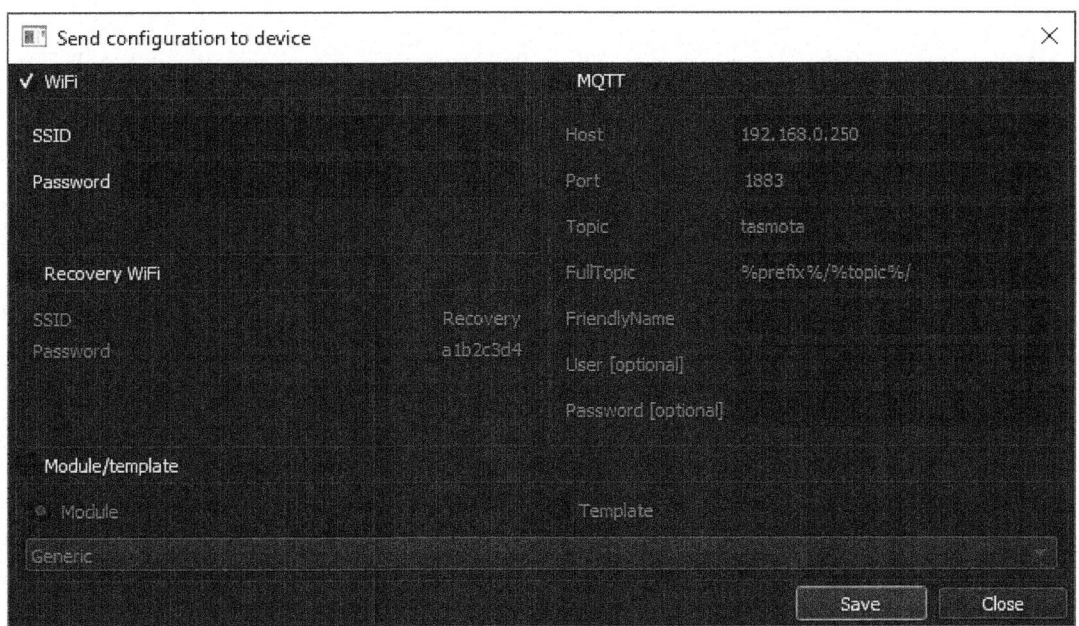

Figure 3.9 – Configuring the initial information in our sensor

11. We will do some initial configuration in our **sensor** so that it can be connected to our home Wi-Fi network. As shown in *Figure 3.9*, specify the **SSID** and **Password** details of your home Wi-Fi network and press the **Save** button.

12. If everything goes well, another screen will appear stating **Configuration sent** and **Device will restart**. Click the **OK** button on this new screen. Click on the reset switch in the **ESP8266 Wi-Fi module**.

13. If the SSID and password were configured correctly, you should be able to get the IP address that was configured to our sensor by clicking on the **Get IP** button presented in *Figure 3.7*. In this case, I got **IP 192.168.0.43** for the sensor, as can be seen in *Figure 3.10*:

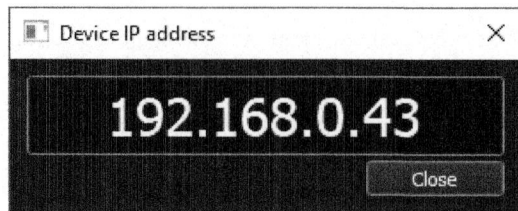

Figure 3.10 – Configuring the initial information in our sensor

14. Take note of this IP address as you will need to use it later. Disconnect the USB cable from your computer.

Important notes

1. If you have issues with *Step 6* of this procedure, check your USB cable to see whether it has all four cable vias available. Usually, some USB charger cables only have the power lines available; we will need a complete four-vias USB cable to connect the computer to the **ESP8266 Wi-Fi module**.

2. The IP address you got for the sensor can change as your home Wi-Fi network changes. You will need it to do the initial configurations or in the future, if you need to change some configurations, such as those for the MQTT IP server. Later in this book, we will learn how to get the IP address for the sensor if the IP changes.

Now that we've completed these steps, our sensor's hardware and software can be configured and integrated into Home Assistant. In the next section, we will configure the sensor so that it's connected to MQTT and set up configuration and adjustment parameters for the **motion** and **environmental sensors**.

Configuring the software of your sensor

Once you have the IP address of your sensor, all **ESP8266 Wi-Fi module** software configurations required to interconnect the sensor elements and connect the double measurement sensor to Home Assistant can be done using a web browser. This section will teach you how to configure the sensor so that it can be integrated into Home Assistant.

You will need to type the sensor's IP address in a web browser to start the configuration process in **Tasmota**. In our case, the IP address that's been assigned to our sensor is 192.168.0.43. Upon typing this IP address and hitting *Enter*, you should get the screen presented in *Figure 3.11*. We will present each item in this default screen and the configurations we will need to do in some of these items:

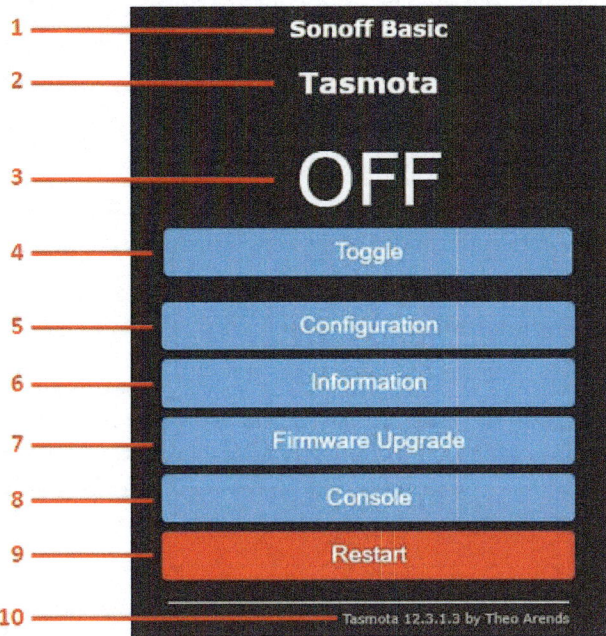

Figure 3.11 – Tasmota's initial default screen

Figure 3.11 specifies numbers for each field or button. Let's take a look at them in more detail:

- **Module configuration name** (**1** in *Figure 3.11*): This field shows the module name that was configured by default. In this case, the default is a **Sonoff Basic** (actuator) device with one relay output. We will change this configuration to a two-sensor input.

- **Device name** (**2** in *Figure 3.11*): This is the default device name (**Tasmota**). We will change this name so that it's closer to our sensor's name so that we can identify it in our home network.

- **Device output status** (**3** in *Figure 3.11*): This shows the default relay status output (**OFF**) for the preconfigured Sonoff device. This status information will disappear after we configure our sensor.

- **Toggle button** (**4** in *Figure 3.11*): This toggles the device's output status. This button will disappear after we configure our sensor.

- **Configuration button** (**5** in *Figure 3.11*): We can use this button to access other buttons to perform different sensor configurations. This button will be used in the next section to configure our sensor.

- **Information button** (**6** in *Figure 3.11*): We can use this button to access all the information that's been configured in the sensor.

- **Firmware Upgrade button** (**7** in *Figure 3.11*): We can use this button to update the firmware. This can be done **over the air** (**OTA**) or by choosing a file directly from a web browser.

- **Console button** (**8** in *Figure 3.11*): We can use this button to access useful information provided by the sensor using a console. It also has a command-line interface so that we can issue some customized commands to configure our sensor.

- **Restart button** (**9** in *Figure 3.11*): We can use this button to restart the software sensor. This is useful when we want to confirm that some configuration was done.

- **Footer information** (**10** in *Figure 3.11*): This area provides general information such as the **software name** (**Tasmota**), **software version** (in this case, 12.3.1.3), and **software author** (**Theo Arends**).

The menu navigation for **Tasmota** is simple. Upon clicking on any of the buttons shown in *Figure 3.11* except for the **Toggle** button (**4** in *Figure 3.11*), you will be taken to another screen with another set of buttons. This new set will have at least one button option called **Main Menu**. When you click the **Main Menu** button, you will be returned to the menu shown in *Figure 3.11*.

Getting data from sensor elements

We will start our **sensor configuration** by doing a pin assignment. This will allow us to start reading **motion detection** and **temperature data** from the **sensor elements**. We will also assign a name to the sensor so that we can correctly identify it when integrating it into Home Assistant.

Configuring the sensor pins

Before we do a proper sensor pin configuration, first, we will configure a **module template** to be used with the sensor. This will help us identify the type of device we are assessing since this module name is displayed at the top of the sensor web page, as seen in *Figure 3.11* (**1** in *Figure 3.11*).

We must follow these steps to configure a template for our sensor:

1. From Tasmota's initial default screen, click **Configuration | Configure Template**. The screen shown in *Figure 3.12* will be presented:

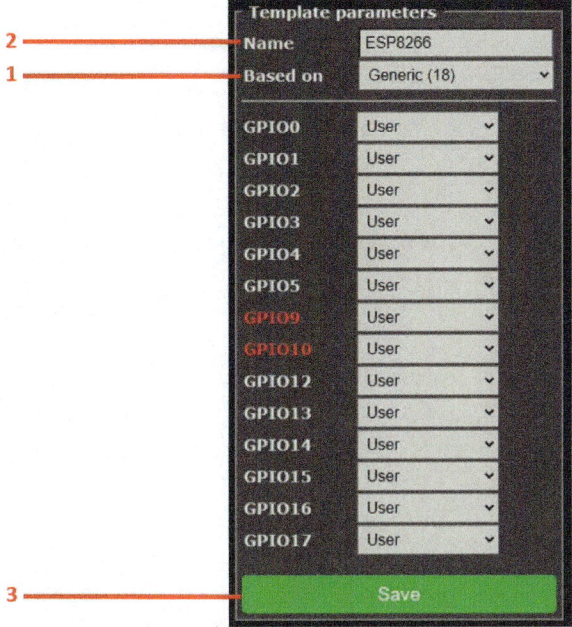

Figure 3.12 – Tasmota template configuration screen

2. On the **Template parameters** screen, click on the **Based on** drop-down field (**1** in *Figure 3.12*) and select **Generic (18)**.

3. In the **Name** field (**2** in *Figure 3.12*), replace **Generic** with **ESP8266**.

4. Click **Save** (**3** in *Figure 3.12*). The software will save the configuration and return you to the main menu.

Now that we've configured a template for our sensor, let's do the pin assignment for it. Follow these steps:

1. Click **Configuration | Configure Module**. You will see the screen shown in *Figure 3.13* but with the parameters to be filled:

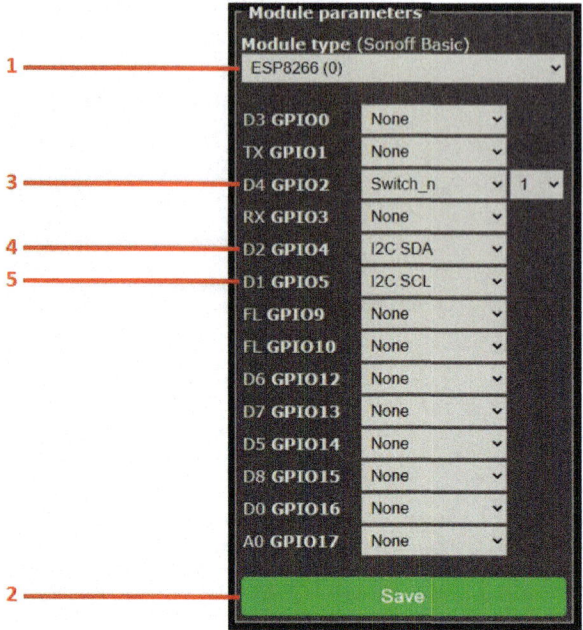

Figure 3.13 – Tasmota module configuration screen

2. In the **Module type** drop-down field (**1** in *Figure 3.13*), select the option we configured before or **ESP8266 (0)**.

3. Click **Save** (**2** in *Figure 3.13*). The software will save the configuration and return you to the main menu.

4. Click **Configuration | Configure Module** again.

5. In the **D4 GPIO2** field (**3** in *Figure 3.13*), change **None** to **Switch_n**. In the following drop-down field in the same line, make sure it is assigned **1**.

6. In the **D2 GPIO4** field (**4** in *Figure 3.13*), change **None** to **I2C SDA**.

7. In the **D1 GPIO5** field (**5** in *Figure 3.13*), change **None** to **I2C SCL**.

8. Click **Save** (**2** in *Figure 3.13*). The software will save the configuration and return you to the main menu.

After making these configuration changes, the sensor's main menu will look similar to the following figure:

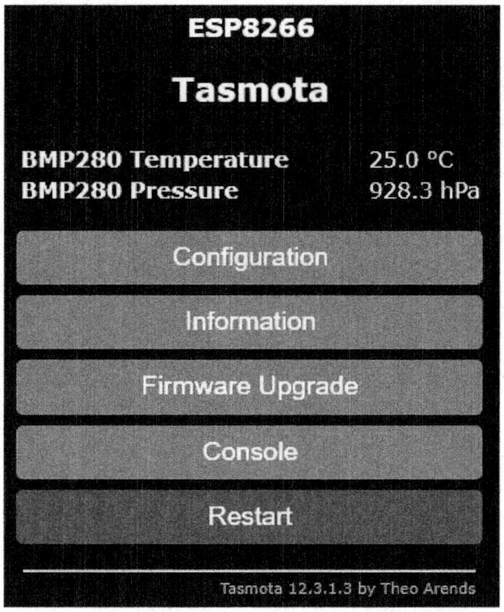

Figure 3.14 – Tasmota screen with sensor pins configured

In *Figure 3.14*, we can see our sensor displaying the temperature and pressure values from the **BMP280 sensor**. Also, at the top, we can see the template of the device we created – that is, **ESP8266**.

With that, we have assigned our sensor pins – that is, the motion sensor has been assigned according to *Step 5* and the environmental sensor has been assigned according to *Steps 6* and *7*.

However, we still need to use a special configuration for the motion sensor pin; we will look at this in the next section. There is nothing else to configure in the temperature and pressure sensor as its data is being processed.

Configuring the motion sensor

We will need to do some extra configurations for the motion sensor to be able to report movement when it is triggered. The way we want the ESP8266 to see the motion sensor input is like an electronic switch. When the motion sensor detects a movement, the ESP8266 will report a **switch closed** or **ON** state; otherwise, it will report a **switch open** or **OFF** state. We can configure this feature by following these steps:

1. From the main menu, click on the **Console** button and then the **Enter command** prompt.

2. Type SwitchModel 1 and hit *Enter*.

We will also need to prepare the sensor so that it reports the data to the MQTT protocol. So, if a movement is detected, we want it to be published to MQTT. The motion sensor's output is mapped in Tasmota by `Switch1` since we configured the **D4 GPIO2** pin as `Switch_n 1`. We will do this by implementing a command sequence using the **Console** button.

3. From the main menu, click on the **Console** button and then the **Enter command** prompt.

4. Issue the following command:

```
Rule1 on Switch1#state=1 do publish sensor/%topic%/PIR1
ON endon on Switch1#state=0 do Publish sensor/%topic%/
PIR1 OFF endon
```

Activate `Rule1` by typing `Rule1 1` in the command input field and hitting *Enter*.

With these two sequences of commands, we have set up `Rule1` at Tasmota to send motion information data to MQTT. We still need to calibrate the motion sensor, but it will be best if we calibrate this while we are installing it. Next, we will configure the **device name**.

Device name

The device name is the final thing we need to configure to get data from the sensor element. This will help you identify the sensor in your home. We can configure the device name by following these steps:

1. From the main menu, click the **Configuration** button.

2. Click the **Configure Other** button.

3. Change the **Device Name** field to **GarageTempPIR**.

4. Change the **Friendly Name 1** field to **GarageTempPIR**.

5. Click the **Save** button.

6. The configuration will be saved and the sensor will be restarted with the new device name being present just below **Sensor Module Type Configuration**, which was previously configured as **ESP8266**. *Figure 3.15* shows what Tasmota's main screen looks like after this configuration:

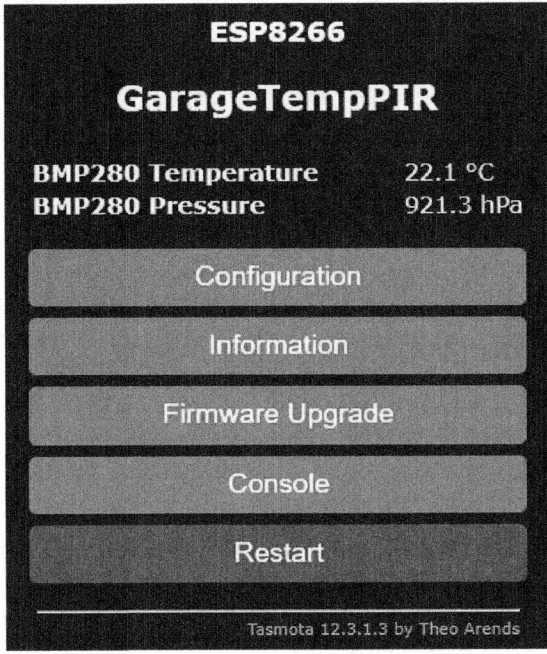

Figure 3.15 – Tasmota's main screen with the device name configured

In the next subsection, we will finalize our sensor configuration by setting up the MQTT protocol to work with it.

Configuring the MQTT information in the sensor

The **MQTT sensor configuration** will allow the sensor to communicate with Home Assistant using the MQTT protocol, as explained in *Chapter 1*. Follow these steps to configure the **MQTT** protocol on our **Tasmota sensor**:

1. From the main menu, click the **Configuration** button.
2. Click the **Configure MQTT** button.
3. Type homeassistant.local in the **Host** field.
4. Type your_name in the **User** field.
5. Type your_password in the **User** field.
6. Type Garage_Temp_PIR in the **Topic** field.
7. Click the **Save** button.

> **Important note**
>
> Make sure the **Port** field in the MQTT parameters is **1883** (default). Also, make sure the user and password match what was configured in *Chapter 2* when we configured the login details that were authorized to connect to the **Mosquitto MQTT broker**.

With that, our configuration for Tasmota is complete. In the next section, we will integrate the sensor into Home Assistant.

Integrating the sensor data into Home Assistant

The last part of the process of creating our sensor is to integrate it into Home Assistant. We will have to return to our installation of Home Assistant, which we did in *Chapter 2*, to do so. Our double measurement sensor will be configured in two steps. In the first step, we will configure the **temperature** part of the sensor; in the second step, we will configure the **motion** part of the sensor.

Integrating the temperature sensor

If you have been following this book since *Chapter 2*, you will have Home Assistant 9.3 or above installed in your home automation server. As mentioned previously, in the case of this book, we are using version 9.3 and above so Home Assistant will automatically discover the temperature sensor and help you configure it.

You will need to execute the following steps to be able to get the data from your temperature sensor:

1. In **Home Assistant**, click **Settings | Devices & Services**.
2. In the **Integrations** tab, verify that the **Tasmota** integration was discovered by Home Assistant. If not, click the **ADD INTEGRATION** button in the bottom-right corner and search for and click on **Tasmota** to install it.
3. Click the **Configure** button in the **Tasmota** window.
4. Click **Submit** on the next screen asking whether you want to set up Tasmota.
5. If everything went well, another screen will be presented with a **Success** message. The **sensor module name (GarageTempPIR)** and **sensor configuration name (ESP8266)** will be presented. We will set up the temperature sensor in a new area of our home by clicking the **Area** drop-down box and selecting the **Add new area** option.
6. Click the **Name** field and type Garage. Then, click **ADD**.

7. A new area called **Garage** will be created. A window with a **Success!** message will appear. Click on the **Finish** button, as shown in *Figure 3.16*:

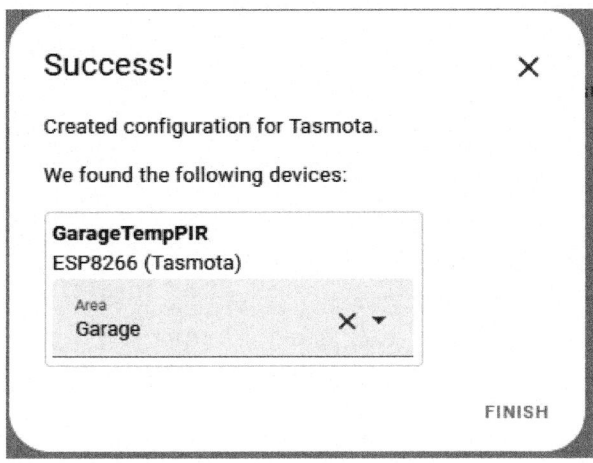

Figure 3.16 – Our sensor being successfully integrated into Home Assistant

The screen presented in *Figure 3.16* will close and the temperature sensor will be integrated into Home Assistant.

With the **temperature sensor** integrated into **Home Assistant**, you can see its name (**GarageTempPIR**) in the **Devices** tab and its data by going to the **Entities** tab. In *Chapter 6*, as part of the **dashboard** configuration, we will arrange the **Entities** data of the temperature sensor to show the information we want.

Integrating the motion sensor

We will need to create a binary sensor in the `Configuration.yaml` file using the MQTT data we configured in `Rule 1` in Tasmota. Before doing that, however, we will need to install a **file editor add-on**, similar to what we did when we installed the MQTT add-on. This process of integrating the sensor is covered in `video ch3-2` and will guide you through this process. Here are the steps to install the file editor and edit `Configuration.yaml` so that you can integrate the motion sensor:

1. In the **Home Assistant** sidebar, click **Settings | Add-ons**. Then, click on the **ADD-ON STORE** button in the bottom-right corner.

2. In the official add-ons area, search for `File Editor`. Click on it. A new window will appear.

3. Click **INSTALL** in the **File editor** window. After some time, the file editor will be installed. Activate the **Show in sidebar** button option. The file editor icon will appear in the sidebar. Click **START** at the bottom of the **File editor** window.

4. Click on **File editor** in the sidebar. Then, click the folder icon at the top left. Search for `configuration.yaml` and click on it. The `configuration.yaml` file will be displayed.

5. After the last line in the file, add the following configuration:

```
mqtt:
    binary_sensor:
      - unique_id: binary_sensor.garage_pir
        name: "garage_pir Sensor"
        state_topic: "sensor/Garage_Temp_PIR/PIR1"
        qos: 1
        payload_on: "ON"
        payload_not_available: "OFF"
        device_class: motion
```

6. If the YAML syntax is correct, including the text indentation, a green check (**1** in *Figure 3.17*) will be presented below the **Settings** icon in the top right of the screen. Click on the first red button (**2** in *Figure 3.17*) in the top right to save the changes:

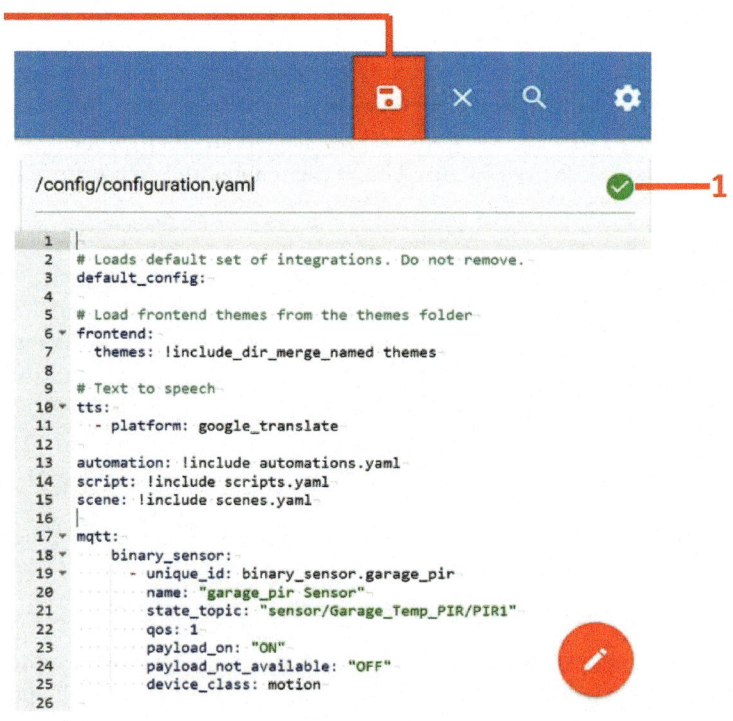

Figure 3.17 – Icons and buttons to look for when editing a file

7. Click on **Developer Tools** in the **YAML** tab. In the **Check and Restart** window, make sure a message stating **Configuration will not prevent Home Assistant from starting!** is presented. Click on the RESTART button and, in the new pop-up window, click **RESTART** again. Home Assistant will restart. Wait until a message stating **Home Assistant has Started!** appears.

8. Click **Settings | Devices & Services**. Click on the **Entities** tab and search for the motion sensor you just integrated. Click on it. Assign its area field to **Garage** and click on the **UPDATE** button.

As we mentioned previously regarding the temperature sensor, we will add this motion sensor entity to the dashboard in *Chapter 6*. We will also create an **automation** in *Chapter 5* using this motion sensor we've created.

In the next section, we will finish this chapter by enclosing the sensor parts, calibrating the motion sensor, and installing the sensor.

Enclosing, calibrating, and installing the sensor

In this section, we will enclose our sensor in a box and calibrate the motion sensor. Once we've done this, we will physically install and test our sensor.

Enclosing our sensor

You can enclose your **sensor** in different ways. All the circuits, including the three boards and harness, can easily fit in an 80 x 80 x 50 mm box. You can purchase or use a pre-fabricated box that has similar dimensions. You can use any material for the box except for metal because it will block or degrade the Wi-Fi signal.

If you have a **3D printer** at home or are familiar with **rapid prototyping**, you can have a more customized enclosure for your sensor. You can make a mechanical design or use some free **3D models** available on the internet. On websites such as https://www.yeggi.com/ and https://www. thingiverse.com/, you can search for and find different **3D models** for **PIR motion sensor cases**. These 3D models are available in **STL file format**, but once you get them, they can be used or translated so that they can be used in your 3D printer. Alternatively, you can send them to be printed by a **3D printer services provider**.

For educational purposes, in this book, we will be using a simple **cardboard box** and other easy-to-find and cheap materials to enclose our sensor. You will need the following materials to build our enclosure:

- A cardboard box (I will use a 130 x 90 x 80 mm box)
- Hot glue stick
- 2x 50 mm 3M dual lock tape pieces

We will need the following tools to help us build the sensor's encloser:

- Knife cutter
- Ruler
- Pen/pencil
- Quarter USD coin (or some other way to make a 23/24 mm circle)
- Hot glue gun

`video ch3-3` will teach you how to build the **sensor's enclosure**. You will need to follow these steps to enclose the **sensor** parts in the **cardboard box**. The dimensions given in the sensor assembly procedure don't need to be measured precisely because a gap and reasonable tolerance have already been considered. So, let's get started:

1. Choose one of the cardboard box faces that is adjacent to the **box lid**.

2. Find the center of this face by tracing, using a ruler, two diagonals of the rectangular face. The intersection point of these diagonal lines will be the center.

3. Get a quarter-dollar coin and position it at the center of the crossing of the two diagonals and make a circle using a pen/pencil.

4. Get a knife cutter and cut the marked circle off.

5. Using a hot glue gun with a hot glue stick, apply the hot glue so that it's surrounding the motion sensor and press it so that it's positioned in the circle you created previously. Make sure the two potentiometers for distance and duration are facing toward the box lid.

6. Use hot glue to make sure the motion sensor will be held to the cardboard box.

7. Make a 10 mm square with a pen approximately in the middle of a side face but not in the opposite face to where the **motion sensor** is located.

8. Cut out the marked square using a knife cutter.

9. Disconnect the USB cable from the **ESP8266** module and pass the cable through the cut-out square in the box.

   This cable will be used to provide power from now on, so we can put a knot in the cable to hold it inside the box.

10. Connect the USB cable to the **ESP8266** and put some hot glue on the base of the USB micro cable connector; press it to the box so that it remains in place.

11. Make another 10 mm square with a pen approximately in the middle of a face opposite to the other we created.

12. Cut out the other marked square using a knife cutter.

13. Disconnect the environmental sensor cables and pass them through the cut-out square in the box. Reconnect the cables back to the sensor outside the box.

14. Put some hot glue on the environmental sensor but just where there is a hole in the board. Do not put hot glue on the **BMP280 sensor**; otherwise, you can damage it. Press the environmental sensor into the box so that it remains in place.

15. Using the dual lock, glue one of the parts to the **sensor** box.

Once you've completed these steps, your **sensor** will look like what's shown in *Figure 3.18*:

Figure 3.18 – Double measurement sensor enclosed

Figure 3.18 shows the side view of the box on the left, with the **environmental sensor** on one side and the **PIR motion sensor** on the other. The top view on the right gives us an idea of how the parts are connected and being held. You can use hot glue to hold the internal cables in the box.

Now that we've enclosed the **sensor**, we can calibrate the **motion sensor** and install it. This will be covered in the next subsection.

Calibrating the sensor

As mentioned previously, the **HC-SR501 motion sensor** has two potentiometers that need to be calibrated or adjusted to work as required. These two potentiometers are the **Distance Adjust** and the **Delay Adjust** shown in *Figure 3.1*.

We will use the trial-and-error method and evaluate the results using the *blue LED* (shown in *Figure 3.3*) of the **ESP8266** connected to the **sensor** output. As mentioned previously, the **sensor** output has an inverted logic, so the blue LED of the **ESP8266** will remain turned *on* until it detects a movement, at which point it will turn *off*.

We will have to leave the **Delay Adjust** potentiometer with its minimum value possible, which means the adjustment mechanism all rotated as far as possible anti-clockwise, as shown in the **Delay Adjust position** indicated in *Figure 3.19*, right. This will give us a time frame of 2.5 to 5 seconds of blocking time until the next movement can be detected. You can play with this potentiometer using a small screwdriver to rotate it clockwise. You will see that as you rotate clockwise, once a movement is detected (*blue LED turned off*), it will take more time for a new movement to be triggered (*blue LED will turn on again*). Since the minimum and maximum values are, as per the sensor specifications, from 5 to 300 seconds if a linear scale could be used for the potentiometer, the center value will be around 147.5 seconds. As discussed previously, we will leave the **Delay Adjust** potentiometer at the minimum value of around 2.5 to 5 seconds to trigger a new movement after an initial one has been detected.

We will calibrate the **Distance Adjust** potentiometer according to the distance between the movement detection and the sensor installation location. We are planning to install the sensor on the garage roof, which is 2,800 mm as referenced in *Figure 3.19*, left. I want movement detection when my car enters the garage. The height of my car is around 1,450 mm, as referenced in *Figure 3.19*, left. So, the distance of movement detection will be around 1,350 mm, as referenced in *Figure 3.19*, left. The maximum distance of movement detection is according to the datasheet specifications, which is 7,000 mm, so the center scale will be 3,500 mm and a quarter of the scale will be 1,750 mm. We will have to adjust the **Distance Adjust** potentiometer so that it's less than one-quarter or one-fifth (20%) of the scale. Using a screwdriver, try to adjust the number marked in the potentiometer adjustment mechanism to approximately the 9 hours indication compared to an analog clock numbering scheme, as presented in the **Delay Adjust position** in *Figure 3.19*, right.

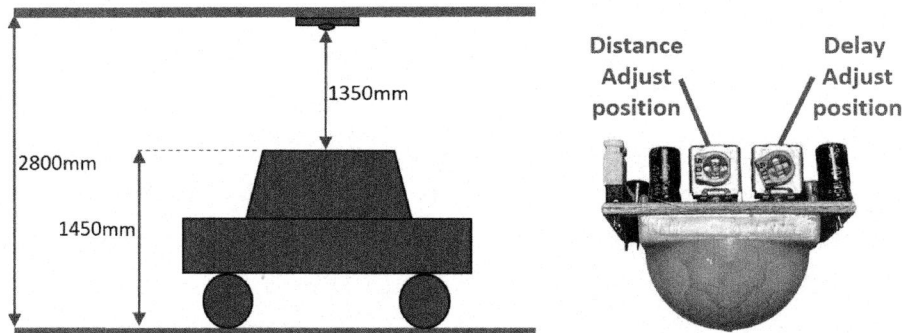

Figure 3.19 – Distances and potentiometer positions in the motion Sensor Calibration

You can improve the distance of movement detection calibration method by installing the sensor in your garage first and then calibrating this distance by checking the movement detection directly in Tasmota. Follow these steps to do so:

1. Using the Tasmota software you installed in your sensor, type the IP address you assigned to the sensor (192.168.0.43) in your web browser.

2. In the **Tasmota** main menu, click the **Console** button.

3. Try to activate the motion sensor by moving in front of it. If your movement is detected, you will see the sensor's status changing according to the following parameters:

```
RUL: SWITCH1#STATE=1 performs "publish sensor/Garage_
Temp_PIR/PIR1 ON"
MQT: sensor/Garage_Temp_PIR/PIR1 = ON
RUL: SWITCH1#STATE=0 performs "Publish sensor/Garage_
Temp_PIR/PIR1 OFF"
MQT: sensor/Garage_Temp_PIR/PIR1 = OFF
```

The RUL and MQT statements indicate the same state status change. If you notice a change in state – that is, from ON to OFF – this means that a movement was triggered.

Installing the sensor

Installing the sensor is very simple – you will need to make sure you will have an outlet available close to where you will install the sensor. First, locate where you will install the **sensor** and the outlet. Once you've figured out where to install it, get a ladder and put it below in the installation location. Detach the **3M dual lock tape** from the other piece of the **sensor** and stick it to the garage roof. Make sure it is attached to it securely. Then, attach the **dual lock tape** attached to the sensor to the one on the garage roof. Connect the **sensor's USB adapter** to the outlet in the garage roof. With that, the sensor will be installed. In my home, it looks like what's shown in *Figure 3.20*:

Figure 3.20 – Double measurement sensor installed

As you can see, the sensor has been installed on my garage roof and connected to an outlet close to the garage gate's control motor.

I have provided a demonstration of the sensor in the Ch3-4 video, including how it can be seen in Home Assistant and the Tasmota interface. I activated the motion sensor in my garage to show how the sensor activation is presented in Home Assistant in real time.

With the sensor installed, we have completed this chapter and can start to prepare for the next one.

Summary

In this chapter, we added another component to our **home automation system**: a **sensor**. We added this component by building it from scratch using electronic parts available on the market. Each part of the sensor was introduced and information about how to interconnect the parts was provided.

We learned about a popular piece of software called Tasmota, which can be used to manage IoT devices, and looked at how to install and configure it in our sensor. After installing and configuring this software, we switched to Home Assistant and integrated the sensor.

We finished this chapter by providing more details on how to enclose the **sensor** in a box, calibrate the **motion sensor module**, and then install it.

In the next chapter, we will look at another type of device called an **actuator**. By doing this, we will have finished looking at the basic components that can be used for a home automation system. This, in turn, will allow us to cover advanced topics so that we can create automations using Home Assistant. Let's continue to build our system!

4
Hacking a Commercial Actuator to Work with Home Assistant

In the previous chapter, we created our own sensor. If you are not interested in creating your own device, you can opt to buy a commercial model instead. One of the great challenges of the home automation industry is ensuring compatibility among the devices offered by each equipment manufacturer. Each manufacturer has its own way of configuring and managing sensors and actuators.

Fortunately, Home Assistant provides several Integrations that allow different devices to be used and controlled through it. Even then, for some devices, an integration to Home Assistant is not available. You may want a different configuration for your device where you can manage its firmware and even adapt it by including features you like that are not available in the original equipment manufacturer's firmware.

This chapter addresses the challenges mentioned previously. The focus will be on guiding you to change the original firmware of a commercial actuator to the one we used in the previous chapter, **Tasmota**. We refer to this operation of changing the original firmware as a **Hardware Hack** or simply **Hacking**.

Besides hacking the firmware of a commercial actuator, you will learn how to do the following in this chapter:

- Understanding hacking a sensor or actuator
- Using tools and hacking the firmware of a commercial actuator
- Configuring your hacked actuator
- Adding another commercial actuator to Home Assistant (non-hacked)
- Installing actuator devices in your home
- Installing other types of devices in your home

By the end of this chapter, you will be able to manage most kinds of sensors or actuators to work with Home Assistant, even if integration is not available. Also, you'll learn how to choose commercial devices to work with Home Assistant. You'll then be able to handle different devices' installation in your home.

Technical requirements

You will need the same skills as for the previous chapter and be familiar with software deployment and configuration to configure the actuator we will be hacking. The core knowledge required for this chapter is familiarity with electronic circuits and devices by disassembling and soldering or connecting wires to them. Using electrical installation tool knowledge could be useful to do some installation-related tasks. Some informative videos will be provided on how to hack and configure actuators. The configuration for the actuator used in this chapter is available at `https://github.com/PacktPublishing/Building-Smart-Home-Automation-Solutions-with-Home-Assistant/tree/main/Chapter%2004`. Check out the following video to view the Code in Action: `https://bit.ly/3KDhnDN`

Understanding hacking a sensor or actuator

As mentioned previously, the hacking operation is accomplished by replacing the original device firmware with other firmware that has some integration with Home Assistant. You might have the following motivations to hack the firmware of a sensor or actuator:

- Integration is not yet available in Home Assistant

- To achieve better control or management than the original device manufacturer's integration

- To change or add features to an integration by changing the sensor or actuator firmware

The main motivation when I started to hack the sensors and actuators for my home was because initial Wi-Fi actuator plugs I purchased some years ago don't have integration to work with Home Assistant. Nowadays, you probably would not need to hack the firmware of your device since most new devices have integration available to work with Home Assistant.

You might opt to hack a sensor or actuator so that it can be managed using **Tasmota** or **ESPHome** integration. This will give a lot of flexibility when you need to update the firmware, if required, or when you want to implement advanced automation using **Node-RED**, for example. Also, using a firmware that's source code is known to you, will allow you to get a better control and understanding of how the data from your home will be shared. There are applications provided by device manufacturers that can store data from your home in the cloud or on their servers, but you do not have control over how this data will be used.

Another advantage of hacking the firmware of your device is that you can write your own code and deploy it or you can change the source code for Tasmota, adding features you want.

In the next subsection, you will learn how to choose and convert the device to be hacked to install Tasmota.

How to choose a commercial sensor or actuator to be used with Tasmota

First, we must mention that as we will hack the system with Tasmota firmware, the device must be compatible with the **ESP8266** and **ESP32** platforms. The issue is that I cannot find a way to discover whether a device is based on these platforms without opening it. So, instead of purchasing these devices and later discovering they are not compatible with Tasmota, this website provides a very complete list of different devices compatible with Tasmota: `https://templates.blakadder.com`. The website lists devices pre-flashed with Tasmota from the manufacturer and devices by type. It also lists devices that are not compatible with Tasmota.

If you purchased a sensor and it has no integration with Home Assistant, look on the web page mentioned to see whether there is compatibility with Tasmota. If it is compatible, follow the instructions for each device to flash and configure Tasmota to it.

> **Note**
> Tasmota can also handle a different chipset, called **Tuya**. This is composed of a microcontroller and a Wi-Fi module. It is possible to flash the firmware to the microcontroller and configure the Wi-Fi module via a serial port. This configuration in Tasmota is called **TuyaMCU**.

In the next section, we will go over the basic tools for hacking a device and proceed with the conversion of its firmware in detailed steps.

Using tools and hacking the firmware of a commercial actuator

In this section, we will teach you about the tools and materials required to hack a commercial actuator. We will also cover the main subject of this chapter, which is effectively hacking the firmware of an actuator. We will do this using an extremely popular actuator that's available on the market.

Learning about the tools and materials used to hack an actuator

The materials we will be using to hack a sensor are as follows:

- 3.3 V DC / 1 A (min) power supply
- Power supply cables
- USB-to-serial converter (+3.3 V option)
- USB type A to USB mini type B cable
- Jump wires

- Soldering iron and solder

- 4-way terminal bar

- A computer with the **Tasmotizer** software installed

> **Note**
>
> Tasmota can also be installed using a web installer. I will provide more details about this firmware deployment tool in *Chapter 10*, in the *Upload the ESP32 Tasmota firmware variant to the temperature hub* subsection.

The power supply can be any that can reach at least 3.3 V DC and 1 A. *Figure 4.1* shows a power supply that will be used to hack the actuator.

Figure 4.1 – Power supply used to hack the actuator

The small bench power supply in *Figure 4.1* is one I have that can supply a variable output for voltage from 0 to 30 V and current from 0 to 5 A. But, as mentioned, you can use a power adapter, a wall plug, or another type that has a specification of 3.3 V DC output voltage and output current of at least 1 A. Another option for the power supply is to use a 5 V DC USB DC-DC step down converter, which can be connected to the computer's USB port and provides the 3.3 V DC output desired.

The power supply cables are banana plug to alligator clip-type probes. They will be useful to connect the power supply to the actuator to be hacked. Usually, these cables use the colors red and black by convention – red for the positive pole and black for the negative of the power supply. These cables are presented in *Figure 4.2*.

Figure 4.2 – Banana plug to alligator clip probes

The USB-to-serial converter is one of the most important tools to be used to hack your actuator. This is because the Wi-Fi module in the actuator is programmed using a **UART** (short for **Universal Asynchronous Receiver Transmitter**) serial port using 3.3 V DC as the signal level. *Figure 4.3* shows a USB-to-serial converter used to hack the actuator.

Figure 4.3 – USB-to-serial converter

The serial-to-USB converter is an extremely useful tool that can be used with other devices, such as Arduino-based microcontrollers. It has a jump to configure the output voltage level to 5 V DC or 3.3 V DC. We will be using the jump configured to 3.3 V DC. This is a very inexpensive tool and you can find it easily on the internet by typing usb serial converter ft232rl FTDI. You may not need to install any drivers to get the serial-to-USB converter working if you are using Windows

10 or above, but if you have trouble doing it, you can visit `https://learn.sparkfun.com/tutorials/how-to-install-ftdi-drivers/all` to install the drivers for different operating systems.

The jump wires are the same kind as presented in *Chapter 3*. In the case of our hacking project, we will be using four jump wires: two male-male and two female-female.

The 4-pin terminal bar will be soldered onto the actuator board using solder and the soldering iron.

These tools will enable you to install the new firmware on the actuator. The next topic will present how to interconnect and use these tools to install Tasmota on the actuator.

How to hack your commercial actuator

The actuator we will hack is one of the most popular used in the market. It is manufactured by the Chinese company **Itead** (`https://itead.cc/`). The model we will use is the **Sonoff BasicR2**, seen in *Figure 4.4*.

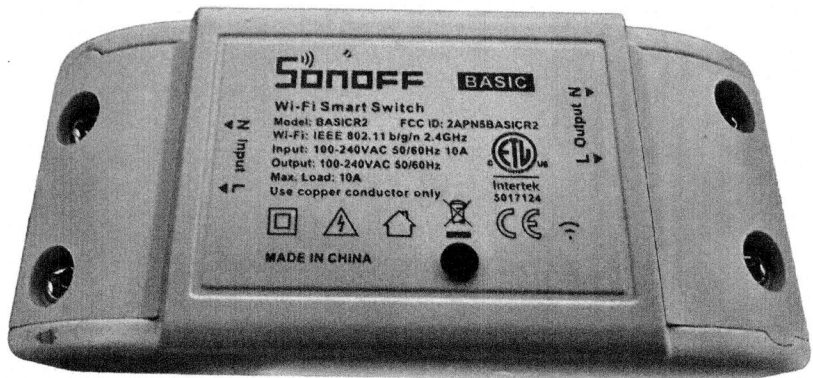

Figure 4.4 – Sonoff BasicR2 – actuator to be hacked

The actuator device shown in *Figure 4.4* is made to be installed inside a wall switch box and can be used to manage a load of up to 10 A. The input and output range has the same voltage, from 100 to 240 V at 50/60 Hz, making it compatible with most voltage systems across the world. The actuator element used in this device is a relay, as mentioned in *Chapter 1*.

There are two inputs where line and neutral input wires are connected and two outputs for line and neutral output wires. There is a black button at the top of the actuator that can be used to manually set the relay status to open or close. This button can also be used to reset the status of the Sonoff BasicR2 and allow the new firmware to be loaded into the unit.

> **Important note**
>
> During the process of uploading the Tasmota firmware to the Sonoff actuator, you will have the option to save the original firmware from the manufacturer in a binary file. We will explore this option during the hacking process. If you want to skip this step and not save the original firmware from the manufacturer, once Tasmota is recorded, there will be no way to return to the original firmware, so do it at your own risk.

In the next subsections, you will follow the steps to prepare the actuator, interconnect the tools, and upload the Tasmota firmware.

Preparing the actuator

We will need to disassemble the Sonoff actuator to access the pins to upload the firmware to the **ESP8285**, which is the Wi-Fi **SOC** (**System On Chip**) used in the sensor used in this chapter. We will also need to solder a four-pin terminal bar to the connector of the actuator electronic board. This will be done to connect the jump wires easily to the actuator, preventing the firmware from being uploaded incorrectly and corrupted.

The sequence to disassemble and solder the four-pin terminal bar is shown in a sequence of pictures in the video `CH4-1` and is explained as follows:

1. Get the Sonoff actuator and, using a screwdriver or any other sharp object, remove the bottom lid. Make sure the four screws are not connected to the unit.

2. Tear apart the bottom lid, the electronic board, and the upper lid. Separate them from the electronic board.

3. Get the four-pin terminal bar and locate the J2 connector in the Sonoff actuator. *Figure 4.5* presents the four-pin terminal bar on the left and the top side of the electronic board on the right with some important internal components, such as the reset switch and the indicator LED represented.

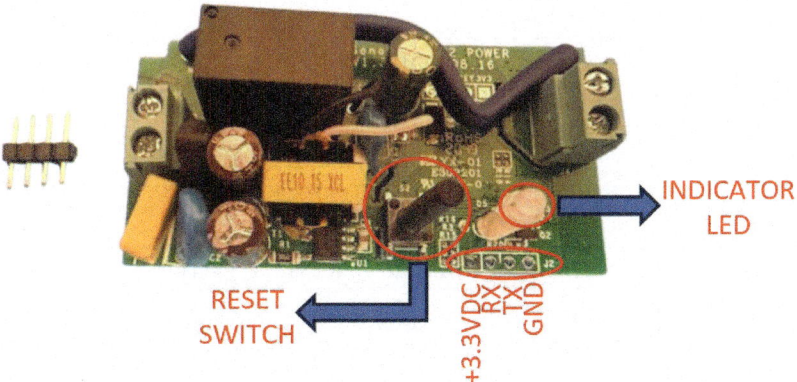

Figure 4.5 – Sonoff BasicR2 electronic board and four-pin terminal bar

4. *Figure 4.5* also presents the J2 connector, circled, and its pinout. Position the four-pin terminal bar on the J2 connector and, using the soldering iron, solder it to the electronic board. Make sure the black part of the four-pin terminal bar sits aligned with the top of the electronic board.

Once the actuator is prepared to be flashed with its new firmware, we will proceed to interconnect the parts.

Interconnecting the tools and parts for hacking

Now, we will need to connect all parts and tools to execute the hacking operation on the actuator. *Figure 4.6* shows the interconnection diagram.

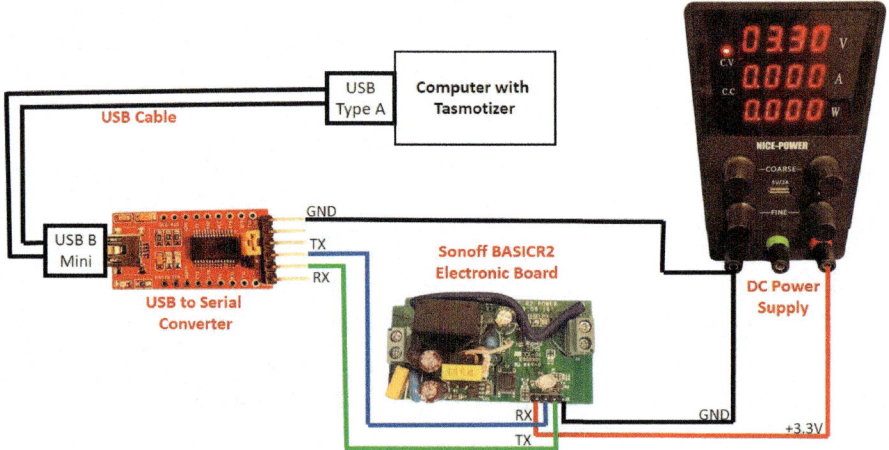

Figure 4.6 – Interconnection diagram for commercial actuator hacking

The complete **Bill of Materials (BOM)** for hacking the actuator is listed in *Table 4.1*.

ID	Quantity	Description
1	1	Sonoff BASICR2 electronic board
2	1	USB-to-serial converter (+3.3 V)
3	1	USB cable (type A to type B mini)
4	1	Computer with Tasmotizer software installed
5	1	+3.3 VDC power supply
6	1	Arduino jump wire male to female – 3 vias (power signals)
7	1	Arduino jump wire female to female – 2 vias (serial data signals)
8	2	Power cable banana plug to alligator clip

Table 4.1 – Actuator hacking – bill of materials

The following sequence is suggested to connect the circuit shown in *Figure 4.6*:

1. Make sure the power supply is turned off and the USB cable is not connected to the computer.

2. Connect item **7** (Arduino jump female-to-female) between item **1** (Sonoff BasicR2 electronic board) and item **2** (USB-to-serial converter +3.3 V). These cables need to be cross-connected in the RX and TX pins, meaning item **1**, RX pin to item **2**, TX pin, and vice versa.

3. Connect item **8** (power cable banana plug to alligator clip) to item **5** (+3.3 VDC power supply).

4. Connect the item **6 Ground (GND**)to the item **8** GND. Two connections should be made: the first connection between the item **8** GND power cable and the item **6** GND signal from item **1** (Sonoff BasicR2 electronic board); the second connection between the item **8** GND power cable and the item **6** GND signal from item **2** (USB-to-serial converter +3.3 V).

5. Connect item **6** +3.3 V to item **8** +3.3 V. A connection should be made between the item **8** +3.3 V power cable and the item **6** +3.3 V signal from item **1** (Sonoff BasicR2 electronic board).

6. Connect item **3** (USB cable) between item **4** (computer with Tasmotizer installed) and item **2** (USB-to-serial converter +3.3 V).

7. Make sure the jump in the USB-to-serial converter is configured to +3.3 V, as shown in *Figure 4.3*.

Important note

During the preceding steps, make sure the connections are not loose, otherwise, the hacking operation will not work properly. Just in case, review the assembly sequence to check whether all connections were done correctly. Also, keep the live power supply connections away from each other to not take the risk of shorting them and damaging the power supply.

Figure 4.7 presents the actuator interconnection after following the steps from *1* to *7*.

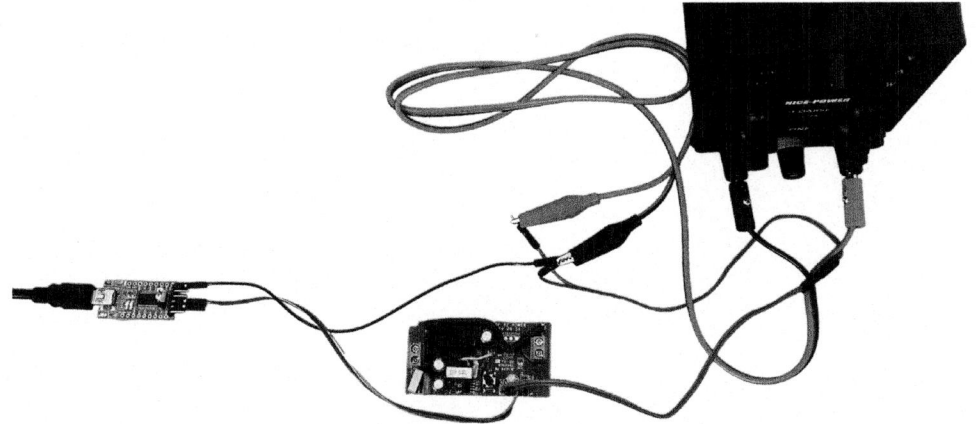

Figure 4.7 – Interconnection diagram for commercial actuator hacking

In *Figure 4.7*, just part of the USB cable is shown and the computer is not presented in the figure.

After connecting all the parts to hack the actuator, the next subsection will explain how to execute the change in the actuator firmware.

Hacking the actuator firmware

If you read *Chapter 3*, specifically the *Installing Tasmota in our sensor* section, you will see the steps to hack the actuator in this chapter are similar. Differences will be related to the USB-serial device to be recognized by the operating system and the firmware name we will be programming in the actuator.

The CH4-2 video clarifies the steps you will need to follow to execute the change in the firmware for the actuator. These steps are also listed here:

1. If your computer does not have Tasmotizer installed yet, download and install the latest release at `https://github.com/tasmota/tasmotizer/releases`.

2. Download the latest `tasmota.bin` file from `http://ota.tasmota.com/tasmota/release/`. The release I'm using is `12.3.1 - Percy`.

3. Connect the **USB-to-serial converter** to the computer using the USB type A connector. When connected, the red power LED on the USB-to-serial converter will be turned on.

4. If you are using a variable power supply, disconnect the positive banana plug from it and turn on the power supply. Adjust the voltage to +3.3 V DC. Connect the positive banana plug back into the power supply. If you are using a fixed 3.3 V DC. output power supply, just turn it on.

5. Use **Windows Device Manager** and check for **Ports (COM & LPT)**. Check whether a device such as **USB Serial Port (COMX)** was added, similar to that shown in *Figure 4.8*. Take note of the **COMX** port. It will be the COM port number to be used in Tasmotizer.

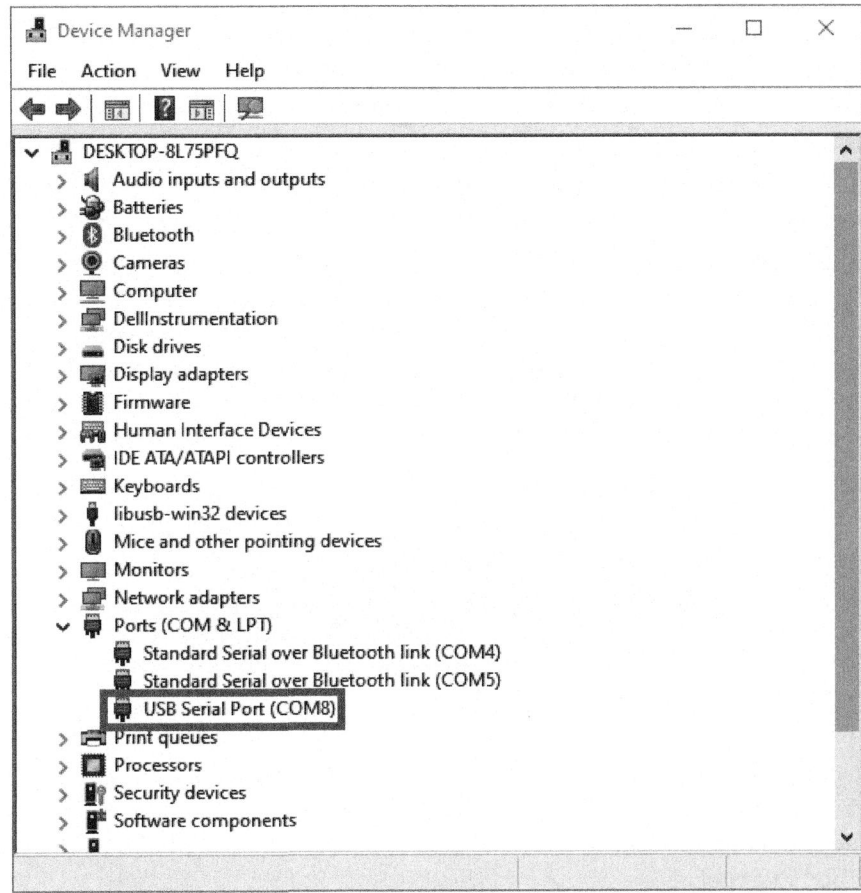

Figure 4.8 – Serial port created by the USB-to-serial converter

6. Open the `Tasmotizer.exe` file. Make sure you are using Admin mode by right-clicking the **Run as administrator** option.

7. Select the **COMX** port found in *step 5*. Click the **Open** button under **Select image**. Choose the `tasmota.bin` file previously downloaded in *step 2*. Check the **Erase before flashing** box.

8. If you want to save the Sonoff BasicR2 original firmware in the **Backup** section, select the **Save original firmware** checkbox, and in the **Flash size** dropbox, select the **1MB** option. Please refer to *Figure 3.7* in *Chapter 3* for the checkbox options to select in *steps 7* and *8*.

9. Click on the **Tasmotize!** button. Another screen will be opened and Tasmotizer will try to connect to the Sonoff device. At this time, you must disconnect the positive banana plug from the power supply, wait for one or two seconds, press and hold the black reset switch on the Sonoff device (please refer to *Figure 4.5* to find it), and reconnect the banana plug. Release the black reset switch.

10. If you choose the backup option, the previous or the original firmware will start to be saved in a file. After saving it in the backup file, the window **User action required** will open with the message **Please power cycle the device, wait a moment and press OK**. Click in the **OK** button.

11. Power cycle the device by again disconnecting the positive banana plug from the power supply, clicking and holding the switch on the Sonoff BasicR2 device, and reconnecting the positive banana plug. Release the button on the Sonoff device.

12. The device will be erased and, in the sequence, the `tasmota.bin` file will be uploaded to it. The Tasmotizer software will present a similar progress screen for the erasing and recording process as in *Figure 3.8* in *Chapter 3*. If everything goes well, after finishing recording, a new pop-up window will be presented, displaying **Process successful! Power cycle the device**, as presented in *Figure 4.9*. Click **OK** and power cycle again by disconnecting the positive banana plug from the power supply and reconnecting it. There is no need to press the switch on the Sonoff now.

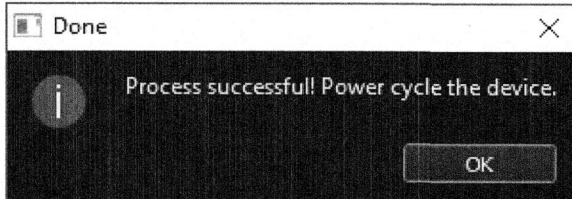

Figure 4.9 – Tasmota recording process successful screenshot

13. We will finish the upload by configuring the Wi-Fi SSID and password on the device. Click on the **Send Config** button at the bottom of the main Tasmotizer screen. A new window will be presented. In this window, enable the Wi-Fi checkbox and type your home network's Wi-Fi SSID and password in the appropriate fields. Click on the **Save** button. Please refer to *Figure 3.9* in *Chapter 3* for the Tasmotizer Wi-Fi configuration screen mentioned in this step.

14. A new pop-up window will be presented confirming that the configuration was sent and the device will restart. A screenshot of this window is presented in *Figure 4.10*. Click on the **OK** button.

Figure 4.10 – Tasmota Wi-Fi configuration sent confirmation screenshot

15. You will have to redo the power cycle operation again. After recycling the power, click on the **Get IP** button on the Tasmotizer software's main screen and you should get an IP configured to your actuator presented on a pop-up screen similar to *Figure 3.10* in *Chapter 3*. In our case, the IP configured for our device this time is **192.168.0.14**.

16. Take note of this IP address to use it later on. Disconnect the USB cable from the computer and turn off the power supply.

17. Your Tasmota firmware was uploaded and initially configured to the Sonoff device. Disconnect all jump wires from the electronic board.

18. Reassemble all parts of the actuator in the reverse order they were disassembled in.

    You now have your actuator hacked and have Tasmota installed on it.

The next steps will be to configure the Tasmota software and, later, Home Assistant to work with it. This content will be covered in the next topic.

Configuring your hacked actuator

The actuator with the new firmware needs to be configured to work as expected. We will do this configuration first on the actuator side. After configuring the actuator side, we will do the Home Assistant configuration so Home Assistant can handle it. After this section, your actuator will be ready to be managed by Home Assistant.

Configuring the Tasmota firmware in your actuator

To configure your actuator, you will need to follow *Figure 4.11*.

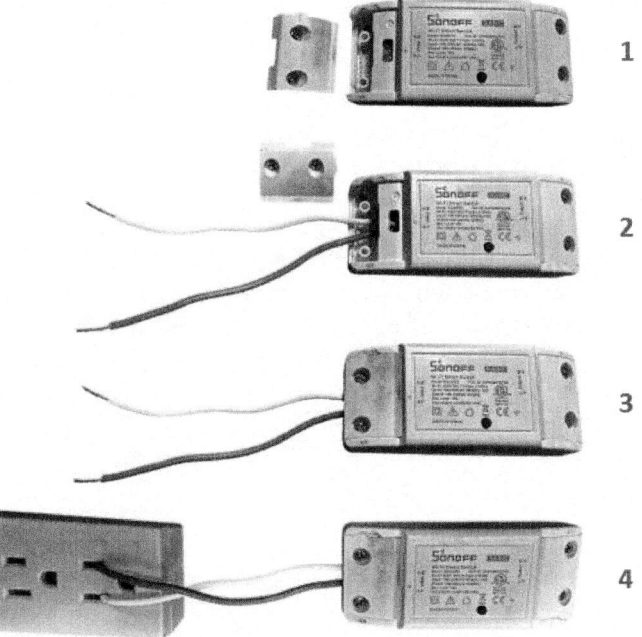

Figure 4.11 – Sequence to install the AC wires to the Sonoff Basic R2

These steps will be required:

1. First, according to item *1* in *Figure 4.11*, you will need to make sure the connector lid on the input side is open. If it is not, unscrew the lid of the Sonoff Basic R2 actuator.

2. Second, according to item *2* in *Figure 4.11*, you will need to put wires in the actuator input. This is needed because we removed the DC power supply connected to the actuator and now, we will connect it to the AC voltage. Get two 20 AWG wires, strip 5mm (about 0.2 inches) of the wire cap on both sides, and connect them to inputs N and L on the Sonoff Basic R2 actuator. You will need to unscrew the two screws in the green connector to attach the wires. Screw the connector lid back on and tighten the screws with the wires connected to them.

3. Following item *3* in *Figure 4.11*, screw the connector lid back on.

> **Important note**
> The next steps will involve the connection of the actuator to the AC voltage. Dealing with AC voltage could involve an electric shock hazard. Make sure to manipulate the sensor and use wires isolated and not exposed to the AC voltage network!

4. Before we start the actuator firmware configuration, we will need to connect it to the AC voltage. According to item *4* in *Figure 4.11*, you should connect it to the outlet. I recommend you to use a outlet power strip and connect the wires in the line and neutral of the outlet power strip turned off. This will be a safer way to safely connect the actuator to the AC line and avoid an electric shock hazard.

After connecting the actuator input to the AC voltage and turning on the outlet power strip, a blue LED will flash twice and turn off. We will then be ready to start our configuration, which is accomplished by similar steps to those presented in *Chapter 3*, and for this reason, they will be simplified by executing the following sequence:

1. Using your web browser, type in the IP configured for your actuator. In this case, for this example, it's **192.168.0.14**. A similar Tasmota main menu page presented in *Figure 3.11* will be shown. The only difference will be the software version, which will be **12.3.1**.

2. Click **Configuration | Configure Module**. In **Module type**, select **Sonoff BasicR2 (0)** as presented in *Figure 4.12*. Click **Save**. The device will restart and return to the Tasmota main menu.

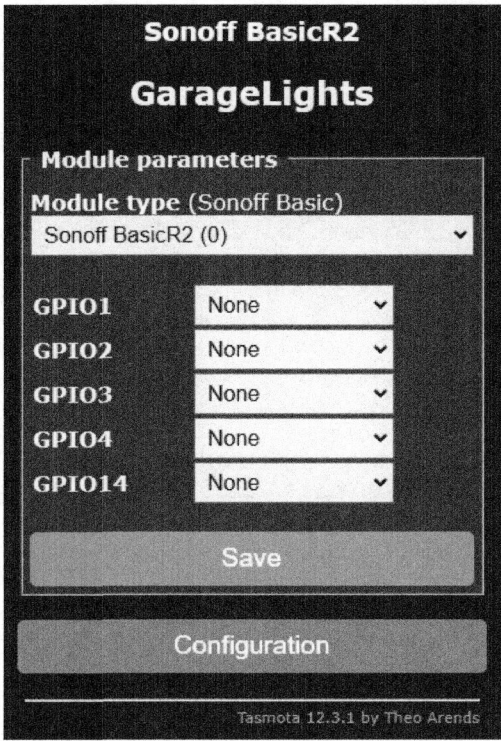

Figure 4.12 – Tasmota module configuration

3.   Click **Configuration | Configure Other**. For **Device Name** and **Friendly Name 1**, put the name you want for this device. We will be using `GarageLights`. Click **Save**. The device will restart and return to the Tasmota main menu.

4.   Click **Configuration | Configure MQTT**. Fill in the information according to *Figure 4.13*. In the **Host** field add the MQTT server, which is `homeassistant.local`. Change the **User** field to `your_name`. Change the **Password** field to `your_password`. Change the **Topic** field to `GarageLights`. Click **Save**. The device will restart and return to the Tasmota main menu.

Figure 4.13 – Tasmota MQTT configuration

Basically, we did the module configuration in *step 6*, the name configuration in *step 7*, and the MQTT configuration in *step 8*. Since Tasmota supports Sonoff devices, there is no need to configure the IO pins in the module configuration. The pins for the LED, push button switch, and relay are software configured automatically. Future commercial devices you want to Flash with Tasmota firmware will follow the steps indicated before, with changes just in the second step when you have to set up the proper commercial device you want to configure if it is different from Sonoff Basic R2.

> **Important note**
>
> As we will use the actuator to turn on and off lights in the garage, we can set an option in Tasmota to force Home Assistant to recognize the actuator switch as a light. This can be done by going to **Console** from the Tasmota main menu and entering the `setoption30 1` command. You should get the `RESULT` message returned in the console as `{"SetOption30":"ON"}`, indicating that the command was configured correctly.

We've done the configuration of the actuator from its perspective, or related to Tamosta. In the next section, we will configure the actuator from Home Assistant's point of view.

Configuring the actuator in Home Assistant

You will be surprised that there is nothing much to do in Home Assistant to have a commercial actuator configured to it. What we will do is just confirm the actuator was integrated and change the location (referenced as area in Home Assistant) where the actuator is located. You will have to go through the following steps to be able to do that:

1. Using your web browser, type in the hostname for Home Assistant, which is `http://homeassistant.local:8123`. If the page for login and password is presented, enter them in the proper fields and click **Login**.

2. Click **Settings | Devices & Services**. In the **Integrations** tab, find the **Tasmota** integration. You will see that there will now be **2 devices** and **21 entities** presented, as shown in *Figure 4.14*.

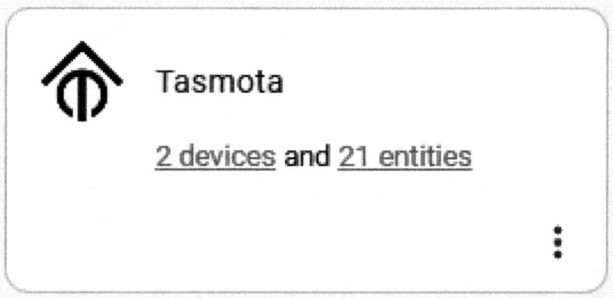

Figure 4.14 – Tasmota integration on Home Assistant

3. Of the Tasmota integration options presented in *Figure 4.14*, click on the **2 devices** link. You will see the **Devices** tab presented and just the devices with Tasmota integration are listed in a table format. Our double-measurement sensor, **GarageTempPIR**, from *Chapter 3*, and our actuator **GarageLights** are listed.

4. Click on the GarageLights actuator line. Click on the pencil icon in the upper-right corner, as presented in *Figure 4.16,* to edit the actuator's properties.

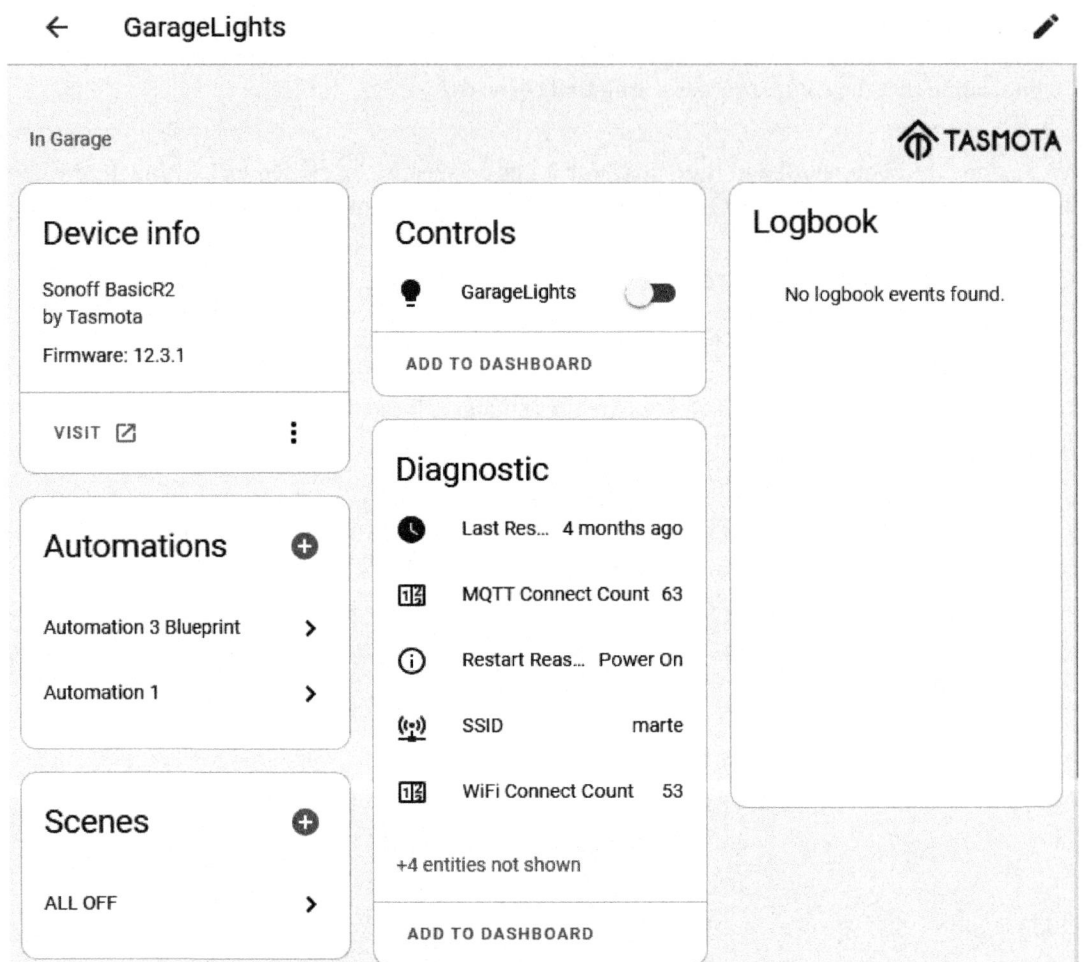

Figure 4.15 – GarageLights actuator configuration in Home Assistant

5. A new window will pop up. Click in the **Area** drop-down box and select the **Garage** option, as presented in *Figure 4.15*. Click on **UPDATE**.

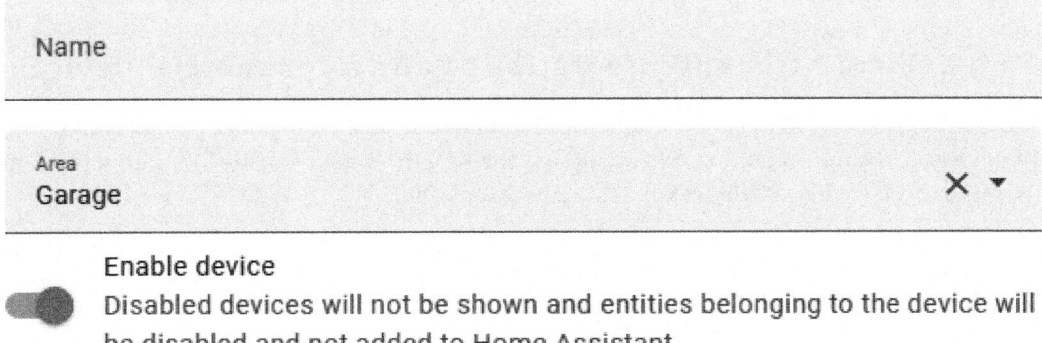

Figure 4.16 – Home Area configuration for the GarageLights actuator

6. Click on the left arrow at the top left of the screen shown in *Figure 4.15* to return to the **Devices** tab. Check whether the **Area** column for the **GarageLights** line has been updated to **Garage**.

This is enough for now in terms of configuration. Feel free to explore and play with these two devices in Home Assistant.

Remember that the actuator, despite being configured to be managed by Home Assistant, is not physically installed. We will still do this in this chapter, but before we do that, let us add one more actuator to Home Assistant so we can explore more opportunities to do automations in *Chapter 5*. The next section will explore this a bit more.

Adding another commercial actuator to Home Assistant (non-hacked)

In this section, we will explore another Home Assistant resource, which I call applications. Applications are integrations provided by the device manufacturer or created by the development community. They allow you to easily integrate a commercial sensor or actuator into Home Assistant without the need to flash or hack your device. If you don't want to change the firmware of your devices, before you buy the next one for your home, check if there is an application for it by searching the integrations available in Home Assistant at https://www.home-assistant.io/integrations/.

We will provide an example of how you can add a device to be managed by Home Assistant directly without any change to the hardware or firmware. The application for the device in the example is available in Home Assistant.

Using a Home Assistant integration to add a commercial device

The device we are going to use in the example is a commercial actuator provided by the manufacturer **TPLink Kasa**. The model used in this example is the **KP115**. It can be easily found in retail stores such as Amazon. *Figure 4.17* shows what this device looks like.

Figure 4.17 – TPLink Kasa actuator to be Integrated into Home Assistant

---

Important note

The steps to be done next assume the TPLink Kasa KP115 plug is already configured to be operated in your home. If the plug is not configured yet, make sure to follow the instructions provided on this page: https://www.tp-link.com/us/support/download/kp115/.

We will need to take the following steps to integrate this actuator into Home Assistant. The CH4-3 video is provided as a reference to assist you in this task:

1. If you are not logged in to Home Assistant, use your web browser to type the hostname http:// homeassistant.local:8123. Input your username and password if required and click **Login**. If you are logged in, jump to the next step.

2. Click on **Settings | Devices & Services**. In the **Integrations** tab, click on the **+ ADD INTEGRATION** button located in the lower-right corner.

3. A window will open and ask you to select a brand. In the **Search for brand name** field, type `tplink kasa`. Select the filtered option **TP-Link Kasa Smart**.

4. On the new screen, leave the **Host** field empty and click on the **SUBMIT** button.

5. Home Assistant will search and will find the **Desk outlet** device, as presented in *Figure 4.18*. If you have more than one device, they will be listed. Select the one you want to add and click **SUBMIT**.

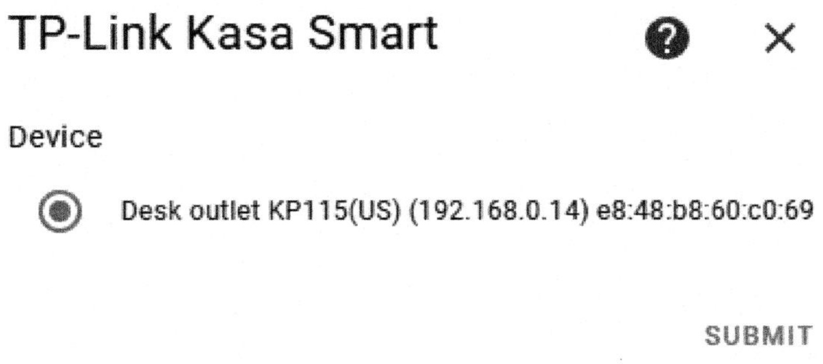

Figure 4.18 – Adding the Desk outlet actuator device to Home Assistant

6. Another screen will be presented indicating **Success!** and prompting you to assign an area for the device. We will create a new area called **kid bedroom 1**. Click in the **Area** field and then on the **Add new area** option.

7. In the new **Add new area** window, click in the **Name** field and type `kid bedroom 1`. Click **ADD**.

8. Back in the **Success!** window, click on **FINISH**. The actuator will be integrated into Home Assistant.

In the **Integrations** tab, you will now find, under the **TP-Link Kasa Smart** integration or application, the KP115 device. Click on **1 DEVICE** to see all actuator properties, as shown in *Figure 4.19*.

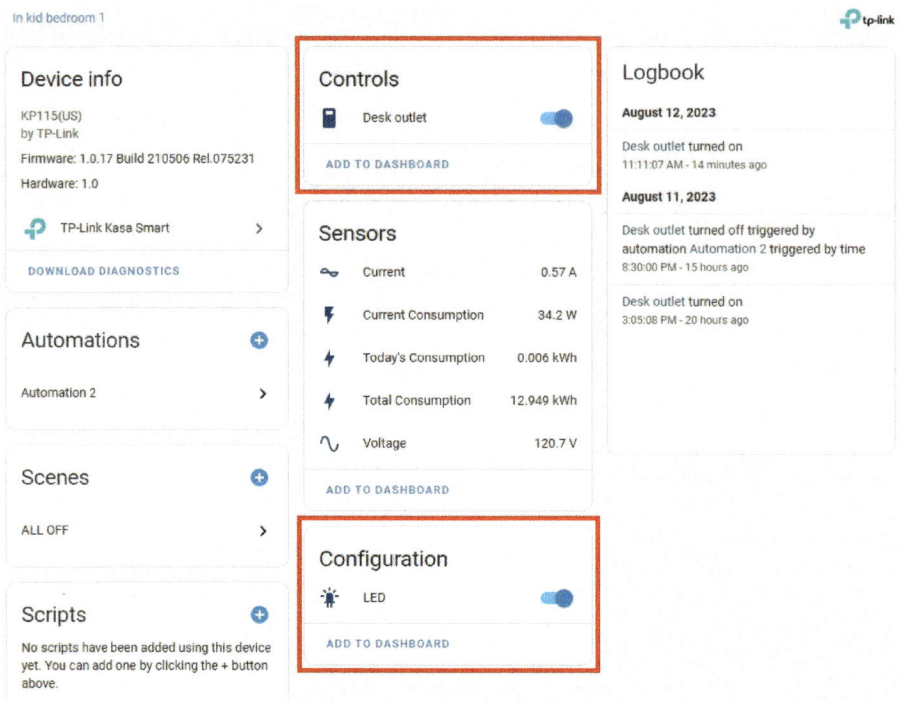

Figure 4.19 – TPLink Kasa Actuator properties presented by Home Assistant

In *Figure 4.19*, you can see the actuator has a sensor that can measure current, voltage, and power consumption. This is especially useful if you want to track power consumption in your home and identify, for example, appliances that are contributing to increasing your electricity bill each month. You can also see that you can control the **Desk outlet** output relay and the LED using Home Assistant. You can do this using the slide switch controls inside the red rectangles in *Figure 4.19*.

We now have at least three devices configured in Home Assistant so far. They are assigned according to *Table 4.2*.

Device	Integration	Model	Area
GarageLights	Tasmota	Sonoff Basic R2	Garage
GarageTempPIR	Tasmota	ESP8266	Garage
Desk outlet	TP-Link KASA Smart	KP115(US)	Kid bedroom 1

Table 4.2 – Devices configured in Home Assistant

Using the devices in *Table 4.2*, we will create some automations, which we will explore in *Chapter 5*.

In the next section, we will provide information about the installation of devices. The focus will first be a hacked actuator and then other types.

Installing actuator devices in your home

After we hacked and configured our actuator, we had to physically install it in our home. The other devices we have in our home, presented in *Table 4.2*, were installed in *Chapter 3*, in the case of the double-measurement sensor, or have a simplified installation, as in the case of the TP-Link Kasa plug. Therefore, we will not need to be concerned about them.

Let us get started with the installation, providing some valuable information prior to the work being done. Later, we will be installing and testing the devices. At the end of the chapter, we will give information about the installation of other types of devices.

Getting started with the actuator installation

Some of the most used devices in your home will be Sonoff actuators. The availability of these devices is high, from assorted brands. They can be used to control lights and appliances in your home, which is involved as part of all automation routines in a home automation system.

Sonoff actuators are made to be installed inside the electrical box of your home. This presents advantages and disadvantages. The main advantages are that the actuator will be hidden in the box so will be clean-looking in your home. The disadvantages are more work for installation and the difficulty of moving the installed actuator from one location to another if needed.

We will provide helpful information to overcome some of the disadvantages presented related to the installation. This includes some tools and accessories used for installation, some safety concerns, and area preparations before starting the installation. This information will be detailed in the next subtopics.

Grouping the tools and materials needed for installation

The tools and materials needed to install the actuator are presented in *Figure 4.20*.

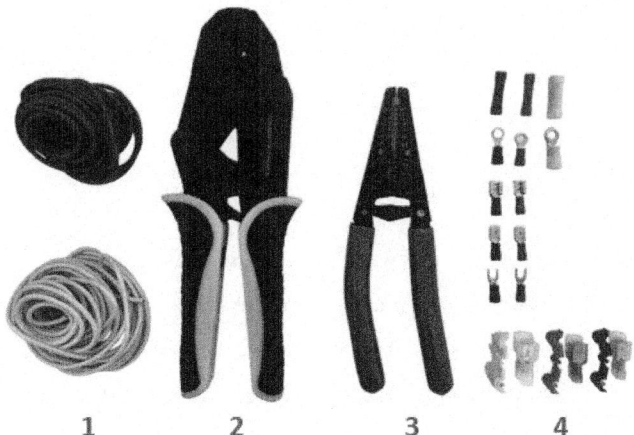

Figure 4.20 – Tools and materials used for the Sonoff Basic R2 installation

You will need two different tools and three diverse types of materials to perform the actuator installation inside the electrical box. The materials and tools needed are enumerated in the following list according to the numbers in *Figure 4.20*:

1. 18 AWG flexible wires

2. Terminal crimper tool

3. Wire stripping tool

4. Assorted electrical wire insulator connectors

The wires, *item 1* in *Figure 4.20*, must be connected to the Sonoff Basic R2 and to the electrical switch or attached to other wires. You will have to strip the wires using a wire stripping tool, *item 3* in *Figure 4.20*. After stripping the wires, you will need to attach an electrical wire insulated connector, *item 4* in *Figure 4.20*. You will need a tool to attach the wire connector, and this is usually done with a terminal crimper tool represented by *item 2* in *Figure 4.20*.

Installing safely

If you intend to use the Sonoff Basic R2 inside an electrical box in your home, you will need to first make sure the power is turned off so you do not risk an electric shock hazard. The easy and safe way to do it is to shut down the general power switch. If you cannot do that, you will need to know which electrical switch is the one related to the outlet or switch where you want to install the actuator. You can also use a multimeter or a multi-phase screwdriver to test whether the circuit is disconnected.

> **Important note**
>
> You will need to do the actuator installation inside an electrical box at your own risk. This is a critical and extremely dangerous operation and should be done by an experienced electrician, a technician, or an electrical engineer. If you do not know how to do it, you should ask for help from a professional to do the installation for you.

Preparing for the installation

In order to prepare to safely install a Sonoff type of actuator in an electrical box, it is recommended to take the following steps:

1. Locate the electrical box where you want to install the actuator.

2. Make sure you have enough clearance to install the actuator.

3. Clean up the area surrounding the electrical box so you have enough room to work.

4. Evaluate whether you have the proper tools to disassemble the electrical box's cover or lid. Get the tools required.

5. Before starting to do any kind of installation, make sure the electrical circuit is switched off.

You can make sure the electrical circuit is switched off by using the following methods:

- Switch off the general circuit breaker in your home.

- If you don't know which circuit breaker is related to your electrical box, turn on lights or appliances connected to the outlet and turn off the circuit breakers one by one until the lights or the appliances turn off.

- Apply the previous method but also measure the voltage to the switch or outlet after removing the cover or lid. The voltage can be measured using a voltmeter or a voltage tester screwdriver.

- Again, be careful when executing *step 5* and applying the methods to turn off the power for your installation. These are key steps in making your installation successful and with no risk. If you are not sure about switching off the power or it is not safe to switch off the electrical circuit related to the installation of your actuator, do not do it. Contact and hire a professional to do this work for you.

After preparing the installation area, you can prepare the Sonoff Basic R2 to be installed. You can do this by following this sequence:

1. Cut 3 x 10 cm (about 3.94 inches) pieces of the 18AWG wire (*item 1* in *Figure 4.20*) – two the same color and one a distinct color. The two of the same color will be connected to the input and output line and the other remaining wire will be connected to neutral.

2. Strip both sides of these three wires by 2 mm or 3 mm (about 0.12 inches) using the wire stripping tool shown in *Figure 4.20*.

3. Open the screws of the Sonoff Basic R2 and locate the line and neutral pins in the input. They are marked as L for line and N for neutral on the left side in *Figure 4.4*. Screw the wires into the input connector of the Sonoff Basic R2.

4. Install the other remaining wire in the line output connector of the Sonoff Basic R2. This connector pin is identified as **Output L** on the right side of *Figure 4.4*. You can install the wire by screwing the wire into the **Output L** connector.

5. Verify the proper way to attach the other side of the stripped wires in the switch. We will be using the circled electrical insulator connector (*item 4* in *Figure 4.20*).

6. We will attach the circled electrical insulator connector on the other side of the wires connected to the line input and output. We will do that using the terminal crimper tool presented in *Figure 4.20* (*item 3*).

7. The last step will be using the electrical insulator connector in the bottom part of *Figure 4.20* (*item 4*) to install the wire connected to the neutral line input of the Sonoff Basic R2. We will do this using the terminal crimper tool.

The result of *steps 1* to *7* are represented in *Figure 4.21*.

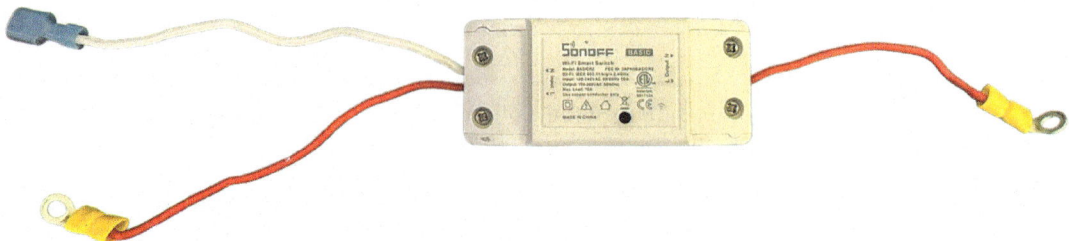

Figure 4.21 – Sonoff Basic R2 with the wires connected and terminal pins crimped

Installing the actuator and testing it The installation of the Sonoff Basic R2 actuator requires a little extra work compared to other devices. In the example in this book, we will install the hacked actuator in a lamp switch box in my garage so we can do some automations in the next chapter using it.

What we will do is install the actuator in parallel with the switch we want to control the garage lights. This is shown in *Figure 4.22*.

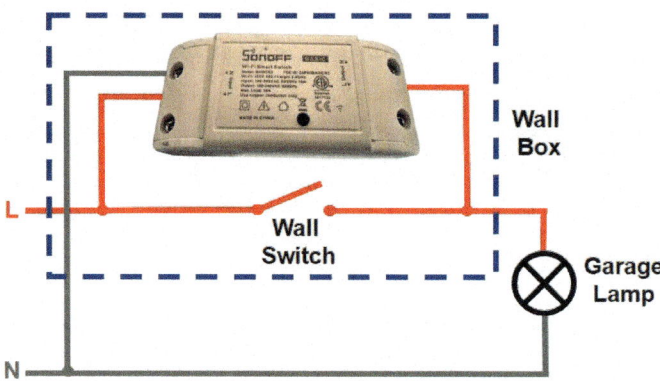

Figure 4.22 – Circuit representation of the Sonoff Basic R2 installation

The dashed rectangle in *Figure 4.22* represents what will be inside the wall box, which includes the wall switch already installed and the Sonoff Basic R2. You will notice that we need to connect just one wire to the output of the actuator. This is because the output relay will switch the line voltage (L) signal connected to the Sonoff basicR2 input on and off. The neutral (N) signal must be connected to the Sonoff Basic R2 to be a return path for the line voltage so the electronic circuit inside the actuator, including what was discussed in *Chapter 1*, can work.

Using the arrangement in *Figure 4.22*, we can still use the switch to turn on and off the lamp if the Sonoff actuator is turned off.

You will basically have to follow this sequence to do the Sonoff Basic R2 installation in an switch electrical box:

1. Make sure you execute *steps 1 to 5* from the *Preparing for the installation* subsection.

2. Disassemble the cover or lid of the switch.

3. Remove the screws attached to the electrical box from the switch.

4. Pull the switch out of the electrical box.

5. Find the phase and neutral wires inside the electrical box. Usually, the phase wire is the one connected to the switch.

6. Get the Sonoff Basic R2 with the wires prepared in advance. Detach the screws connected to the switch terminals. Reattach them, installing the wires with the insulator connectors.

7. Using the tap wire part of the terminal, install it to bite the neutral wire associated with the lamp circuit. Attach the tap wire part to the neutral wire connector.

8. After these steps are completed, you will have the Sonoff Basic R2 attached to your lamp switch circuit. I recommend you test it now before assembling it inside the electrical box. You will do the test by turning the circuit breaker on. Make sure you have the area cleaned before you turn it on.

9. If everything is connected correctly, you will see the Sonoff Basic R2's blue LED light being turned on and off twice. You can repeat the procedure presented in the *Configuring your hacked actuator* section.

10. Before continuing with the installation, turn off the circuit breaker. Push the Sonoff Basic R2 inside the electrical box.

11. Reattach the switch using the screws to hold it in the electrical box.

12. Put the switch cover or lid back.

13. Turn on the circuit breaker and repeat the test done in *step 9* to check that the actuator is still working. If not, disassemble the lid and check for any wire disconnections.

By executing these steps, you will have your actuator installed inside your box. In the next section, we will learn how to install other types of devices. You will see that the installation is more simplified for the other devices than for the Sonoff Basic R2.

Installing other types of devices in your home

As I mentioned in *Chapter 1*, I have different devices installed in my home, including sensors and actuators. Some of them do not require proper installation, while others require minimal work to be installed. In the following subsections, I will briefly comment on and show some of the devices I have at home and how to install them.

Installing small actuators in electrical wall boxes

Some electrical wall boxes I have at home are small, and the size of the Sonoff Basic R2 was a problem for me to install an actuator inside it. The solution I found was to purchase small actuators for electrical wall boxes, such as the **Sonoff Mini R2** model shown at the bottom of *Figure 4.23*.

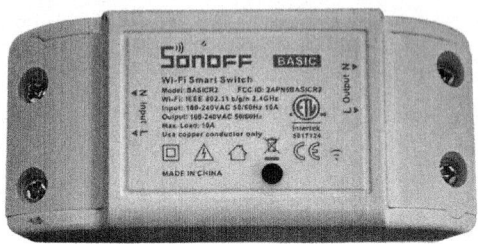

Figure 4.23 – Sonoff Basic R2 x Sonoff Mini R2

The Sonoff Basic R2 at the top of *Figure 4.23* is used as a reference to compare the sizes. The Sonoff Mini R2 model can also be hacked to install Tasmota, following a different procedure where the firmware is installed using the **Over The Air** (**OTA**) method called **Sonoff DIY** (`https://tasmota.github.io/docs/Sonoff-DIY/`). The installation and wire connection also follow the same idea that was explained before, represented in *Figure 4.22*.

Installing outlet plug actuators

I prefer to use outlet plugs like the one shown in *Figure 4.17* to control appliances or table lamps. This is because the installation is very straightforward, not requiring any additional effort besides connecting it directly to the outlet. These outlet plugs offer the flexibility of being easily removable and allocated to another outlet if required.

An actuator such as the Sonoff Basic R2 can also be installed to control an outlet, but the connection diagram used will be different from what is presented in *Figure 4.22*. Instead of the actuator being installed in parallel, it must be installed in series with the line (L) voltage signal connected to the outlet. I do not have an actuator installed to control an outlet in my home.

Installing smart lamps (bulbs)

The installation of **smart lamps** or **smart bulbs** is simple and can be done directly by attaching the lamp to the socket. I use some smart lamps at home but they are not connected to Home Assistant because, to turn them on and off, they need to always be connected to the energy system, and they are not because I want to keep the original manual switch to turn the lamp on and off. The use of smart lamps in my case is just to take advantage of the multiple colors and the dimmer capability. I use smart lamps with the Alexa voice assistant after I make sure they are turned on by their correspondent lamp switch.

Home Assistant supports different Integrations to add smart lamps, which can be found at this link: `https://www.home-assistant.io/integrations/#light`. I suggest you first look at the integrations supported by Home Assistant if you want a smart lamp integrated into it.

You can use a smart lamp connected to an actuator such as the Sonoff Basic R2 hacked in this chapter and then create an automation so that once the actuator is turned on, the smart lamp will be turned on as well, in a specific color and the desired brightness. Thus, you will avoid the issue of not being able to control the smart lamp if the manual switch is not turned on. I will leave this automation as an exercise after you complete the content of *Chapter 5*.

Regarding lights, a device I really like to use at home is an LED strip and string lights. We will see more about that in *Chapter 9*.

Installing battery-powered devices

Examples of battery-powered devices I have in my home are door sensors and Bluetooth thermometers. The thermometers are very small and have adhesive tape behind them, which allows easy attachment to a wall or any other place. The flatter the surface, the better the attachment will be.

The door sensors are also attached using adhesive tape so the same surface flatness requirement can be applied. As commented on in *Chapter 1*, these door sensors use an electronic component called a reed switch connected to the main electronic circuit, which usually is physically separated from the remaining part of the sensor, which is a magnetic device.

The door sensors I use in my home were bought at **AliExpress** (`http://www.aliexpress.com`) and the model is **WKD-D03**. One of the sensors installed on my doors looks as in *Figure 4.24*.

Figure 4.24 – Door sensor installation

You can see in *Figure 4.24* that there is a need to have a certain distance between the reed switch and the remaining part. The distance in this case from one part to the other cannot be more than 2 cm (about 0.79 inches) in general, otherwise, the sensor element will not be detected by the remaining circuit.

This concludes the content of this chapter. We now have a minimal system installed in our home that will allow us to start to play with Home Assistant to do some interesting things in the next chapters.

Summary

In this chapter, we enhanced our knowledge related to sensors and actuators by focusing on hacking a commercial device. This was accomplished by installing firmware that can be customized according to what is needed. We presented some motivations behind the hacking execution and highlighted how to choose a device to be hacked.

You learned about the tools required to perform the hacking process and the steps required to upload Tasmota firmware, and later, how to configure it from the actuator perspective and Home Assistant perspective.

We added more information to this chapter by explaining how to configure commercial integration in Home Assistant for an outlet plug device without the need to hack it.

We wrapped up the content by teaching you how to install the actuator we hacked in this chapter. This included the presentation of the common tools and materials used and a step-by-step sequence of physical preparation, installation, and testing. In addition to that, a brief explanation of different device installations was provided.

If you are following the chapters of this book, at this point, we have a Home Assistant automation server, sensors, and actuators installed and configured to work. This allows us to explore other resources from Home Assistant, which will start to enable our home to be automated. That is the purpose of the next chapter.

I want to invite you to join me to deep dive into Home Assistant automations. Let's make it happen!

Part 3: Automations, Customizations, and Integrations Using Home Assistant

In this part, you will learn how to create automations in Home Assistant to control your home based on real examples implemented in my house. You will understand how to customize dashboards to present information about your home and use integrations in Home Assistant.

This part has the following chapters:

- *Chapter 5, Creating Automations Using Home Assistant*
- *Chapter 6, Doing More Using Integrations and Customizations*

5

Creating Automations Using Home Assistant

Now that we have our minimal home automation system created and configured, we will explore one of the main features of Home Assistant, which are **automations**. We will learn what automations and their components are. We will also create automations based on the system implemented until now. We will cover the following main topics in the chapter:

- Learning what automations are

- Components of an automation in the context of Home Assistant

- Creating your own automations

- Testing and debugging your automation

- Expanding the Home Assistant automation capabilities – using and creating pre-formatted automations (blueprints)

- More examples of automations

By the end of this chapter, you will understand the power of Home Assistant in integrating automation into the devices in your home. You will be inspired by the examples and ideas to create your own automations to make your home automated and smart.

Technical requirements

This chapter will not deal with any hardware or other electronic device installation or physical configuration. Only software skills will be used. If you are familiar with programming development and the use of programming debug tools and methods, you will be able to follow this chapter easily. Some informative videos will be provided on how to create some of the automations, scripts, and scenes. All the `.yaml` files used in this chapter are available at `https://github.com/PacktPublishing/Building-Smart-Home-Automation-Solutions-with-Home-Assistant/tree/`

main/Chapter%2005. Check out the following video to view the Code in Action: `https://bit.ly/3KCPR9O`

Learning what automations are

Generally speaking, an automation could be defined as a process that uses some kind of logic or intelligence to produce an action or output automatically depending on an input or event. In the context of the home, automation refers to using the information provided by input devices such as sensors and processing this information by verifying whether the data input meets some decision criteria. If this is the case, the **Home Automation Server** (or in our system, the Raspberry Pi with Home Assistant installed) sends a command or a data output to the actuators or other devices. Usually, the automation runs in an infinite loop, reading and analyzing the information and making the proper decision. When an automation is configured to operate without feedback or monitoring from the output actuators, it is referred to as having an open-loop configuration. *Figure 5.1* shows a flowchart representation of a typical open-loop home automation.

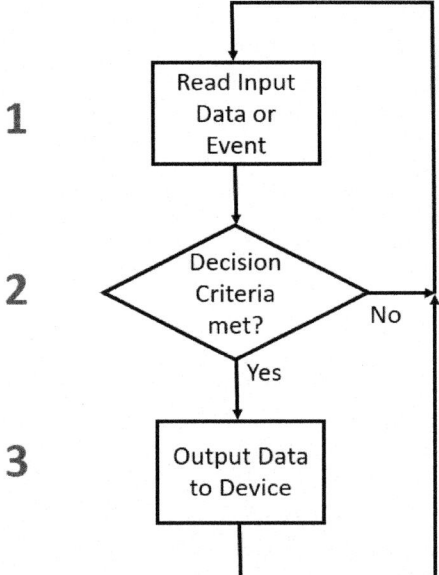

Figure 5.1 – Open-loop automation flowchart

The first rectangle (numbered **1** in *Figure 5.1*) is a data input, which can be from a sensor or an event. An event could be information not associated with a sensor, such as, for example, sunrise. In the flowchart sequence, the diamond (numbered **2** in *Figure 5.1*) implements the logic to decide whether the input data matches what is expected. If it matches, the criterion is satisfied and the automation process triggers output data to send to some device, which is usually an actuator, represented by the second rectangle (numbered **3** in *Figure 5.1*). After the data is sent to the output device, the automation returns to the initial status to read the input information or event. If the input data information does not match, the criterion is not satisfied, the automation will not send any control information to an output device, and will it return to the read input status.

> **Important note**
>
> If you are not familiar with flowcharts, in *Figure 5.1*, the rectangles are actions and the diamond is a decision. The flowchart should be read from top to bottom following the arrow direction.

Automations are convenient routines that can help you to reap the benefits of having an automated home, as mentioned in *Chapter 1*. Automations can help you to save time, feel comfortable, save money, and/or be safe. You have to be creative and think about what will help and support you best in your home. In this chapter, in the *Creating your own automations* section, I will provide you with some automation examples by explaining to you how I created them so you can start to think about what you can create.

Home Assistant has a powerful editor where automations can be configured to work based on the different situations mentioned in this section. In the next section, we will explore the components of an automation so you can properly create one in the following section.

Components of an automation in the context of Home Assistant

It is important to understand what are the names assigned by Home Assistant to some components of an automation, which will be helpful when you create your own automation. Before detailing what the components are, let's first understand what an entity is in Home Assistant.

Understanding entities

Before we can discuss the components of an automation, we will need to know what an **entity** is. An entity is what Home Assistant calls a data structure that can be associated with a **device**. An entity basically has three main parts:

- **ID**: The identifier for the entity
- **State**: The current state of the entity
- **Attributes**: Extra information related to the entity or state

A device can have one or more entities, and each one, with its parts, can be included in an automation. As an example, the off-the-shelf plug device, `desk_outlet`, that we configured in *Chapter 4* has the entity structure shown in *Table 5.1*:

Entity ID	Possible States	Possible Attributes

`sensor.desk_ outlet_current`	Numeric values	`state_class: measurement`
		
		`unit_of_measurement: A`
		
		`device_class: current`
		
		`friendly_name: Desk outlet Current`

`sensor.desk_ outlet_current_ consumption`	Numeric values	`state_class: measurement`
		
		`unit_of_measurement: W`
		
		`device_class: power`
		
		`friendly_name: Desk outlet Current Consumption`

`sensor.desk_ outlet_today_s_ consumption`	Numeric values	`state_class: total_increasing`
		
		`unit_of_measurement: kWh`
		
		`device_class: energy`
		
		`friendly_name: Desk outlet Today's Consumption`

`sensor.desk_ outlet_total_ consumption`	Numeric values	`state_class: total_increasing`
		
		`unit_of_measurement: kWh`
		
		`device_class: energy`
		
		`friendly_name: Desk outlet Total Consumption`

`sensor.desk_ outlet_voltage`	Numeric values	`state_class: measurement`
		
		`unit_of_measurement: V`
		
		`device_class: voltage`
		
		`friendly_name: Desk outlet Voltage`

`switch.desk_ outlet`	Binary values (on/off)	`friendly_name: Desk outlet`

Entity ID	Possible States	Possible Attributes
switch.desk_ outlet_led	Binary values (on/off)	icon: mdi:led-on friendly_name: Desk outlet LED

Table 5.1 – desk_outlet plug device entities

As noticed in *Table 5.1*, the desk outlet has two groups of entities: a **sensor** and a **switch**. The sensor entity can measure the input current and voltage and the switch entity can be controlled to be turned on or off. Besides the sensor and switch, there are other groups of entities depending on the device you have installed in your home. Some other common entity groups are **Lights**, **Alarm**, **Camera**, **Person**, and **media_player**. You will not need to be concerned about entity structure creation as Home Assistant does this for you. You can configure some attributes of the entities, such as friendly_name, to better serve your needs.

Understanding the automation components

We can redraw *Figure 5.1* to look as in *Figure 5.2* with the nomenclature provided by Home Assistant:

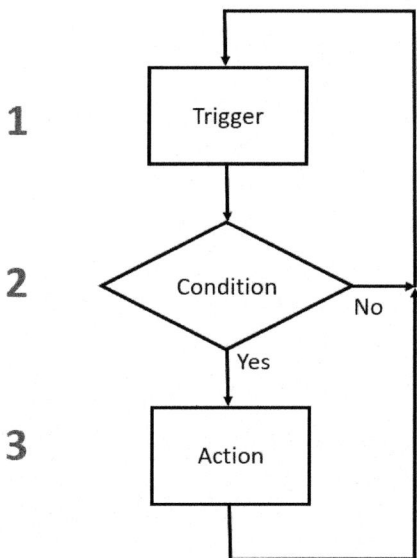

Figure 5.2 – Home Assistant automation components

A **trigger** (represented by the number **1** in *Figure 5.2*) is the starting point of an automation in Home Assistant. This automation component is usually associated with a state change or event. As we explained before, a state is always associated with an entity, which could be a sensor, an actuator, or a person, for example. We will see, in this chapter, that we can monitor or change the state of an entity using the **Developer Tools**.

At the time I'm writing this book, there are 19 different types of triggers supported by Home Assistant. We will be using the **state trigger** and **time trigger** in the examples we will be creating in this chapter.

The next automation component is a **condition** (shown as number **2** in *Figure 5.2*). Once the automation is triggered, the Home Assistant automation will verify whether the state change meets the condition for the automation. If the condition is met, then the next automation component, the **action**, is executed. **Action** is represented by the number **3** in *Figure 5.2*. If the condition is not met, then no action is executed and the automation will be returned to the initial status of continuing to monitor the state change to initiate the trigger component. The same initial status will be reached after the automation executes the action component. An action, as we will see later in this chapter, can be tested by calling a service using the Developer Tools.

At the moment, there are nine types of conditions that could be used to evaluate automations. We will be using the **state** and **time** conditions in our automations. Likewise, as the actions are implemented through the services, there are more than 200 types that can be used to control output devices.

Another configuration found for automations in Home Assistant is their modes. Home Assistant offers four types of modes, which basically deal with the way an automation will execute the actions based on multiple triggers happening while the automation is being executed. The ways available are **single**, **restart**, **queued**, and **parallel**. We will be using just the single mode in our automations in this chapter. If you want to learn more about these automation modes, please take a look at `https://www.home-assistant.io/docs/automation/modes/`.

Now that you know how an automation works in Home Assistant and understand its key components, we will create our own automations based on the devices we installed in our home in the previous chapters.

Creating your own automations

We will create two automations in this section using the Home Assistant automation editor. The first automation will use the two entities we created in *Chapter 3* and *Chapter 4* and the second automation will be using the off-the-shelf actuator we installed using an application integration in *Chapter 4*.

The Home Assistant automation editor can be accessed by clicking on **Settings | Automations & Scenes**. The automations can be created using the **Automations** tab. In the next subsections, we will detail how to create the two automations.

Automation 1 – convenient light for your garage

The first automation we will create was the first I created in my home. I created it because my street at night is very dark; there is no public light. I wanted my garage lights to turn on when I arrive home at night on the weekend with my family. This would help me to unload everybody from the car safely.

The automation is very basic and can be explained as follows:

Turn the garage lights on if car movement is detected in the garage and it is after sunset. Turn the garage lights off after two minutes.

This example contains two separate sets. Let's identify the components of our first automation set, which are as follows:

- **Trigger**: Car movement detected
- **Condition**: After sunset
- **Action**: Turn the garage lights on

The trigger component is provided by the **motion sensor** created in *Chapter 3*. The motion sensor will need to have its state change to trigger the automation. This will happen when there is car movement in the garage since the sensor will be installed where a car is usually parked, as presented in *Figure 3.15* in *Chapter 3*.

The condition to be verified is that the action will just be executed if the sun is in the sunset state. I included this criterion because I just want the garage lights to be turned on when it is becoming dark or it is nighttime, which means after sunset.

The action of turning the garage lights on is executed if the condition evaluated by the Home Assistant automation is true. The garage lights will be turned on using the actuator we hacked in *Chapter 4*. Let's identify the second set of the automation:

- **Trigger**: Two minutes after the garage lights are turned on
- **Condition**: After two minutes
- **Action**: Turn the garage lights off

The automation components in the second automation set are trickier to identify. The trigger is when the state timer associated with the garage lights actuator reaches two minutes. The condition to be evaluated is the timer value state for the garage lights actuator being longer than two minutes, and the action will be *turn the garage lights off*.

In order to implement these two automation sets, you will need to execute the following steps using Home Assistant. You can also find this sequence of steps in the Ch5-1 video:

1. On the Home Assistant logged-on screen, click on the **Settings | Automations & Scenes** sidebar option.

2. Click on the **CREATE AUTOMATION** button, located in the bottom-right corner of the screen.

3. A window will pop up asking you how you want to create your new automation. We will select the **Start with an empty automation** option.

4. The three automation components will be presented. Click on the + **ADD TRIGGER** button. Choose **State**.

5. Fill the **Entity** field with the name of the motion sensor, which is garage_pir Sensor.

6. Click on the + **ADD CONDITION** button. Choose the **Sun** option. On the **After** option, check the **Sunset** option.

7. Click on the + **ADD ACTION** button. Choose the **Call Service** option. Choose the **Light: Turn on** option. Click on the green + **Choose entity** button and then choose **GarageLights**. At this point, we've completed the first set of the automation and we will continue with the second set.

8. Click on the + **ADD ACTION** button. Choose the **Wait for time to pass (delay)** option. Fill the **Duration** field with 02 minutes in the field **mm**.

9. Click on the + **ADD ACTION** button again. Choose the **Call Service** option. Choose the **Light: Turn off** option. Click on the green + **Choose entity** button and then choose **GarageLights**.

10. Click on the **SAVE** button. In the new pop-up window, add the Automation 1 example name in the **Name** field, and in the **Description** field, type Turn on and off the Garage lights at night if a movement is detected. Click on **SAVE**.

Our first automation in Home Assistant will look like this:

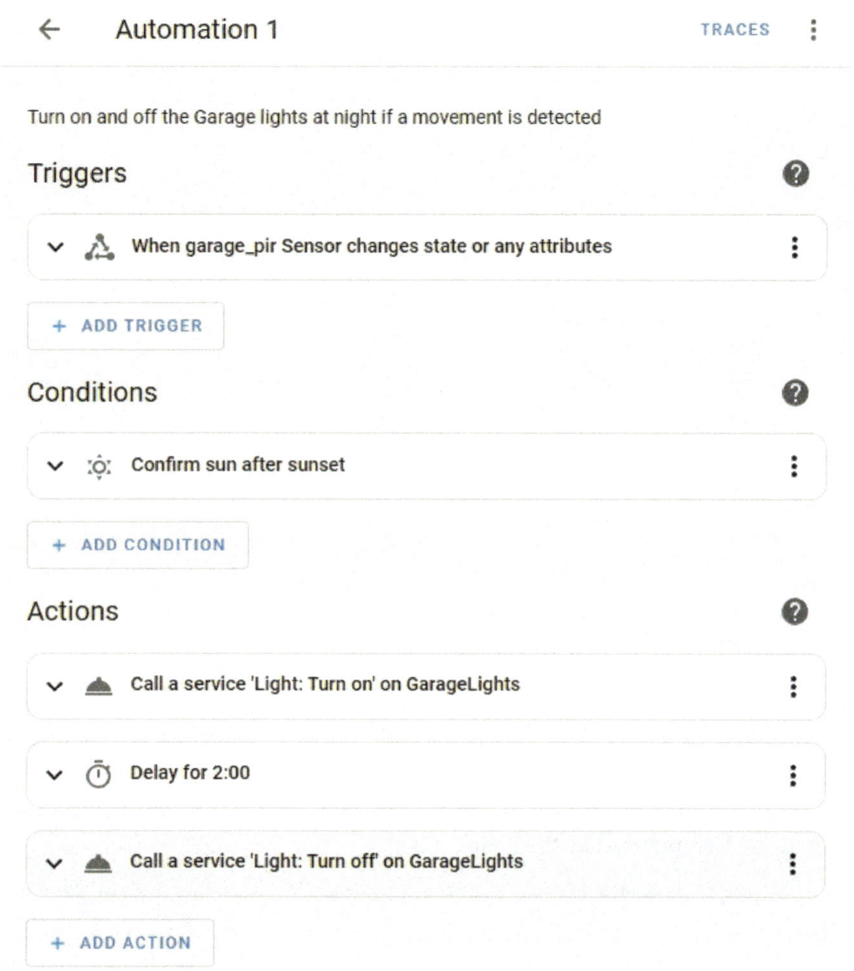

Figure 5.3 – Automation 1 represented in Home Assistant

Figure 5.3 shows the three main components of automation 1, which we've created, and a simplified description of each one. This automation is also created in YAML format by Home Assistant. You can see and edit the automation in YAML format by clicking on the three vertical dots and selecting **Edit in YAML** on the top right of the screen, which can be accessed after you click on **Automation 1** listed in the **Automation** tab. The following code will be displayed:

```
alias: Automation 1
description: Turn on and off the Garage lights at night if a movement
is detected
```

```
trigger:
  - platform: state
    entity_id:
      - binary_sensor.garage_pir_sensor
condition:
  - condition: sun
    after: sunset
action:
  - service: light.turn_on
    data: {}
    target:
      entity_id: light.garagelights
  - delay:
      hours: 0
      minutes: 2
      seconds: 0
      milliseconds: 0
  - service: light.turn_off
    data: {}
    target:
      entity_id: light.garagelights
mode: single
```

The preceding YAML code has a header composed of the `alias` and `description` fields. By changing the content of these two fields, you will change the name (`alias`) and description of `Automation 1`. The rest of the code are the automation components referenced as `trigger`, `condition`, and `action` words. Within these automation component words there are an indentation code delimiting what is required to be configured by the code.

The `trigger` component indicates that we are looking for a change in the state (`- platform: state`) of the entity (`entity_id`) called `binary_sensor.garage_pir_sensor`.

The condition component of the automation is represented by the codeword `condition`. The condition component is looking for the sun after sunset condition to be met. This is done in the code by the expressions `condition: sun` and `after: sunset`.

The action component is delimited by the word `action` and has three parts. The first part is to use the service called **Light: Turn on** represented by the code expression `- service: light. turn_on` and make a reference to the entity called `light.garagelights`, represented in the code by the expression `entity_id: light.garagelights`. This service will act to to turn the **GarageLights** actuator on. The second part of the action is a delay (`- delay:` codeword) of two minutes, represented by the `minutes: 2` line in the preceding code. The third part of the `action` component is to use the service **Light: Turn off** represented by the code expression `- service: light.turn_off` and reference it to the entity called `light.garagelights`, represented by the codeword `entity_id: light.garagelights`. This service will turn off the **GarageLights** actuator. The preceding code finishes by configuring the automation mode to `single`.

> **Important note**
>
> You can view and change the automation modes by clicking on the three vertical dots (called ellypsis) in the top-right corner of the screen, presented in *Figure 5.3*. Click on the **Change mode** option to see the current mode and change it. You can also change the automation mode by editing the word after the `mode:` syntax in the automation YAML code. As discussed before, the mode options available are `single`, `restart`, `queued`, and `parallel`.

Automation 2 – turn off screen monitor at bedtime

The second automation we will create is even simpler than the first one. Automation 1 used one sensor and one actuator. In automation 2, we will be using just one actuator. Automation 2 can be described as follows:

Turn off the screen monitor plug in my kid's room after 8:30 P.M. on the weekdays.

I created this automation to make sure my oldest kid will know when it is time for bed on weekdays. This will be accomplished by turning off the plug where the screen monitor is attached. Other devices, such as a table lamp, are also connected to the actuator plug using an outlet extender, so this plug can turn off different devices at the same time and he will be alerted when it is time to sleep.

Doing the same evaluation as we did for automation 1, let's identify the components for automation 2:

- **Trigger**: After 8:30 P.M.
- **Condition**: On weekdays
- **Action**: Turn the screen monitor plug off

I implemented this automation using the following sequence, which can also be found in the `Ch5-2` video:

1. On the Home Assistant logged-on screen, click on the **Settings | Automations & Scenes** sidebar option.

2. Click on the **CREATE AUTOMATION** button, located in the bottom-right corner of the screen.

3. A window will pop up asking you how you want to create your new automation. We will select the **Start with an empty automation** option.

4. Click on the **+ ADD TRIGGER** button. Choose **Time**. Check the **Fixed time** option and set the **At time** field to **8:30:00 PM**.

5. Click on the **+ ADD CONDITION** button. Select **Time**. In the first **After** field, check the **Fixed time** option, and in the second **After** field, set to blank spaces with no time configured. Do the same as you did for the **After** field to the **Before** field, checking the **Fixed time** option and

setting the second **Before** field to blank spaces. In the **Weekdays** list box, check from **Monday** to **Friday** options.

6. Click on the + **ADD ACTION** button. Select **Call service**. In the **Service** field, select **Switch: Turn off**. Click on the + **Choose device** option and then choose **Desk outlet**.

7. Click on the **SAVE** button. In the new pop-up window, add the example name `Automation 2` to the **Name** field, and in the **Description** field, type `Turn off the Screen Monitor plug in my kid's room after 8:30PM on weekdays`. Click on **SAVE**.

Our second automation in Home Assistant will look as in *Figure 5.4* in the Home Assistant automation editor:

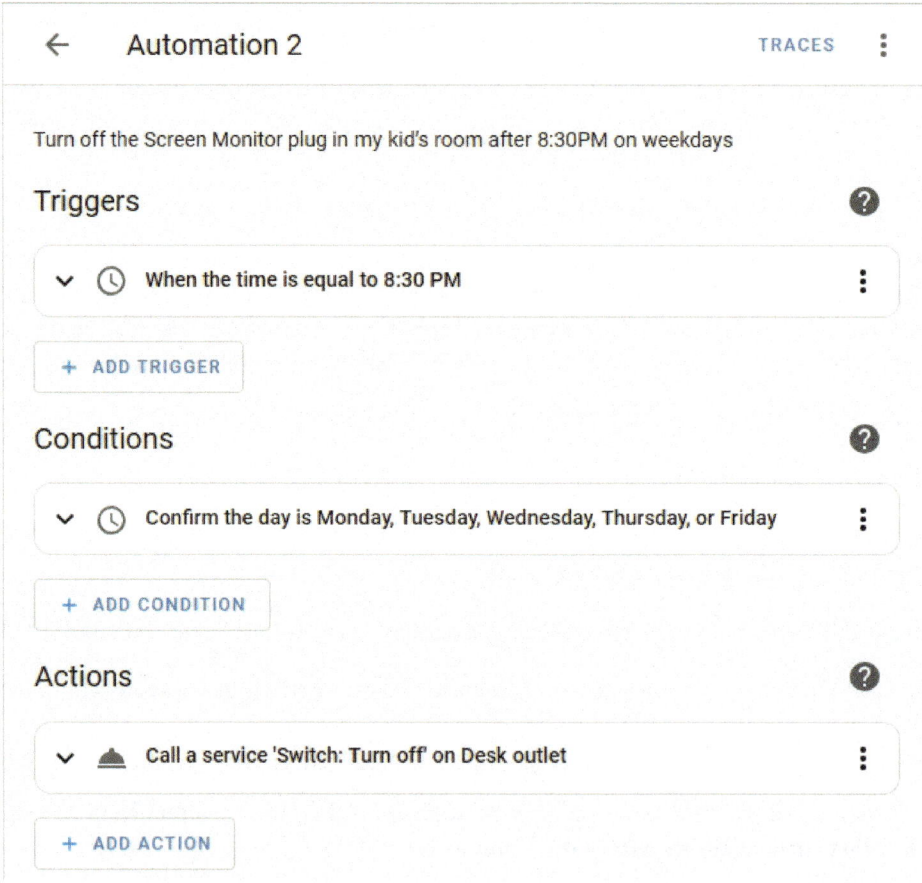

Figure 5.4 – Automation 2 represented in Home Assistant

The YAML code generated by Home Assistant for automation 2 is presented next:

```
alias: Automation 2
description: Turn off the Screen Monitor plug in my kid's room
after 8:30PM on weekdays
trigger:
- platform: time
  at: '20:30:00'
condition:
- condition: time
  weekday:
  - mon
  - tue
  - wed
  - thu
  - fri
action:
- service: switch.turn_off
  data: {}
  target:
    device_id: e9f3cf638163b4c94f453c0a103fa407
mode: single
```

1. Like automation 1, the YAML code for automation 2 has three parts: `trigger`, `condition`, and `action`. The trigger is configured using the `platform: time` directive at a fixed time, `20:30:00`. The code within the codeword `condition` tests whether `weekday:` is a day value between mon (Monday) and `fri` (Friday). If the `condition` is met, the automation executes `action` to turn off the switch with `device_id: e9f3cf638163b4c94f453c0a103fa407` using `service: switch.turn_off`. The automation execution mode is configured to **Single** using the codeword `mode: single`.

   As I mentioned before, the `automation.yaml` code is generated by Home Assistant when you use the automation editor and some codes or identification numbers, such as the device ID `e9f3cf638163b4c94f453c0a103fa407`, are also created by it. Directly editing the `Automation.yaml` file is not recommended since it can cause issues and errors that may be difficult to diagnose and troubleshoot.

2. After creating these two automations, they will be listed in the **Automations** tab under the **Settings | Automations & Scenes** menu.

Now that we have our automations created in Home Assistant, let's understand how we can test and debug them. This will be the topic of the next section.

Testing and debugging your automation

In the process of creating an automation, many times you will create it and want to test it right away to verify it is working. In other situations, even if you can test the automation immediately, for some reason it won't work and you will want to know what to fix. Home Assistant provides Developer Tools, which can help you to test and debug your automations. We will explore Developer Tools in the next subsections.

Setting and checking the state of entities

While I'm writing this subsection in my office, I want to test automation 1. One way to do that is to go to my garage, trigger the motion sensor, and see whether the garage lights turn on. Another option is to set the state of the motion sensor entity and check the state of the garage light entity. We can do this by using the **STATES** tab using the Developer Tools in Home Assistant.

Let's test our automation 1 by setting and checking the state of the entities. We will do this by following this procedure, which is also covered in the *ch5-3* video:

1. On the Home Assistant logged-on screen, click on **Developer Tools** and then on the **STATES** tab.

2. Find the motion sensor, `binary_sensor.garage_pir_sensor`. Click on its hyperlink.

3. In the **Set State** window area, find the **State** field for the `Garage_pir Sensor` entity. Edit **State**, changing it from **off** to **on**. Click on the **SET STATE** button.

4. You just manually set the state of the `Garage_pir` sensor. If it is after sunset, automation 1 should be working. You should check the state of the `light.garagelights` entity, which must be **on**.

5. Wait for two minutes, then check the `light.garagelights` state on the screen. The `light.garagelights` entity should return to the **off** state.

The preceding sequence will just work if it is after sunset. If you are testing automation 1 during the day, before sunset, you will also need to add, in *step 3*, the state setting of the `sun.sun` entity and change it to `below_horizon`. As noticed, state change is a powerful developer tool and can be very useful to test and also debug an automation. You can set the sun state inside Home Assistant without needing to wait for a particular event or situation, such as sunset, to happen.

Setting the state of an entity does not change the real state of the entity. It just changes what Home Assistant sees, or in other words, forces the state representation in Home Assistant to be changed to some configured value. In order to effectively change the state of an actuator, for example, we will have to use another feature in Home Assistant called **services**, as we will see in the next subsection.

Changing the state of output devices using services

In the process of creating an automation, besides testing to see whether it is working, you will also want to find issues and whether your automation is behaving as you expect. In this case, you have to debug it.

We will imagine a scenario where we will need to debug automation 2. Let's suppose we test automation 2, but after 8:30 P.M. on weekdays, the desk outlet plug is not working for some reason. One thing we can do in this case is test the actuator desk outlet plug directly, independent of automation 2. We can do that by using a developer tool that will be able to control the desk outlet plug using a service. A service is used to control one of the entities of a device or to call an external script or a scene. The service we will be using to control the desk outlet plug will be `switch: turn_off`.

You will need to use the **Services** tab under the Home Assistant Developer Tools accessed through the sidebar and follow the procedure listed here to be able to turn off the desk outlet plug:

1. Navigate to the **Developer Tools | Services** tab and in the **Service** listbox field choose the **Switch: Turn off** service.
2. Click in the + **Choose device** blue button. Select **Desk outlet**.
3. Click on the **CALL SERVICE** button. You will see that the switch will turn off immediately.

As you can see, we can manage the output of an entity (`Switch`) of a device (`Desk_outlet`) using services (`switch: turn_off`). This tool is very useful to directly control devices using Home Assistant even if they are not part of an automation. Also, some services allow some attributes to be controlled as well, providing the possibility to test and debug different features of an output device.

> **Important note**
>
> To explore this further, try to set the state of the desk outlet using the **State** tab under **Developer Tools**. You will notice that the desk outlet's real status will not change but the entity state will change momentarily to the state set, returning after a short time.

In the next subsection, we will learn about a powerful tool to debug your automation within Home Assistant. This tool will allow you to inspect, step by step and in detail, what happened with the executions of the automations we created.

Using traces to debug your automation

Home Assistant provides a tool if you want to understand how your automation is behaving. This allows you to check how your automation is being executed so you can evaluate it if a problem occurs and work out what is needed to fix it. This tool is called **traces** and basically are the steps recorded by Home Assistant when an automation is executed.

We will examine the traces of the last execution of automation 1. In order to do that, you will need to do the following:

1. From the sidebar, click on **Settings | Automations & Scenes**. Click on the **Automations** tab.

2. Make sure **Automation 1** has the **Last Triggered** column filled with any value aside from **Never**. Click on **Automation 1** to open it.

3. In the top-right corner, click on **TRACES**.

After accessing the traces, you will see something similar to *Figure 5.5*.

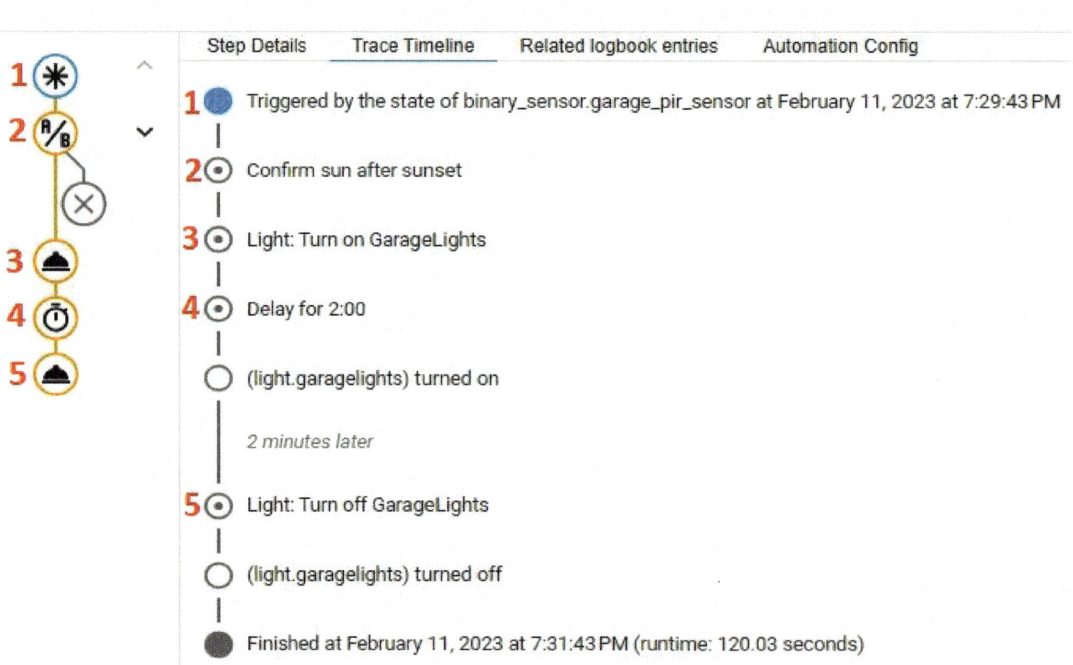

Figure 5.5 – Automation 1 traces debug tool

In *Figure 5.5*, you can trace each step of the automation by clicking on each circle on the left, numbered from **1** to **5**. In the case of *Figure 5.5*, the trigger circle is the one at the very top on the left and it is represented by the top filled circle in the trace timeline indicating when the trigger happened. In *Figure 5.5*, you can also see the automation steps on the left numbered from **1** to **5** and the timeline representation of the steps, also numbered from **1** to **5**. You can click on the other tabs to learn more about the step details, related logbook entries, and how the automation is configured.

In the case of the trace inspected for automation 1, we can see that it took *120.03 seconds* to execute. This means that removing the *2* minutes included as a delay, Home Assistant took *0.03* seconds to execute the entire automation 1.

In the next section, we will discuss some ways to expand the Home Assistant automation capabilities by using features such as **pre-formatted automations** or **blueprints**. They can speed up the process of creating automations and also provide some ideas of automations you can easily create. We will also cover the creation of **scripts** and **scenes** so you will be able to improve and do more with automations.

Expanding the Home Assistant automation capabilities

Home Assistant offers more resources to automate your home. If you don't have many ideas about what to do to automate your home, you can use a pre-formatted automation or import one. You can also create a pre-formatted automation and share it to be used in your home or by the development community. You can use scripts that will help you to execute coordinated actions, increasing the power of your automation. Your automation can be structured by creating scenes that can manage specific areas of your home. We will discuss these options in the next subsections.

Using and creating pre-formatted automations (blueprints)

In the previous sections, we learned how to create our own automations from scratch using the Home Assistant automation editor. You can also use the pre-formatted automations available in Home Assistant or import them. These pre-formatted automations are known as **blueprints**. If you think your automation can be reused in your home or by the community, you can transform it into a blueprint. In this subsection, we will learn how to use and how to create our own blueprint.

> **Important note**
> A blueprint also works for scripts. You can reuse blueprint scripts and import or create them.

Using and importing automation blueprints

For the example in this section, we will be using a blueprint already available in Home Assistant. This blueprint will work similarly to automation 1 we created before. The name of this blueprint is **Motion-activated Light**. You can use this automation blueprint by using the following procedure:

1. From the sidebar, click on **Settings | Automations & Scenes**. Click on the **Blueprints** tab.
2. Select the **Motion-activated Light** option and click on **CREATE AUTOMATION**.
3. The **Blueprint** screen will be presented. Fill the **Motion Sensor** entity with the **garage_pir Sensor** in the **Entity** list box.
4. Click on the blue + **Choose device** button and select the **GarageLights** device.

5. In the **Wait time** option, leave the time field as **120 seconds**. Click on the **SAVE** button in the bottom-right corner of the screen.

6. In the **Rename** pop-up window, include the name `Automation 3 - Blueprint` and the description `Example of how to use an Automation Blueprint`. Click on the **RENAME** button.

When you return to the **Automations** tab under **Settings | Automations & Scenes**, you will see that **Automation 3 - Blueprint** was created. This automation will be triggered if a motion is detected in the garage and will turn the garage lights on for 2 minutes, or 120 seconds, and then turn them off. It is slightly different from automation 1, which includes an *after sunset* condition. If you want to import blueprints into your Home Assistant installation, follow these steps:

1. First, click on the **Blueprints** tab.

2. If you want to search through more of them, click on the **DISCOVER MORE BLUEPRINTS** button. This will guide you to the Home Assistant blueprint community forum, where you can find different blueprints resources to be used in your home.

3. Click in the **IMPORT BLUEPRINT** button in the bottom-right corner.

4. A pop-up window called **Import a blueprint** will be presented. Input the GitHub URL address for the blueprint you want to import in the **Blueprint address** field and click on **PREVIEW** to see the automation blueprint to be imported.

5. Another pop-up window with the title **Import a Blueprint** will be presented. You will see a description of the automation to be imported. Click on the **IMPORT BLUEPRINT** button. The imported blueprint automation will be loaded into your blueprints list.

Another easy way to import an automation is by visiting the Home Assistant blueprints exchange page at `https://community.home-assistant.io/c/blueprints-exchange` and clicking on one of the automation blueprints. After clicking on it, you will see a badge to import the blueprint. This blueprint badge is shown in *Figure 5.6*. If you click on it, a web browser page will be presented asking you to input the Home Assistant installation URL. For this book, it is `http://homeassistant.local:8123`. If you click on **SAVE** after inputting the Home Assistant web address, a page will open asking whether you want to open a page in your Home Assistant installation. Click on the **OPEN LINK** button. Your Home Assistant installation opens with the same pop-up window, **Import a Blueprint**, presented, and the Git URL address with the automation blueprint filled in. Click on **PREVIEW** and then on **IMPORT BLUEPRINT** to import the automation blueprint into your Home Assistant installation.

Figure 5.6 – IMPORT BLUEPRINT badge

Creating automation blueprints

For this example, we will convert automation 1 into a blueprint automation. This means we will make automation 1 reusable by making the configuration for the motion sensor and the lights actuator available for readers of the book. We will not go into too much detail about how to create your own blueprint; just the main details will be provided. The Ch5-4 video details the process to create your own blueprint as in this example.

You will need to follow this sequence of steps to be able to create your own blueprint:

1. The first step to create a blueprint automation is to create a YAML file and save it to the blueprint/ automation folder from the Home Assistant root folder. Create an empty file and save the file as `Automation1_blueprint.yaml` using the **File editor** add-on.

2. Add the following code content to the `Automation1_blueprint.yaml` file and save it:

```yaml
blueprint:
    name: Automation 1 Blueprint
    description: Turn on and off a light after sunset if a
movement is detected
    domain: automation
    input:
        motion_sensor:
            name: Motion Sensor
            description: Motion Sensor to activate lights
            selector:
                entity:
                    domain: binary_sensor
                    device_class: motion
        target_light:
            name: Lights
            description: Lights activated by Motion Sensor
            selector:
                target:
                    entity:
                        domain: light

trigger:
    - platform: state
      entity_id: !input motion_sensor
condition:
  - condition: sun
    after: sunset

action:
```

```
- service: light.turn_on
  target: !input target_light

- delay:
    hours: 0
    minutes: 2
    seconds: 0
    milliseconds: 0

- service: light.turn_off
  target: !input target_light
```

3. Open the **Blueprints** tab under **Settings | Automations & Scenes**. You should be able to see the blueprint you just created. Use it as you did in the last subsection.

Blueprints can facilitate the process of creating an automation you have to use often in your home. Instead of creating one after the other from scratch each time, you can just do it using blueprints.

> **Try this out!**
>
> In the blueprint created, we kept the delay fixed at two minutes. As a challenge, I will leave it to you to figure out how to make the delay configurable so you can enter as input the amount of time you want the lights to stay on.

In the next subsection, we will use another feature of Home Assistant that can help with executing many tasks in sequence and also be used to improve the automation execution process: scripts.

Creating and using scripts

Scripts are another feature available in Home Assistant. They can be defined as a set of actions that should be created to be used multiple times. They can be used alone or as part of a service execution used by an automation. You can create a script and it can be referenced as an entity. Like what we learned while using automations, scripts can also have execution modes (*single*, *restart*, *queued*, and *parallel*), and we can use and create blueprints for scripts.

The basic difference between a script compared to an automation is that scripts do not have a trigger component. You will have to execute the script manually or use it as part of an automation action component.

For the example in this section, we will create a script called *Time for Bed*, redo the automation 2 example using the script instead of the direct action, and save it as automation 4. The sequence of commands to implement the *Time for Bed* script is the following, which can also be found in the *ch5-5* video:

1. From the sidebar, click on **Settings | Automations & Scenes**. Click on the **Scripts** tab and then on the **+ ADD SCRIPT** button in the bottom-right corner.

2. Fill in the fields with the following data:

    *   **Name**: Time for Bed
    *   **Icon**: mdi:bed-clock
    *   **Entity ID**: timeforbed
    *   **Mode**: Single

3. Click on the **+ ADD ACTION** button. Select **Condition** and then **Time**. Set **After condition** to **Fixed time** and the **After** time field to **8:30:00 PM**. In the **Weekdays** listbox, check **Monday** to **Friday**.

4. Click on the **+ ADD ACTION** button again. Select **Call service**. In the **Service** field, select **Switch: Turn off**. Click on **+ Choose device** and then choose **Desk outlet**. Click **SAVE SCRIPT**.

We now have our first script created. It can now be used in automation 2 and many other automations that we can create with different triggers but the same action. Let us see how we can add the *Time for Bed* script to automation 2:

1. From the sidebar, click on **Settings | Automations & Scenes**. Click on the **Automations** tab. Click on the three vertical dots at the end of the **Automation 2** line. Click on **Duplicate**.

2. Click on the three vertical dots, or overflow, menu at the end of the **Conditions** line. Select the **Delete** option, and in the pop-up window that will be presented, click on the **Delete** button.

3. Click on the three vertical dots at the end of the **Actions** line. Select the **Delete** option, and in the pop-up window that will be presented, click on the **Delete** button.

4. Click on **+ ADD ACTION**. Click on the **CALL SERVICE** button. Select **Script: Time for Bed**. Click on **SAVE**.

5. In the **Save** window, include the name Automation 4 in the **Name** field. Click **SAVE**.

A screenshot of automation 4, which we just created, can be seen in *Figure 5.7*.

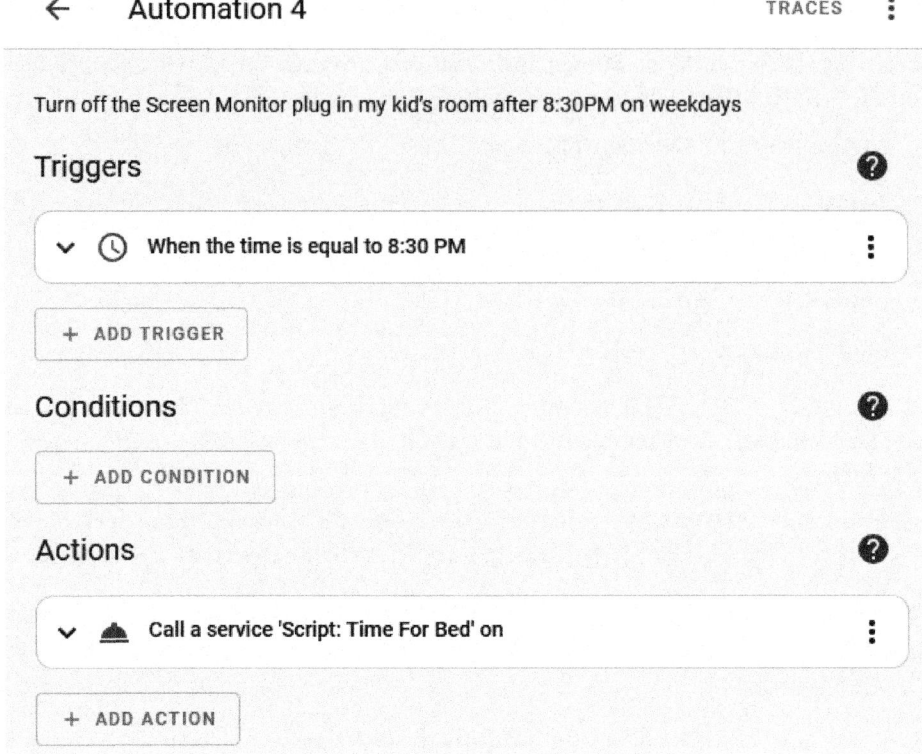

Figure 5.7 – Automation 4 created using a script as an action

You can see the *Time for Bed* script that we created in *Figure 5.7*, which simplifies the configuration process for the automation. You can notice a difference by comparing *Figure 5.7* with *Figure 5.4*, where automation 2 was presented. In *Figure 5.4*, the **Conditions** and **Actions** fields are configured, while in *Figure 5.7*, only the script is required in the **Actions** field since it includes the **Conditions** field in it.

Since automation 2 and automation 4 are doing the same thing, we can disable automation 2 to test automation 4. We can do that by clicking on the three dots on the **Automation 2** line and then selecting **Disable**.

> **Tip**
> An easy way to test automation 4 is by changing the **Time** condition from **8:30PM** to some other time close to when you are carrying out your experiment. I will leave it to you to discover how this can be done.

As you will notice, the script can simplify a lot the automation flow and execution mainly if a complex action needs to be executed multiple times by different automations. Another advantage of scripts is that they can be changed a single time and all automations using it will automatically be changed.

In the following subsection, we will learn a bit more about scenes and how they can be used in your home to create a combination of different states.

Creating scenes

Scenes are another resource available in Home Assistant. Their purpose is to define states for different devices or entities and combine them to happen at the same time. Like scripts, they can be used as actions for automations. For example, you can create a scene to make a room in your home cozier by lowering the light brightness, turning the heater on to a specific temperature, and turning on some relaxing music on your smart speaker. You can combine this with an automation that is triggered by a lower temperature outside or a condition such as after 9 P.M., for instance.

We will create a scene that will put all actuator devices in our home in the off state. We will call this scene *ALL OFF*. Use the following sequence to do it. You can also find this sequence in the *ch5-6* video:

1. From the sidebar, click on **Settings | Automations & Scenes**. Click on the **Scenes** tab and then on the **+ ADD SCENE** button in the bottom-right corner.

2. Fill in the fields with the following data:

    *   **Name**: ALL OFF

    *   **Icon**: mdi:home-off

    *   **Area**: Empty

3. We will not add anything to the **Devices** option. We will use the **Entities** option instead. In the **Add an entity** option, click on the **Add an entity** field and select **Desk outlet**. Do the same again, this time selecting **GarageLights** as the entity. Click on **SAVE** in the bottom-right corner. The **ALL OFF** scene will be created.

4. Unfortunately, Home Assistant does not allow state configuration using the **Scenes** tab directly. You will have to use the **File editor** and edit the scenes.yaml file in the config folder to do it. If you open the scenes.yaml file, you will see the following content:

```
- id: '1676691530760'
  name: ALL OFF
  entities:
    switch.desk_outlet:
      friendly_name: Desk outlet
      state: 'off'
    light.garagelights:
      supported_color_modes:
```

```
       - onoff
     friendly_name: GarageLights
     supported_features: 0
     state: 'off'
 icon: mdi:home-off
 metadata:
   switch.desk_outlet:
     entity_only: true
   light.garagelights:
     entity_only: true
```

5. In the case of the YAML code for the scene created, Home Assistant created the states and configured them correctly, as you can see by the state: 'off' syntax for both the switch. desk_outlet and light.garagelights entities. There will be some situations, for example, if you want to set a specific color for each smart bulb in a scene, where you will have to edit the scenes.yaml file to do it.

6. To add a scene to your automation actions, you must choose the **Call Service** option and then **Scene: Activate**. Click on the green + **Choose entity** button and select the **ALL OFF** scene. Click **SAVE** to save your automation.

With this look at scenes, we complete the technical content of this chapter on automations. In the next section, I will provide you with some examples of automations I am using or planning to use in my home.

More examples of automations

Here are some examples of automations I use in my home:

- *When a door is opened, announce it through a smart speaker.*

- *Turn on the lights at the front of the house at sunset and turn them off four hours later.*

- *Turn on the lights in the laundry room when the garage door is opened. Keep them turned on for two minutes and then turn them off.*

The following are examples I intend to include in my home soon:

- *After midnight, if a movement is detected in the corridor, turn on the corridor lights for two minutes and then turn them off.*

- *If there is no one at home, put the AC in eco mode and make sure the lights and some plugs are turned off.*

- *When returning home, set the lights at the same status as they were before leaving.*

Now that you know what automations are, have an idea of how to create them, and have seen some examples, my suggestion is that you think about what will best suit you and what your needs are. Think about what you have to do every day and what automations can do for you. You will find useful ways to automate your home by using automations and the features associated with them provided by Home Assistant.

Summary

In this chapter, we learned in detail what automations are both in general and in the context of Home Assistant. We also learned about the components associated with an automation and other features used by Home Assistant, such as entities and services.

During the course of this chapter, several practical examples were provided to create automations. Various tools were explained and used to debug and verify their functionality. We were able to expand the capabilities of an automation by learning how to create and use blueprints and doing the same with the scripts and scenes. Finally, some examples of automations used in my home were provided, as well as some others I am planning to create in the near future. Hopefully, they will inspire you to create your own automations and think of ways to smart control your home.

In the next chapter, we will add more devices to our home and include them in the dashboard so you can have visibility and direct control of them using the Home Assistant user interface. We will also learn about some other add-ons we can use inside Home Assistant. You will see how powerful Home Assistant is and what else you can do with it.

Doing More Using Integrations and Customizations

This chapter will focus on customization, which involves the setup of Home Assistant dashboards. You will be able to create your own dashboards and customize how the sensors, actuators, and other device data will be presented and managed. Also, you will be able to understand and change what parts of the Home Assistant dashboard can be customizable using YAML.

We will cover the following content in this chapter:

- Adding more devices to your home using integrations

- Using dashboards in Home Assistant

- Customizing your dashboards

- Using extra resources to customize your dashboard

After reading this chapter's content, you will understand what Home Assistant can deliver in terms of the features and functionalities related to integrations and dashboards, preparing you to explore other IoT software using add-ons in the next chapter.

Technical requirements

The technical requirements for this chapter are the same as those in *Chapter 5*, and the basic knowledge you will need is software configuration. Some informative videos will be provided on how to create some parts of the dashboards. All the `.yaml` files and code for the dashboard used in this chapter are available at `https://github.com/PacktPublishing/Building-Smart-Home-Automation-Solutions-with-Home-Assistant/tree/main/Chapter%2006`. Check out the following video to view the Code in Action: `https://bit.ly/47wuUqN`

Adding more devices to your home using integrations

Before we start to play with the dashboards, you will have to add more devices to your home. The way Home Assistant allows this to be done is by using **integrations**. We encountered some flavors of integrations using **MQTT** in *Chapter 2*, **Tasmota** in *Chapter 3*, and **TP-Link KASA Smart** in *Chapter 4*, and now we will use some others. You can create integrations for Home Assistant, but that is out of the scope of this book. Instead, we will use the built-in integrations provided by Home Assistant. At the time of writing, there are 2,412 built-in integrations available.

The built-in integrations in Home Assistant can be divided into two main types:

- Home Assistant-based integrations
- Device manufacturer-based integrations

Home Assistant-based integrations are natively provided directly by Home Assistant. They allow you to create sensors based on other types of information available in Home Assistant, add more features to automations, and so on. One example of a built-in Home Assistant-based integration is the automation blueprints we learned about in *Chapter 5*. This type of integration can be used in different situations when a generic item, not associated with a specific physical device, needs to be handled by Home Assistant. An example of a generic item could be a shopping list, person, or time.

Device manufacturer-based integrations are integrations developed to integrate third-party devices' hardware or software. They must be used always when you want Home Assistant to manage a new third-party manufactured device. You will find different built-in integrations for your 3D printer, alarm, camera, car, doorbell, fan, light, media player, and so on. Examples of popular devices and manufacturers supported in this type of integration are **Google Cast**, **Google Assistant**, and **Alexa** (via a **Nabu Casa** subscription), **Philips Hue**, **Shelly**, **SmartThings**, and **Sonos**. They are very well documented on the Home Assistant web page where you can find out how to use them. You can check them out here: `https://www.home-assistant.io/integrations/`.

We will use both types of integrations to add more devices to our home, which we will cover in the next subsections.

Using Home Assistant-based integrations

As an example of how to use Home Assistant-based integrations, we will add two sensors in Home Assistant related to date and time. The first sensor will be used to display the current date and time. The second sensor will be used to display a specific time in a different timezone.

We will add the time and date sensor by using the `time_date` integration in Home Assistant. We will execute the following steps to do so. The `Ch6-1` video is a good reference to follow as well:

1. From the Home Assistant sidebar, click on **File editor**. Click on the folder icon in the top-left corner of the screen, as shown in *Figure 6.1*. Open the `configuration.yaml` file.

Figure 6.1 – The File editor top bar icons

2. At the end of the `configuration.yaml` file, add the following content:

```
sensor:
  - platform: time_date
    display_options:
      - 'date_time'
```

The `sensor` codeword will set up a sensor in the `platform` called `time_date`, and the information we want to display using the `display_options:` codeword is in the `date_time` format, which is the current date followed by the current time.

3. Click on the **Save** icon, as shown in *Figure 6.1* (the fourth icon from right to left in the top-right corner).

    For the changes in the `configuration.yaml` file to take effect, you will need to restart Home Assistant by performing the following steps.

4. From the sidebar, click on **Developer Tools | YAML**. In the first rectangle, titled **Check and Restart**, click on **CHECK CONFIGURATION**. If the YAML syntax is correct, a green message will appear saying **Configuration will not prevent Home Assistant from starting!**, as shown in *Figure 6.2*.

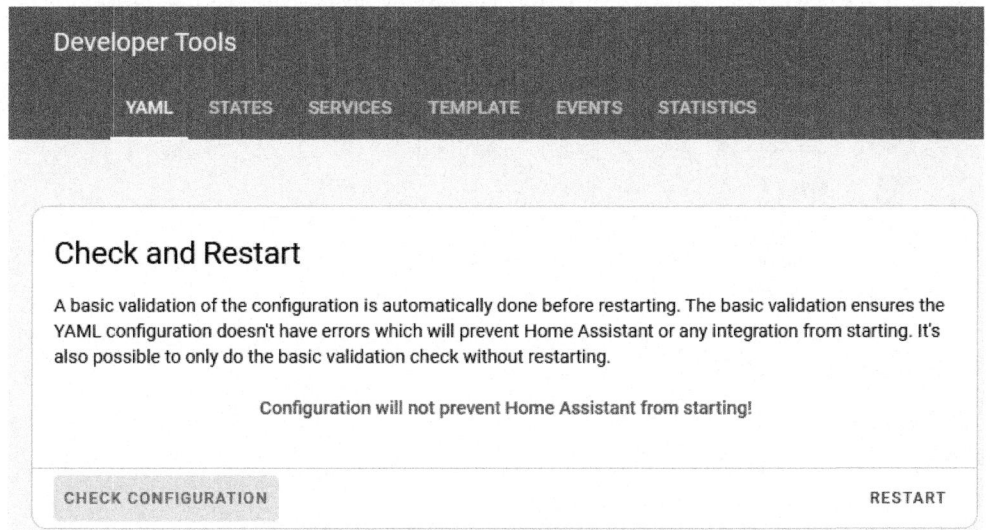

Figure 6.2 – The Configuration.yaml file checker

5. Click on **RESTART** and then **RESTART** again in the pop-up window. Wait until Home Assistant restarts.

6. After Home Assistant restarts, check whether your **Date & Time** sensor was created by going to **Settings | Devices & Services | Entities**.

After creating the date and time sensor, we will integrate our specific timezone sensor by using the `worldclock` sensor platform. As we did before, we need to edit the `configuration.yaml` and follow the same steps done to add the `time_date` sensor, with the addition of the following content to the `Configuration.yaml` file, just one line after the last part of the code shown before in the *step 2* after the codeword - `'date_time'`:

```
- platform: worldclock
    time_zone: America/Sao_Paulo
```

In the same way, make sure to check the `Configuration.yaml` file content to see whether the syntax is OK, and then restart Home Assistant so that the configuration changes take effect. If you want to add just the `worldclock` sensor platform and not the `date_time` sensor added previously, do not forget to add the world `sensor:` at the top of the preceding pseudo-code. Conversely, if you want to add more sensors by editing the `Configuration.yaml` file, keep the `sensor:` codeword at the top of the first sensor configuration and continue to add them, using the `platform` codeword and their specific parameters with the appropriate code indentation. Check out the `Configuration.yaml` file in the *Chapter 6* book repository to see how both these sensors were created.

After restarting, if the `worldclock` sensor was created correctly, you should be able to check whether the new **Worldclock sensor** was integrated by going to **Settings | Devices & Services | Entities**.

Now, as shown in *Figure 6.3*, we have two more sensors integrated into Home Assistant using the integration provided by it.

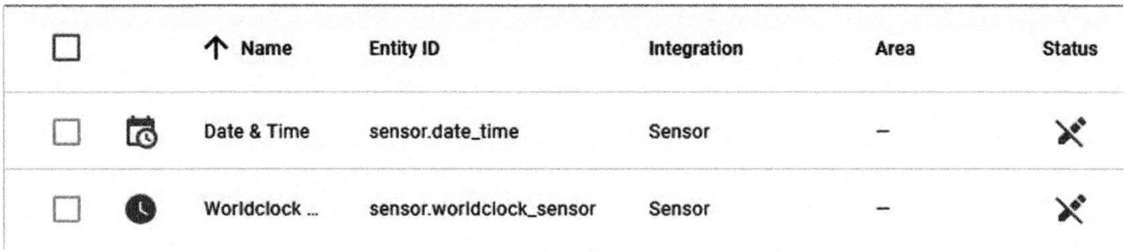

		Name	Entity ID	Integration	Area	Status
☐	📅	Date & Time	sensor.date_time	Sensor	–	✕
☐	🕐	Worldclock ...	sensor.worldclock_sensor	Sensor	–	✕

Figure 6.3 – The created sensors listed in Home Assistant

In the next section, we will use a couple of different device manufacturer-based integrations to add more sensors and actuators to our home.

Using device manufacturer-based integrations

We will add more sensors and actuators to our home using device manufacturer-based integrations. There are several ways to add devices using device manufacturer-based integrations, and they can vary according to the manufacturer. Most of them will require access to an external manufacturer website that will manage the integration, and then the devices will be integrated into Home Assistant. They will also require you to create user accounts with a username/password so that you can manage your devices, using an external application for the most common cellphone operating systems available on the market today. There is no common recipe or standard way to do this, although most of the integrations can be started using the **Sidebar | Settings | Devices & Services** option in Home Assistant.

In the next subsections, we will add some other devices, and I will go through how we will do it step by step.

Adding Sonoff actuators to your home

I decided to not convert all of my **Sonoff** actuators to Tasmota so that I am able to evaluate them using a device manufacturer-based integration. We can add the Sonoff actuators using the **eWeLink** Smart Home add-on provided by the Sonoff manufacturer **Itead**.

> **Important note**
> The procedure described in the following steps to add Sonoff actuators in Home Assistant assumes you have an eWeLink account already created and the actuators pre-configured and working with it. If you don't have them pre-configured, visit `https://www.youtube.com/watch?v=2hfuJz6U7Nk` and watch the video to do so.

We will do this integration by following these steps:

1. Go to the sidebar menu and then click on **Settings | Add-ons**. Click on **ADD-ON STORE** in the bottom-right corner.

2. Click on the vertical three dots in the top-right corner, and then click on the **Repositories** option. In the **Manage add-on repositories** screen, type the following GitHub web address: `https://github.com/CoolKit-Technologies/ha-addon`. Click on the **ADD** button. The **Manage add-on repositories** screen will appear, as shown in *Figure 6.4*.

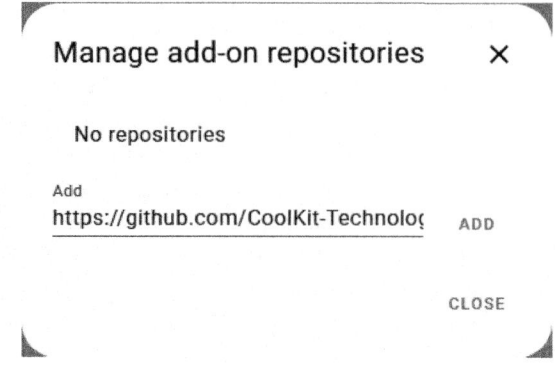

Figure 6.4 – The Manage add-on repositories screen

3. From the sidebar, click on **Developer Tools | YAML**. Under the **Check and Restart** options, click on **RESTART**. Wait for Home Assistant to restart.

4. From the sidebar, open **Settings | Add-ons** again. Search for the `eWelink Smart Home` application under **eWeLink add-ons**. In the new window that appears, click on the **INSTALL** button, as shown in *Figure 6.5*.

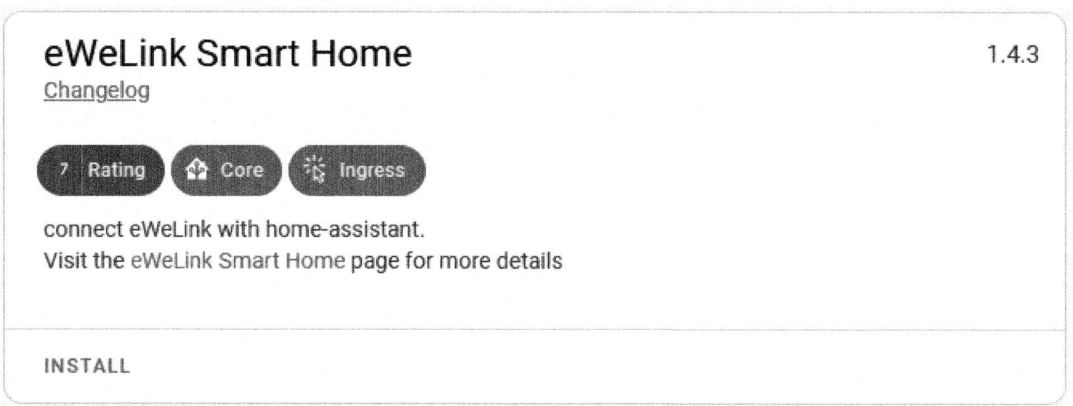

Figure 6.5 – The eWeLink Smart Home installation screen

5. Wait for about two minutes until the installation has finished. Then, proceed to restart Home Assistant by repeating *step 3*.

6. From the sidebar, return to **Settings | Add-ons**. Search for the `eWelink Smart Home` application under **eWeLink add-ons**. Click on the **START** button and then the **OPEN WEB UI** button.

7. The **eWelink Smart Home** sign-in screen will appear. Click on **Sign in** at the top right of the screen. Input the country, login (email), and password details for your eWelink application, and then click on the **Sign in** button. The login screen is shown in *Figure 6.6*.

Figure 6.6 – The eWelink login screen

8. Finally, all the Sonoff actuators previously added to your eWeLink account will be integrated into Home Assistant.

The only difference with this integration is that your actuators will be integrated not as devices but as entities, and because of that, your actuators will be limited to just working as switches in Home Assistant. I was able to integrate six more actuators using device manufacturer-based integration, as shown in *Figure 6.7*.

	Name	Entity ID	↑ Integration
	MB Lamp	switch.100125c00d	Switch
	Vitor Fan	switch.10011f1632	Switch
	LaundryLights	switch.10011ec33d	Switch
	Front Light	switch.10011dc05f	Switch
	MB Fan	switch.1001257d12	Switch
	MasterBedroom corridor light	switch.1001252709	Switch

Figure 6.7 – Sonoff actuators added as entities

As previously mentioned, to implement this integration, you have to have your devices configured in the eWelink application beforehand. If you have not yet done that, go to the website at `https://ewelink.cc/` to verify how to install eWelink.

In the next subsection, we will add more sensors to your home using another device manufacturer-based integration.

Adding Tuya door sensors to your Home

I use door sensors that use software from a company called **Tuya** (`https://www.tuya.com/`). They are very compact and easy to install. I have four of these sensors installed on my doors. One of the sensors installed is shown in *Figure 4.23* in *Chapter 4*. The doors where the sensors are installed give me access to external areas of my home, so these sensors can detect any attempt to enter or leave my home.

In order to complete the installation of the Tuya door sensors, you will need to create two different accounts. The first account will be to configure your sensors using your cellphone. This application is called **Smart Life**, and you can find out all about it and download it by using the following link: `https://www.tuya.com/product/app-management/all-in-one-app`. The other account you will need to create is for Tuya IoT Platform, which can be accessed at the following website: `https://auth.tuya.com/`.

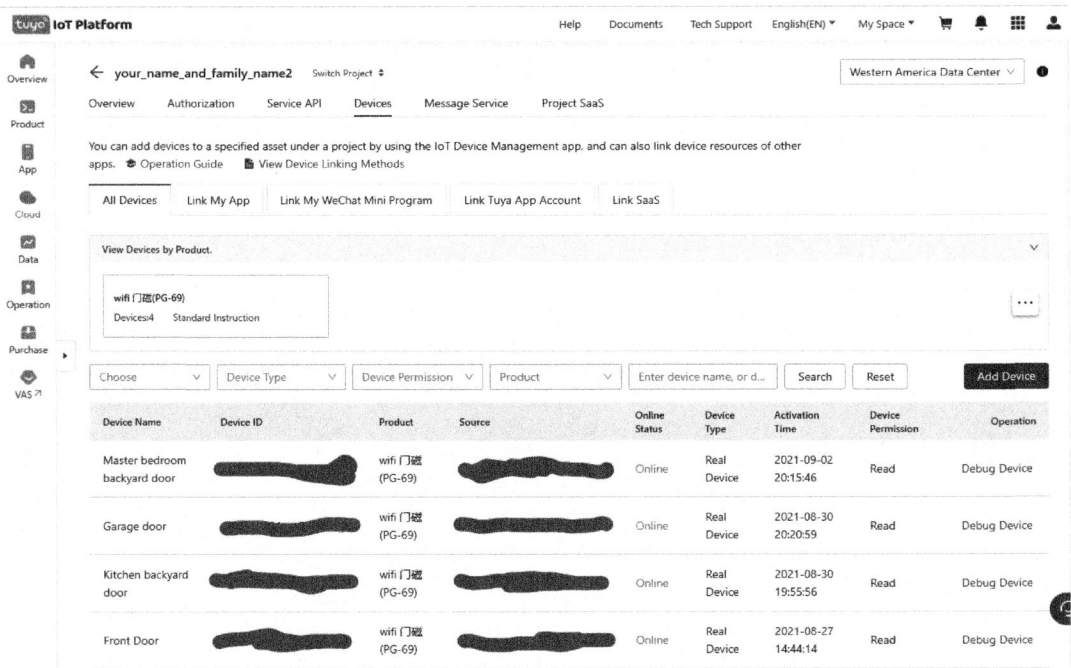

Figure 6.8 – Tuya door sensors configured in Tuya IoT Platform

The software configuration and installation for the door sensors in Home Assistant can be done using the following website: `https://www.home-assistant.io/integrations/tuya/`. After the installation, if everything goes well, you should see your door sensor as I have it in my home, as shown in *Figure 6.9*.

↑ Device	Manufacturer	Model	Area	Integration	Battery
Front Door	Tuya	Contact Sensor...	–	Tuya	0% 🔋!
Garage door	Tuya	Contact Sensor...	–	Tuya	37% 🔋
Kitchen backyard ...	Tuya	Contact Sensor...	–	Tuya	47% 🔋
Master bedroom ...	Tuya	Contact Sensor...	–	Tuya	0% 🔋!

Figure 6.9 – Tuya door sensors integrated into my home

The Tuya integration has more features than the Sonoff integration. The sensors are integrated as devices, and there are three different entities that can be managed by Home Assistant, including battery status. I realized by checking the screen in *Figure 6.9* that the door sensor installed in my front door needs a battery replacement.

In the next subsection, we will complete the integration of our devices by listing what other integrations I used to add them to my home.

Adding other devices to your home

In this section, we will list what other integrations I used to add more devices to my home.

Tasmota integration

Before I hacked the Sonoff Actuator with Tasmota, I hacked some plugs I bought in 2017. They were the **CT-065W** model from the manufacturer **Eco Plugs**. Their conversion to Tasmota is more complex compared to the BasicR2 from Sonoff, but ultimately, Tasmota software works in the same way on both devices. In the case of the Tasmota devices, as mentioned, they are automatically recognized in Home Assistant as soon as your MQTT configuration is done. Refer to the *Configuring your hacked actuator* section in *Chapter 4* to review how to do it.

The Tasmota devices in my home are listed in the screenshot in *Figure 6.10*.

	Device	Manufacturer	Model	Area	Integration
	Coffeemaker	Tasmota	CT-65W	Kitchen	Tasmota
	DiningRoomLam...	Tasmota	CT-65W	Dinning Room	Tasmota, Chan...
	ESP32_TEMPERA...	Tasmota	ESP32-DevKit	—	Tasmota
	FireplaceLights	Tasmota	Sonoff MINIR2	Living Room	Tasmota
	GarageLights	Tasmota	Sonoff BasicR2	Garage	Tasmota
	GarageTempPIR	Tasmota	ESP8266	Garage	Tasmota
	MB_tv	Tasmota	CT-65W	Master Bedroom	Tasmota

Figure 6.10 – Tasmota integration

Ring integration – doorbell

The **Ring integration** allows me to add my front doorbell to Home Assistant. Its integration is very straightforward and is done using the standard integration method of adding integrations using the **+ ADD INTEGRATION** button from the sidebar and the **Settings | Devices & Services** path. You should select **Ring** as the brand name in the search pop-up window, as shown in *Figure 6.11*, after clicking on the **+ ADD INTEGRATION** button.

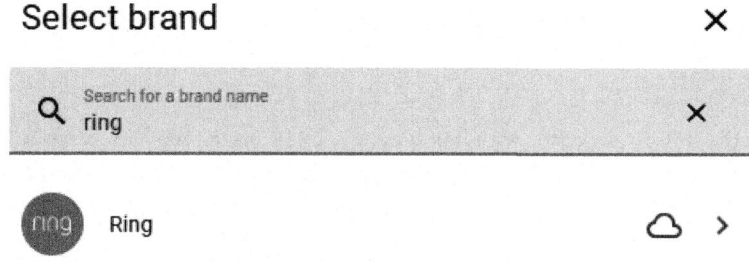

Figure 6.11 – Selecting the Ring integration

Like the other integrations, the Ring doorbell integration will ask for your login and password from the application previously configured. You will have to include them to be able to include the doorbell in your home. It is interesting to note that these integrations that require access to an external account or website will be shown with a gray cloud symbol in the bottom right corner of it, as shown in

Figure 6.11. This means this device is controlled by a cloud application and will only be available if Home Assistant is connected to the internet.

After I add the Ring integration, it allows me to access nine different entities, as shown in *Figure 6.12*. These entities include the binary sensor for the doorbell (**Ding**) and another binary sensor for a motion sensor (**Motion**), which is embedded into the doorbell device. The doorbell and motion sensor are binary sensors because they have two statuses to be reported – **Clear** and **Detected**.

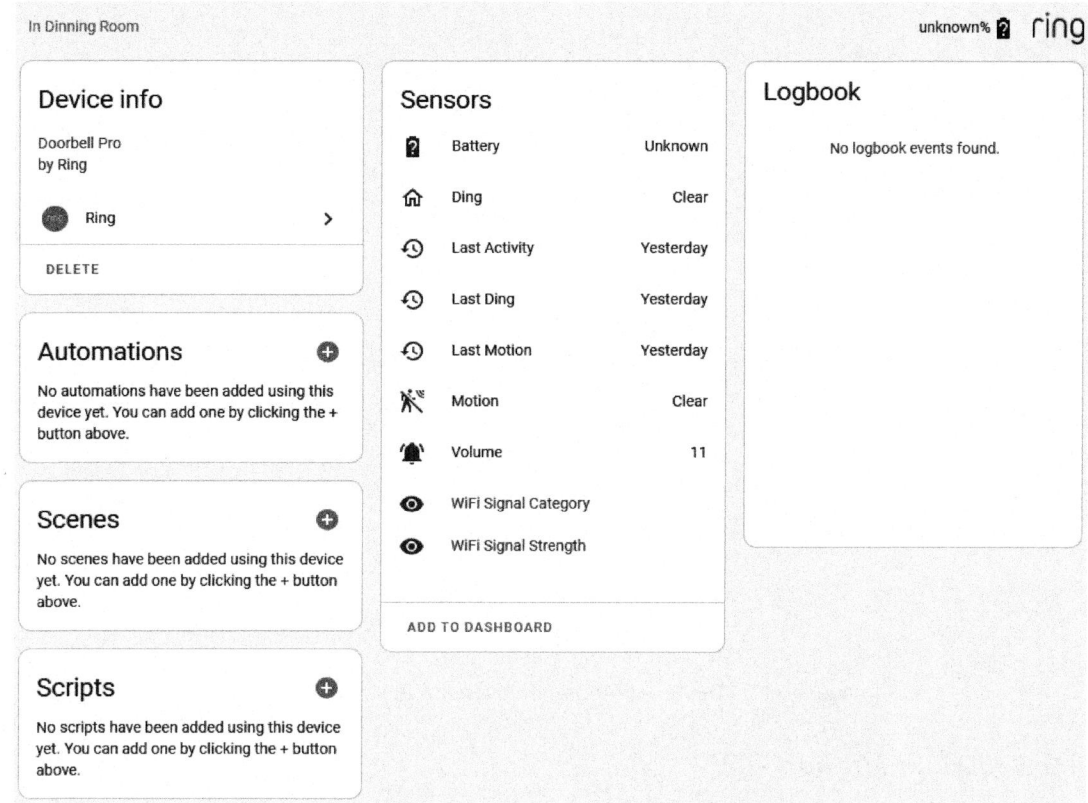

Figure 6.12 – A Ring integration overview in Home Assistant

Blink integration – the camera monitor

I used the **Blink integration** to add a camera monitor that is installed in my youngest kid's bedroom. This integration is done in the same way as the Ring integration, and you just need to select **Blink** as the brand name in the search pop-up window after clicking the + **ADD integration** button. You will have to include your login and password, previously configured in the application outside Home Assistant.

The Blink integration is also a cloud application, so you can access the camera when the internet is connected to Home Assistant. This integration adds one device and seven different entities, as verified in *Figure 6.13*. Some of them cannot be used, such as the battery status, because the device in use does not have a battery.

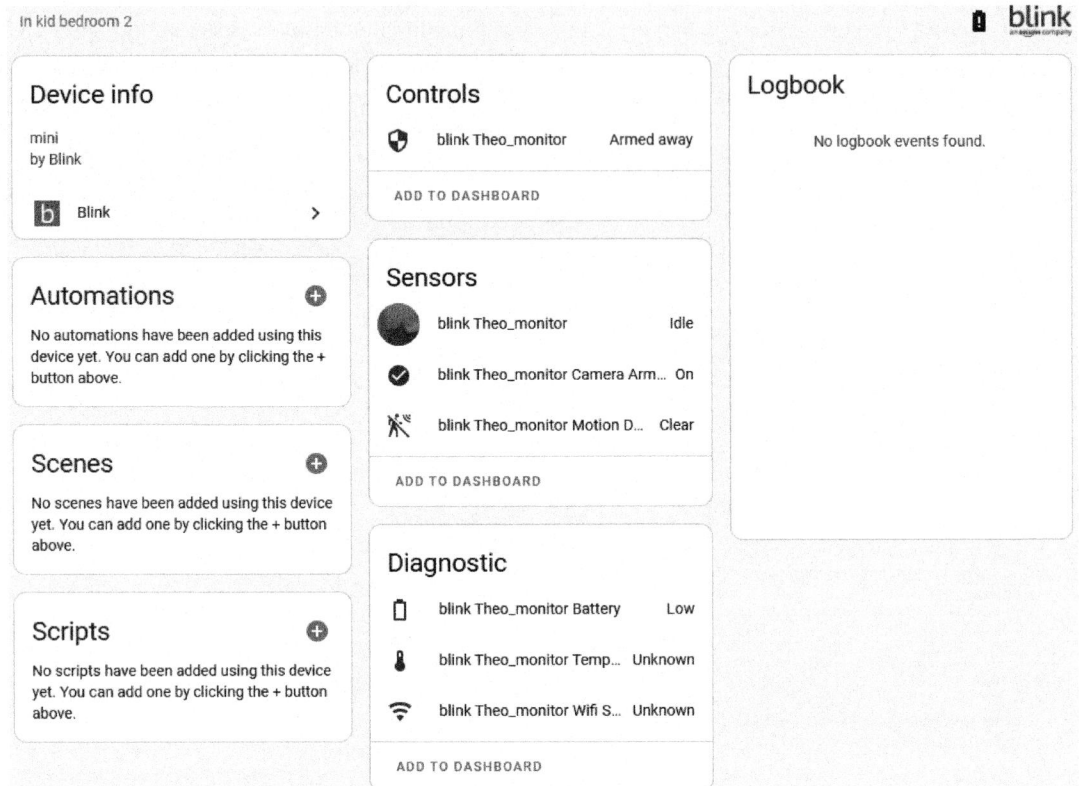

Figure 6.13 – The Blink integration overview in Home Assistant

LG WebOS integration – TV

The **LG WebOS integration** allows me to integrate my LG TV into Home Assistant. This was an integration automatically discovered and suggested by Home Assistant, so all I had to do was just click on the configure button on the integration screen and follow the instructions to pair it with the TV.

After the integration was added to Home Assistant, it included one device and one entity. I can control the TV main switch to turn it on or off, pause and play the current program, and control the TV volume. It is worth commenting that Home Assistant allows other TV manufacturer models to be integrated into it, such as Sony Bravia and Samsung smart TVs.

After performing these device manufacturer integrations, we have about 19 devices added and 2 more devices that use Home Assistant-based integrations. This will offer a lot of different information to populate our dashboards, which we will cover in the next section.

Using dashboards in Home Assistant

Using the knowledge that you have gained so far in this book, you can add devices to your Home Assistant and test them. You can also create automations, scripts, and scenes and test them. When adding devices to your home, you can manage them individually by clicking on them using the **Settings | Devices & Services | Devices** path. By clicking on this path, you will be able to see the device and its entities, as shown in *Figure 4.9* in *Chapter 4*. When using this method, you must repeat it every time for each device if you want to manage its data using its entities. You should be able to access all the entities of a device you want to manage in a customized window. The good news is that you can do it using **dashboards** in Home Assistant.

In the next subsections, we will learn what dashboards are and how we can populate them.

Understanding and creating dashboards

Dashboards are what Home Assistant implemented to present various information from the devices you can configure and manage in your home. It is the main screen you will see after logging into Home Assistant, as shown in *Figure 2.3* in *Chapter 2*.

Home Assistant is configured with a main dashboard, formerly known as **Lovelace**, and you can create different dashboards for your home, depending on your needs and the amount of information you want to handle through them. By default, the main dashboard is automatically created by Home Assistant as you install the system, and you can access it by using the sidebar and clicking on the **Overview** menu option. Another dashboard is created by default in Home Assistant, and you can access it by clicking the **Energy** menu option from the sidebar.

Another concept involving dashboards is the use of **views**. Each dashboard has at least one view, and the views are where the data from the devices and entities are shown. Home Assistant creates a default view called **Home** on the **Overview** menu page. Each view can be customized with its own type, theme, or background.

The views can be configured to become **subviews**. Subviews are not accessible directly through the dashboards, and they can be used to provide specific information about one sensor or group of devices, for example. The subviews are accessible using a card, which has the **Navigate** option as an action. We will see an example of subviews in the next section.

You can create more dashboards by using the **Settings | Dashboards** path and clicking on the **+ ADD DASHBOARD** button in the bottom-right corner of the screen. When you do that, a new pop-up **Add new dashboard** window will be shown, asking for a title and icon. We will input the `Test-dashboard` and `mdi-devices` values for the icon and click on **CREATE**. Home Assistant will automatically create a generic dashboard, including all areas of our home and some other devices and entities. This dashboard will partially look like *Figure 6.14*.

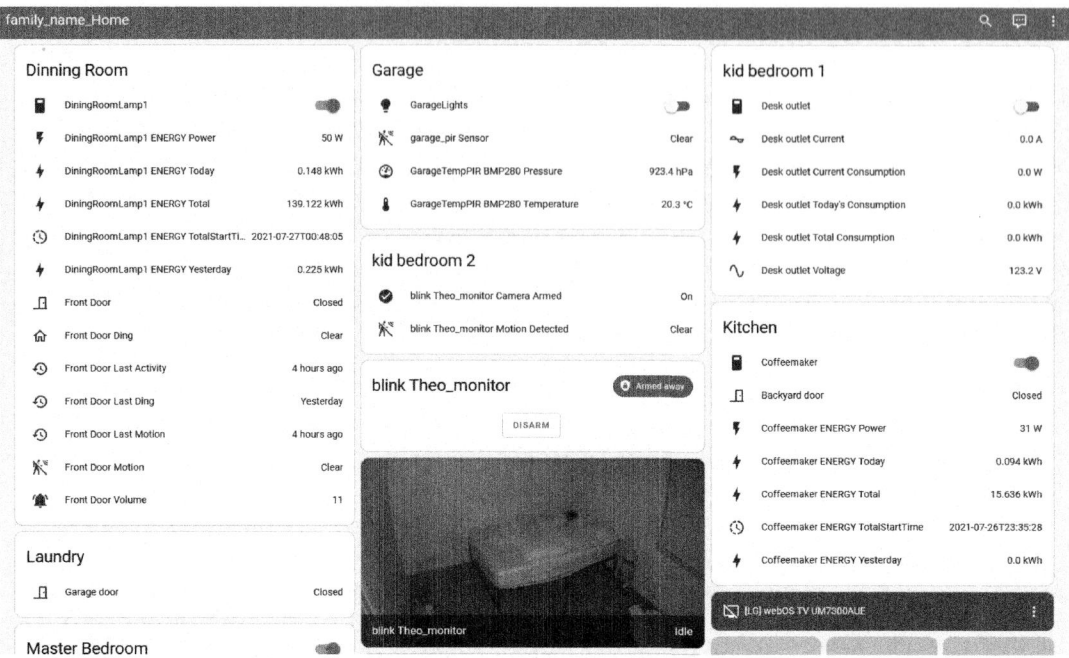

Figure 6.14 – A dashboard automatically created by Home Assistant

The dashboard shown in *Figure 6.14* is controlled by Home Assistant and will be updated each time a new device or entity is added to a system. This is a convenient way to quickly have your devices and entities populated, shown, and controlled on one screen. The disadvantage of this method is that more devices and entities will be added than you need, and you cannot customize the way the dashboard is created. You can edit this created dashboard by clicking on the three vertical dots, known as an **ellipsis**, in the top-right corner of the screen (as shown in *Figure 6.14*), and selecting the **Edit Dashboard** option. When you do that, a new popup will appear, asking if you want to take control of your dashboard. When you take control of the dashboard, Home Assistant will not update the dashboard for you when a new device or entity is added. If you want to take control of the dashboard, click on the **TAKE CONTROL** option; otherwise, hit **CANCEL**. We will not take control of this dashboard right now, so when you reach this option, click on **CANCEL**.

In the next subsection, we will see how we can populate dashboards by adding formatted ways to view and manage the devices and entities.

Important note

You can get an idea about the assorted styles of dashboards by visiting `https://demo.home-assistant.io/#/lovelace/0`. This is a demo environment created by the Home Assistant, where you can explore different dashboards created by different users.

Populating dashboards by using cards

After you know what dashboards to edit, you can start to populate them. There are some pre-formatted ways to do this by using what is called **cards**. These cards can only be displayed in the user interface if they have a view available in the dashboard. Currently, there are more than 30 different cards included in Home Assistant. All of them can be configured. You can also create your own card or use the options available from the Developer community. Some examples of cards developed by the community can be found here: `https://github.com/custom-cards`.

You can start populating your dashboard by going to the **Overview** menu option from the Home Assistant sidebar. By clicking on the ellipsis in the top-right corner in the **Home** view and then on the **Edit Dashboard** option, you will can then access the cards by clicking on the **+ ADD CARD** button, shown in the bottom-right of the screen. After clicking on the **+ ADD CARD** button, you will be able to choose the cards with two options, **BY CARD** or **BY ENTITY**, as shown in *Figure 6.15*, where the **BY CARD** option is selected by default.

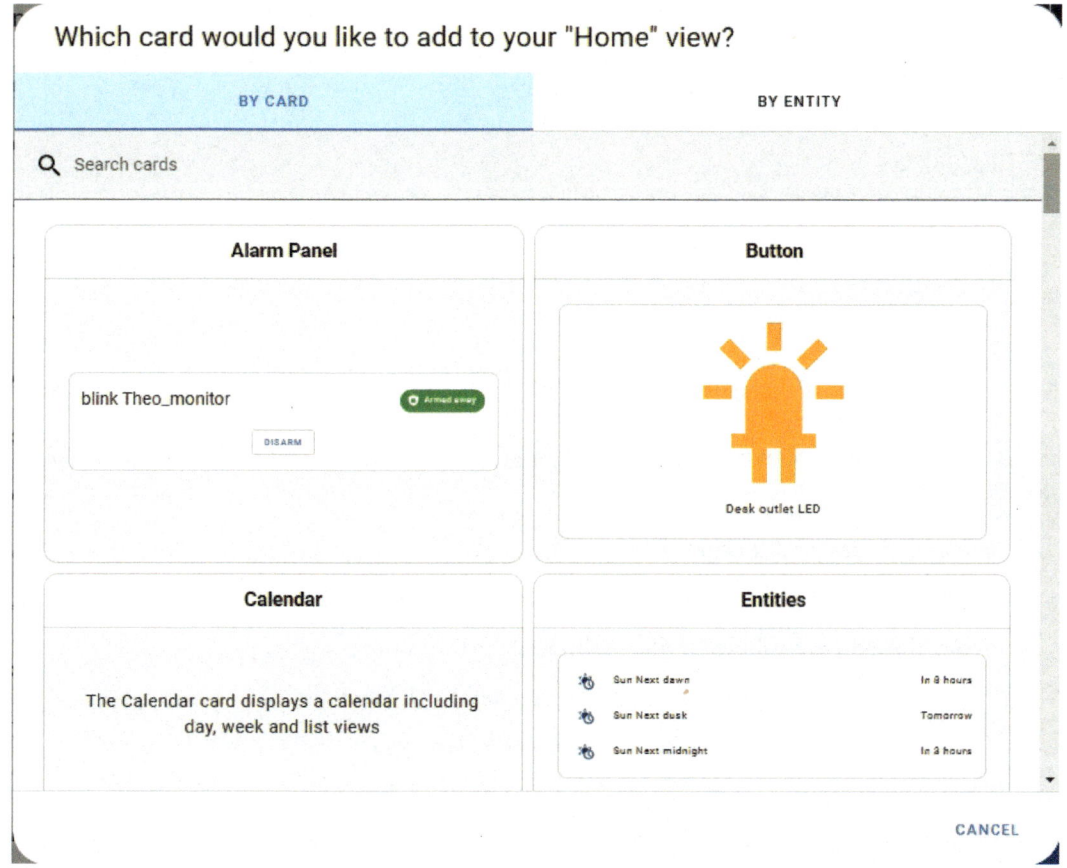

Figure 6.15 – Home Assistant cards configuration

In the **BY CARD** option, as shown in *Figure 6.15*, we can choose how the information will be shown. You can create a button with one device or entity, or represent sensor data, using a gauge or statistical data, for example. If you click on the **Button** card, for example, the pop-up window in *Figure 6.16* will be shown.

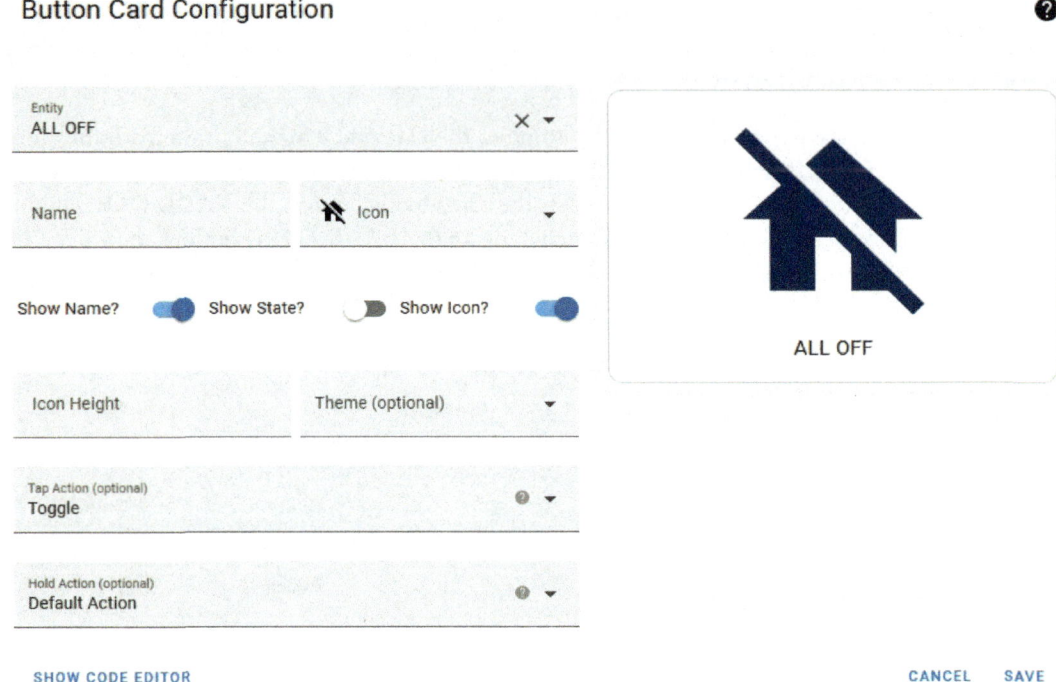

Figure 6.16 – Adding items to a dashboard using the BY CARD option

Just to give you an idea about what can be configured in a card, I will list for you what parameters can be configured in the card shown in *Figure 6.16*:

- **Entity**: Entities you will control
- **Name**: The name of the entity that will be shown in the dashboard
- **Icon**: The icon to be shown in the dashboard for the button
- **Show Name?**: Configure whether the button name will be shown
- **Show State?**: Show when the button state was last changed
- **Show Icon?**: Configure whether the icon name will be shown
- **Icon Height**: Configure the icon height in pixels
- **Theme**: Configure the theme used by the button (optional)

- **Tap Action**: Configure the action when the button is clicked

- **Hold Action**: Configure the action when the button is clicked and held

It is good to remember, as mentioned, that each card is configured and the configuration parameters will change from one card to another.

Here is where you will have to put your creativity to work because countless possibilities of combinations are available when adding a card to a dashboard.

In the **BY ENTITY** card configuration option, Home Assistant will present all entities and you will have to select, by clicking in a list box, one or more to be added to the dashboard. The **BY ENTITY** card configuration option is shown in *Figure 6.17*.

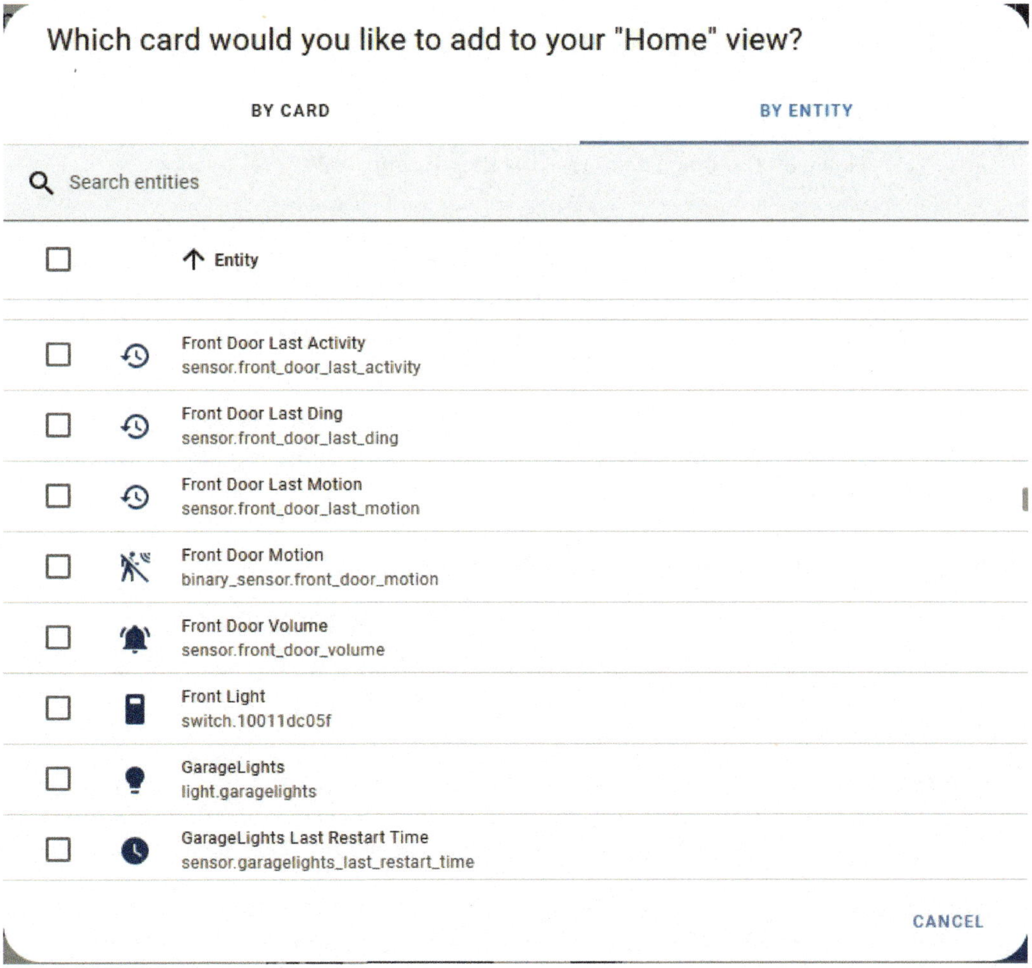

Figure 6.17 – Adding entities to a dashboard using the BY ENTITY option

When you finish the selection, Home Assistant will present a suggestion for a card to be added to the dashboard. As an example, I picked two switch entities to be added to the dashboard, and the suggestion is shown in *Figure 6.18*.

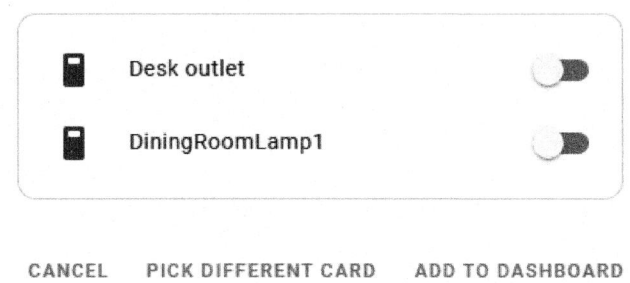

Figure 6.18 – Adding items to a dashboard using the BY CARD option

You can add the suggested card in *Figure 6.18* in a dashboard by clicking on the **ADD TO DASHBOARD** option, pick a different card by clicking on the **PICK DIFFERENT CARD** option, or **CANCEL** to cancel the operation. If you choose the **PICK DIFFERENT CARD** option, you will return to the original screen in *Figure 6.15*, showing the two **BY CARD** and **BY ENTITY** options. Choose the **BY CARD** option, select the card you want, and click on the **SAVE** button to include the card with the selected entities in the dashboard.

Another way to represent the information or status of devices and entities in dashboards and views is by using **badges**, which is what we will see in the next subsection.

Populating the dashboards by using badges

Another feature provided by Home Assistant to show the information from devices and entities is badges. I should say that badges are a hidden Home Assistant resource because, currently, with Home Assistant version 2023.6.3, they are not directly available graphically, and you have to include them manually using the Raw configuration editor.

Badges are useful graphical resources defined as widgets. They can quickly capture the status of certain devices and are easily seen because they are located above all cards, so they are the first information to be seen from top to bottom of the Home Assistant dashboard screen. There are two kinds of badges:

- **State Label Badge**: This is used to display the status of an entity. It supports **actions**, which means if you click on it, an action such as a status toggle, call-service, or navigation to a URL will be triggered.

- **Entity Filter Badge**: This groups a list of entities that can be tracked if they meet certain conditions.

An example of a State Label Badge can be seen in *Figure 6.19*. I used the following code to discover the status of my kid, and the badge quickly says that he is at home:

```
badges:
  - type: state-label
    entity: person.your_kid1
```

Figure 6.19 – A State Label Badge example

The preceding pseudo-code defines a code area for badges using `badges:`, then a state-label badge is defined using `- type: state-label`, and the entity we want to track is listed using `entity: person.your_kid1`.

If we want to use badges to track who is at home, we will have to use an Entity Filter Badge, and in this case, the pseudo-code to track this filter is the following:

```
badges:
  - type: entity-filter
    entities:
      - person.your_kid1
      - person.your_name_and_family_name
      - person.your_wife
    state_filter:
      - home
```

The result in my home at the time of writing is shown in *Figure 6.20*, which shows that my wife, my kid, and I are at home.

Figure 6.20 – An Entity Filter Badge example

The pseudo-code syntax for the Entity Filter Badge is similar to the previous State Label Badge. Again, a code area for badges using `badges:` needs to be defined. In the sequence, all entities we want to track need to be listed under `entities:`. We list my kid (`- person.your_kid1`), me (`- person.your_name_and_family_name`), and my wife (`- person.your_wife`). We will use `state_filter:` to track the status at `- home`.

You should add both sets of pseudo-code by clicking on the dashboard you want to create the badges, then the ellipsis, and then **Edit Dashboard**. Click on the desired view, then on the ellipsis again, and then **Raw configuration editor**. The pseudo-code should be added just after the view `title:` syntax.

There are other options to customize the badges, such as assigning an image or an icon to it. I recommend you visit `https://www.home-assistant.io/dashboards/badges/` to know more about these options.

In the next section, we will create and customize some dashboards based on different approaches so that you can control and manage your home better using them.

Customizing your dashboards

In this section, we will explore one of the most fun activities in this book, which is to customize some dashboards in Home Assistant. The dashboards will be where you will interface with your home, controlling actuators and verifying the status of the sensors, so this will need to be somewhat easy for you to access and manage. The views will be where you can see the cards and badges.

I will provide you with three main approaches to configuring your dashboards with different cards so that you can have an overview of the possibilities that can be used to interface with your home. These approaches are as follows:

- **By home dependencies**: The *by home dependencies* dashboard approach will group devices and entities based on the dependencies of my home. Currently, I have eight dependencies with devices installed, so we will explore different cards that can better be reshown by this configuration.

- **By device type**: The *by device* type dashboard approach will group devices and entities by device type. They can be sensors, actuators, or media types. Again, different cards will be used to provide you with ideas to explore.

- **By home assistant integrations**: The last approach evaluated is *by Home Assistant integrations*. This will group and present the entities created in the *Using Home Assistant-based integrations* subsection. We will also group the automations, scripts, and scenes created in *Chapter 5* and add them to this dashboard.

Dashboard approach 1 – by home dependencies

This approach was created automatically by Home Assistant when we created the dashboard using the **Settings | Dashboards** option, but we want to customize it to our needs. Instead of taking control of the dashboard, we will create one from scratch and populate it including the home dependencies. We will do that by following the following steps:

1. From the sidebar, click on **Overview**. Click on the ellipsis in the top-right corner, and then click on the **Edit Dashboard** option. We will leave our **Home** view and create another view by clicking on the + symbol in the top-left corner of the screen.

2. In the **View Configuration** window under the **SETTINGS** tab, fill the fields with the following data:

    -   **Title**: Home dependencies
    -   **Icon**: Leave blank
    -   **URL**: d
    -   **Theme**: Leave blank
    -   **View type**: Select the default option, **Masonry (default)**

3. Under the **BADGES** tab, leave the **Entity** field blank.

4. Under the **VISIBILITY** tab, leave all users selected. Click on the **SAVE** button.

5. We have our dashboard dependencies created. Now, let us start to populate the dashboard using the + **ADD CARD** button.

6. Click on the + **ADD CARD** button, and then in the **BY CARD** option, choose the **Entities** card.

7. In the **Entities** card configuration, I will group first the devices in my garage, so I will fill the fields according to *Figure 6.21*.

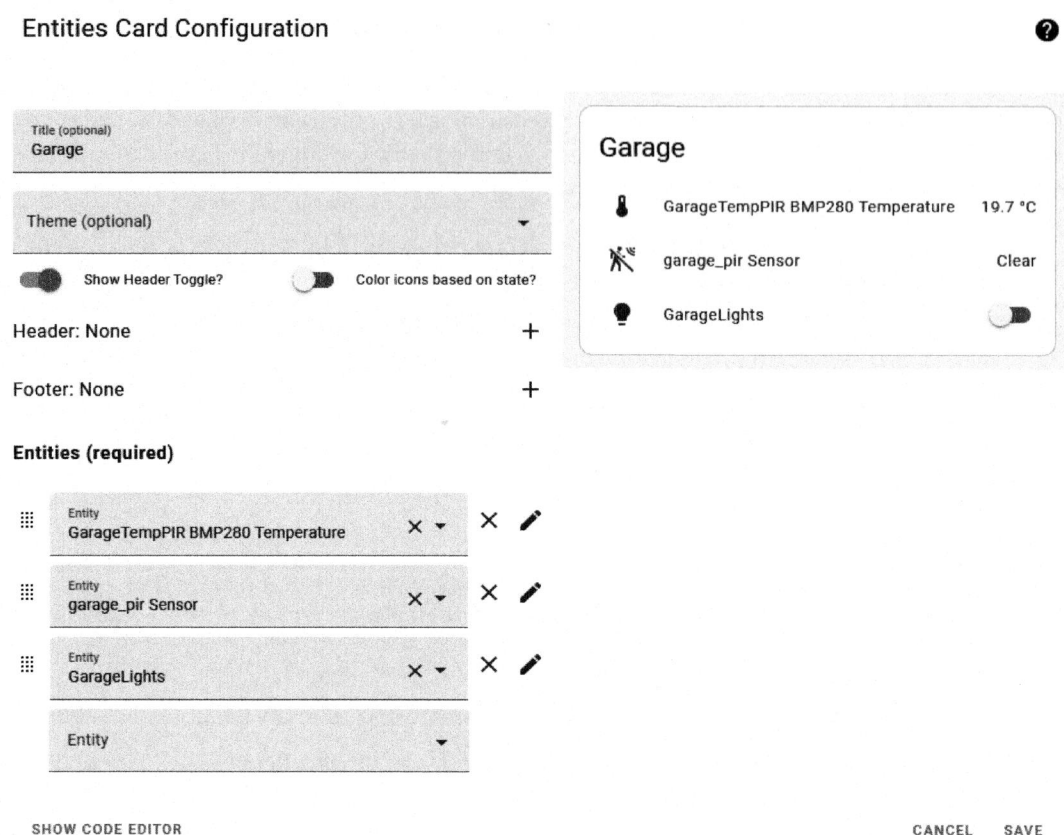

Figure 6.21 – Configuring devices by dependency (garage)

You can see in *Figure 6.21* that as you configure the fields on the left, the card will be updated accordingly on the right.

8.   Click on the **SAVE** button.

9.   At this point, the first card is shown in the **DEPENDENCIES** dashboard. We will be repeating *steps 5* to *7* eight times, but adding the different dependencies of my home. When you have finished, click on the **DONE** button at the top-right corner of the screen. The result will be the dashboard shown in *Figure 6.22*.

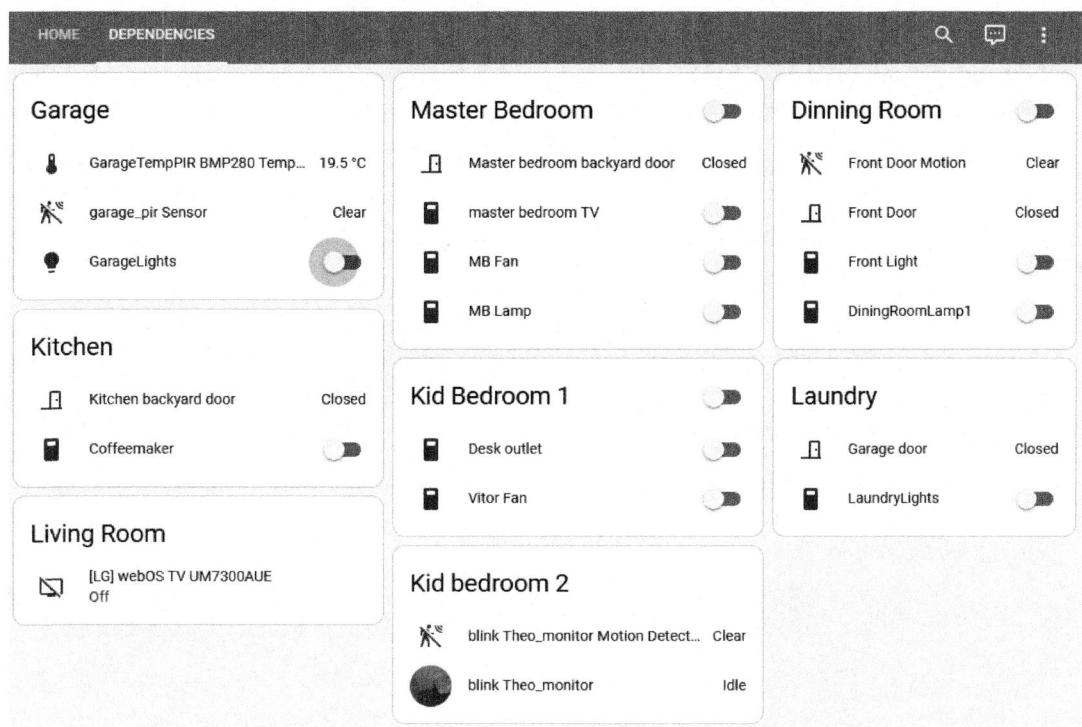

Figure 6.22 – A dashboard configured by home dependencies

You can play with other different cards to change the appearance of the dashboard shown in *Figure 6.22*. For example, if you choose the card named **Glance**, the entities will be shown in columns instead of lines. Other cards will be available to configure how the dashboard will be arranged. These cards are the following:

- **Grid**: Show multiple cards in a grid configuration
- **Horizontal Stack**: Stack together multiple cards so that they can be aligned horizontally
- **Vertical Stack**: Stack together multiple cards so they can be aligned vertically

We will comment on other types of cards, as we will create and configure the other approaches.

Another way to structure dashboards using the by home dependencies approach is, instead of creating one view page including all Home Dependencies, you can create several view pages, and in each one, you can include all information for that dependency. To do that, you can create an empty dashboard by going to the **Settings** | **Add a dashboard** option. Name the dashboard title Dependencies, enter mdi:home in the **Icon** field, make sure that the **Show in Sidebar** option is activated, and then click on the **CREATE** button. Home Assistant will create a dashboard populated for you, but this is not what we want, so we will click on the ellipsis in the top-right corner of the screen and click on the **Edit**

Dashboard option. In the next pop-up window, we will select the **Start with an empty dashboard** option and click on the **TAKE CONTROL** option. This will create an empty dashboard, so we can populate it with cards by following the sequence:

1. In the top-left corner, next to **Edit UI**, click on the **pencil** symbol and enter the name Dependencies. Click on the other pencil symbol next to **HOME**.

2. In the pop-up window that appears, fill the **Title** field with Garage, leave all other options as they are, and click on **SAVE**.

3. Begin to populate the dashboard by choosing all devices or entities located in this bedroom. We will use the **Light** and **Sensor** cards to add a control to the light and to see the sensor data in this dependency, respectively. I will also use the **History Graph** and **Entity** cards to display more information about the motion sensor and garage door sensor.

We will create more views for each home dependency by clicking on the + button in the top-left corner and repeating *steps 2* to *3*, changing the dependencies and populating more information in the dashboards created. The result is shown in *Figure 6.23*.

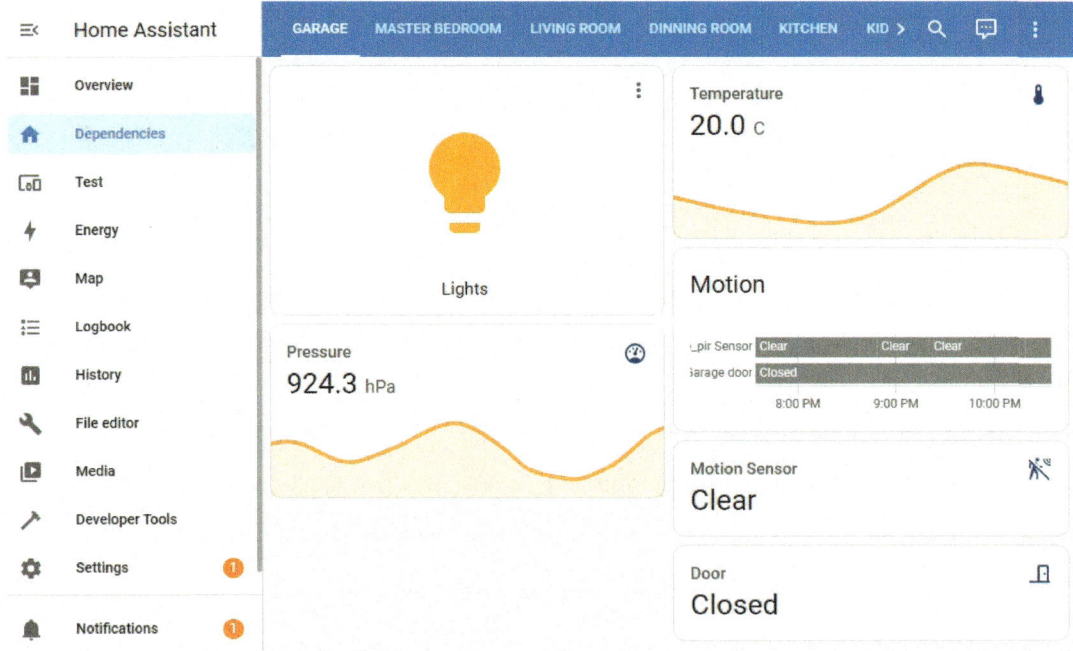

Figure 6.23 – Individual dashboards configured by home dependencies

You can see in *Figure 6.23*, on the top bar, the name of the views created for each home dependency. You can see that the devices or entities reshown in the views are more spaced out and easier to read, as opposed to the views shown in *Figure 6.22* The view configuration shown in *Figure 6.23* are more suitable for smartphones and tablet screens where the size is a constraint.

In the next subsection, we will create another dashboard configuration based on the device type.

Dashboard approach 2 – by device type

The second approach we have to configure our dashboards is by device type. This approach allows you to basically monitor or control three types of devices – sensors, actuators, and media. Like the by home dependencies approach, we can also create all the devices in one view or split them into several views, named per device type. In this section, we will create just one view, including all the device types. I encourage you to create separate views indexed by device type.

We will start this approach by creating an empty view under the **Overview** menu dashboard on the sidebar. We will do this and create the view by following these steps:

1. Under the **Overview** tab, click on the ellipsis in the top-right corner of the screen and then the **Edit Dashboard** option. At the top left of the screen, click on the + symbol.

2. In the pop-up window that appears, fill the **Title** field with `Devices`, leave all other options as they are, and click on **SAVE**.

To populate the dashboard view, follow the following steps:

1. Click on the + **ADD CARD** button in the created dashboard view, **Devices**.

2. We will organize the sensors in one column, so click on the **Vertical Stack** card.

3. In the pop-up window that appears, click on the **Entities** card, and in the following window, fill in the fields as follows:

    *   **Title**: `Door Sensors`

    *   **Entities**: `Garage door`, `front door`, `Master bedroom backyard door` and `kitchen backyard door`

4. Click on the + icon that is present at the top, close to the trash symbol.

5. Repeat *steps 3* and *4* for the temperature and motion sensors.

6. Click on the **SAVE** button.

We will also use *steps 1* to *3* to add all actuators. We will add the media devices by using the **Media Control** card and filling in the entity information for the smart speaker and the TV. After adding all the devices, click the **DONE** button in the top-right corner of the screen. After all the steps are executed, we will have a dashboard view configuration, like the one shown in *Figure 6.24*.

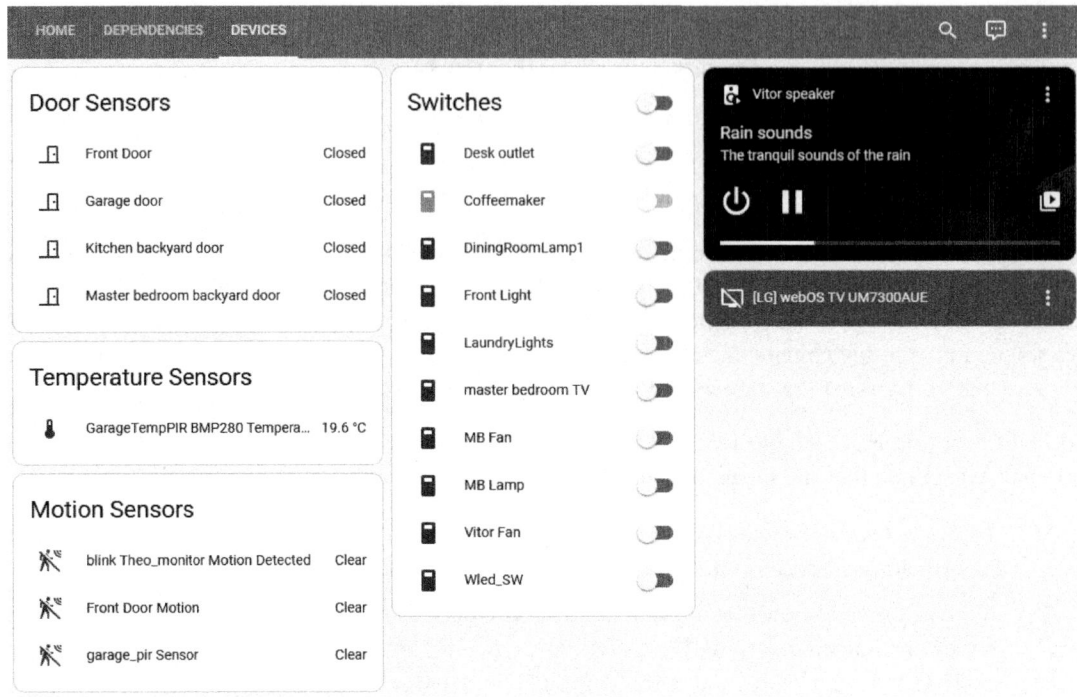

Figure 6.24 – A dashboard configured by device type

As you can see in *Figure 6.24*, the devices are organized in a vertical column using the **Vertical Stack** card. In the first column, several types of sensors are listed. In the second column, the actuator switches are listed, and in the third column, the media devices are listed.

We will finish this subsection for now and move to the other one, where we will add a new dashboard view for the Home Assistant integrations.

Dashboard approach 3 – Home Assistant integrations

The third approach focuses on Home Assistant integrations. We will take the opportunity to use the remaining cards that were not used and also explore the person configuration and the presence sensor. As a bonus, we will finish by creating a **subview** and associating it with one of the cards in this view.

We will make all the configurations in our original **Home** dashboard view under the **Overview** option from the sidebar. We will edit the view and delete the two cards we had originally configured. This can be done by clicking on the ellipse at the bottom right of each of the cards and then the **Delete card** option.

After cleaning the **Home** dashboard view, we will start creating weather information using a previously unused card. We will do so by following these steps:

1. Click on the + **ADD CARD** button in the **Home** view.

2. Select the **Weather Forecast** card. Leave **Entity** as **Home**. In the **Weather to Show** option, click on the **Show current Weather and Forecast** option. Click **Save**.

3. We will add a horizontal card by choosing + **ADD CARD** and clicking on the **Horizontal Stack** card. We will choose the **Date & Time** entity and click on the + symbol.

4. Next, we will choose the **Worldclock Sensor** entity and click on the + symbol. In the sequence, choose the **Sun** entity. Click **Save**.

5. We will choose the **Glance** card to add the person entities. Click on the + **ADD CARD** and click on the **Glance** card. Choose the people that are in your home. In my case, I will include myself, my wife, and one of my kids in the **Entities** fields. Click **Save**.

6. In the sequence, we will create a vertical card, and inside it, we will include a horizontal card. We will do this by clicking on + **ADD CARD** and clicking on the **Vertical Stack** card. In the first card of the vertical stack, we will use the **Entities** card. Click on the **Entities** card and enter the title Automation, and in the **Entities** field, add all the automations created in *Chapter 5*.

7. Click on the + symbol and select the **Horizontal Stack** card. We will configure the cards, as shown in *Figure 6.25*. Select the **Button** card for the first column of the horizontal line card. In the **Entity** field, look for the **ALL OFF** scene we created in *Chapter 5*. Leave all the other fields as they are.

8. Click on the second + symbol inside the window, and select the **Button** card again for the second column of the horizontal line card. In the **Entity** field, look for the **Time for Bed** script we created in *Chapter 5*. Leave all the other fields as they are and click on **Save**.

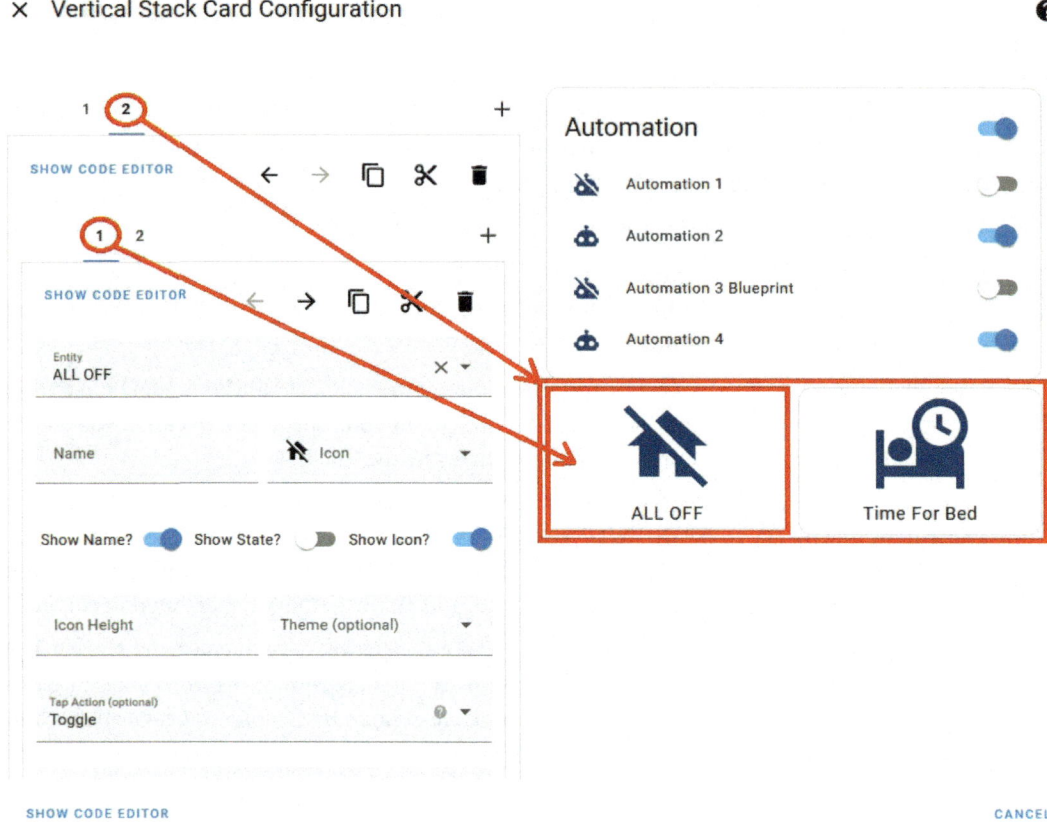

Figure 6.25 – Configuring a horizontal stack card inside a vertical stack card

Figure 6.26 shows what the dashboard for the Home Assistant integrations looks like and indicates the cards used to represent each one of the entities.

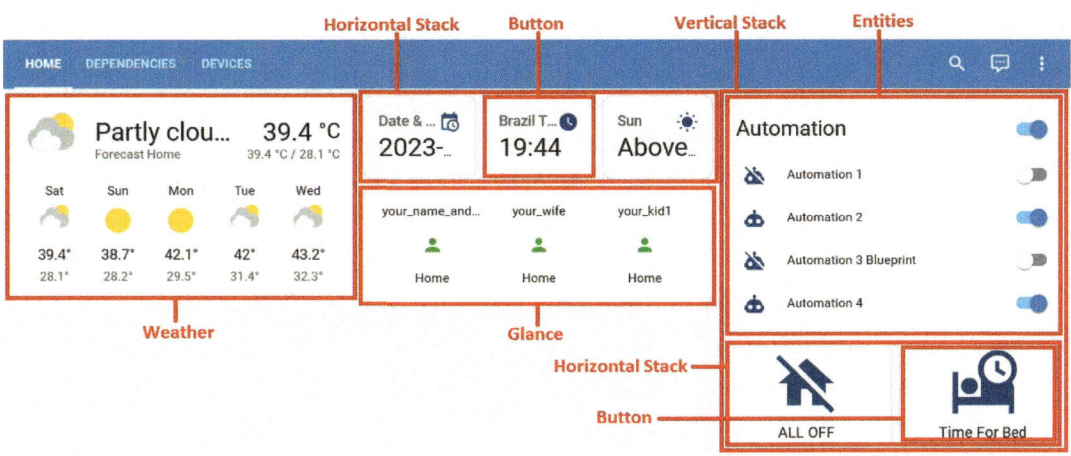

Figure 6.26 – Home Assistant-based integrations with cards explained

The entire code used to represent all dashboards in the **Overview** menu, including **Home**, **Dependencies**, and **Devices**, can be viewed by clicking on the ellipse at the top right of the screen, as shown in *Figure 6.26*, and then the **Edit Dashboard** option. Once in Edit mode, click on the ellipse again and then on the **Raw configuration editor** option. A small part of the code used to represent the code for the **Glance** card is shown here as an example:

```
title: family_name_Home
views:
  - path: default_view
    title: Home
    cards:
  - type: glance
    entities:
      - entity: person.your_name_and_family_name
      - entity: person.your_wife
      - entity: person.your_kid1
```

Each card is reshown by the codeword `cards`, and each type is reshown by the codeword `- type: card name`. Each card has its own configuration field type, which is different from the others. In the case of the code previously shown, the only fields configured for the glance card were the **Entities** field (`entities`), including each **Entity** field name (`- entity:`), which is mandatory.

We will finish this approach by creating a subview. This subview idea will be a hidden page that will list the outside temperature of my sensors. We will include these temperature sensors in *Chapter 10*, so for now, let us just use their data. We will associate this subview with a new **Button** card to be created in the **Home** view. When we click on this **Button** card, the subview will be shown with the outside temperature I get from my outside temperature sensors.

We will create a subview dashboard and a **Button** card by following these steps:

1. Under the **Overview** tab, click on the ellipsis and then the **Edit Dashboard** option. At the top left of the screen, click on the + symbol.

2. In the pop-up window that appears, as shown in *Figure 6.27*, enter Outside Temperature in the **Title** field and turn on the **Subview** option. Leave all other options as they are and click on **SAVE**.

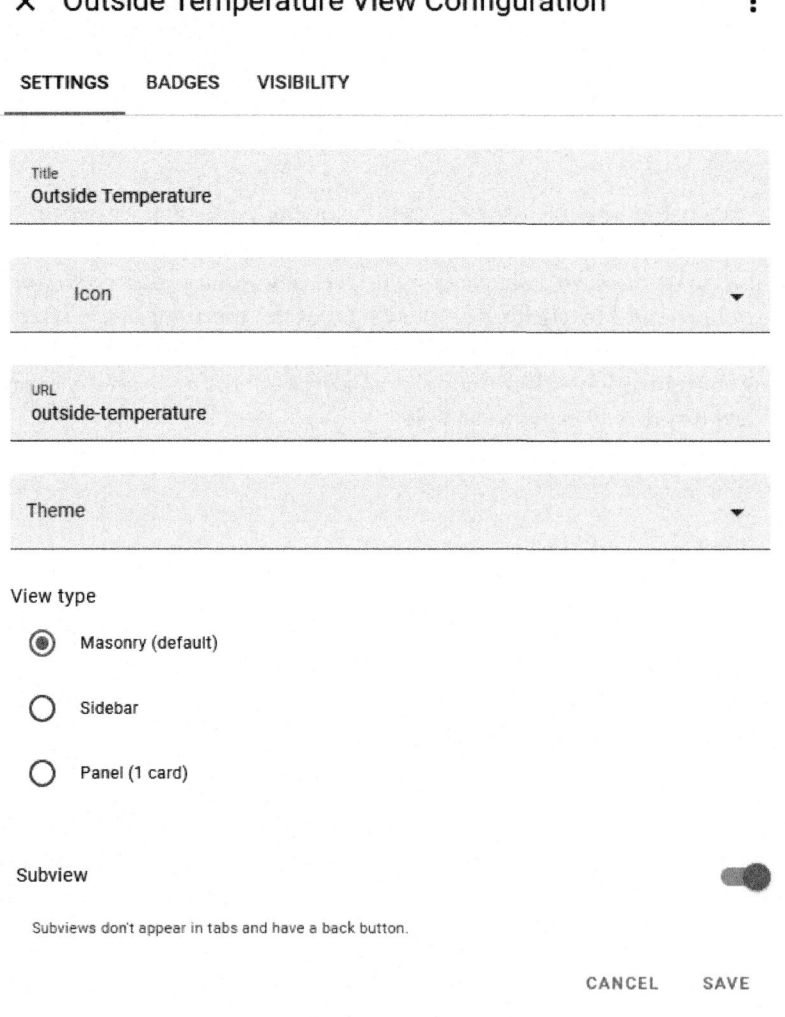

Figure 6.27 – The dashboard subview creation screen

3. A subview will be created, and we will add an **Entities** card by clicking on + **ADD CARD |
Entities**.

4. On the **Entities card Configuration** screen, we will enter `Outside temperature` in the **Title**
field, and in the **Entities** field, we will select the `GarageTempPIR BMP28- Temperature`
and `Backyard Temperature` entities. Click on **SAVE**.

5. Then, to conclude the creation of the subview dashboard, we will click on the **DONE** button
in the upper-right corner of the window.

6. You will see that the subview is hidden, and now, we will associate the **Button** card to show the
subview. Click on the ellipsis | **Edit Dashboard** on the **Overview** tab.

7. We will create a **Button** card by clicking on + **ADD CARD** in the **Home** view. Fill in the fields
as follows:

   • **Entity**: `Sun`

   • **Name**: `Outside Temperature`

   • **Icon**: `mdi: sun-thermometer`

   • **Tap Action**: `Navigate`

   • **Navigation Path**: `/lovelace/outside-temperature`

8. Click on **SAVE** and then the **Done** button in the upper-right corner of the window.

You can now test the link to the subview by clicking on the **Outside Temperature** button just created.
You will see that the subview dashboard page is shown with the two temperature sensors displayed.

Using these three approaches for your dashboard, we will cover all possibilities of their use. You have
more resource options available if you want to further customize the dashboards. We will discuss
some of these options in the next section.

Using extra resources to customize your dashboard

Home Assistant allows you to customize the dashboards even more, providing extra resources that can
be uploaded or installed with it. In the upcoming subsections, we will explore some of these resources
so that I can show you the benefits of a well-designed dashboard.

Using the Picture Elements card

The **Picture Elements** card is a powerful card where you can represent the floor plan of your home,
using an image in the `.png` format, and assign the devices you have on it. This is something I
discovered recently in Home Assistant, and I did not dedicate too much time to exploring it. I will
provide a quick example to you using just the floor plan of my master bedroom so that you have an
idea of how you can use the card.

First, you need a floor plan of your home. Then, create a drawing or image from it. I created my master bedroom floor plan using **MS Visio**, but you can use another of your preference. After you have a floor plan image of your home, you must upload it to a www folder to be created under the `config` folder from Home Assistant. You can create the www folder using the **File editor** add-on installed in *Chapter 5*. After uploading the file, you must restart Home Assistant so that it can recognize the folder and uploaded file.

Using the sidebar menu and choosing the **Overview** option, you can add the Picture Elements card by editing the dashboard and choosing this option when clicking on the + **ADD CARD** button. I have four devices installed in my master bedroom, and by adding them to the floor plan, I will have a Picture Elements card configuration that looks like *Figure 6.28*.

Picture Elements Card Configuration

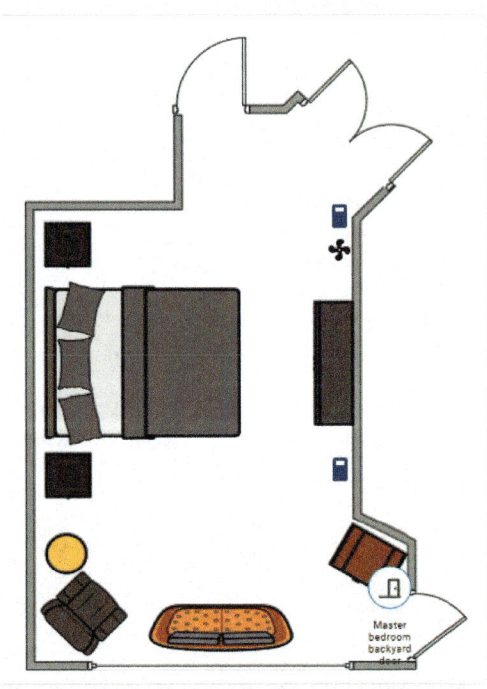

```
 1  type: picture-elements
 2  elements:
 3    - type: state-icon
 4      title: Master Bedroom Switch TV
 5      entity: switch.master_bedroom_tv
 6      style:
 7        top: 68%
 8        left: 70%
 9        font-size: 10px
10    - type: icon
11      title: Master Bedroom Fan
12      icon: mdi:fan
13      entity: switch.1001257d12
14      style:
15        top: 35%
16        left: 70%
17        font-size: 10px
18    - type: state-icon
19      title: Master Bedroom Lights
20      entity: switch.100125c00d
21      style:
22        top: 30%
23        left: 70%
24        font-size: 10px
25    - type: state-badge
26      title: Master Bedroom Door Sensor
27      entity: binary_sensor.master_bedroom_backyard_door
28      style:
29        top: 90%
30        left: 80%
31        font-size: 10px
32  image: /local/mb_floorplan.png
33
```

No visual editor available for type 'picture-elements'.

SHOW VISUAL EDITOR   CANCEL

Figure 6.28 – The Picture Elements card configuration

You can see in *Figure 6.28* that there is no visual editor for this card, so all configuration is done using YAML code. I used different configuration types to set up the four devices in the picture – `state-icon`, `icon`, and `state-badge`. Each one has diverse types of parameters, but some of them are similar, such as `style:`, where the position of the device in the image can be controlled by percentages in the `top:` and `left:` parameters. The image location is set up in the `image:` parameter. The floor plan image is reshown on the left of *Figure 6.28*, and the parameters are updated in the image as you are typing them in the editor on the right. There is a syntax checker that works automatically as you type in the editor.

The floor plan image, reshown on the left of *Figure 6.28*, shows four devices on the left – two reshown as switches, one reshown as a fan, and the door sensor on the bottom right reshown as a door with its name written on it.

In the next subsection, we will see other customized cards and items and what type of dashboards you can generate using them.

Installing and using other customizable cards and items

Customizing a dashboard allows you to be highly creative by changing the configuration of the card information per your needs. As mentioned and exemplified before, each card you add to your dashboard is highly configurable with different options. You can also use **themes**, which can change the Home Assistant frontend default color and other parameters that are used to present the screen elements to the end user.

A straightforward way to add more customized cards and themes to Home Assistant is by using **Home Assistant Community Store (HACS)**. You will have to install **HACS** in Home Assistant with the following guide: `https://hacs.xyz/docs/setup/prerequisites`. Using HACS, you will also be able to install integrations developed by the Home Assistant development community. Note that you will have to install and use HACS at your own risk, since it is explicitly mentioned during the installation process that everything inside HACS is custom and untested by Home Assistant.

Two example cards and themes that I recommend you install using HACS are the following:

- **Button Card**: `https://github.com/custom-cards/button-card`
- **Mushroom**: `https://github.com/piitaya/lovelace-mushroom`

Button Card adds only one customized card and applies just to buttons. You can create customizable buttons using YAML code only, and Button Care allows you to change the different parameters of a button, such as size, color, disposition, value, and description.

Mushroom added 18 new customized cards and allows you to create dashboards with views suitable for smartphones and tablets. I was able to quickly create a very minimalist dashboard using Mushroom. This dashboard uses the three combined approaches shown in this chapter, each one shown on a different line. I took a phone screenshot of this dashboard, which is partially shown in *Figure 6.29*.

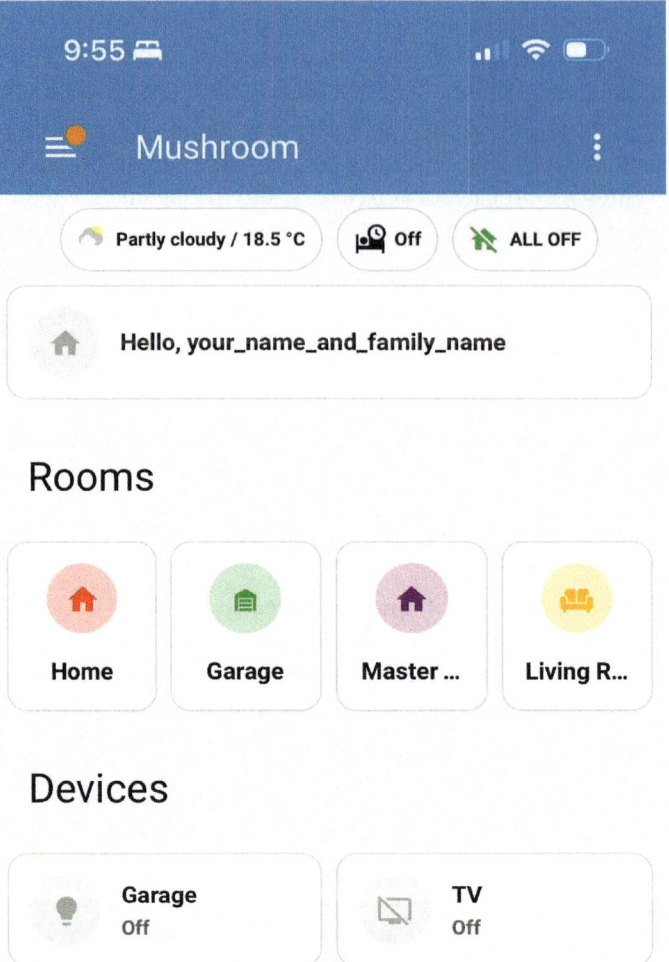

Figure 6.29 – A dashboard smartphone screenshot created using Mushroom cards

Most of the cards used on the screen shown in *Figure 6.29* are from Mushroom. Not all entities, devices, and rooms are reshown in the Dashboard screenshot. It is just to give you an idea of how to customize even more dashboards using the customized cards.

Using this last example of how to customize a dashboard, we are able to learn how to configure and organize the information we want to have about our home. This will help us to access and manage how we interact with our devices and entities. I consider that with this chapter, we have covered most of the basic content you will use with Home Assistant. In the next chapter, we will explore how to extend the capabilities of Home Automation using some IoT software add-ons.

Summary

In this chapter, we learned how we can do more using integrations and dashboard customizations. We saw how I can configure the remaining devices in my home using distinct types of integrations for sensors and actuators that I have at home. Different setups and configurations were demonstrated so that you can understand the integration process used by Home Assistant.

After we installed and configured more devices to work with Home Assistant, we learned about the dashboard and views configuration, enabling us to represent the information we have for the devices in diverse ways, which can be managed according to our needs. We did that by providing examples of using badges and three approaches to configuring dashboards in incremental steps using cards. We finished the chapter by providing extra resources that can help you to further customize your dashboard using cards and themes developed by the Home Assistant Developer community.

The next chapter will take you to another level of Home Automation knowledge, since we will learn another add-on software that you can use to automate and provide information about your home.

Part 4: Expanding Home Assistant's Capabilities

In this part, you will enhance your Home Automation system with features and add-on software tools that expand Home Assistant's usability and capabilities. You will learn how to back up and recover your Home Assistant installation. We will end this part by presenting a new installation approach for Home Assistant and other IoT software tools.

This part has the following chapters:

- *Chapter 7, Extending Home Automation Capabilities Using Add-ons*
- *Chapter 8, Installing and Setting Up Home Assistant Container*

Extending Home Automation Capabilities Using Add-ons

This chapter will present the main add-ons that can be installed with Home Assistant and that I currently use in my home. These add-ons are software applications that will extend the capabilities of Home Assistant, allowing you to go beyond it with the ability to program, present, and store data generated by your home automation system.

The following main topics will be covered in this chapter:

- What are add-ons in Home Assistant?
- Performing automations without Home Assistant using Node-RED
- Using database and chart tools to present data from your home
- Managing your network of Tasmota devices using TasmoAdmin
- Accessing Home Assistant remotely

By the end of this chapter, besides Home Assistant, you will know and be able to evaluate the applications for use in your next project for home automation.

Technical requirements

In this chapter, it is helpful if you know the concept of a visual programming logic sequence (**Node-RED**) and how to deal with database applications (**InfluxDB**). If you have the skills to handle charts and know how to configure them, you will be better prepared to handle the chart application (**Grafana**). In some sections, links to videos are provided to exemplify some steps to be followed. Information used in the chapter, including these videos, is available at https://github.com/ PacktPublishing/Building-Smart-Home-Automation-Solutions-with-Home-Assistant/tree/main/Chapter%2007. Check out the following video to view the Code in Action: https://bit.ly/3OVMsFy

What are add-ons in Home Assistant?

The content learned so far has shown that Home Assistant can handle most of the resources required to automate your home. The concept of **add-ons** was introduced to include more features to Home Assistant besides its main purpose. Add-ons are software applications that extend Home Assistant's usability. They can be used as part of Home Assistant's functionality or work totally independent to it. We already briefly covered the installation of some add-on software such as the **Mosquitto** MQTT broker in *Chapter 1* and **File editor** in *Chapter 5*. All the add-on software provided by Home Assistant is free to use.

Add-ons can be installed in the same way by following the **Settings | Add-ons** path and then clicking on the **ADD-ON Store** button in the bottom-right corner of the screen. They are split into two categories – **Official add-ons** and **Home Assistant Community Add-ons**. The official add-ons are maintained by the Home Assistant team while the Home Assistant community add-ons are handled by the Home Assistant community. *Figure 7.1* and *Figure 7.2* show screenshots of both official add-ons and community add-ons, available in the Home Assistant 2023.5.2 release.

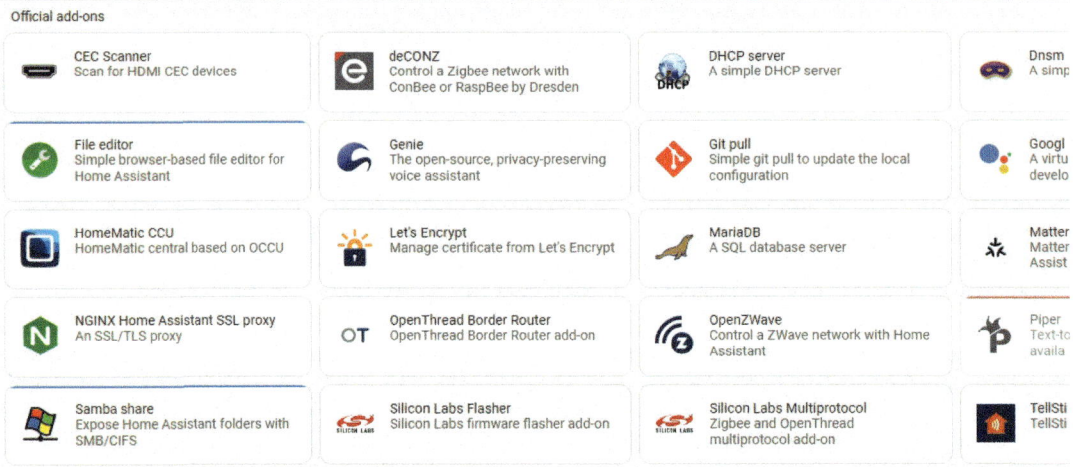

Figure 7.1 – Official add-ons

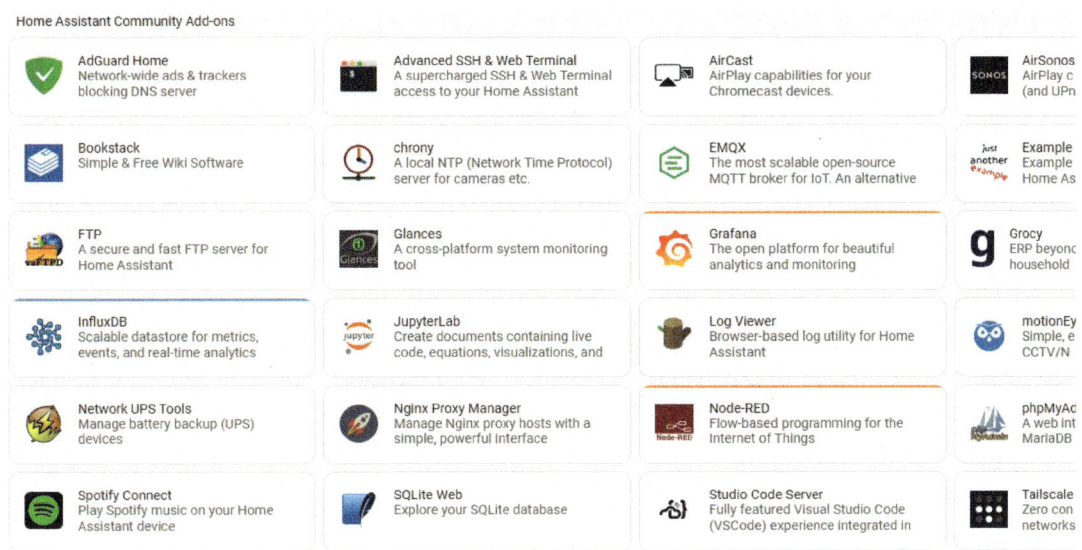

Figure 7.2 – Home Assistant community add-ons

The add-ons can vary in use, from file manipulation to access to a database. Some examples of add-ons are grouped in *Table 7.1*:

ID	Application name	Category	Main function	Home assistant-integrated?
1	File editor	File manipulation	Editing files in Home Assistant	Yes
2	SSH server	Remote access	Logging in remotely to Home Assistant using SSH	Yes
3	Mosquitto broker	MQTT server	Providing an MQTT server to be used by Home Assistant	Yes
4	Studio Code Server	File manipulation	An enhanced file editor suitable for YAML code manipulation. Embedded with a Visual Studio Code editor.	Yes
5	Node-RED	Programming tool	A programming tool suitable for IoT applications	No
6	Duck DNS	DNS IP address manipulation	Performing automatic updates of the Duck DNS IP address	Yes
7	Grafana	Chart manipulation and presentation	Creating, exploring, and presenting charts using data from sensors and others	No

ID	Application name	Category	Main function	Home assistant-integrated?
8	InfluxDB	Database	Time-series database	No
9	MariaDB	Database	Database for Home Assistant	Yes
10	TasmoAdmin	Devices manager	Managing Tasmota-based devices	No

Table 7.1 – Examples of add-on software

The examples in *Table 7.1* show two valuable bits of information. The first important thing is that the first three applications listed, **File editor**, **SSH server**, and **Mosquitto broker** are now, at the time of writing, the most common add-ons installed by users, being available in 65.9%, 55.4%, and 52.5% of Home Assistant installations, respectively. More statistics about the add-ons can be found at this link: `https://analytics.home-assistant.io/add-ons/`. The second important thing presented in the table is in the right-most column. It shows whether the applications are integrated or not with Home Assistant.

If an application is integrated into Home Assistant, it makes sense for it to be used in a Home Assistant context. **File editor**, for instance, is used primarily to edit files within Home Assistant and will not work outside of it. On the other hand, applications not integrated into Home Assistant can run independently of it. In other words, these applications do not need information from Home Assistant to be used. These non-Home Assistant-integrated applications allow you to expand the capabilities of using Home Automation devices once they outgrow some feature or functionality poorly covered by Home Assistant. Therefore, in this chapter, we will explore the use of all the *non-Home Assistant-integrated applications* presented in *Table 7.1*, which means **Node-RED**, **Grafana**, **InfluxDB**, and **TasmoAdmin**.

These add-ons will also be discussed in *Chapter 8* and *Chapter 10* when we build our **five-zone temperature logger**. We will also explore the **Duck DNS** application so that we can use Home Assistant remotely when we are not at home.

Let's begin our add-on software exploration, starting with Node-RED in the next section.

Doing automations without Home Assistant using Node-RED

Node-RED is an open source, flow-based visual programming tool, based on **nodes** that are interconnected using **wires** to create execution **flows**. Flows can be created and edited using a web browser, and nodes can be plugged together through a flow editor. This programming environment in our current Home Automation system runs as separate software but does not need to be integrated into Home Assistant, meaning that any program developed in Node-RED can run independently of Home Assistant. Sensors and actuators can pull or push their data using MQTT topic messages. Using the nodes grouped by functionalities or features, the data from sensors or actuators can be manipulated by the nodes to create automations, based on the data status. These grouped nodes create a **palette** that can be expanded by installing new groups of nodes.

As part of a programming tool the, Node-RED development environment offers the capability of debugging in real time, and data can be manipulated using preformatted functions or even by writing functions using **JavaScript**. Despite Node-RED having a visual programming flow, programming source code is generated in the background using the **JSON** format, which can be copied and pasted to new or different flows, or imported and exported using files created by Node-RED.

In the following subsections, we will learn how to install and use Node-RED by implementing a similar automation, created beforehand using Home Assistant.

Installing and using Node-RED

You will be able to install Node-RED by using the **Settings | Add-ons** path from the Home Assistant sidebar. In the bottom-right corner of the screen, click on the **ADD-ON STORE** button. Continue the installation by following these steps, which also are presented in the ch7-1 video:

1. On the **Add-On Store** screen, scroll down to the Home Assistant community add-ons and look for **Node-RED**. Click on the **Node-RED** button.

2. On the next screen, in the first rectangle titled **Node-RED**, click on **INSTALL**.

3. After one minute or so, Node-RED will be installed in your Home Automation server. Slide the **Show in sidebar** button to enable Node-RED to be initialized from the sidebar.

4. Click on the **Configuration** tab at the top. In the **credential_secret*** field, set a password type configuration of your choice. For the example in this book, we will use my_home.

5. Disable the **ssl** option to avoid possible initialization errors. Click on the **SAVE** button. Wait for Node-RED to save the information.

6. Click on the **Info** tab at the top of the screen. Then, click on the **START** button in the first rectangle titled **Node-RED**. Node-RED will start up.

7. Click on the **OPEN WEB UI** button. Node-RED will open inside Home Assistant, as presented on the screen in *Figure 7.3*.

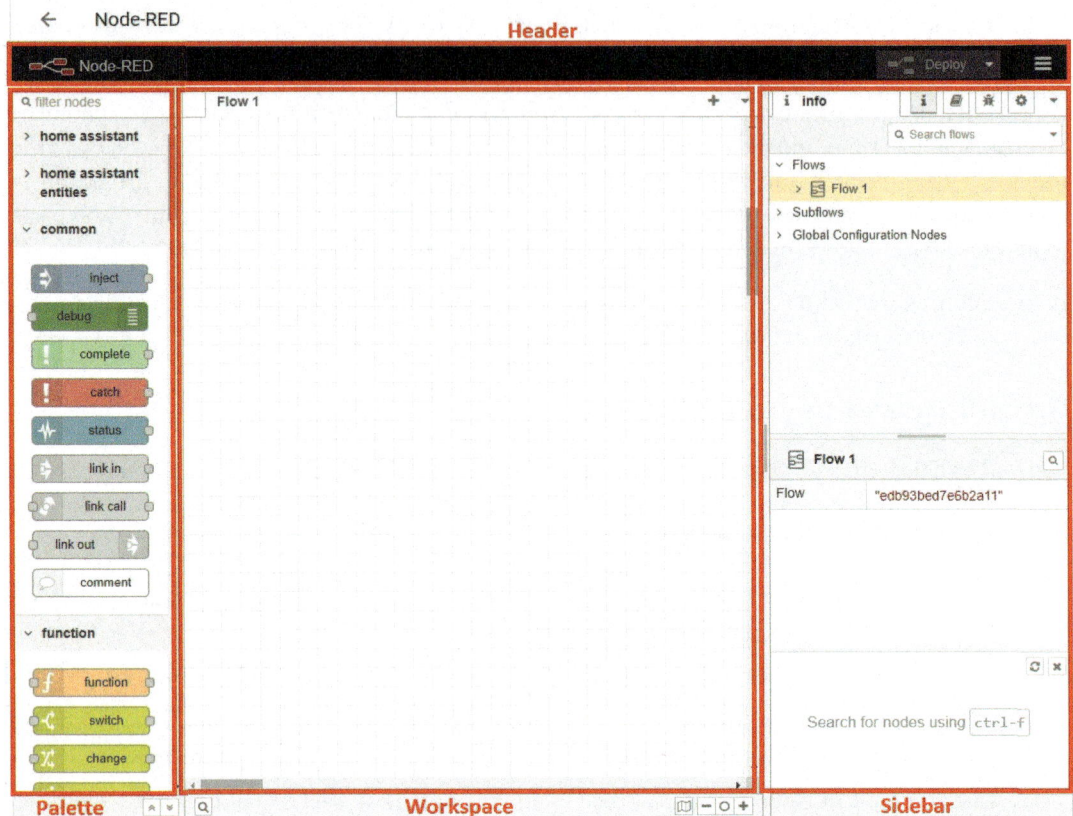

Figure 7.3 – Node-RED editor configuration

Figure 7.3 presents how the Node-RED editor is configured. There are four main components, described as follows:

- **Header**: Contains the **Deploy** button and main menu.
- **Palette**: Contains the nodes grouped by sets, according to application.
- **Workspace**: This is where the flows are created. Flows are presented by tabs activated at the top.
- **Sidebar**: This shows how flows are configured and structured. It presents debug and output information.

The Node-RED programming concept is based on flows created in the workspace. The flows are made by nodes located in the palette. Nodes are organized in a programming logic sequence and connected using wires. The node programming flow can be read or executed from the left to the right of the screen. Nodes are inserted in the workflow by dragging and dropping them from the palette. A set of nodes joined together can create a group and be moved or copied as a single object within the workspace area. Another concept used by Node-RED to simplify the programming read is the use of **subflows**. Subflows are collections of nodes that are collapsed into a single node in the workspace.

The workspace editor offers distinctive features to make the nodes programming easy to use. These features include a selection tool, a nodes arrangement tool, and a search tool. Another important feature that can simplify the programming process is the ability to import or export flows using the JSON format, which can be done using files or by directly copying and pasting in the import area. There is also the possibility to install a new set of nodes using the **Palette Manager**, accessed through the main menu.

Besides Home Automation, common Node-RED use cases include IoT applications, workflow automation, industrial automation, and cloud and web service integration. In the next subsection, we will present an example of these use cases in the Home Automation area, which is how to use Node-RED to recreate an automation we did in *Chapter 5*.

Recreating an automation using Node-RED

After installing and discussing how Node-Red works, let's recreate **Automation 1**, which we made in *Chapter 5*. Automation 1 is described as follows:

Turn the Garage Lights on if car movement is detected in the Garage and it is after Sunset. Turn the Garage Lights off after two minutes.

The first aspect we will need to understand in Automation 1 is that we will have to listen for a motion sensor to detect movement. As all the devices, including sensors, communicate using Wi-Fi and MQTT, we will need to listen to MQTT messages and act from there. Node-Red implements a node, **mqtt in**, under the **Network** group (check out the left side of *Figure 7.4*), which can connect to an MQTT broker and subscribe or listen for messages related to a specific topic. We will use this node to detect the trigger condition of Automation 1. You will need to locate the **Network** group and the **mqtt in** node, then drag it from the palette, and drop it in the workspace area. After that, double-click on the **mqtt** in node and configure the properties, according to the right side of *Figure 7.4*:

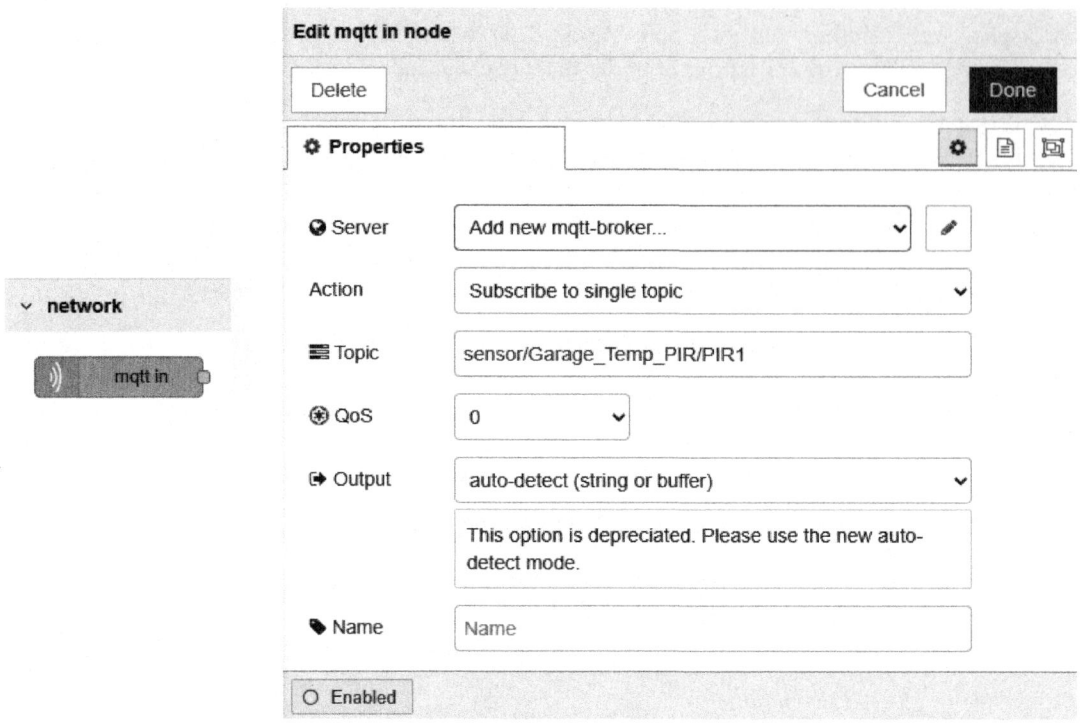

Figure 7.4 – mqtt in icon and node configuration

The two most essential pieces of information to be filled in on the **Edit mqtt in node** pane presented in *Figure 7.4* are the **Topic** and **Server** fields. The **Topic** field must be filled with the information sensor/Garage_Temp_PIR/PIR1. The **Server** field can be configured by clicking on the pencil button beside the **Server** field and configuring the properties, as shown in the **Connection** tab on the left side of *Figure 7.5* and then in the **Security** tab presented on the right side of *Figure 7.5*.

> **Important note**
>
> It is possible to subscribe to multiple topics in Node-RED for troubleshooting purposes using the **MQTT wildcard #**. In the case of our example, if we want to subscribe to multiple topics coming from the main sensor topic, the information in the **Topic** field must be filled as sensor/#.

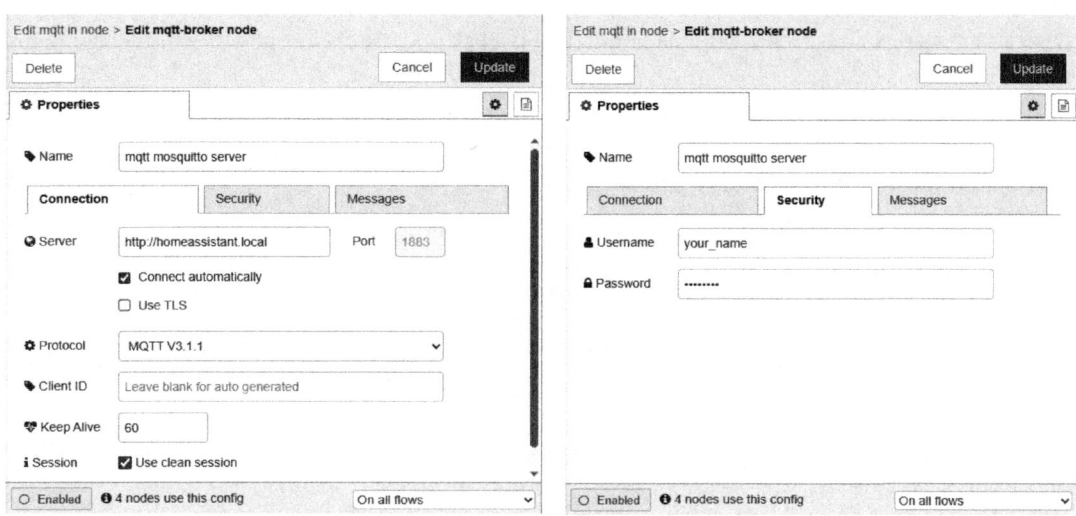

Figure 7.5 – The mqtt broker configuration in Node-RED

In *Figure 7.5* on the left, there is only one parameter to be filled in. It is the **Server** field in the **Connection** tab, and the content should be `http://homeassistant.local`. Fill in the **Username** and **Password** parameters under the **Security** tab with the configuration made in *Chapter 2*, or with the `your_name` and `your_password` values, as shown on the right of *Figure 7.5*. The MQTT broker server name should be configured using the **Name** field. I will use the generic name `mqtt mosquitto server`. We must click on the **Update** button at the top right of the pane for the configurations to take effect.

We now need to include a node that can inform us about the sunset event. Node-RED has the **sunrise** node in the **time** group, as presented in *Figure 7.6*.

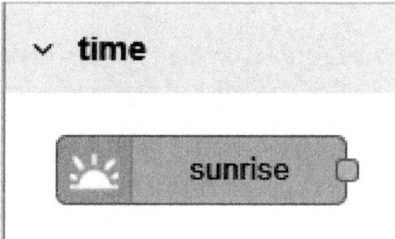

Figure 7.6 – The sunrise node icon under the time group

Drag and drop this node to the workplace and double-click on it. In the properties window, configure the parameters as follow:

- **Latitude**: The latitude of your location.
- **Longitude**: The longitude of your location.
- **Name**: The name of your location. I will use the generic name `your_location`.

Click on the **Done** button at the top right of the window so that the configuration saves.

Node-RED works with the concept of messages, and the default message has the object **payload** as the main content of the information provided by each node output. In the case of the **mqtt in** node, when a movement is detected, a payload, **ON**, is created. In the **sunrise** node, a payload called **1** is created when it is day, and a payload called **0** is created when it is night. We will combine the two output messages of the **mqtt in** and **sunrise** nodes in a single message by using another node called **join** under the **sequence** group. Drag and drop the **join** node to the workspace and connect the output from both the **mqtt in** and **sunrise** nodes to the input of the **join** node using wires, as shown in *Figure 7.7*.

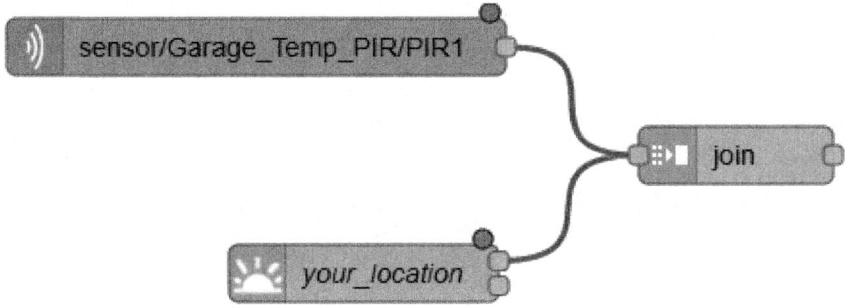

Figure 7.7 – The first nodes interconnected in the Node-RED automation

Double-click on the **join** node to configure it. In the **Edit join node configuration** box, change the **Mode** field to **manual** and fill the **After a number of message parts** field with **2**. Click on the **Done** button to save the node configuration.

Next, we will create a function to check for detected movement and a night condition, and we will configure a new message payload with values 1 and 0, depending on these two parameters' statuses. We will use the node called **function** in the function group to do this. Drag and drop this node to the workspace and double-click on it. We will select the **On Message** tab and insert the following JavaScript code into it:

```
var newmsg = {};
if (msg.payload["sensor/Garage_Temp_PIR/PIR1"] == "ON" && msg.payload.
sun == 0) {
    newmsg.payload = 1;
} else {
```

```
      newmsg.payload = 0;
}
return newmsg
```

In the preceding code, a new variable, `newmsg`, is created and initialized. After that, a verification is made using the `if` clause. This verification is for the condition that we want to trigger our automation when a movement is detected and it is night. These two conditions are represented by the `msg.payload["sensor/Garage_Temp_PIR/PIR1"] == "ON"` and `msg.payload.sun == 0 statements, respectively`. If these conditions are satisfied, the value 1 is attributed to the `newmsg.payload` object (`newmsg.payload = 1`); otherwise, the value 0 is assumed (`newmsg.payload = 0`). The code finishes by returning the `newmsg` variable. This variable will be available in the output of the **function** node.

Depending on your configuration, you can change the device name and topic name you want to subscribe to. In this case, in the preceding code, the `msg.payload` content should replace `sensor/Garage_Temp_PIR/PIR1` with `sensor/your_device_name/your_topic_to_be_subscribed`, where `your_device_name` is the name of your device and `your_topic_to_be_subscribed` is the topic name to be subscribed.

After including the previously described code, let's enter a name for the function, Check Sunset and Movement, in the **Name** field. Click on the **Done** button at the top right of the **Edit function node** configuration window. Link the output of the **join** node to the input of the function just created. We will now have the nodes configured according to *Figure 7.8*.

Figure 7.8 – The function node included in the automation flow

The next node we will include in our flow is the **switch** node, as shown on the left of *Figure 7.9*. The **switch** node is used for route messages based on their values or sequence position. In the case of our example, the **switch** node will be used just to evaluate whether the payload for the new message created in the previous function node satisfies the required condition, which is the payload value being equal to the number *1*. The switch node can be found in the **function** group. Drag and drop the node from the palette to the workspace. Double-click on the switch node to configure it. In the **Edit switch node** window, configure the **Property** field according to the right side of *Figure 7.9*.

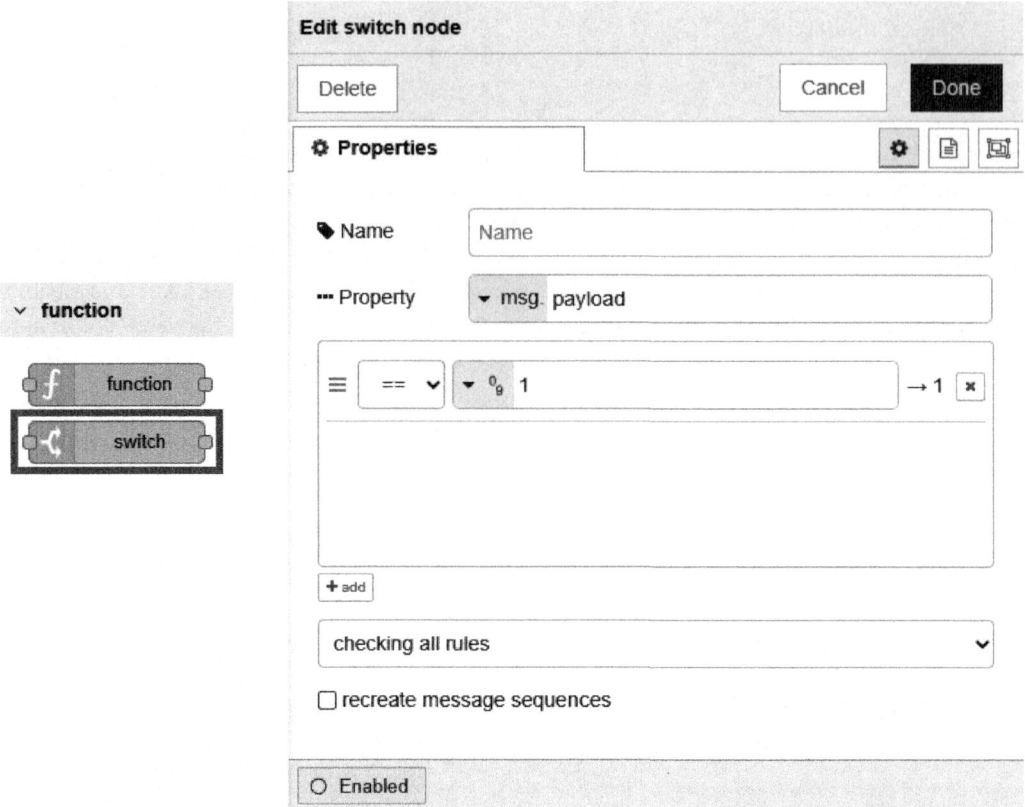

Figure 7.9 – The switch node icon and configuration

In *Figure 7.9*, make sure the condition clause is set as a number (0 9). Click on the **Done** button to save the configuration. Link the output of the **function** node to the input of the **switch** node using the wires.

Next, we will add a **trigger** node. The **trigger** node works by sending a message when it is triggered and then a second message after some configurable delay. We will use it to send an **ON** message to the GarageLights actuator hacked in *Chapter 4* and then, after one and a half minutes, send another message to the same actuator with the **OFF** content. The trigger node can be found in the **function** group. Drag and drop the trigger node into the workspace. Double-click to configure it. Make sure to have all the fields configured according to *Figure 7.10*.

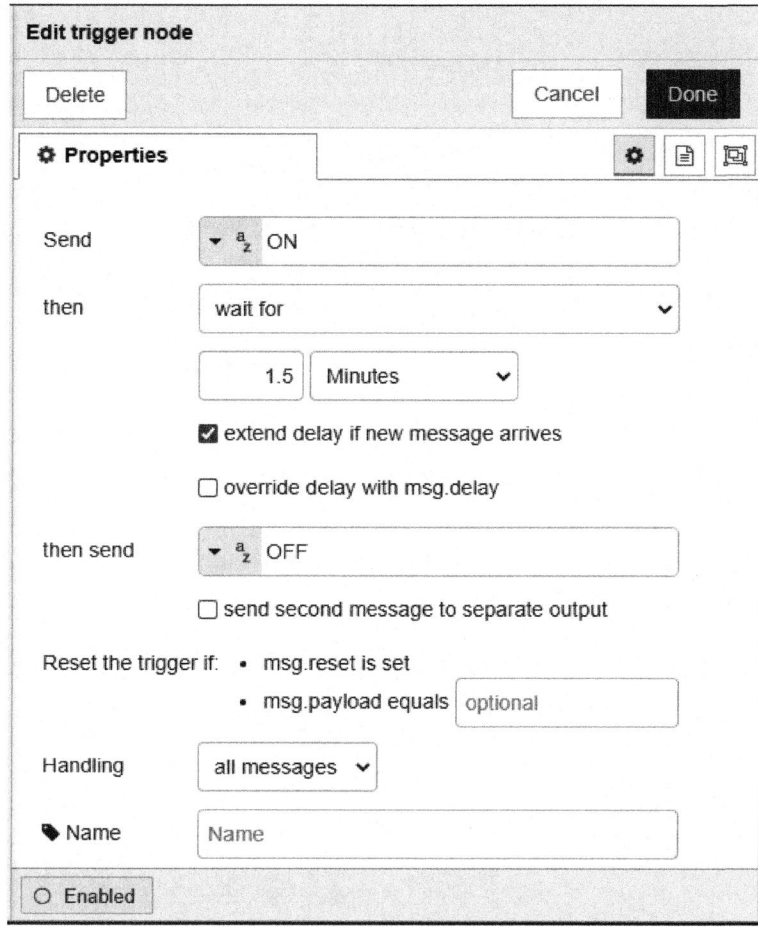

Figure 7.10 – The switch node configuration

Important configurations to be done in the trigger node are in the **Send** field, which is set as **ON**, and the **then** field, using the **wait for**, 1.5, and **Minutes** values. It is also important to configure the **then send** field using the **OFF** value. After all configurations are done according to *Figure 7.10*, make sure to click the **Done** button to save the trigger node configuration. We must link the **trigger** node input to the **switch** node output using the wires.

The last part of the automation created in Node-RED is to include a reference to our actuator installed in the garage. We will do that using the **mqtt out** node, found in the **network** group. *Figure 7.11* shows the **mqtt out** icon.

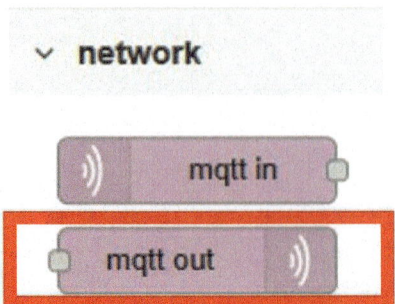

Figure 7.11 – The mqtt out node icon under the network group

Following the same process as the other nodes, drag and drop the **mqtt out** node into the workspace. Double-click on it to proceed with the configuration. Fill the following fields with data in the **edit mqtt out node** window:

- **server**: mqtt mosquito server or another name you choose for your MQTT server

- **Topic**: cmnd/GarageLights/POWER

Click on the **Done** button at the top right of the window and link the output of the trigger node to the input of the **mqtt out** node. We now have all nodes configured and linked. We should have the Node-RED flow now configured according to *Figure 7.12*.

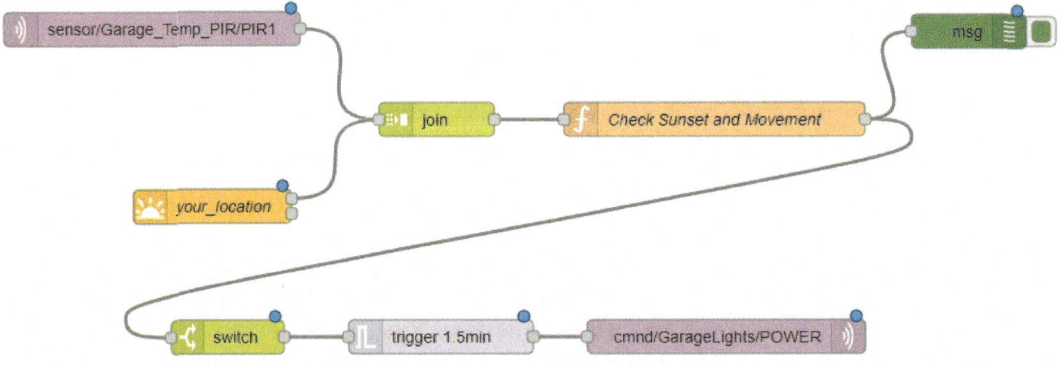

Figure 7.12 – The Node-RED flow for Automation 1

In *Figure 7.12*, I included a **debug** node named **msg**, located under the **common** group. It can be included in the output of any node to check the status of the messages. It is a useful tool when you create a flow using the nodes. This debug message's status is shown in the debug window on the Node-RED sidebar.

The next step after creating the flow with the nodes is to execute it. We will do that by clicking on the **Deploy** button at the top-right corner of the Node-RED window, as presented in *Figure 7.13*.

Figure 7.13 – The Node-RED Deploy button

After clicking on the **Deploy** button, it becomes disabled and the flow executes. You can see in *Figure 7.14* that the MQTT nodes are connected by showing the **connected** status below the node. The **sunrise** node also presents its status below the node representation. In this case, the status of sunrise indicates **night**, as represented in *Figure 7.14*.

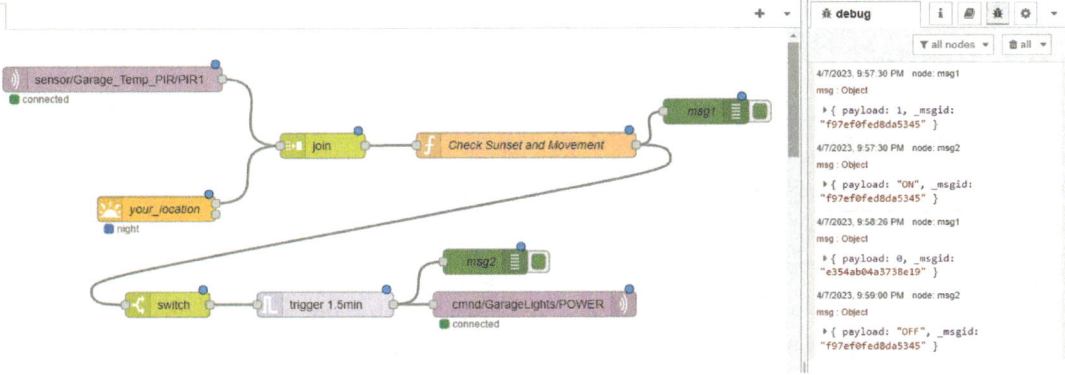

Figure 7.14 – Node-RED Automation 1 being executed

You can see in *Figure 7.14* that I included two nodes for debugging, one after the **function** node and another after **trigger**. You can include as many as you want to support the creation of your automations. In the sidebar on the right, you can see some debug messages that can present all the message parameters, supporting you to depurate the flow for correct execution.

> **Important note**
>
> I saved the code in *Figure 7.14* in the JSON format. It is available in the *Chapter 7* reference folder in GitHub. To import the script into your Node-RED installation, click on the main menu (in the top-right corner) and then the **Import** option. In the **Import nodes** window, select the `garage Motion at night.json` file, available in the book's GitHub repository, and then click on the **Import** button.

In general, you can create your own Node-RED-based home automations that read data from sensors using the **mqtt in** node, manipulating the data accordingly by validating the data conditions, using functions and other nodes available in the groups and performing actions by sending commands to the actuators using the **mqtt out** node. Another example of a home automation using Node-RED will be seen in *Chapter 10*.

You can see that Node-RED can handle multiple ways to manipulate data coming from sensors and send it to actuators. Numerous other nodes can be used to create execution flows. There are groups in the Node-RED palette that can be used to integrate information from Home Assistant, but as you can see in the example, none of the information or data from Home Assistant was used. Node-RED is a very powerful tool, used for IoT devices, and it can simplify some tasks in Home Automation that don't necessarily need a user interface. This concludes our section about Node-RED, and in the next section, we will learn about the use of database and chart tools using data from your home.

Using database and chart tools to present data from your home

In this section, I will present two other add-ons that can be installed using Home Assistant. These two add-ons, despite being installed at the top of Home Assistant, run independently of it as a separated application. These two add-ons will be introduced, but no examples will be provided for now. I will provide an example using these two add-ons and also Node-RED in *Chapter 10*, when we create a five-zone temperature logger for use in your home.

The first add-on we will introduce is one that stores data from your home in a database format. The data can be stored and retrieved later. The database add-on is called InfluxDB. The other add-on introduced in this section is called **Grafana**. This is used to create charts from data series. In the next two subsections, I will detail how to install InfluxDB and Grafana from Home Assistant.

Installing and creating databases using InfluxDB

InfluxDB is an open source database tool that can be used to collect, store, process, and visualize data. This data is called time-series data because it is indexed and ordered by time. Usually, the time series comes from a single data source where the same data pattern is sometimes presented.

A use case for applying influxDB to Home Automation could be, for example, to store data from an analog sensor, such as a temperature or energy consumption sensor. In the case of the five-zone temperature logger that will be presented in *Chapter 10*, an example of data stored by influxDB is presented in the following table:

```
time                             room_id    temperature value
----                             -------    ----------- -----
2022-12-11T21:20:30.498671239Z   backyard   19.8
2022-12-11T21:20:29.513091689Z   kid2room   22.1
2022-12-11T21:20:29.512643463Z   kid1room   22.8
2022-12-11T21:20:28.570822492Z   kitchen    22.3
```

```
2022-12-11T21:20:28.569671658Z Master    22.2
2022-12-11T21:18:39.911856251Z garage    23.5
2022-12-11T21:15:30.493028232Z backyard  19.8
2022-12-11T21:15:29.473516259Z kid1room  22.8
2022-12-11T21:15:29.473140748Z kid2room  22
```

The data in the table presented here is from an output command issued in the InfluxDB command line. Nine lines of data are presented, indexed by the column time. The table has three columns of data – `time`, `room_id`, and `temperature` values. Each table line in the InfluxDB database is called a **point**, and each set of data is called a **series**. In the example of the temperature table, the data is stored in the database each time one of the thermometers installed in one of the five locations in my home sends data. The table also stores the room ID, so I can index it later when presenting the data using Grafana.

InfluxDB uses **InfluxQL**, which is a SQL-like query language that you can use to interact with data created in InfluxDB. Another way to explore data using InfluxDB is by using **Flux**, which is a functional data scripting language designed to handle time-series data. InfluxQL and Flux are out of the scope of this book. For more information about Flux, visit `https://docs.influxdata.com/influxdb/v2.0/query-data/get-started/`.

InfluxDB is the core of the **TICK stack**, which includes three other pieces of software that support data manipulation and presentation. These software are **Telegraf**, **Chronograf**, and **Kapacitor**. Chronograf will be briefly explained after installing InfluxDB, while Telegraf and Kapacitor are out of the scope of this book.

To install InfluxDB, we will follow the standard using the **Settings | Add-ons** path from the Home Assistant sidebar. In the bottom-right corner of the screen, click on the **ADD-ON STORE** button. Continue the installation by following these steps:

1. On the **Add-On Store** screen, scroll down to **Home Assistant Community Add-ons** and look for **Node-RED**. Click on the **InfluxDB** button.

2. On the next screen, in the first rectangle titled **InfluxDB**, click on **INSTALL**.

    After one minute or so, InfluxDB will install.

3. Click on the **START** button in the first rectangle titled **InfluxDB**. InfluxDB will start.

4. Click on the **OPEN WEB UI** button. **Chronograf** will open inside Home Assistant, as shown in the screenshot presented in *Figure 7.15*.

←   InfluxDB

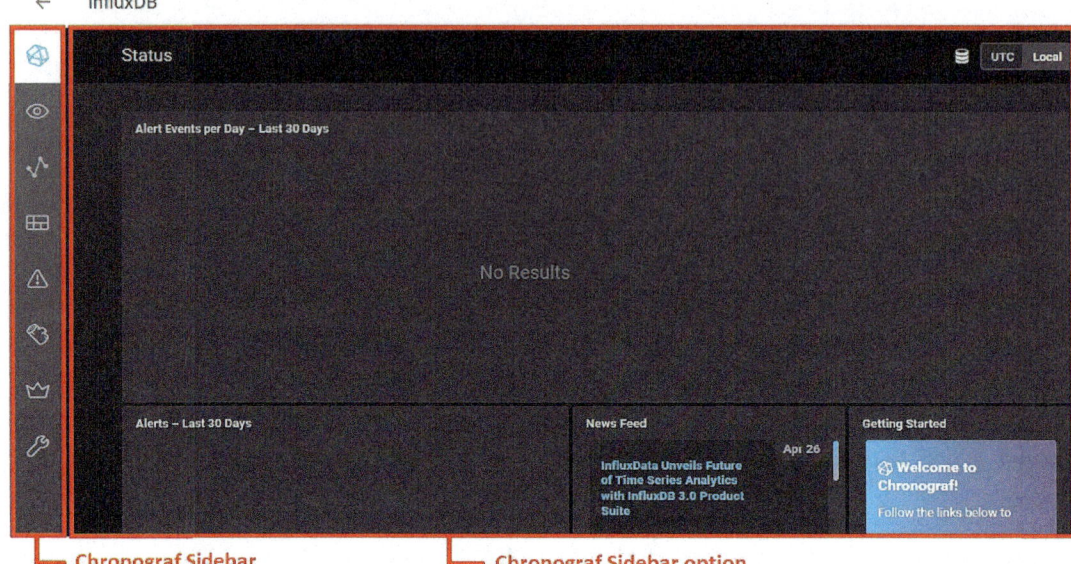

Figure 7.15 – Chronograf screen configuration

Chronograf, as presented in *Figure 7.15*, can handle all the three other software parts of the TICK stack, and its main function is to provide a user interface for InfluxDB data and the ability to create dashboards to monitor and present data, as Grafana does. By choosing one of the options in the Chronograf sidebar, the options will be presented in the space I called the **Chronograf Sidebar Option** in *Figure 7.15*.

For now, using Chronograf, what we will do is just create a temperature database where we will log the five-zone temperature data in *Chapter 10*. We will do this by clicking on the **crown** icon (the second icon from the bottom in the sidebar) and then the **+ Create Database** button. In the field that is shown, type Temperatures, and then click on the **check** button on the right to save and create the database.

In the next subsection, we will introduce Grafana, which is a versatile tool to present and monitor data.

Installing and presenting data using Grafana

Grafana is another open source add-on software that can be installed through Home Assistant. It is a powerful tool to monitor and present data. In contrast to Chronograf, Grafana can handle not just InfluxDB data sources but also many others, which makes it more versatile compared to Chronograf.

Let's move straight to the installation so that we can see what Grafana can do. We will need to use the **Settings** | **Add-ons** path from the Home Assistant sidebar to install Grafana. In the bottom-right corner of the screen, click on the **ADD-ON STORE** button. Follow the same process that we used with Node-RED and InfluxDB by choosing the Grafana button and then the **INSTALL** button. Click on the **Show in the Sidebar** slide button to enable Grafana to be presented in the sidebar. After the installation, click on the **START** button to start Grafana and then the **OPEN WEB UI** button to open the Grafana web interface, as presented in *Figure 7.16*.

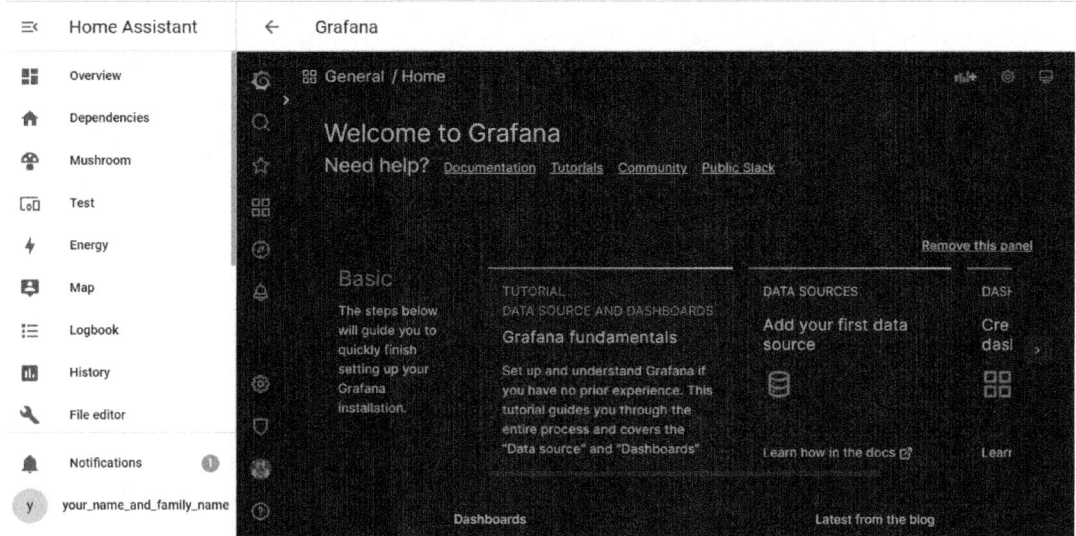

Figure 7.16 – The Grafana web interface

As you can see, the Grafana screen configuration presented in *Figure 7.16* has the same format as Chronograf, using a sidebar on the left and a sidebar option on the right.

Grafana utilization is simple, and you will need two configurations. The first configuration is the data source. You will need to configure the data source so that Grafana knows where to pull the data from. You can set the data source by clicking on the **configuration gear** icon in the sidebar and then using the **Data Sources** tab. Click on the **Add data source** button to see what types of databases can be added. Click on the **InfluxDB** option to see what can be configured. Fill the **URL** field with the value `http://homeassistant.local:8086`, which is the URL address where InfluxDB can be accessed. If we want to pull data from the database we created in the last subsection, we will have to fill the **Database** field with the value `Temperatures`. You can leave all the other fields with their default values. Click on the **Save & Test** button.

The second configuration to do with Grafana is creating a **dashboard**. Hover the mouse on the **Dashboard** icon (the fourth option from the top of the sidebar) and click on the **+ New dashboard** option. On the new screen, click on the **Add a new panel** option. The screen shown in *Figure 7.17* will appear.

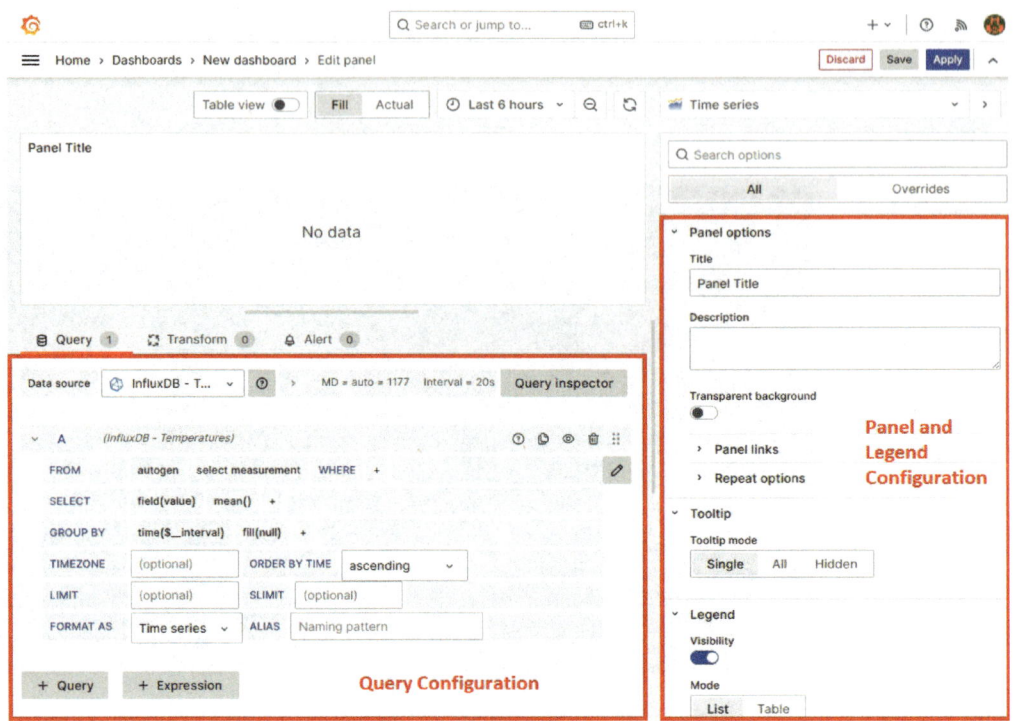

Figure 7.17 – The Grafana Edit Panel screen

If your database source is populated with data from *Chapter 10*, you can perform a query in the database by using the query configuration presented in *Figure 7.17*. In the panel options shown in *Figure 7.17* on the right, you can include basic configurations such as the panel title and legend. To give an idea of how data can be presented using Grafana, *Figure 7.18* shows one of the charts obtained from the `Temperatures` database.

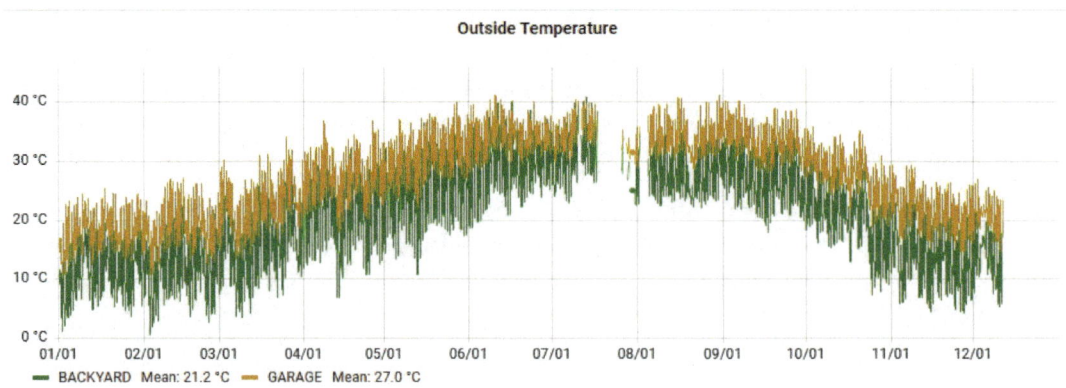

Figure 7.18 – A Grafana chart example

The chart presented in *Figure 7.18* shows two outside temperatures in my house during the year 2022. One temperature is in the garage, and the other is in my backyard. Using this chart, I can extract several types of information. I can see, for example, when my router was damaged; I was traveling with my family in July, so I could not log the temperatures during this time (note that between **07/01** and **08/01**, no data is displayed). Another significant piece of information is the maximum and minimum temperatures achieved in my backyard in 2022. I can see values in the range of **0** to **40** degrees Celsius.

As commented several times in this subsection, we will explore Grafana more thoroughly in *Chapter 10*. For now, just know that this powerful tool can support you to present data from sensors and other sources of information you have in your home. In the next section, we will comment on another add-on, which is especially useful to manage **Tasmota devices**.

Managing your network of Tasmota devices using TasmoAdmin

If you plan to use Tasmota on many devices in your home as I do, the add-on that I will present in this section might be useful to you. It is called **TasmoAdmin**. This is used to manage devices such as sensors and actuators installed with Tamosta. It scans your network to find Tamosta devices, allowing you to see their status, configure them, and even send firmware updates over the air to one or more devices at once. TasmoAdmin is very handy for me when I need to configure something in particular on a Tamosta device and do not know the IP address it is configured for. It scans and finds the Tasmota device IP for me.

We will install TasmoAdmin with the same procedure used to install other add-ons. I will not repeat the installation procedure; instead, I invite you to try to follow the process presented in the previous sections to install the other add-ons. It starts the same way – looking for **Settings | Add-ons**.

After the installation and initialization, before clicking on the **OPEN WEB UI** button, you must click the **Configuration** tab, disable the **SSL** option, and click on **Save**. Click on the **OPEN WEB UI** button, and a login screen will be presented. Enter a username and password, and then click on the **Register** button. For the educational purposes of this book, we will use `your_name_and_family_name` as the username and `your_password` as the password.

On first login, the **Start** screen will not present any devices, so you will have to scan your network to find them. Click on the **AutoScan** button to do so. The **AutoScan** screen will fill the **From IP** field with `192.168.0.2`, and the **To IP** field will include the IP `192.168.0.255`. Leave the other fields with their default values. Click on the **Start AutoScan** button to search for the devices. After some seconds, the devices found in your network will appear, including the device IP and configured name. Click on the **Save All** button at the bottom of the screen.

If you click on **Devices** at the top left of the screen after you add them, you will find the following options:

- **List**: Allows you to list all devices in your network

- **Update**: Allows you to update the Tasmota firmware of your devices

- **Backup**: Allows you to back up your Tasmota devices individually, in a group, or all at the same time

- **AutoScan**: The option we just used to scan your network to seek devices

As an example, if you click on the **List** option, the screen shown in *Figure 7.19* will appear.

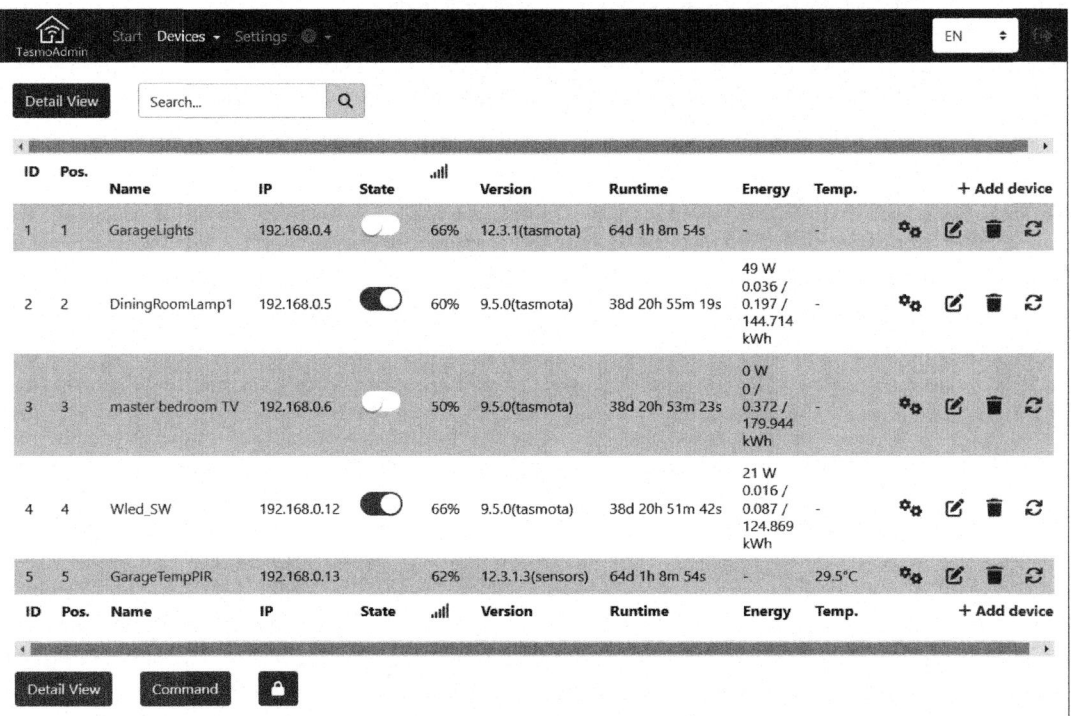

Figure 7.19 – The TasmoAdmin List option

Figure 7.19 lists five of my devices currently activated. I can see a lot of information such as IP addresses, state, Wi-Fi signal strengths, Tasmota firmware versions, runtime, and even specific information, such as energy consumption for some actuators and temperature information for the **GarageTempPIR** sensor created in *Chapter 3*. In the icons presented on the right of *Figure 7.19*, I can configure parameters from the devices using the TasmoAdmin interface, edit some basic device parameters, delete the device from the TasmoAdmin management list, or restart the device. I can also get more detailed information about the Tasmota devices, such as hostnames and Mac addresses, by clicking on the **Detail View** button. Clicking on the **Command** button, you can send a command to specific devices or all of them at the same time.

TasmoAdmin is another add-on that can be used without any interaction with Home Assistant. TasmoAdmin is even more independent, since it runs in a separate web browser window.

After this brief overview of TasmoAdmin, we will present in the next section another add-on that is more integrated into Home Assistant and will be useful if you want to access Home Assistant when you are not at home.

Accessing Home Assistant remotely

The add-on in this section will allow you to access Home Assistant remotely using an external domain. The add-on used to do so is Duck DNS. **Duck DNS** (which stands for **Duck Domain Name System**) is a free dynamic DNS service that allows users to assign a custom domain name to their home network or any device with a changing IP address. It provides a way to access devices and services on your home network, even if your internet service provider assigns you a dynamic IP address that changes periodically. In other words, Duck DNS will allow you to use Home Assistant even if you are away from your home.

The first step to use this add-on is to create a Duck DNS account. To do that, we will need to follow these steps:

1. Go to `https://www.duckdns.org/` and create an account using your preferred credential method. There are currently five credential methods available, including Google and GitHub. I will use my GitHub account.

2. After authorizing Duck DNS to have access to your account, Duck DNS will give you the option to create an internet subdomain in the format of `http://your_domain.duckdns.org`. Type the subdomain you want to create for your home. For educational purposes, I created the domain `homeassistantbook` for this example. If the domain is available, the screen in *Figure 7.20* will be presented.

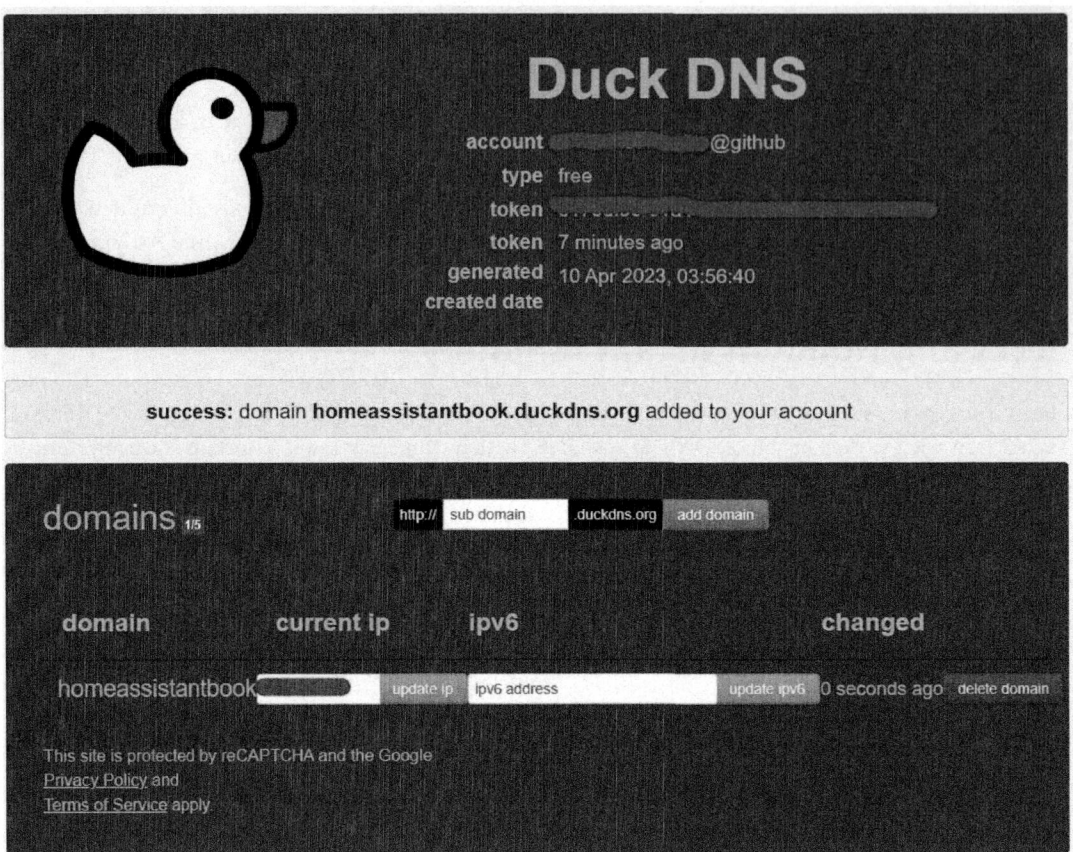

Figure 7.20 – The Duck DNS domain creation screen

Note that I omitted some information in *Figure 7.20* for security reasons.

The next step in the process is to install and configure the Duck DNS add-on in Home Assistant. We will do that by following these steps:

1. Start from the Home Assistant sidebar and use the **Settings | Add-ons** path. Click on the **ADD-ON STORE** button, and on the **Add-On Store** screen, go to the official add-ons and look for **Duck DNS**. Click on the **Duck DNS** button.

2. On the next screen, in the first rectangle titled **Duck DNS**, click on **INSTALL**.

    After one minute or so, Duck DNS will install.

3. Click on the **Configuration** tab and fill in the following fields:

    *   **Domains**: your_domain.duckdns.org

- **Token**: This is token information provided when a domain was configured (the parameter is omitted in *Figure 7.20*)

- **Let's Encrypt**: `Accept_terms: true`

4. Click on the **SAVE** button.

5. Go to the **Info** tab and click on the **START** button.

6. Go to the **Log** tab, and make sure you get the final initialization messages as follows:

   ...

   + Checking certificate...

   + Done!

   + Creating fullchain.pem...

   + Done!

Now, we will have to make the IP of Home Assistant static and include external access. We will do that by following these steps:

1. From the Home Assistant sidebar, go to **Settings | System | Network**. In the **Configure network interfaces** box, click on the **IPv4** option on the **WLAN0** tab.

2. Mark the **Static** radio box option, and take note of the current IP address in the **IP address/Netmask** field.

3. In the **Home Assistant URL** box, the **Internet** field includes the domain created using Duck DNS. Click on the **SAVE** button.

The next configuration to be made will be in your router. You will need to find where to configure a **virtual server** or **port forwarding**. In my case, I have an **Arris 7400** router and found this configuration under the **Firewall** tab. Configure the router parameters as follows:

- **Description**: Any thing you want. I will use `Home Assistant`.

- **Inbound Port**: `443`.

- **Type**: `TCP`.

- **Private IP Address**: The static IP address of your Home Assistant installation (which we got in *step 2* of the previous steps).

- **Local Port**: `8123`.

> **Important note**
>
> If you want to continue accessing your home using the address `http://homeassistant.local:8123/`, you need to add another configuration in your router, as shown previously, by changing the **inbound port** to `8123`. Unfortunately, my router doesn't support two different configurations pointing to the same IP address and local port, so by doing this configuration, I lost the ability to access Home Assistant using the standard address.

The last configuration to be made is in the `configuration.yaml` file. Open File editor, add the following lines to the `configuration.yaml` file, and then save the file:

```
http:

  ssl_certificate: /ssl/fullchain.pem

  ssl_key: /ssl/privkey.pem
```

Restart Home Assistant by using **Developer Tools | YAML**. In the **Check and Restart** box, click on the **RESTART** button. If everything goes well, you should now be able to access your Home Assistant remotely using the domain created in Duck DNS.

We can now finish the installation and configuration for Duck DNS and finish the content of this chapter.

As you can see, Home Assistant functionalities can be extended using add-ons. Some of these features are integrated into Home Assistant while others do not have any relationship with it.

Summary

In this chapter, we learned what add-ons are and how they can be used to support the automation of your home. You know understand more about the installation and utilization of the main add-ons that I use in my home.

We learned about Node-RED, a new tool to create automations. InfluxDB and Grafana were discussed, and examples were given so that you could verify how data is stored and monitored using these two tools.

A very important tool to manage your Tasmota devices was introduced, TasmoAdmin, and you saw what it can do.

Finally, we enabled Home Assistant to be accessed remotely by using the Duck DNS add-on.

This chapter gave you an overview of the add-ons available and introduced you to new tools and software so that you can go beyond what Home Assistant offers.

In the next chapter, we will explore another type of Home Assistant installation, showing you additional ways to use more resources of your hardware and software besides using Home Assistant.

8
Installing and Setting Up Home Assistant Container

We will try another Home Assistant installation approach in this chapter. We will first learn how to create backups of Home Assistant installations. We will then learn how to back up and keep the data and information for the work done until now safe before we go ahead and learn how to do a new type of installation.

The chapter will provide instructions on how to use **IOTstack**, which will allow you to understand how to handle a new type of installation for Home Assistant: **Home Assistant Container**. The pros and cons of this type of installation will be presented and evaluated. The IOTstack software architecture will be explained and details about how to run each software application will be provided.

By the end of this chapter, you will be able to create and restore backups of your Home Assistant installation. You will also know how to set up automation to create backups automatically for you. The main content of the chapter will teach you how to handle a new installation type for Home Assistant and add-ons using a container approach so you can use it with the Raspberry Pi **Operating System (OS)**.

We will cover all of this in the following sections in this chapter:

- Creating backups in Home Assistant
- Understanding the architecture of the IOTstack
- Installation of the IOTstack
- Configuring the IOTstack
- Running and managing the applications in IOTstack

Technical requirements

You will make faster progress through this chapter if you are familiar with the concept of Docker containers. Also, if you have read the previous chapter about add-ons, you will be able to better understand some of the software installed with IOTstack. If you are used to using Linux or Raspberry Pi OS commands, you will easily be able to manage the configuration of IOTstack. The resource information needed for this chapter is located at `https://github.com/PacktPublishing/Building-Smart-Home-Automation-Solutions-with-Home-Assistant/tree/main/Chapter%2008`.

Creating backups in Home Assistant

By this point, since we started creating our Home Automation system in *Chapter 2*, a lot of configuration, setup, and customizations have been made to Home Assistant. You never know when things can go wrong, so it is best to be safe and back up your system regularly so you don't lose the work done up to this point, as well as saving future changes we make to the system. In this section, we will cover how you can manually create Home Assistant backups, how to retrieve them, and how you can automate backup creation.

Creating and retrieving manual backups using Home Assistant

You can create and retrieve backups manually using a Home Assistant built-in backup tool. Follow these steps:

1. From the sidebar, go to **Settings | System | Backups**. Click on the + **CREATE BACKUP** button on the bottom right.

2. The pop-up window shown in *Figure 8.1* will be presented. Include a backup name in the **Backup name** field. Choose the option you need for backup (**Full backup** or **Partial backup**) and click **CREATE**. We have filled in the information shown in *Figure 8.1*.

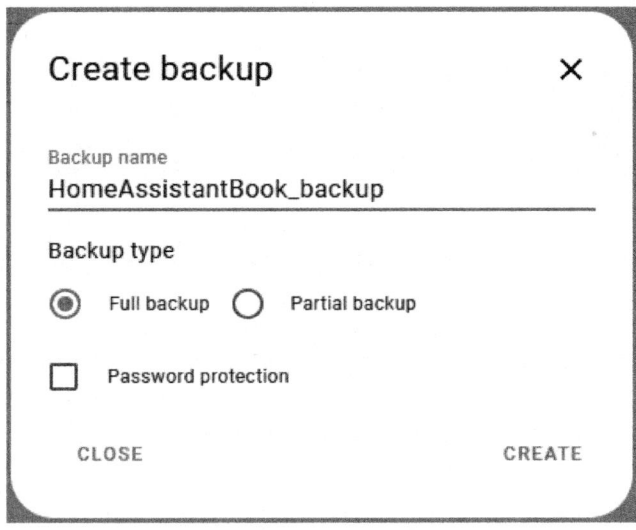

Figure 8.1 – Backup creation screen in Home Assistant

3. The backup process will start and a backup will be created. At the end of the backup creation process, the backup name you chose will be listed in the backup table.

The backups are stored in the /backup folder. The difference between **Full backup** and **Partial backup** is that **Full backup** will back up all Home Assistant folders, including add-ons, while in **Partial backup**, you can choose what folders you want to back up.

Now that you have a backup of your system, if something goes wrong, you can retrieve the data from the previous backup done using Home Assistant by following these steps:

1. From the sidebar, follow the same path as before, **Settings | System | Backups**. In the backup list, click on the backup you want to retrieve.

2. A pop-up window will be presented indicating the backup name as the window title. In the case of this example, the HomeAssistantBook_backup backup name will be presented. Choose **Full backup** and click **RESTORE**.

3. A pop-up window will be presented asking whether you want to wipe your system and restore the backup. Click **RESTORE** if you want to proceed. We will not proceed at this point; instead, click **CANCEL**.

If there is a problem, for example, you lose your SD card or your system is damaged or corrupted, so you can't access the Home Assistant installation anymore, you will need to carry out some extra configuration to access your backup outside the Home Assistant installation. One of the ways you can retrieve data is by using the **Samba share** add-on, which looks as in *Figure 8.2*.

Figure 8.2 – Samba share installation icon

You can install Samba share by following the same procedure as for the majority of the add-ons installed in *Chapter 7*. You will need to configure a password in the **Configuration** tab before starting the Samba share add-on. After starting the application, if you are using a Windows OS like me, you can follow these steps to access the Home Assistant folders and copy the backup files to your computer:

1. Go to **Windows File Explorer** by typing `File Explorer` in the search area (the magnifier icon) or double-clicking on the File Explorer icon (the yellow folder icon).

2. After File Explorer is opened, click in the folder access area and type the Home Assistant IP address in the format `\\ip address`. In my case, my Raspberry Pi has the IP `192.168.0.32`, so I have to type `\\192.168.0.32` and press *Enter*. Refer to the following important note about how to find the local IP address of your installation.

    You will have access to the files presented in *Figure 8.3*.

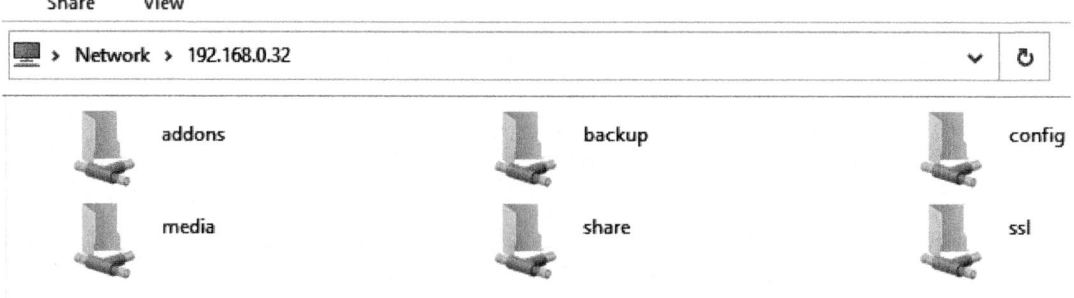

Figure 8.3 – Home Assistant files accessed using Windows OS

3. You can now copy the files in the `backup` folder, shown in *Figure 8.3*, to your computer. They are now safely stored and can be retrieved in the case of a catastrophic installation failure.

> **Important note**
>
> Home Assistant has an integration which will allow you to have access to the local IP assigned to your installation. The name of this integration is **Local IP Address** and you can install it using the default method for integration installation, that is, by going to **Settings | Devices & Services | + ADD INTEGRATION** and looking for **Local IP Address**. Follow the basic instructions on the screen and the integration will be installed. After the integration installation, double-click on the **1 ENTITY** link, and then in the **Entities** tab, click on the **Local IP** so you will see the local IP address of your installation.

The files in the `backup` folder are compacted files in the `.tar` format. The only detail you need to be aware of in the compacted file is the **Date modified** property so you know when the backup was created, helping you to manage what files you want to restore. Talking about restoration, if you copy the backup files from your computer's operating system back to Home Assistant `backup` folder, Home Assistant will automatically index the file and present details about the backup when you access **Settings | Systems | Backups**. Both Windows and Home Assistant backup representations are captured in *Figure 8.4*.

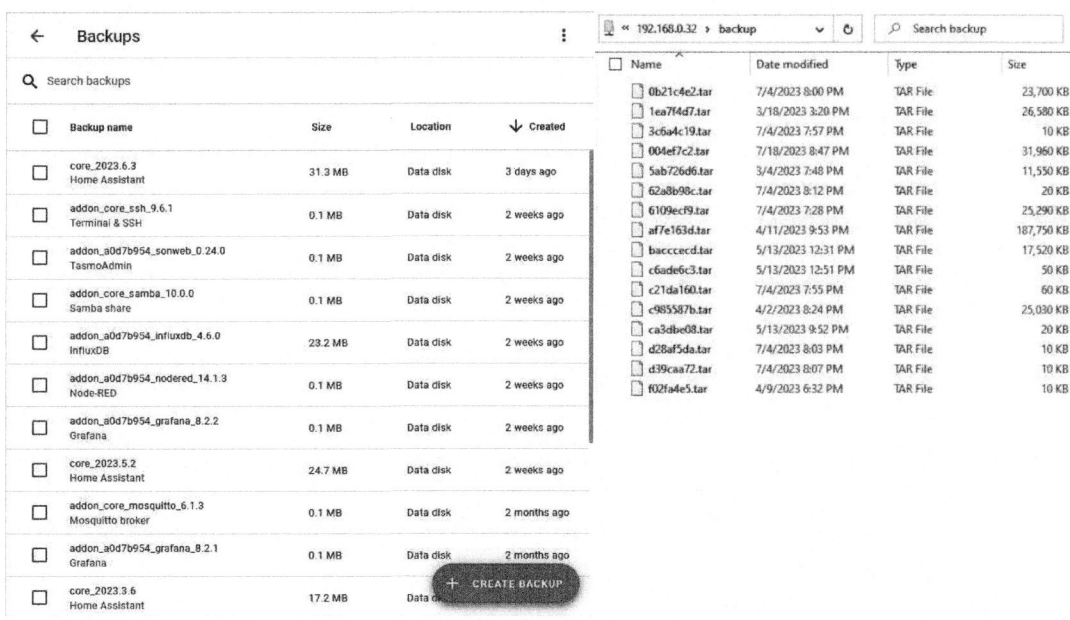

Figure 8.4 – Backup files in Windows and Home Assistant representation

On the left of *Figure 8.4*, you will see the backup files created by Home Assistant and presented in Windows File Explorer. As mentioned, they are compacted TAR files and named with eight hexadecimal characters. You can see other properties information on the Windows File Explorer screen, such as **Date modified** and **Size**. On the right of *Figure 8.4* is the Home Assistant backup representation, where you can see the same content as the Windows File Explorer but now, the **Backup name** column is clear, adding what is included in the backup and the version of some Home Assistant installation or add-ons. It is worth commenting that when you update the installation of Home Assistant or add-ons, you can choose the option to create a backup of the installation before installing the new one. So, you can see some backups on the right of *Figure 8.4*, for example, `addon_core_ssh_9.6.1`, which were created using this option during the installation update.

It is a best practice to keep regular full backups of your Home Assistant on your computer or in the cloud. In the case of a crash of your Home Assistant system, I recommend you start a new Home Assistant installation from scratch following the procedure described in *Chapter 2*, in the *Installing Home Assistant in Raspberry Pi* section. Follow the process up to *Figure 2.7*, where you will find the **Alternatively you can restore from a previous backup** option below the **CREATE ACCOUNT** button. Click on it and follow the process to restore your system installation.

If you don't want to save your Home Assistant backup on your computer, there are several add-ons available to save your backup in the cloud. Here are some options:

- **Google Drive backup**: `https://github.com/sabeechen/hassio-google-drive-backup`
- **Dropbox sync**: `https://github.com/danielwelch/hassio-dropbox-sync`
- **OneDrive backup**: `https://github.com/lavinir/hassio-onedrive-backup`
- **Nextcloud backup**: `https://github.com/Sebclem/hassio-nextcloud-backup`
- **Remote Backup**: `https://github.com/ikifar2012/remote-backup-addon`
- **Samba backup**: `https://github.com/thomasmauerer/hassio-addons/tree/master/samba-backup`
- **Syncthing**: `https://github.com/Poeschl/Hassio-Addons/tree/main/syncthing`

Now that you have learned how to create and retrieve backups, we will see in the next subsection how quickly you can create an automation to back up your system every day.

Creating an automation to back up your system

We will create an automation to automatically back up your system. We will need to use the **Home Assistant Supervisor: Create a full backup** service to do a full backup of the system. The automation will have just a trigger and an action. You will need to follow these steps to create the automation:

1. From the sidebar, go to **Settings | Automation**.
2. Click **Create Automation** and choose **Start with an empty automation**.

3. Click +**Add Trigger** and choose **Time**. Enter the time you would like to do the backup in the format **HH:MM:SS**.

4. Click +**Add Action** and choose **Call a service**.

5. In **Service**, search for the **Home Assistant Supervisor: Create a full backup** option.

6. Click on the **SAVE** button.

Using these backup options, we will be safe in case some unexpected happens. We are now ready to move on to the next section, where we will learn about a new installation type we can use with Home Assistant.

Understanding the architecture of IOTstack

In *Chapter 2*, we mentioned ways to install Home Assistant. We were using the Home Assistant OS, which is the most common one in use. Another type of installation used by Home Assistant is the **Home Assistant Container**. A **Container** is a lightweight and standalone package that contains what is needed to run an application, including code, libraries, dependencies, and system tools. **Docker** (https://www.docker.com/) is an open source platform that allows developers to build, ship, and run applications in containers. Docker provides a way to manage containers using **Docker Compose** (https://github.com/docker/compose), which is a tool for defining, managing, and running multi-container Docker applications.

In this section, and until the end of this chapter, we will explore the Home Assistant Container installation using Docker Compose. This type of installation was the first one I tried and was how I discovered how to use Home Assistant and other IoT software. The main advantage of Home Assistant Container installation, in my view, is that you can continue to use your Raspberry Pi with the Raspberry Pi OS (formerly Raspian) installed. In other words, you have more flexibility to use your Raspberry Pi with other software and not just the ones you are limited to with Home Assistant OS.

The disadvantage of the Docker installation approach is that you will need to do more work to maintain the software stack and the containers since they will not be updated using the software. You will have to update the containers to update the software applications inside them.

We will be using a pre-formatted configuration tool with some scripts, including Docker Compose, for the Home Assistant Container installation, which will allow us to run not only Home Assistant but also the other add-ons we saw in *Chapter 7*. This installation tool is called **IOTstack** and is located at https://github.com/SensorsIot/IOTstack. IOTstack was originally created by *Graham Garner* and later forked in GitHub. It is currently maintained by *Andreas Spiess*. At the time of writing this chapter, IOTstack supports more than 50 different types of software, which can be installed in containers. IOTstack has the architecture represented in *Figure 8.5*.

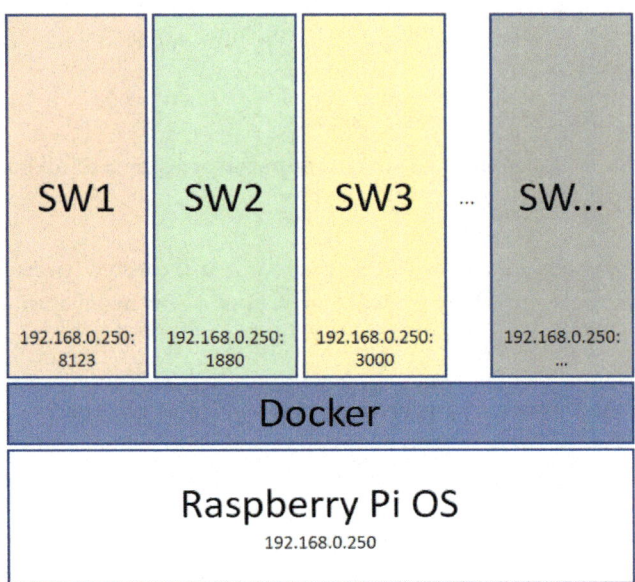

Figure 8.5 – IOTstack architecture

From the bottom of *Figure 8.5* to the top, we will find the first level of IOTstack, which is the Raspberry Pi OS. This is the standard Raspberry Pi OS, which has to be installed in your Raspberry Pi prior to any other installation. This OS must have a fixed IP to make references to it and other software later installed using IOTstack.

On top of the Raspberry OS, we will find the Docker platform. Docker Compose runs as part of Docker and is the tool to be used for defining and running multi-container Docker software applications.

The software applications are represented by SW1-SW... in *Figure 8.5* and refer to Home Assistant, Home Assistant add-ons, and many other IoT software that can be used with Raspberry Pi. These software applications are packaged in containers that are isolated from each other. Most software applications are accessed using the fixed IP from Raspberry Pi OS and a specific port.

After this brief explanation of the IOTstack architecture, we will see in the next section how to install it.

Installation of IOTstack

In this section, we will cover how to install IOTstack. As mentioned in the last section, IOTstack runs on Raspberry Pi OS. So, you have to install the Raspberry Pi OS prior to installing IOTstack. I will not explain how to install the Raspberry Pi OS since it is very well covered on the internet; you can find installation instructions by visiting this link: https://www.raspberrypi.com/software. You have to do some basic configuration to use the system, such as setting up your cable or wireless network. The next procedure will assume you have internet access in your Raspberry Pi.

If you already have the Raspberry Pi OS installed, you will need to make sure you have the latest software version. You can do that by running the following commands on the Raspberry Pi terminal console:

1. Update the list of repository packages using the **Advance Package Tool** (**APT**) command:

```
sudo apt update
```

2. When the preceding command is done, run the update command to get the latest software packages:

```
sudo apt dist-upgrade
```

3. Follow the instructions and wait for Raspberry Pi to update. When it is done, issue the command to remove unnecessary package files:

```
sudo apt clean
```

4. Reboot the system by using the following:

```
sudo reboot
```

After making sure you have the Raspberry OS up and running with the latest version, follow these steps to install IOTstack:

1. Install the `curl` command-line tool using the following command:

```
sudo apt install -y curl
```

2. Run the following command to install IOTstack:

```
curl -fsSL https://raw.githubusercontent.com/SensorsIot/
IOTstack/master/install.sh | bash
```

3. If you are prompted to install any software, install it by choosing the <**Yes**> option. Reboot the system using the following:

```
sudo reboot
```

4. Wait for it to reboot and run the `menu` shell script command to choose the software to be installed:

```
cd ~/IOTstack
./menu.sh
```

The menu in *Figure 8.6* will be presented:

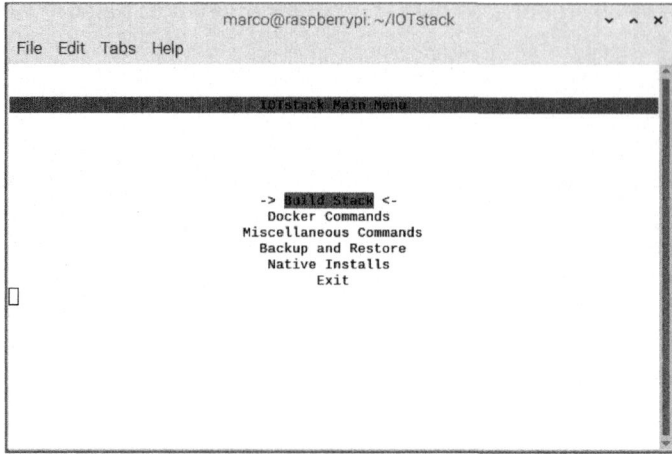

Figure 8.6 – IOTstack main menu

5.   Choose the first option highlighted in *Figure 8.6*, -> **Build Stack** <-, and press *Enter*. On the other screen, titled **Select containers to build,** for the educational purposes of this book, select at least the following software using the keyboard space bar key and the other controls detailed in *Figure 8.7*: **duckdns**, **grafana**, **home_assistant**, **influxdb**, **mosquitto**, **node-red**, **portainer-ce**, and **tasmoadmin**.

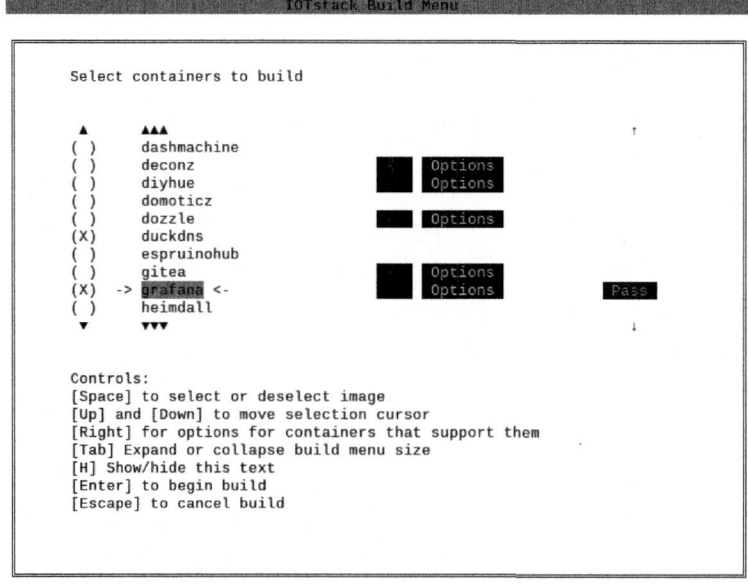

Figure 8.7 – Selecting containers to build

6. Make sure, when choosing **node-red**, to press the right arrow key and select -> **Select & build addons list** <- by pressing *Enter*. Choose the default options on the **Select NodeRed Addons (npm) to install on initial run** screen, as shown in *Figure 8.8*, and press *Enter*.

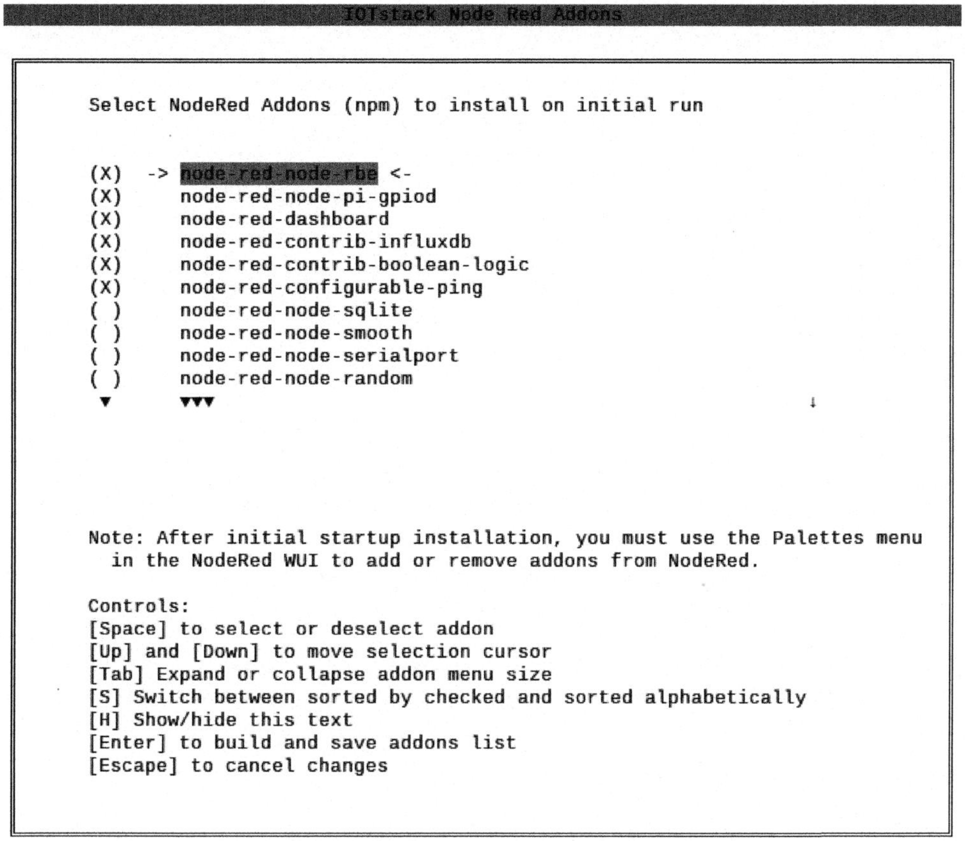

```
                          IOTstack Node Red Addons


        Select NodeRed Addons (npm) to install on initial run


        (X)    ->  node-red-node-rbe <-
        (X)        node-red-node-pi-gpiod
        (X)        node-red-dashboard
        (X)        node-red-contrib-influxdb
        (X)        node-red-contrib-boolean-logic
        (X)        node-red-configurable-ping
        ( )        node-red-node-sqlite
        ( )        node-red-node-smooth
        ( )        node-red-node-serialport
        ( )        node-red-node-random
         ▼        ▼▼▼                                              ↓




        Note: After initial startup installation, you must use the Palettes menu
          in the NodeRed WUI to add or remove addons from NodeRed.

        Controls:
        [Space] to select or deselect addon
        [Up] and [Down] to move selection cursor
        [Tab] Expand or collapse addon menu size
        [S] Switch between sorted by checked and sorted alphabetically
        [H] Show/hide this text
        [Enter] to build and save addons list
        [Escape] to cancel changes
```

Figure 8.8 – Selecting node-red add-ons

7. Exit the IOTstack main menu by choosing the **Exit** option and pressing *Enter*.

8. Put docker-compose to work by using the following command:

```
cd ~/IOTstack
docker-compose up -d
```

After this last command, all container installations will be downloaded. If everything goes well, you will not receive an error and the cursor prompt will return to the command-line terminal interface. The `docker ps` command will return the status of all containers and will return information as in *Figure 8.9*.

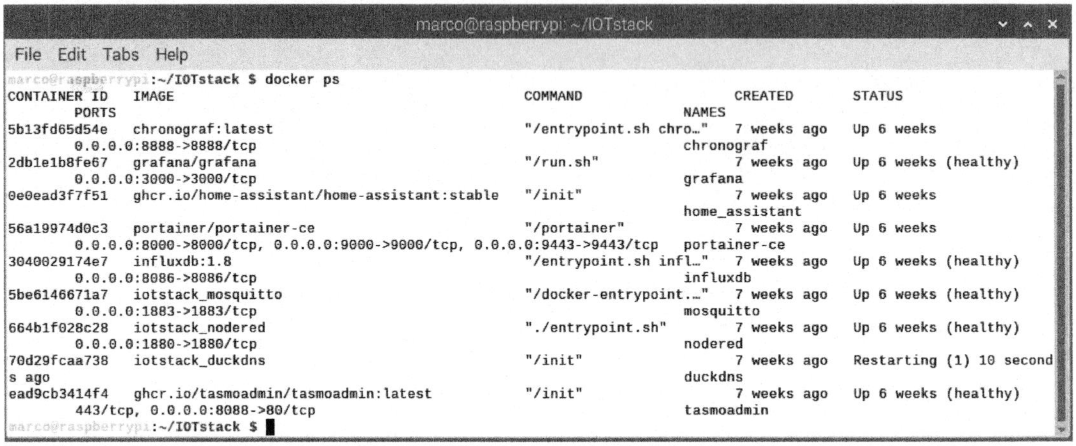

Figure 8.9 – Checking the container installation status

You can see in *Figure 8.9* that the last STATUS column lists all the containers, except duckdns, indicated as Up. The STATUS Up means the containers are ready to be configured and used.

Now that we have all of our containers installed, we will proceed to the next section, which will inform you of how to configure some parameters to properly run the software applications inthe containers.

Configuring the IOTstack

We will have to do some configurations to put IOTstack to work as a Home Automation Stack. The following configurations will be required:

- Raspberry Pi static IP configuration
- Accessing and configuring the container software applications
- MQTT server configuration in Tasmota devices
- Configuring Home Assistant in IOTstack

We will discuss each of them in the next subsections.

Raspberry Pi static IP configuration

The first configuration we will have to do to run the Home Automation Stack properly is to set up a static IP in Raspberry Pi. We will see that making the IP static on Raspberry Pi will help with accessing the software applications and also configuring the MQTT server address for sensors and actuators. To configure the static IP, you have to execute the following steps:

1. Open a terminal console in your Raspberry Pi and find the IP address of your router by using the following command and hitting *Enter*:

   ```
   ip r | grep default | awk '{print $3}'
   ```

2. Take note of the IP address that is returned. This will be your router's IP address. In my home, my default router's IP address is 192.168.0.1.

3. Next, we will make the IP static on Raspberry Pi. Right-click on the wireless network standard symbol on the top right of the screen, indicated in *Figure 8.10*, and select **Wireless & Wired Network Settings…**. On the screen that opens, in the first dropbox, click on **Interface**, and in the other dropbox, select **wlan0** if you are using a wireless network and **eth0** if you are using a cable network.

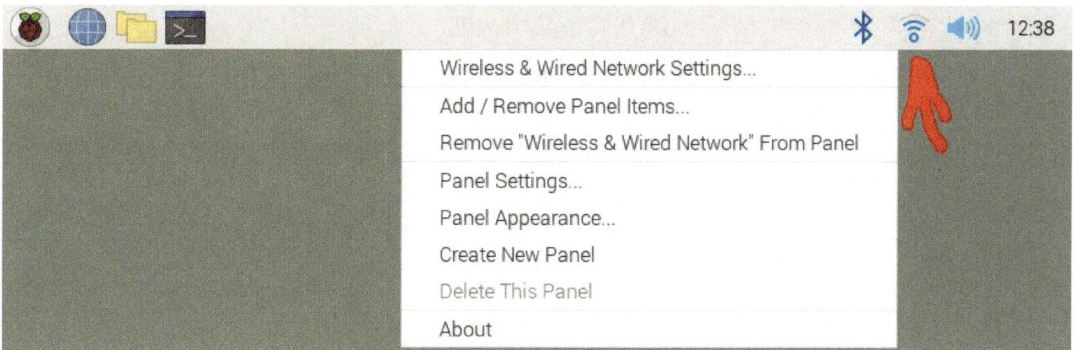

Figure 8.10 – Changing wireless configuration on Raspberry Pi

4. Fill in the **IPv4 Address** field with the static IP address you want for your Raspberry Pi. The IP address chosen should be the first three sets of numbers of your router IP address and the last number set should be a number different from your router's last number set and up to the number 255. In my home, I chose the last number set of the IP address to be 250, so my Raspberry Pi static IP is **192.168.0.250**. In the end, the fields that have to be filled are as shown in *Figure 8.11*:

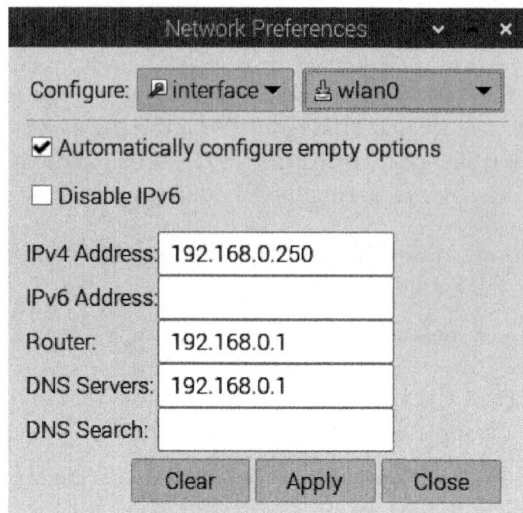

Figure 8.11 – Raspberry Pi static IP configuration

5. The **DNS Servers** field configuration in *Figure 8.11* is typically configured as the same IP address as the router. Once done, click on the **Apply** button.

6. Reboot your Raspberry Pi by opening a terminal window and running the sudo reboot command.

7. After the reboot, check whether the configuration was done properly by opening a terminal console and issuing the following command:

```
hostname -I | awk '{print $1}'
```

The static IP configured will be returned. In the case of this book's example, the IP returned is 192.168.0.250.

In the next subsection, we will see how to access and configure the software application containers.

Accessing and configuring the container software applications

After configuring the static IP for Raspberry Pi, we will see how we can access and configure the container software applications.

The docker-compose creates a YAML file where you can evaluate how each container is configured. This file is called docker-compose.yml and can be accessed by using the following commands:

```
cd ~/IOTstack
cat docker-compose.yml
```

You will see that after the word `Services` in the `docker-compose.yml` file, each container name will be listed with its properties. As an example, you can see the `tasmoadmin` configuration is as follows:

```
tasmoadmin:
    container_name: tasmoadmin
    image: ghcr.io/tasmoadmin/tasmoadmin:latest
    restart: unless-stopped
    environment:
    - TZ=Etc/UTC
    ports:
    - "8088:80"
    volumes:
    - ./volumes/tasmoadmin/data:/data
```

The important parameters in each configuration are `ports` and `volumes`. `ports` lists what ports should be used after the Raspberry Pi static IP address is configured in the last section to access the application. Therefore, to access the application in the containers, you should use the following combination:

`Static IP address:Application Port`

In the case of `tasmoadmin`, for example, you can access the application by typing `192.168.0.250:8088` in your web browser. All the other software will have their ports configured according to *Table 8.1*.

Application Name	Port	Accessible Using Web Browser?	IP Address and Port to Access Web Browser Application
Duck DNS	1000	No	-
Grafana	3000	Yes	192.168.0.250:3000
Home Assistant	8123	Yes	192.168.0.250:8123
Influxdb	8086	No	-
Mosquitto	1883	No	-
Node-RED	1880	Yes	192.168.0.250:1880
Portainer-CE	9000	Yes	192.168.0.250:9000
TasmoAdmin	8088	Yes	192.168.0.250:8088

Table 8.1 – Ports used by each IOTstack container software application

The other important information is that the `volumes:` are where the data created by each application on the IOTstack is stored. The volume information is configured in the format: `external path:internal path`. This means the container data is directly linked to an external path in the

Raspberry Pi external storage device (an SD card in our case). In the case of `tasmoadmin`, the `data` folder inside the container is mapped to the external `IOTstack/volumes/tasmoadmin/data` folder. You can use the `IOTstack/volumes` folder's content to back up important information from all containers installed in IOTstack.

Now that you know how to access each application installed in IOTstack, we will see how to configure devices with Tasmota firmware installed.

MQTT server configuration in Tasmota devices

Tasmota devices use MQTT to exchange messages with Home Assistant and NodeRED. Therefore, if you want your sensors and actuators installed with Tasmota to operate with IOTstack, you must configure Tasmota with the MQTT server address used in IOTstack. You can do this configuration change by taking the following steps:

1. Access the Tasmota device by typing its IP address in the web browser. In the Tasmota main menu, click on **Configuration | Configure MQTT**, as circled in *Figure 8.12*.

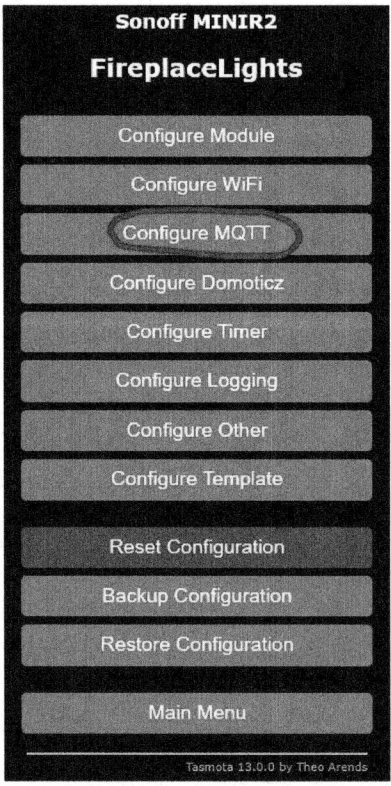

Figure 8.12 – Accessing the MQTT configuration option in Tasmota

2. Change the **Host** field to the static IP address you configured for your Raspberry Pi, 192.168.0.250, as shown in *Figure 8.13*. Change the **Port** field to 1883. You don't need to configure **User** and **Password**; just leave them as they are.

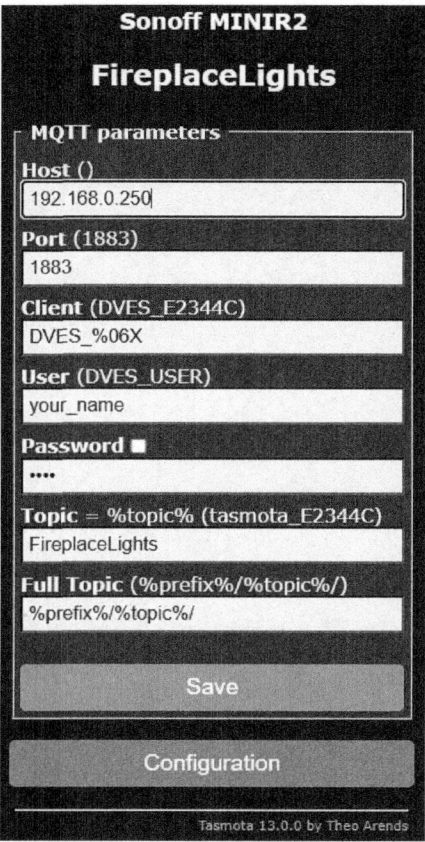

Figure 8.13 – Changing the MQTT server to work with IOTstack

3. Click on **Save** and wait until your Tasmota restarts.

You will have to repeat *steps 1* to *3* for each device you will be using with Tasmota.

Let's now see, in the next subsection, what needs to be configured in the Home Assistant container to operate under IOTstack.

Configuring Home Assistant in IOTstack

If you type the Home Assistant container IP address and port, which in my case is 192.168.0.250:8123, in your web browser, you will be prompted to create a new user account for Home Assistant using similar steps as we used in the *Home Assistant initial configuration* section in

Chapter 2. Fill in the name, username, and password and click on the **CREATE ACCOUNT** button, as presented in *Figure 2.6* in *Chapter 2*. The next screen will be the same as in *Figure 2.7*. Fill in the fields and click on the **NEXT** button. I will be using `family_name_Home_IOTStack` in the **Name of your Home Assistant installation** field to make it different from what was used before.

After configuring the initial parameters, the Home Assistant dashboard will be presented, similar to as in *Figure 2.9*. You can explore the Home Assistant menus, and you will notice the only difference between the installation in the container and the Home Assistant Operating System installation done in *Chapter 2* is the absence of the add-ons installation option. You can check this by comparing *Figure 8.14* with *Figure 2.10*.

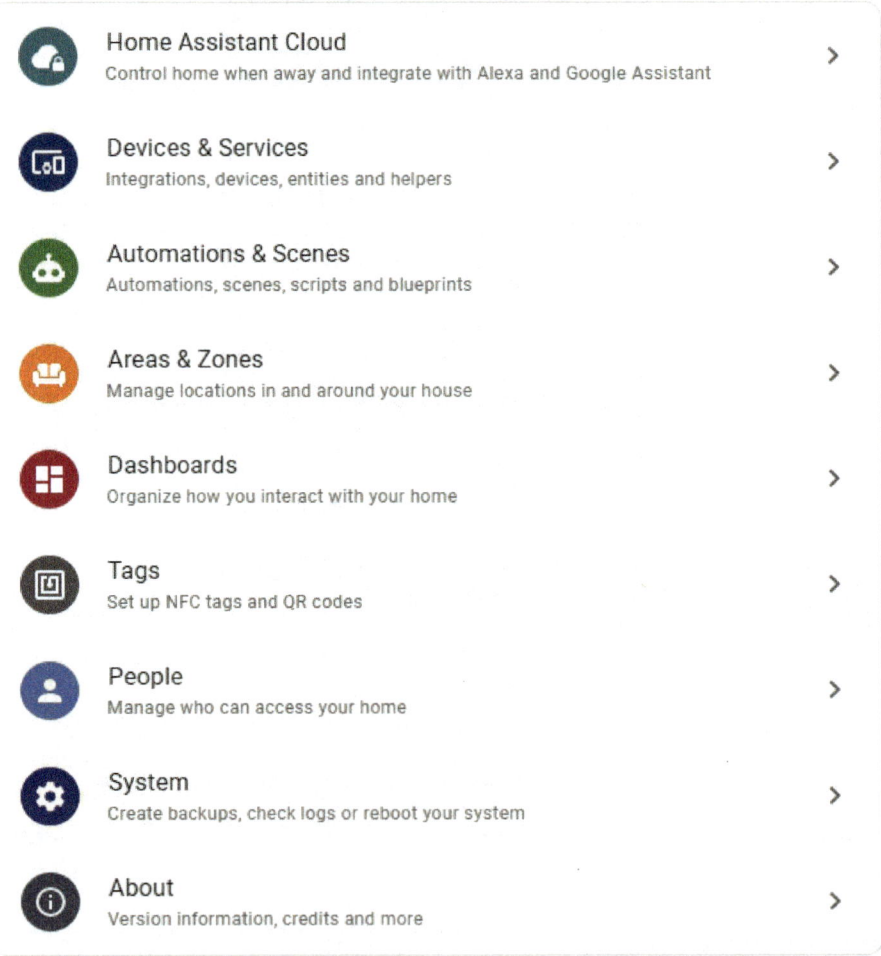

Figure 8.14 – Settings options in Home Assistant Container installation

We will need to configure the MQTT server in Home Assistant to communicate with the Tasmota devices. We will do that by clicking on **MQTT Integration** after clicking, from the Home Assistant sidebar, on the **Settings | Integrations | + ADD INTEGRATION** button. The configuration fields in *Figure 8.15* will be presented.

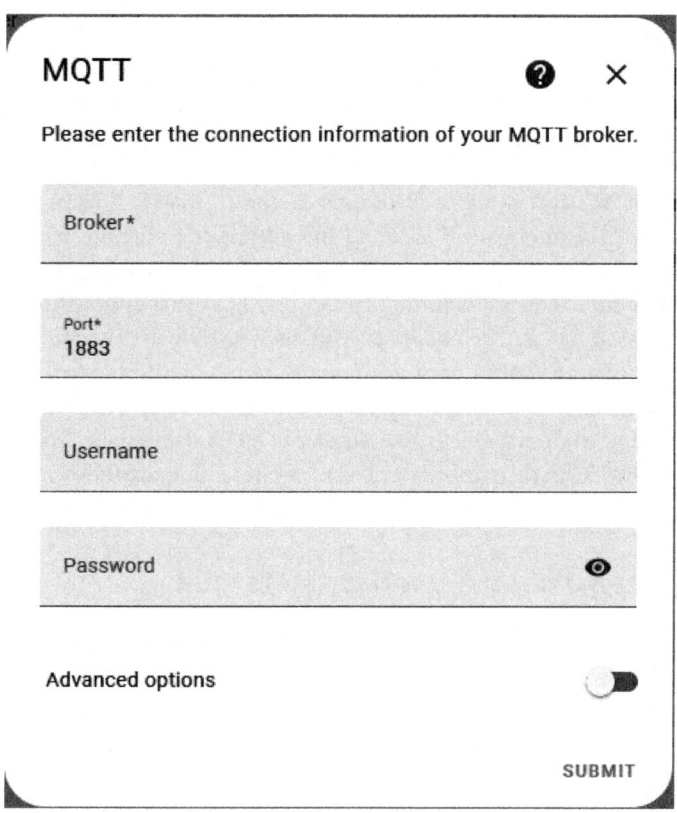

Figure 8.15 – MQTT configuration options

On the screen shown in *Figure 8.15*, fill in only the **Broker** field with the static IP address 192.168.0.250 and leave the others at their default values. Click on the **SUBMIT** button. On the **Success** screen presented after, just click on the **FINISH** button. In my case, I didn't change all the sensors and actuators from the previous installation, so I have just one Tasmota device configured in the new IOTstack installation, which is my five-zone temperature, which we will see in more detail in *Chapter 10*.

All other configurations and utilization we saw in the other chapters, except the add-ons we learned about in *Chapter 7*, can be done using the Home Assistant container installation.

> **Important note**
>
> We will have to configure the MQTT server in the Node-RED container, and we will do that by including the **Server** name presented in *Figure 7.5*, which is 192.168.0.250 for this book's example, and leaving the **Port** as 1883. You will have to fill this in according to the static IP you chose to use for the Raspberry Pi and configured in the *Raspberry Pi static IP configuration* subsection in this chapter.

Running and managing the applications in IOTstack

As explained in the last section, some applications can be accessed and run using the web browser by pointing to the static Raspberry Pi IP address and adding the port number to the end of it using a colon (:) in the middle. The applications we installed in the last section that have access using the web browser can be found in the last column of *Table 8.1*. The other applications, such as Duck DNS, which cannot be accessed using a web browser, will need to follow a specific configuration process, which will mostly consist of changing or adding a parameter to the docker-compose.yml configuration file. I will not go over the configurations for running applications that are not accessible using a web browser since they are well explained on the IOTstack website. You can understand more about how to run the IOTstack container installations by accessing the following address: https://sensorsiot.github.io/IOTstack/Containers/AdGuardHome/.

Maintaining the software used by IOTstack

If you look at the list of software in *Table 8.1* that was installed in this chapter in the *Installation of the Home Automation Stack* section, you will see that new software was installed that wasn't mentioned in other chapters. The software I'm talking about is **Portainer-CE (Community Edition)**. Portainer-CE is a web-based **graphical user interface (GUI)** for managing Docker environments. It provides an easy-to-use interface for visualizing and managing containers, images, networks, and volumes. With Portainer-CE, you can easily manage the Docker containers on IOTstack.

You can access Portainer-CE by using a web browser pointing to 192.168.0.250:9000. You will have to create a user account using the default **Admin** username and create a password, which I will leave you to choose. After the login, you will see the home screen presenting the **Environments** section. If you click on **local**, you will see the dashboard for IOTStack, as presented in *Figure 8.16*.

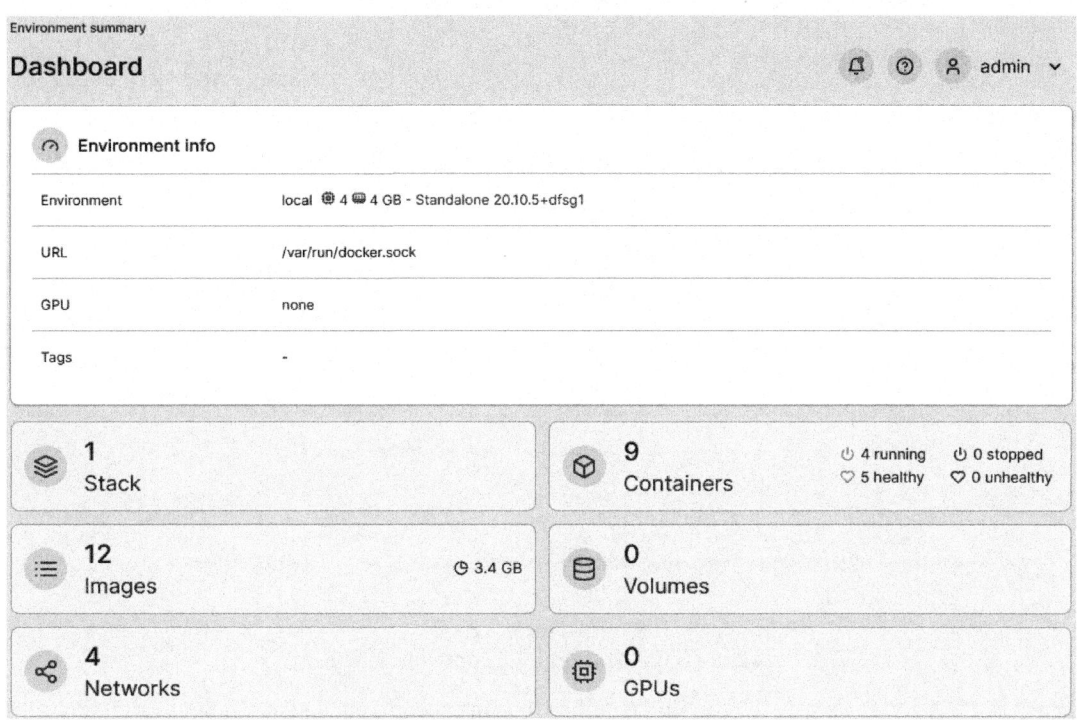

Figure 8.16 – Portainer-CE dashboard screen

You can evaluate the information from *Figure 8.16* and see, for example, that 12 images were installed with IOTStack and they are using 3.4 GB of disk space. You can also see that we installed nine containers with IOTstack and four of them are running and five are healthy. If you click in the **9 Containers** rectangle in *Figure 8.16*, the containers will be listed as represented in *Figure 8.17*.

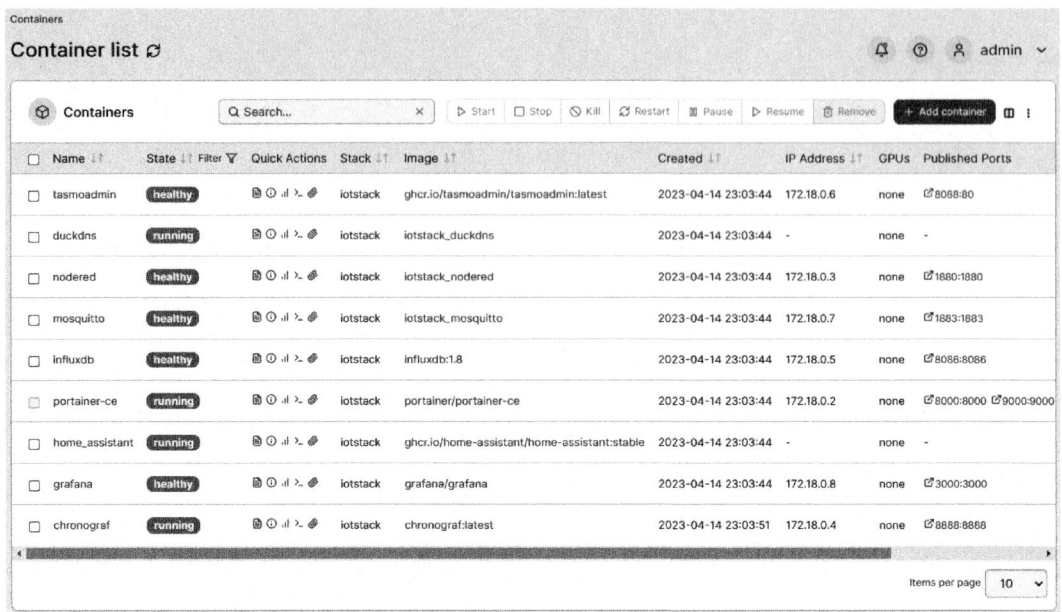

Figure 8.17 – Portainer-CE container screen

In *Figure 8.17*, you can see all the container applications installed in my IOTstack and information such as **state**, **Published Ports**, and **image** that can be evaluated. By clicking on each container **Name**, you will be able to stop, kill, restart, or pause it. You could also remove the container as well. Portainer-CE is a useful tool to help in the management of IOTstack.

As we have covered the main aspects and features of IOTstack, we can finish this chapter. We can now prepare to the next chapter, where I will share an exciting hands-on project idea to decorate your home during the holiday season.

Summary

In this chapter, we covered a very helpful topic, which is how you can create backups for Home Assistant using the Home Assistant operating system installation.

After learning how to do backups, we guided you through how to explore a new type of Home Assistant installation, which is the Home Assistant Container. We did that by using a pre-formatted installation tool called IOTStack. IOTStack is an open source project that not only includes Home Assistant Container installation but also many other types of software that can be used with IoT devices. In our case, it was used to install software to handle Home Automation applications.

We understood how the IOTStack architecture is configured, how to install container applications, and how to configure, use, and manage them.

In the next chapter, we will cover another hands-on project, which is a fun idea to support you during the festive holiday season. I hope you enjoy it!

Part 5:
Learn by Doing and
Future Trends

In this part, you will be working through two hands-on projects, which will help you to create sensors and actuators for your home and use them with Home Assistant and other software tools. New trends and technologies will be presented. A list of frequently answered questions regarding Home Automation and Home Assistant will help to consolidate what you learned in the book. This part will be helpful in providing a list of resources for your continuous learning in the home automation area.

This part has the following chapters:

- *Chapter 9, Hands-On Project 2 – Creating an LED Strip Controller and Adding It to Home Assistant*

- *Chapter 10, Hands-On Project 3 – Creating a Five-Zone Temperature Logger for Your Home*

- *Chapter 11, The Road Ahead in Home Automation Technologies*

Hands-On Project 2 – Creating an LED Strip Controller and Adding It to Home Assistant

This second hands-on project will teach you how to create an LED strip controller using a wireless microcontroller module and an application developed specifically to do it. The steps to create the controller, and later the software deployment, will be explained. You will be able to configure the LED strip controller using the application directly and also using Home Assistant.

Using what we learned in *Chapter 5*, we will create an automation that will be attached to the controller so that it will be very useful for ambient decoration, mainly on holidays such as Halloween and Christmas, which is the purpose I'm using it for in my home today.

In this chapter, we will be covering the following topics to build the project:

- How an LED strip controller works
- Grouping the materials and connecting the parts
- Deploying the controller software
- Configuring the LED strip controller using the WLED software application
- Integrating the LED strip controller into Home Assistant
- Creating an automation using the LED strip controller
- Installing the LED strip controller in your home

By the end of this chapter, you will be able to create your own LED strip controller and configure and control it by using a computer or your cell phone, using a specific application, a web browser, or Home Assistant. You will learn how to create an automation in Home Assistant to manage the controller functionality.

Technical requirements

There are similar technical requirements to *Chapter 3* and *Chapter 4* to complete the project described in this chapter. You will also need to apply the knowledge learned in *Chapter 5* to create a Home Assistant automation using the LED strip controller in a later section of this chapter. If you know any programming language, it will help to understand the automation example where you will be using templates for Home Assistant. All resources used in this book are available at `https://github.com/PacktPublishing/Building-Smart-Home-Automation-Solutions-with-Home-Assistant/tree/main/Chapter%2009`. Check out the following video to view the Code in Action: `https://bit.ly/451EGiZ`

How an LED strip controller works

Before understanding how an LED strip controller works, we will have to learn what an LED strip is. An LED strip, also known as LED tape or LED ribbon, is a flexible electronic circuit board with multiple **light-emitting diodes** (**LEDs**) mounted on it. It is a type of lighting solution that can be used in a variety of applications, such as accent lighting, task lighting, and decorative lighting. There is a variation of the LED strip that follows the same work principle but instead of the LED connection being set up using a flexible circuit, it is done using wires. This variation is called an **LED string**. I use LED strings to decorate my Christmas tree. *Figure 9.1* shows a photo of an LED strip on the left and an LED string on the right.

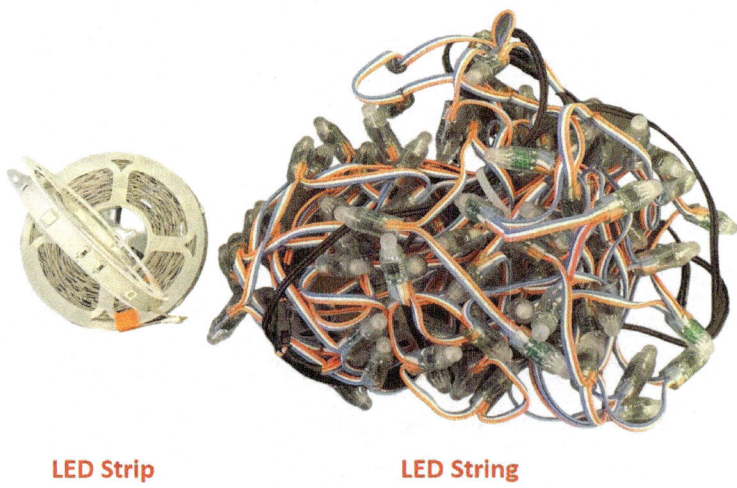

LED Strip   **LED String**

Figure 9.1 – LED strip x LED string configuration

LED strips come in a range of colors and color temperatures, and they are available in various lengths and densities. They are typically powered by low-voltage **direct current** (**DC**) and can be cut to fit the desired length, making them customizable to fit almost any application. The LED strip power supply and brightness are directly related to their length or density.

LED strip common voltage values are 5, 12, and 24V DC. There are different LED types that can be used in LED strips and the types are not so important. The important specification parameters to consider in an LED strip, including the measurement unit, are as follows:

- **Supply voltage**: Measured in V DC
- **Density**: Measured in LEDs per inch or LEDs per meter
- **Color**: Single color, dynamic tunable white, multicolor, RGB, RGBW, RGBCCT/RGBWW
- **Length**: LED strip length. Typically, 1, 2, or 5 meters
- **Power consumption**: Measured in **Watts (W)**
- **Ingress Protection (IP)**: IP30, IP65, IP67
- **Addressable or Non-Addressable**: LEDs individually controlled or LEDs not individually controlled

The first four parameters in the specification list are straightforward. Power consumption is the power consumed by an LED used in the strip. We will comment more on power consumption when commenting on the power supply in this section. The Ingress Protection or IP value measures the capability of the strip to prevent dust and water ingress. You can understand the IP as a number where the higher it is, the more the LED strip is able to prevent or be protected from the ingress of dust and water. The last parameter in the preceding list identifies whether the LED is addressable or not. This is an interesting feature that allows LEDs to be individually controlled, allowing different combinations of colors, brightness, and effects to be produced by the strip. The addressable feature is part of the LED type used in strip lights. An addressable LED has a small **Integrated Circuit (IC)**, which can be addressed and controlled individually. Examples of addressable LEDs are the WS2811, WS2812B, and WS2813 models.

In this book, we will be using LED strips connected to a wireless microcontroller module to compose what I am calling an LED strip controller. A block diagram for the LED strip controller is represented in *Figure 9.2*.

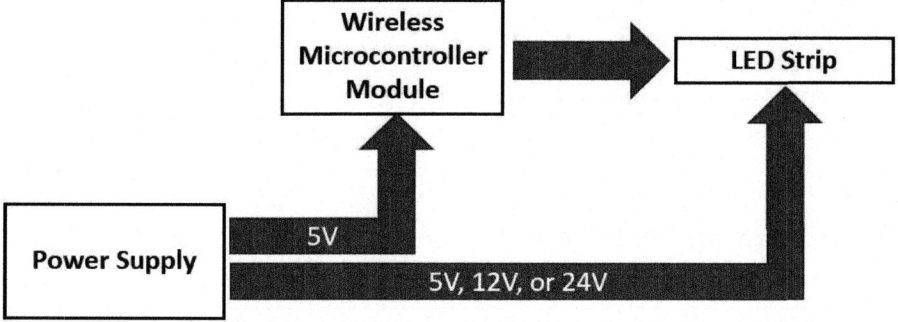

Figure 9.2 – LED strip controller block diagram

The wireless microcontroller module shown in *Figure 9.2* can customize and control – depending on the LED type used in the strip – the brightness, color, or individual LED status. Addressable LED strips have an integrated circuit inside the LED package that allows individual control of the LED properties. This control is done using a single serial communication line, which means you will need to use just one IO pin from the wireless microcontroller module to send commands to the entire LED strip.

The LED strip block presented in *Figure 9.2* is an LED arrangement separated by a fixed distance, which defines the LED strip's density. This LED arrangement is connected by a flexible circuit or by wires. The LED element in the LED strip is normally one model and can have all features or specifications commented on before. Both blocks – the wireless microcontroller module and the LED strip – are powered by a power supply.

Regarding the power supply shown in *Figure 9.2*, the wireless microcontroller accepts just 5V maximum as the power voltage, while the LED strip usually accepts 5V, 12V, or 24V. Using the same 5V voltage for the wireless microcontroller module and LED strip, a single output power supply can be used. If you use a voltage different from 5V for the LED strip, then you will need a dual output power supply or another DC-to-DC converter installed to convert the voltage from the power supply to 5V or the LED strip voltage. The power supply range is an important parameter and should be dimensioned according to the LED strip power consumption. Each LED has a power consumption measured in Watts and the power supply range should be calculated by multiplying the LED power consumption by the total quantity of LEDs used in the strip.

After this explanation about how the LED strip controller works, we can start to build the project by grouping and connecting the circuit parts. We will do this in the next section.

Grouping the materials and connecting the parts

In this section, we will group the materials required to build the LED strip controller. The specifications of these materials will also be discussed. In sequence, we will present how the circuit should be interconnected and the steps to assemble it.

Materials required to build the LED strip controller

Before we list all the materials required to build the LED strip controller, I would like to comment on the LED strip that will be used. In my projects, I prefer to use an LED strip with the following specification:

- **Supply voltage**: 5V DC
- **Density**: Min of 30 LEDs/meter
- **Color**: At least RGB
- **Ingress Progression (IP)**: IP30 for indoor installations and IP67 for outdoor installations
- **Length**: 5 meters
- **Addressable**

For this project, we will build an LED strip controller to be placed outdoors at the front of my house so we will have to use IP67 as the IP rating. The LED strip we will use is based on the LED **WS2812B**, powered by 5V DC, RGB, and addressable. I need to cover a considerable length of the front of the house so 5 meters is the size I picked for this project.

The power supply we will be using is 5V DC and we will need to calculate the power range. The specification of the WS2812B LED says that it consumes 0.3 Watts. As we will be using at least 30 LEDS/meter and the total length is 5 meters, we will need 150 LEDs consuming 0.3 Watts each or 45W for the power supply range. You can use a power supply with a lower power range but the effect will be that the last LEDs in the chain will have reduced brightness due to the lower current and voltage drop along the strip.

It is worth mentioning that one of the reasons to choose 5V DC for the LED strip is compatibility with the voltage supply required for the wireless microcontroller module so we will not need an extra DC/DC converter or a dual output power supply.

The LED strip and power supply are the critical items in this project so if you pick them right you will not have issues. That said, we can now look at the bill of materials to build this project, listed in *Table 9.1*.

ID	Quantity	Description
1	1	ESP8266 Wi-Fi module
2	1	LED strip WS2812B, 5 meters, 30 LEDS/meter, IP67
3	1	Power supply adapter 5VDC / 45W or above
4	1	LED strip light connector (male)
5	1	3-pin terminal bar (male)
6	1	Power supply adapter plug

Table 9.1 – Bill of materials required to build the LED strip controller

The ESP8266 Wi-Fi module (*ID 1* in *Table 9.1*) is the same one used in *Chapter 3*. You can use any variation of the ESP8266, and even the ESP32, but as we will just need to use one IO pin, the **Wemos D1 Mini** presented in *Figure 3.3* is more than enough.

The LED strip (*ID 2* in *Table 9.1*) is based on the WS2812B LED powered by 5VDC and has an **RGB** (short for **Red Green Blue**) LED capable of reproducing 16 million distinct colors. We will be using a length of 5 meters, 30 LEDs/meter, and IP67, able to support the outdoor environment. The LED strip I used is from the manufacturer **BTF-LIGHTING** (https://www.btf-lighting.com). *Figure 9.3* shows the LED strip we will be using in this project, which is already installed at the front of my house.

Figure 9.3 – LED strip used in the project

The power supply adapter (*ID 3* in *Table 9.1*) used in this project has a single 5VDC output power supply adapter able to power the ESP8266 Wi-Fi module and the LED strip at the same time. You can use power supply adapter from the same supplier as the LED strip, **BTF-LIGHTING**. For this project, I used the **Alitove** model **ALT-0510**, as shown in *Figure 9.4*.

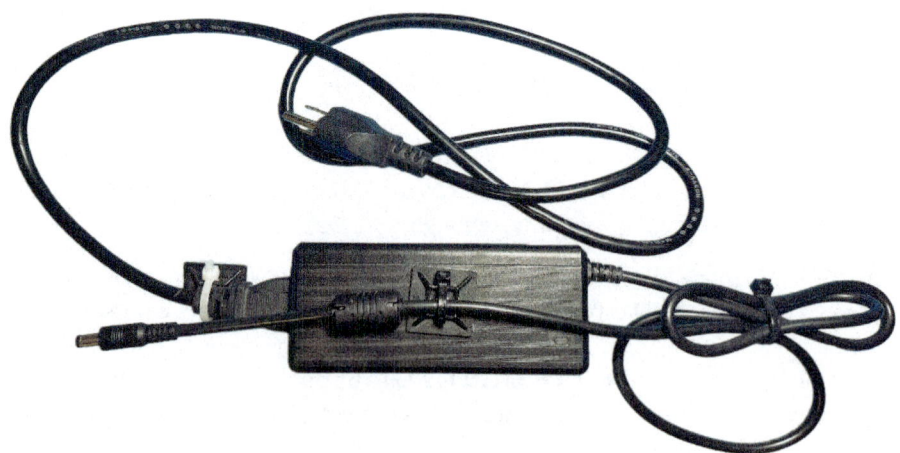

Figure 9.4 – Power supply used in the LED strip controller project

The 45W power supply adapter range was dimensioned based on the LED density and length of the LED strip. You can use a different power range depending on the density and length used, according to *Table 9.2* where typical values found are listed.

Density (LEDs/meter)	Length (meters)	Power Range (W) Min
30	1	9
30	5	45
60	1	18
60	5	90
100	1	30
144	1	43.2

Table 9.2 – Power supply range for various LED strip densities and lengths

The LED strip light connector (*ID 4* in *Table 9.1*) is included when you buy the LED strip and you will need to connect the Wi-Fi module to the LED strip. This cable is presented in *Figure 9.5*.

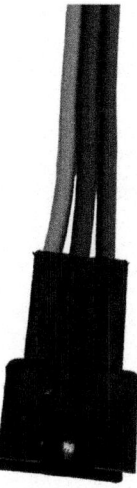

Figure 9.5 – Cable used to connect the Wi-Fi module to the LED strip and power supply

I use the 3-pin terminal bar male (*ID 5* in *Table 9.1*) to provide a better connection between the cable presented in *Figure 9.5* and the ESP8266 Wi-Fi module (*ID 1* in *Table 9.1*). The 3-pin terminal bar male is the same type presented in the 4-pin terminal bar shown in left side of *Figure 4.5* in *Chapter 4*.

The last item from the list is the power supply adapter plug (*ID 6* in *Table 9.1*), which will help to convert the power supply standard output plug to a socket able to attach the LED strip wires. This will be helpful to easily make power supply connections and disconnections to and from the LED strip. This adapter plug is presented in *Figure 9.6* and is provided with the power supply adapter purchased from **Alitove** and **BTF-LIGHTING**.

Figure 9.6 – Power supply adapter plug

As you know about all of the materials needed to build the LED strip controller now, let us see how we can assemble them in the next subsection.

Connecting the parts to build the LED strip controller

The LED strip controller circuit diagram is shown in *Figure 9.7*.

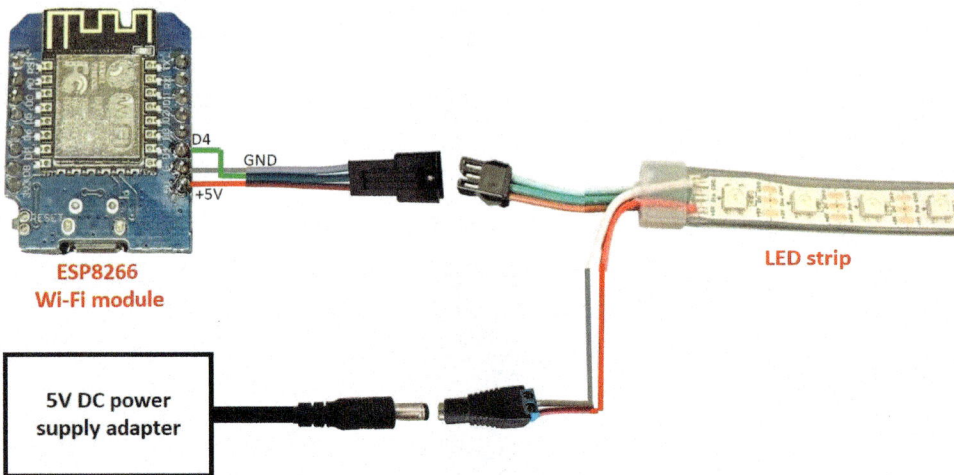

Figure 9.7 – LED strip controller circuit diagram

I will use the material ID column in *Table 9.1* to reference the parts to be interconnected. I suggest you follow this sequence to build the LED strip controller project:

1. Start with the ESP8266 Wi-Fi module connection to the LED. We will have to use a soldering iron and solder to interconnect the 3-pin terminal bar (male) (*ID 5* in *Table 9.1*) to the LED strip light connector (*ID 4* in *Table 9.1*). The pins should be soldered according to the pinout represented in *Figure 9.7*, meaning the pin in the middle of the connector should be the GPIO2

connected to the ESP8266 D4 pin. After soldering the pins to the terminal bar, connect the male side of the 3-pin terminal bar of the connector to the ESP8266 and the other connector side to the LED strip bar female connector.

2. Check the power supply adapter plug. There should be symbols indicating the positive (+) and negative (-) terminal bourne. Get the two remaining wires coming from the LED strip and connect the positive wire, normally in the color red, to the positive terminal bourne, and the negative wire, usually in the color black or white to the negative terminal bourne. You will need a screwdriver to make these connections.

3. Connect the power supply plug to the power supply adapter plug to the LED strip wires attached in *Step 2*.

As seen, it takes just three steps to connect all the LED strip controller parts.

In the next section, we will learn about the software we will use to manage the LED strip controller and also deploy this software so we can start using it.

Deploying the controller software

I was grateful when I was building my LED strip for the first time. I thought I could develop one from scratch but I was running late to get it ready for Halloween. Then I started to look at some options on the internet, when I found the software I am using today to manage all the strip lights I built. This software is called **WLED**.

The WLED software was created by *Christian Schwinne* and made to run under **Expressif Systems'** popular **ESP8266** and **ESP32** wireless microcontroller modules. It implements a web server in these devices and is intended to control some LED types, including the WS2812B we are using in this project. It has multiple features and configurations we will be exploring in this chapter. For example, it has over 100 integrated special effects and can control 3 different LED outputs independently if we are using EP8266, and 10 LED outputs if an ESP32 is used. It has everything we will need for this project and more. Another key factor that was one of the motivations to include it in this book is native Home Assistant integration, which means that once some configurations are done in the WLED software, it will be automatically recognized by Home Assistant.

The WLED software is available to be installed in several ways. We can download the software and install it using the Tasmotizer software used in *Chapter 3* and *Chapter 4*. We can also install it using the online tool available at `https://install.wled.me/`. We will instead be using another tool to deploy the software, which is a popular one to deploy software or firmware for the ESP platform, called **esptool**. Esptool is a software deployment tool developed in **Python** and maintained by the ESP8266/ESP32 manufacturer, Expressif Systems. Python is a high-level, general-purpose programming language.

You will have to follow these instructions to deploy the WLED firmware to the ESP8266 using esptool:

1. To install and run esptool, you will need to first install Python on your computer. You will need to download and install the installation files according to your operating system. In my case, as I use Windows, I downloaded and installed the latest installation files from https://www.python.org/downloads/windows/.

2. Once Python is installed, assuming you have the Windows operating system as I have, type cmd in the Windows search bar and hit *Enter*.

3. In the Windows command prompt, type the Pip install esptool command and hit *Enter*. The esptool software will be installed.

4. Download the latest stable WLED installation file, available at https://github.com/Aircoookie/WLED/releases. In the case of this book, I will use release *0.13.3* and the file to be downloaded is WLED_0.13.3_ESP8266.bin. Take note of the path to where you download the WLED software because it will be useful in the next step.

5. Execute this command to deploy the WLED firmware to the ESP8266:

```
esptool.py write_flash 0x0 ./<your_path>/WLED_0.13.3_ESP8266.bin
```

Replace <your_path> with the path where you saved your WLED file. The WLED file will be deployed to your system. *Figure 9.8* shows the steps esptool takes to program the WLED binary file to your ESP8266.

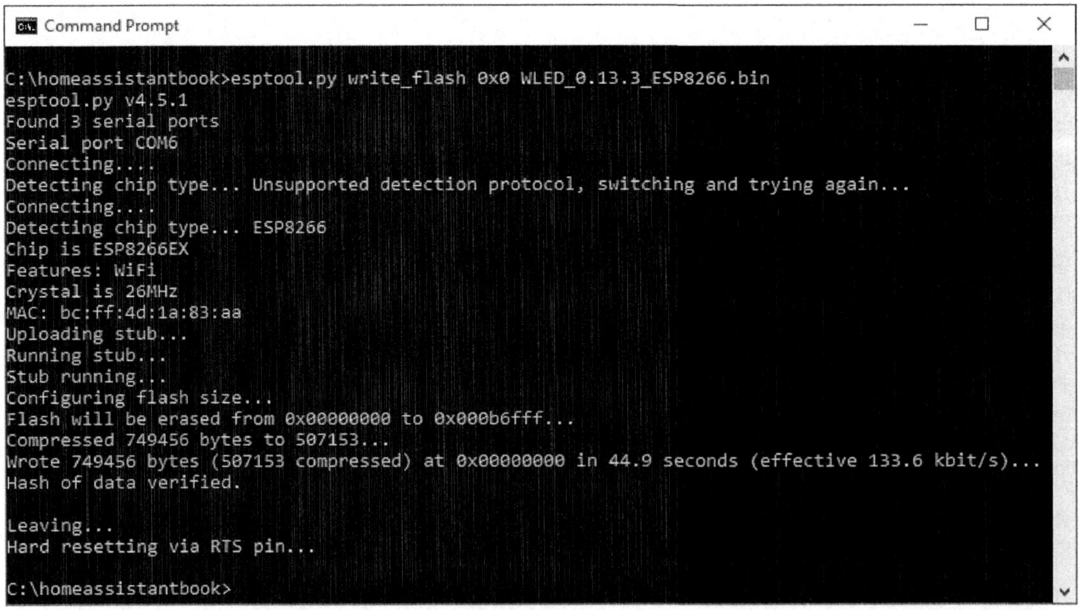

```
C:\homeassistantbook>esptool.py write_flash 0x0 WLED_0.13.3_ESP8266.bin
esptool.py v4.5.1
Found 3 serial ports
Serial port COM6
Connecting....
Detecting chip type... Unsupported detection protocol, switching and trying again...
Connecting....
Detecting chip type... ESP8266
Chip is ESP8266EX
Features: WiFi
Crystal is 26MHz
MAC: bc:ff:4d:1a:83:aa
Uploading stub...
Running stub...
Stub running...
Configuring flash size...
Flash will be erased from 0x00000000 to 0x000b6fff...
Compressed 749456 bytes to 507153...
Wrote 749456 bytes (507153 compressed) at 0x00000000 in 44.9 seconds (effective 133.6 kbit/s)...
Hash of data verified.

Leaving...
Hard resetting via RTS pin...

C:\homeassistantbook>
```

Figure 9.8 – esptool programming WLED file to ESP8266

Figure 9.8 shows the command used according to *step 5*. I stored the WLED binary file to be recorded in the `homeassistantbook` folder. The esptool software detects the serial ports on your computer, connects to the ESP8266 via this port, erases the flash, writes the entire WLED binary file, and verifies it. Esptool doesn't provide a clear output of success for the program operation so you can understand that if you get outputs such as `Wrote <WLED_binary_file_amount_of_bytes>` `bytes (<amount_of_bytes_compressed> compressed) at 0x00000000 in XX` `seconds...` and `Hash of data verified`, it should be confirmation that the binary file was deployed successfully. This confirmation can be seen in *Figure 9.8*.

> **Important note**
>
> If you have your ESP8266 already programmed with the previous firmware, it could be required that you have to erase everything else off the device prior to program it with the WLED firmware. You can do this by issuing the `esptool.py erase_flash` command. You can check the `esptool.py` documentation at `https://docs.espressif.com/projects/` `esptool/en/latest/esp8266/esptool/index.html`.

Now that you have the WLED firmware installed in your ESP8266 Wi-Fi controller module, in the next section, we will start to configure some parameters to later connect it to Home Assistant.

Configuring the LED strip controller using the WLED software application

You should not face many issues configuring and testing the WLED application. The application offers a lot of configuration options and it is very intuitive. You need to have the ESP8266 Wi-Fi module connected to the power supply used to power the LED strip controller. We will first connect our project to the home Wi-Fi network, and after we will go over the main configurations to be done using the WLED application. We will cover these two subjects in the next subsections.

Configuring the Wifi network in the WLED application

Once the power is connected, you will need to use the WLED software application using your web browser. Follow these steps to configure the LED strip controller:

1. Using your cell phone or your computer, check for the *WLED-AP* Wi-Fi network. Connect to it using the default password, `wled1234`.

2. Once connected to the WLED-AP Wi-Fi network, if you are using a computer and the web browser is open, it will automatically open the page using the IP `4.3.2.1`, presented in *Figure 9.9*.

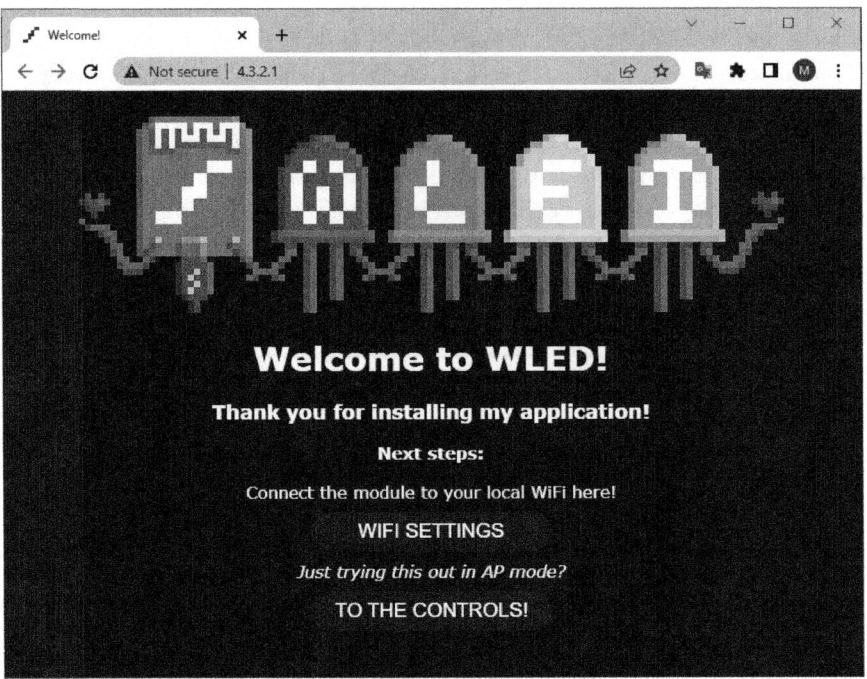

Figure 9.9 – WLED application start screen

3. Click on the **WIFI SETTINGS** button on the screen presented in *Figure 9.9*.

4. Another screen, titled **WiFi setup**, will be presented. Fill in your SSID network name and password in the fields **Network name** and **Network password**. I like to use a static IP to make the remote configuration easy using the application, so we will add the IP 192.168.0.200 in the **Static IP** field, but another IP address can be used per your convenience (vide note that follows). You will have to fill in the **Static gateway** field using your router IP. The router IP I have at my home is 192.168.0.1, so I will fill in this value in the **Static gateway** field.

5. Click on the **Save & Connect** button at the bottom of the screen. After the application processes the information, another screen will be presented saying that the Wi-Fi settings were saved. The WLED-AP network connection will be dropped now.

6. Connect to your regular Wi-Fi network and point your web browser to the IP 192.168.0.200, previously configured to access the WLED application.

So, after this configuration, if the Wi-Fi configuration is not changed, you can always access the WLED application using the static IP configured, or in my case, using the IP 192.168.0.200.

> **Important note**
>
> You can assign IP addresses to your devices by looking at your home network and checking the IP addresses already in use by other clients. You must choose an IP that is not yet assigned to a device. An easy way to check the list of client IP addresses currently in use is to look in your router configurations for something such as **Wireless Client List**.

The next subsection will support you in the main configurations to be made for your WLED application, and also some preparations to use it for Home Assistant.

Configuring the main parameters of the WLED application

When you open IP 192.168.0.200 in the web browser, you see the screen presented in *Figure 9.10*. Initially, you will see a screen in dark mode but I changed this configuration, as shown in *Figure 9.10*, to be better presented in the book.

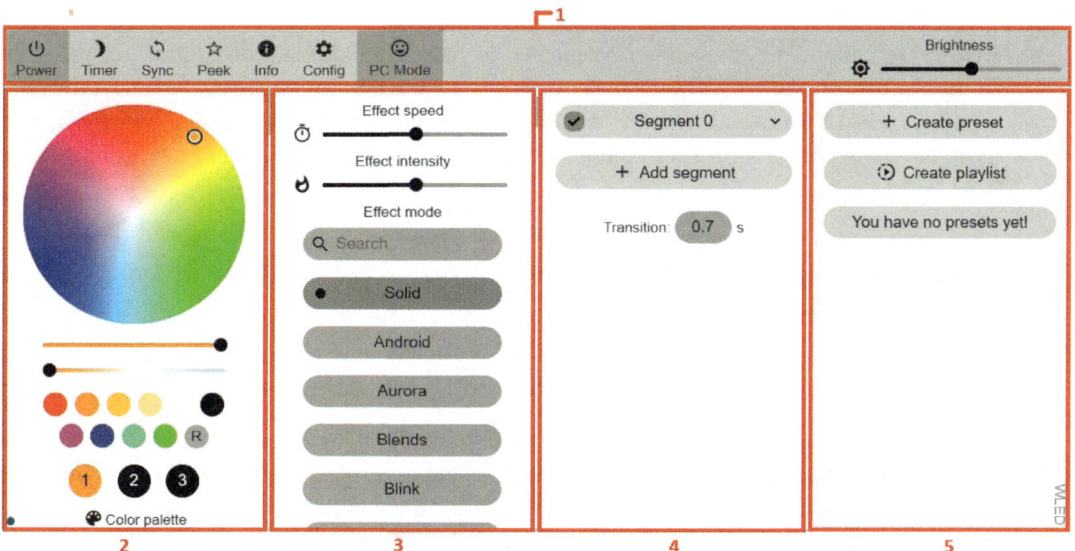

Figure 9.10 – WLED application main screen

Starting at the top of *Figure 9.10*, there are some buttons and a brightness slider control, as presented in the rectangle numbered as *1*. The buttons outlined by the rectangle number *1* have the following functions:

- **Power**: Turn on/off the LED strip. The ESP8266 Wi-Fi module is still turned on. It also turns on/off the blue LED attached to pin D7.

- **Timer**: When clicked, triggers a timer to turn off the LED strip for over one hour.

- **Sync**: When clicked, makes all other LED strips with the WLED firmware installed synchronize with the one we are building in this project.

- **Peek**: Shows a color bar below the button area representing the animation currently configured in the LED strip.

- **Info**: Show the LED strip's basic configuration.

- **Config**: Allows access to another button menu to configure many parameters in the WLED software. We will go over some details about the configurations in the next paragraph.

- **PC Mode**: When clicked show the screen as in *Figure 9.10*. When unclicked, shows one screen representation at a time and you need to click on the buttons at the bottom to access each screen.

The **Config** button allows general configuration according to the following options:

- **WiFi Setup**: Allows configuration related to the Wi-Fi network. All configuration parameters required were set in *Step 3* in the last subsection.

- **LED Preferences**: We will need to configure some parameters here according to our LED strip. In the **Hardware setup | LED outputs** option, change the **Length** parameter to reflect the total quantity of LEDs on the strip. In the case of this project, there will be 30 LEDs per meter and a total of 5 meters – 150 LEDs in total, so **Length** should be configured to **150**. Click on the **Save** button at the bottom to save the configuration.

- **User Interface**: This manages the configuration related to the user interface. If you want to configure the main screen as in *Figure 9.10*, you have to check the **I hate dark mode** option and click on the **Save** button.

- **Sync Interfaces**: This option configures how external software interacts with WLED. We will change the **Device topic** field to **LED_STRIP1**. This is the MQTT device topic parameter.

- **Time & Macros**: Configure the location, time zone, and NTP server to set up the WLED time configuration. You will configure the **Time zone** field according to your location. In my case, I will need to set this field to *US-AZ* and click on the **Save** button. In this menu, you can also configure macros. For macro configuration, visit `https://kno.wled.ge/features/macros/`.

- **Usermod**: This menu is intended to present any customized configuration to be done using the WLED software source code. You can customize options by changing the WLED source code and adding customized configurations using this menu.

- **Security & Updates**: This option allows configurations for **Over The Air** (**OTA**) software updates, enabling and disabling the OTA configuration. Also, you can save and restore backups for presets and configurations.

All configurations related to the LED strip's behavior and sequencing are done using four options named **Colors**, **Effects**, **Segments**, and **Presets**, which are numbered *2, 3, 4,* and *5* in *Figure 9.10*.

Using the **Colors** option, you can configure the palette of colors that will be used in your LED strip. You can use whatever colors you want. It can be used in around 70 different palettes. You'll see that changing any configuration in this tab will immediately change the color on the LED strip.

The **Effects** option allows you to configure a sequence of effects or animations for your LED strip. Each effect has its own color sequence but you can change it using the **Colors** option explained previously.

The **Segments** option can break your LED strip into different segments so you can control each one with a different **Color** and **Effects** scheme. You could, for example, split our 150 LEDS into 3 segments of 50 LEDs each or 5 segments of 30 LEDs each.

The last option, **Presets**, allows you to create presets. Presets store the current setup of **Color** and **Effects** and save it under a name and a label number. You can then create a playlist and sequence the presets from a certain number to another. You can configure the time each configuration will be presented and the transition time between the two configurations.

What I did in my home was set up two playlists, one for Halloween and the other for Christmas. For Halloween, I set up the base colors as orange and purple, while for Christmas I used the colors white, red, and green. I created 41 presets in total by looking at the LED strip and using basic colors for Halloween, and by changing the effects, I created preset numbers 1 to 14. I did the same using the Christmas color scheme and created presets 15 to 41.

To create a preset, you will have to click on the + **Create preset** button in the **Presets** tab. The screenshot in *Figure 9.11* will be presented, and in the **Presets** tab (please check *Figure 9.10* for it), you will then need to enter a name in the **Enter name…** field and leave the options **Use current state**, **Include brightness**, and **Save segment bounds** checked. Click on the **Save preset** button to save it.

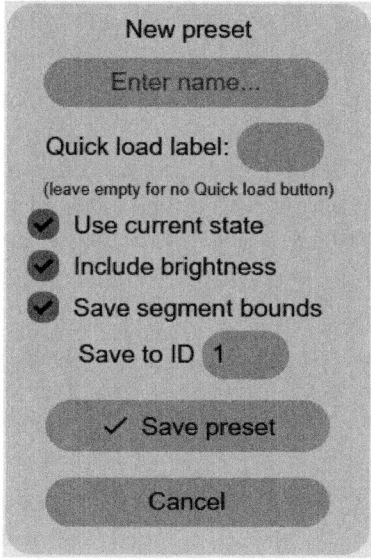

Figure 9.11 – Create a new preset in WLED

To create a playlist, you have to click on the **Create playlist** button. You will have to create at least one preset first to create a playlist, otherwise, WLED will not accept it. The screen shown in *Figure 9.12* will be shown.

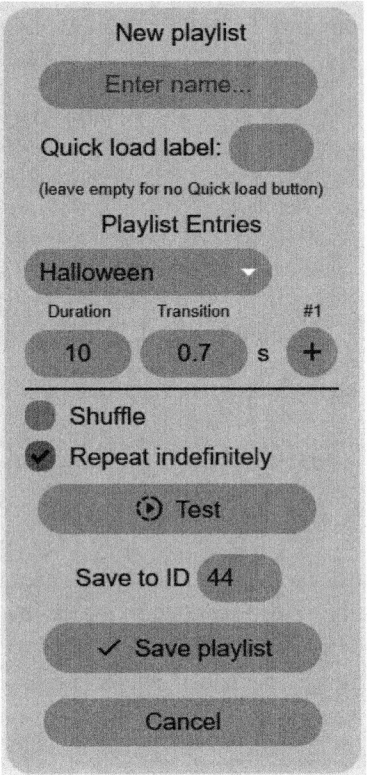

Figure 9.12 – Create a new playlist in WLED

Following *Figure 9.12*, you will need to include a name in the **Enter name...** field and choose the presets you want to include in the playlist by selecting them in the **Playlist Entries** dropbox, set up the **Duration** and **Transition** times (in seconds), and click on the + button to add the preset to the playlist. You will need to repeat the process to select the preset in the **Playlist Entries** dropbox as many times as you want to add the different presets to the playlist. Click on **Save playlist** to save your playlist.

I included the following parameters in the **Presets** tab to create both playlists:

- Playlist name: **Halloween**:
  - **Repeat indefinitely**: Checked
  - **First preset**: 1 (Halloween)
  - **Last preset**: 14 (Tri chase)

- **Duration**: 30 s

- **Transition**: 0.7 s

- **ID**: 42

• Playlist name: **Christmas**:

  - **Repeat indefinitely**: Checked

  - **First preset**: 15 (Christmas-1)

  - **Last preset**: 41 (Christmas-27)

  - **Duration**: 30 s

  - **Transition**: 0.7 s

  - **ID**: 43

You can use the presets I used in my home using the `presets led_strip1 ch9.json` file available in this chapter's folder of the book's GitHub repository. To upload the presets to your WLED configuration, from the main screen, go to **Config** | **Security &Updates** and you will find the **Restore presets** option. You can also see the `ch9-1` demonstration video on how these two playlists work using the WLED application.

Important note

If you want your LED strip controller to start a playlist after it is turned on, you must click on **LED preferences** and, under **Defaults**, fill in the numbers `42` (Halloween) or `43` (Christmas) in the **Apply preset at boot** option.

You can use the WLED application and the LED strip controller in standalone mode if you want, but you can also integrate it into Home Assistant so you get the benefit of using it with other devices using automations, for example. You will see how to integrate the LED strip controller into Home Assistant in the next section.

Integrating the LED strip controller into Home Assistant

The WLED integration with Home Assistant is simple. After you execute the steps from the previous section, open the command palette using the *C* hotkey, type `integrations`, and select it (or use **Settings** | **Devices & Services**), as can be seen in *Figure 9.13*.

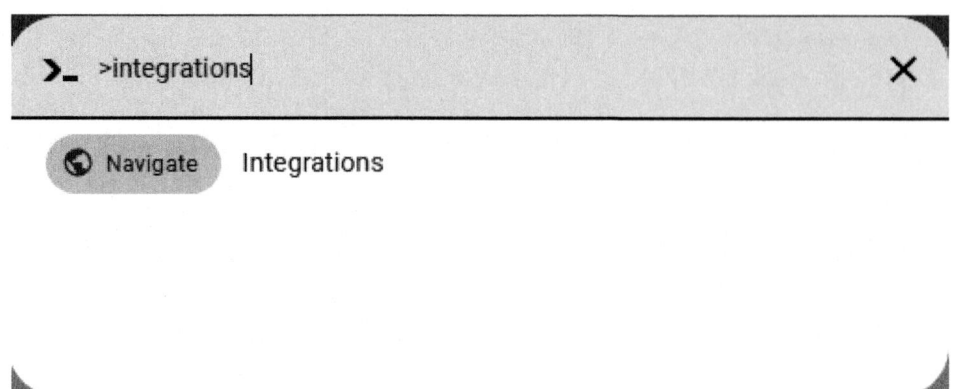

Figure 9.13 – Integrations configuration from the C hotkey

You will see the WLED integration ready to be configured as presented in *Figure 9.14*.

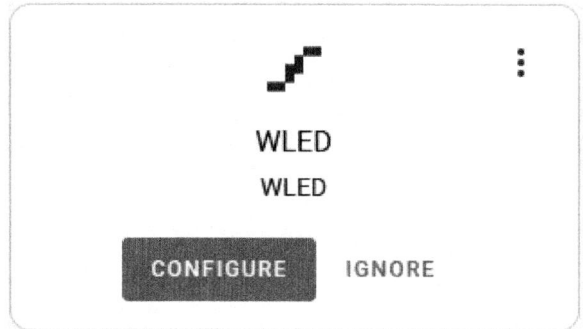

Figure 9.14 – WLED final configuration screen in Home Assistant

Click on the **CONFIGURE** button to configure the WLED integration within Home Assistant. A pop-up window will be presented asking you if you want to add the WLED to Home Assistant. Click on the **SUBMIT** button. The screen presented in *Figure 9.15* will ask you to assign the WLED to an area. We will leave it blank for now and click on the **FINISH** button.

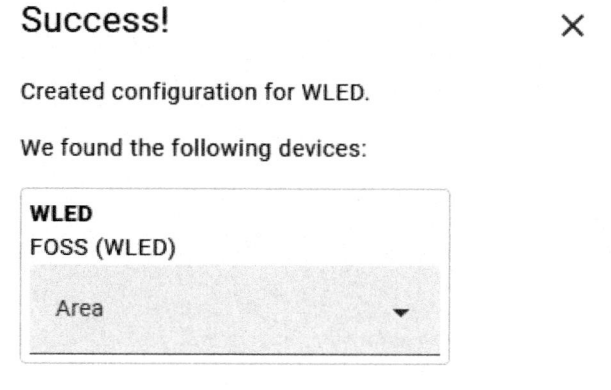

Figure 9.15 – WLED final configuration screen in Home Assistant

After clicking on the **FINISH** button, still in the **Integrations** tab, in the WLED configuration box presented in *Figure 9.16*, click on **1 device**.

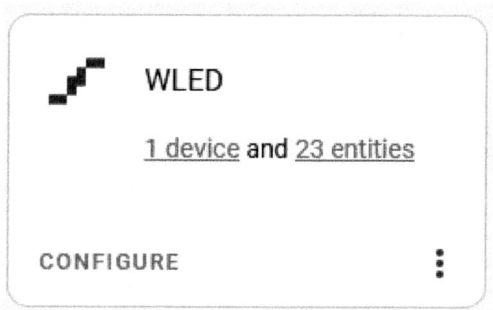

Figure 9.16 – WLED configuration box

Once you click on **1 device**, the screen shown in *Figure 9.17* will be presented.

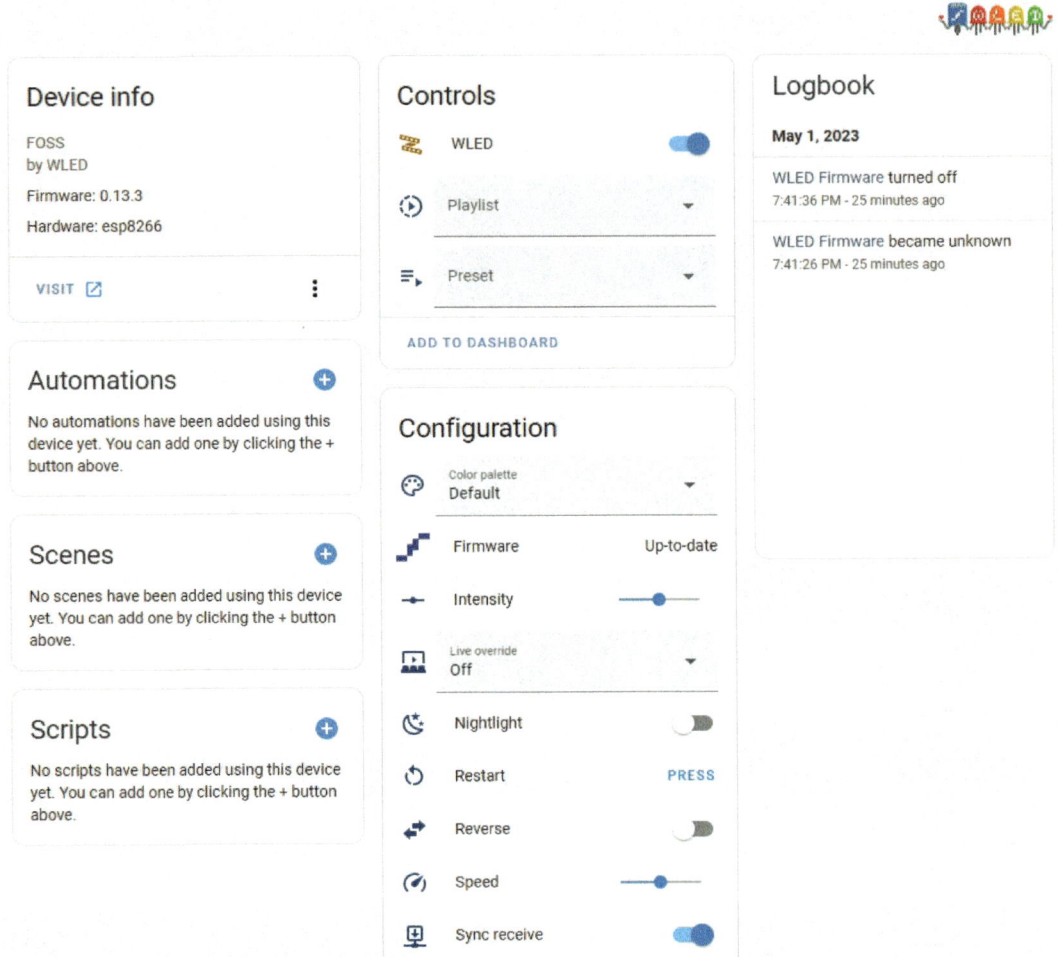

Figure 9.17 – WLED device configuration in Home Assistant

You can see all the information about and the configuration for the WLED device we just added in Home Assistant. It is possible to verify information about the device using the **Device info** box. Using the **Controls** box, it is possible to turn on/off the WLED device and configure a playlist or preset created in the last section. In the **Configuration** box, it is possible to make changes to the color palette, intensity, speed, and so on. In the **Logbook** box, you can see the activity involving the WLED, including significant changes in the status of the device. There is another box not shown in *Figure 9.16*, which is called **Diagnostic**. In this box, it is possible to see the estimated current to power the LED strip, LED count, and maximum current. In total, for our example, there are 23 entities associated with the LED strip controller we can monitor and control.

We will add the **Controls** box to the dashboard by clicking on the **ADD TO DASHBOARD** button just below the **Controls** box. A pop-up window will be presented to choose the dashboard to include it in. Choose the **Default** dashboard and click on the **NEXT** button. The next screen will ask you whether the current controls can be used or whether you want to pick a different card. Click on **ADD TO DASHBOARD**. The WLED controls box will be added to the **Home Default** dashboard, as can be seen in *Figure 9.18*.

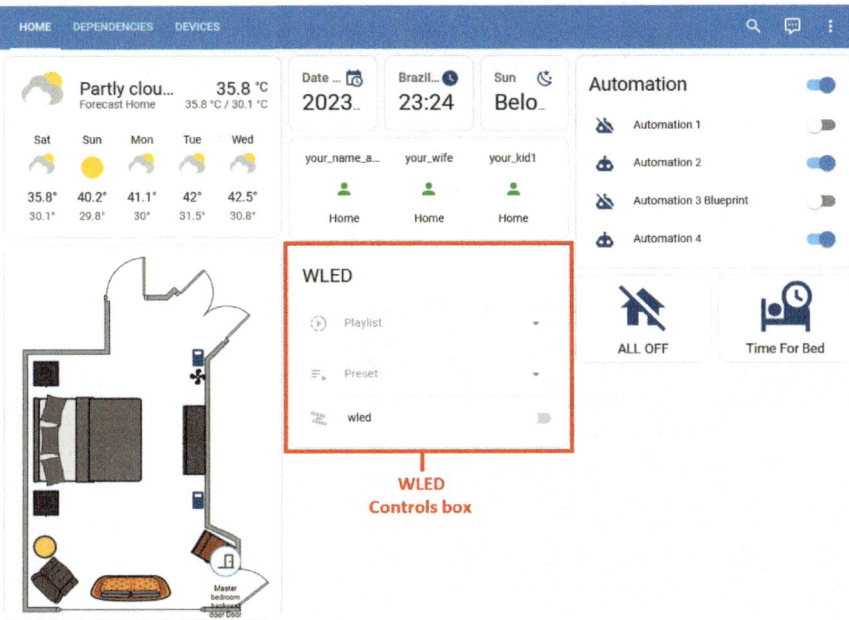

Figure 9.18 – WLED Controls box added to the Home Assistant dashboard

You can now easily control some WLED parameters using the Home Assistant dashboard. I created the demo video ch9-2 showing the WLED integration and control using Home Assistant.

The next part of this chapter will be focused on implementing an automation involving the LED strip controller. We will do this in the next section.

Creating an automation using the LED strip controller

As mentioned, the advantage of having the LED strip controller integrated into Home Assistant is being able to use the WLED integration entities in coordination with other parameters to create an automation.

In the case of our LED strip controller, we will need to consider what we can associate to use the two playlists created for the Halloween and Christmas seasons. The first thing we can associate is daytime. We only need the LED strip controller to be turned on at night and not the entire night – maybe until midnight or for four hours after sunset. So I decided that we need both playlists to be executed after sunset for 4 hours. The second factor to associate and distinguish between the two playlists is the time of the year. The Halloween playlist should be executed in October (or month number 10) and the Christmas playlist should be executed in December (or month number 12). In summary, the automation to be created can be explained as follows:

"After sunset, if we are in the months of October or December, turn LED_STRIP1 on and configure the Halloween playlist if we are in the month of October(10); otherwise, configure the Christmas playlist if we are in the month of December(12). Turn LED_STRIP1 off 4 hours after sunset."

Doing the same as was done in the automation created in *Chapter 5*, we have the following:

- **Trigger**: After sunset

- **Condition**: If month is October(10) or December(12)

- **Action**: Turn LED_STRIP1 on. If the month is October(10), configure the Halloween playlist; otherwise, configure the Christmas playlist. Wait until four hours after sunset and turn it off.

We will create this automation using the *C* hotkey and type Automation in the Home Assistant Quick Bar. We will select the **Navigate | Automations** option. This will lead us to the **Automations** tab. Click on the **+ CREATE AUTOMATION** button to start creating the automation. In the next window, click on the **Create new automation** option.

We will go over each part of the automation and explain how I implemented this automation in my home. First, let us start with the trigger condition, which is shown in *Figure 9.19*.

Figure 9.19 – LED strip controller – automation trigger configuration

We will have to use the **+ ADD TRIGGER** button to create the trigger for the automation. We will choose the **Sun** option and then mark the **Sunset** option as shown in *Figure 9.19*.

The next automation component to be added is the condition. We will click on the + **ADD CONDITION** button and choose the **Template** option. A template is an advanced Home Assistant feature allowing users to control information leaving and entering the system. It is used primarily for formatting outgoing messages, processing or parsing incoming data from sources that provide raw data such as **MQTT**, and is used in automations, as we are doing in this example. We will need to use a template to verify the current month and check if the month is October or December. We need to use a template because Home Assistant does not have a direct way to test in which month of the year we are. We will have to use the template code presented in *Figure 9.20*.

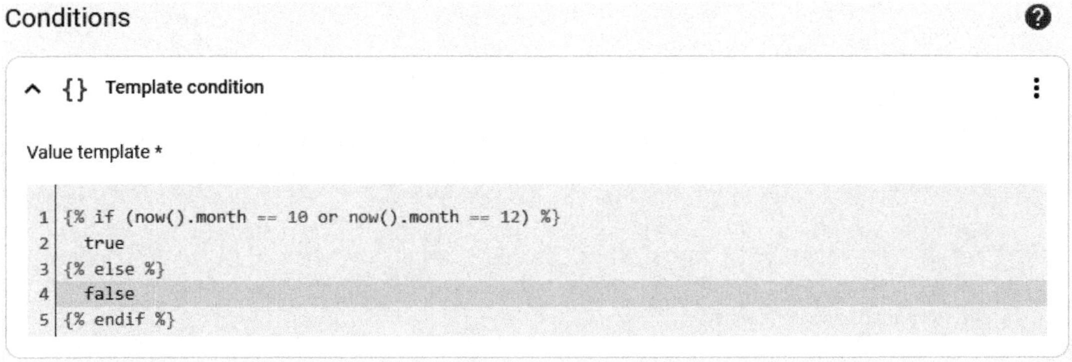

Figure 9.20 – LED strip controller – automation condition configuration

The code presented in *Figure 9.20* checks if the current month (now().month) is October, represented by the number 10, and if it is December, represented by the number 12. If this condition is satisfied, then the template returns the value true, otherwise, it returns the value false.

> **Important note**
>
> You can test template code using the **Developer Tools** option (Hotkey *c* | **Navigate** | **Developer Tools**) and type your code in the template editor window. You will see the result of your code in the result window on the right of the screen. More information about templates can be found at https://www.home-assistant.io/docs/configuration/templating/.

The last part of the automation example will be to create the actions. We will do that by clicking on the + **ADD ACTION** button. The first action to be added is **Call Service** and we will be looking for the **Light: Turn on** service. In the **Targets** field, we will click on the + **Choose device** button and then add the **WLED** device. In the sequence, we will have to add more template code, as we did before in the condition step. We will have to click on + **ADD ACTION** again and choose the **If-then** option. You will have to click on + **ADD CONDITION** under the **If-then** option to include the code presented in *Figure 9.21* under the If* : clause.

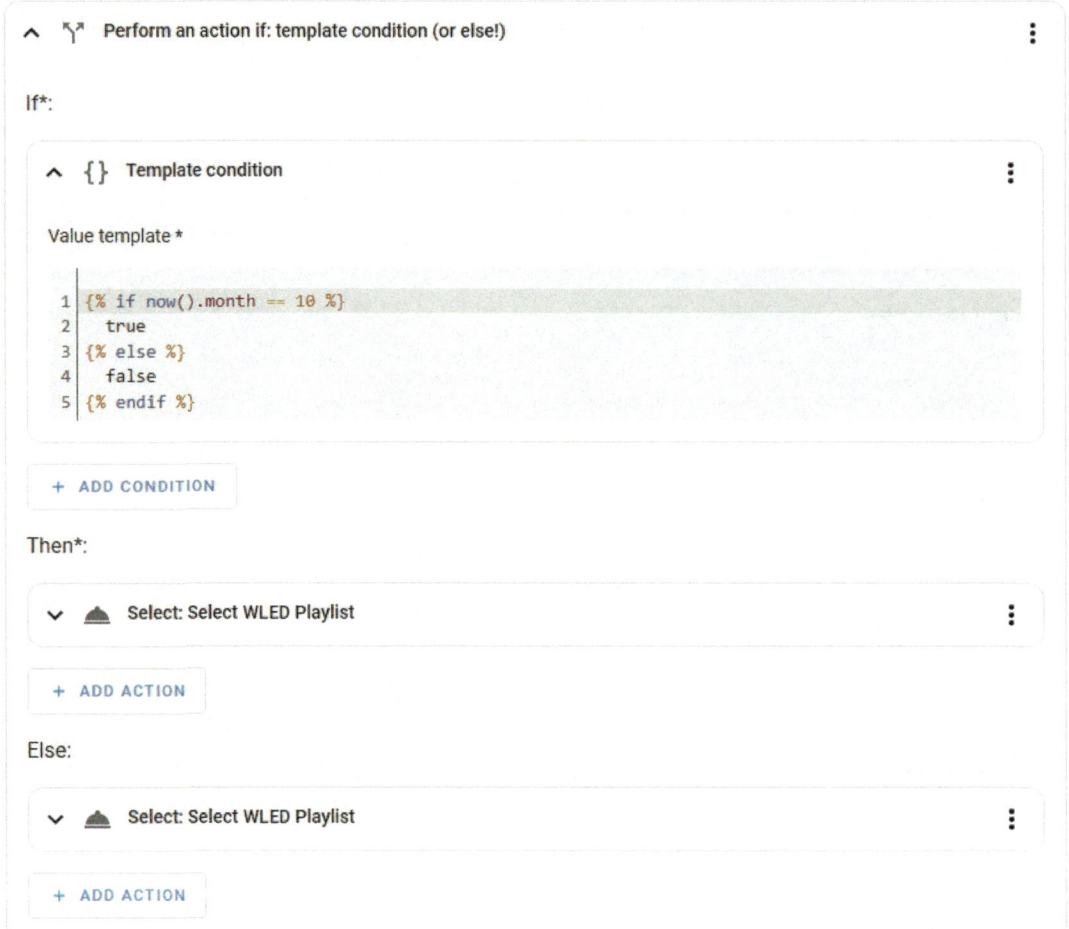

Figure 9.21 – LED strip controller – automation action configuration – part 1

The template code will now check only if the current month (now().month) is October, represented by the number 10, and if it is, return the value true, and otherwise returns false. If the condition is true, we have to add the action to select the Halloween playlist. We will do that by clicking on the **+ ADD ACTION** button under the **Then*:** clause. We will choose the **Call Service** option and will choose the **Select: Select** option. We will now click on + **Choose entity** and select the **WLED Playlist** option. In the **Option** field, we will include the **Halloween** playlist. We will click on the **Add else** link and add an else condition. We will click on the **+ ADD ACTION** button under the **Else:** clause. We will repeat the process done before for the Halloween playlist to the Christmas playlist by choosing the **Call Service** option, and will choose the **Select: Select** option. We will now click on the + **Choose entity** and select the option **WLED Playlist**. In the **Option** field, we will include the **Christmas** playlist.

After including the playlist selection, we will add the delay and turn off actions. We will include the delay by clicking on the **+ ADD ACTION** button outside of the **If-Then** option presented in *Figure 9.21*. You will have to choose the **Wait for time to pass (delay)** option and fill in the information, as in *Figure 9.22*, by including the number 4 under the **hh** field.

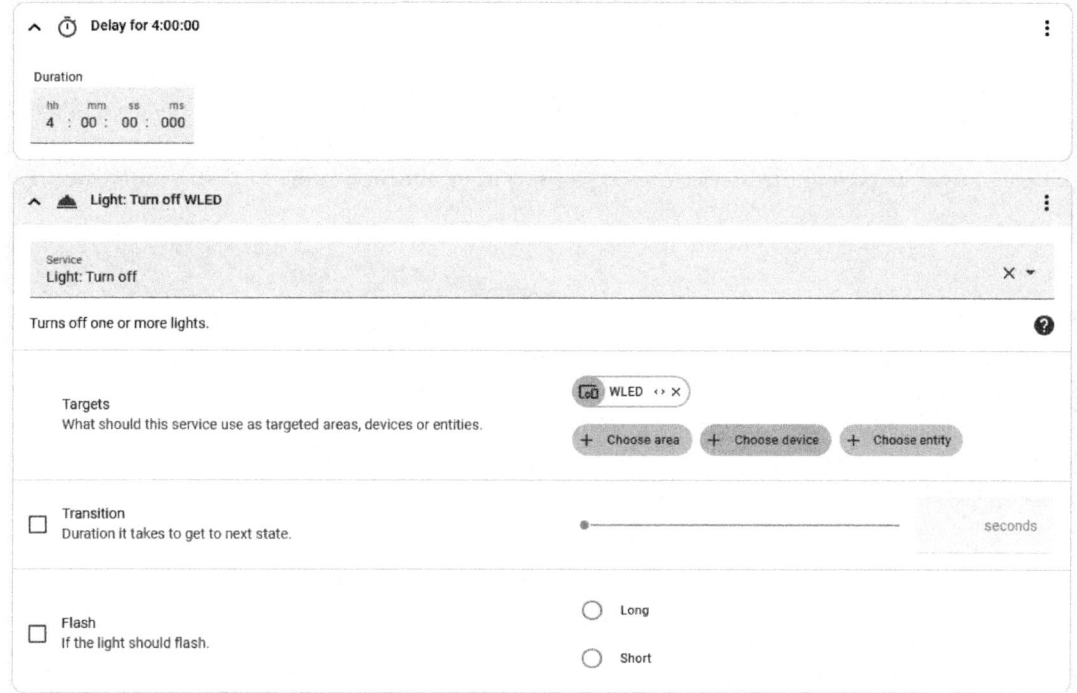

Figure 9.22 – LED strip controller – automation action configuration – part 2

After adding the 4-hour delay, we will have to include the last part of the automation, which is to turn off the LED strip controller. We will do that by clicking on the **+ ADD ACTION** button and selecting **Call Service**. We will look for the **Light: Turn off** service. In the **Targets** field, we will click on the **+ Choose device** button and then add the **WLED** device, as presented in *Figure 9.22*.

We can conclude the automation addition by clicking on the **SAVE** button at the bottom right of the screen. In the **Save** pop-up window, fill in the **Name** and **Description** fields using the **LED strip controller** and **Automate the LED Strip controller during Halloween and Christmas seasons** options respectively. Click on the **SAVE** button to finally save the automation.

You can test your automation now by clicking on the ellipsis in the top-right corner of the Home Assistant screen and clicking on **Run**. The automation will be triggered automatically and if the conditions match with the month of October or December, the LED strip will be turned on, select the appropriate playlist, and run it for 4 hours before turning off.

That concludes this section. We'll now move on to the next section, where we will provide some guidance and ideas on how to install the LED strip controller.

Installing the LED strip controller in your home

As you will have noticed from *Figure 9.3* and the *Ch9-1* and *Ch9-2* videos, I installed the LED strip controller project at the front of my house as a decorative light for Halloween and Christmas. I found a perfect spot for the installation that perfectly fits my entire LED strip and with the possibility of attaching some hooks to it so I can easily remove the LED strip. I used some type of carton paper and put hot glue to attach it to the house. You can see one hook attached to the LED strip in *Figure 9.23*.

Figure 9.23 – LED strip installation

On the ESP8266 Wi-Fi module side, I have to make sure to install it to somehow protect it from rain and any type of severe weather. I always keep glasses cases so I can use them in small projects like this. They are usually made of plastic, so it is quite easy to make holes and manipulate them. I made three holes in the glasses case – two to install a cable clamp and the other to pass through the cable to interconnect the Wi-Fi module to the LED strip. *Figure 9.24* illustrates what the ESP8266 Wi-Fi module installation inside the glasses case looks like.

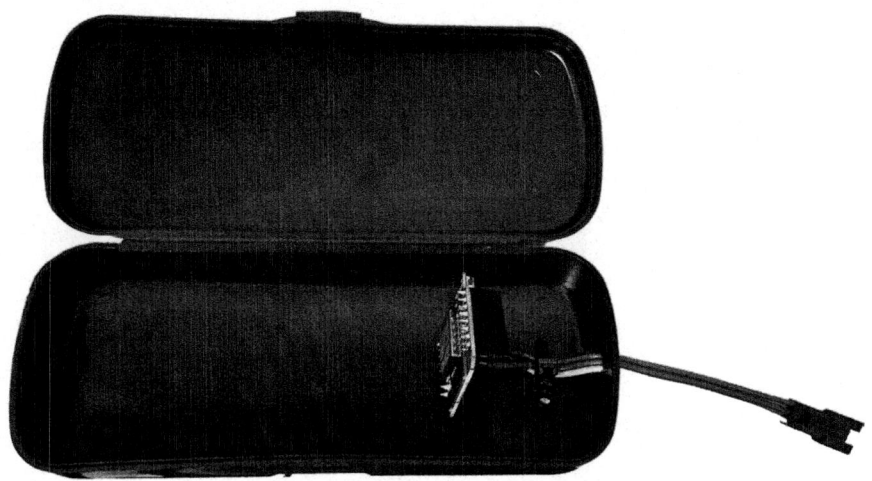

Figure 9.24 – ESP8266 Wi-Fi module installation

I created two more videos, ch9-3 and ch9-4, showing some other details of the installation. It will be interesting for you to look at so you can grab some ideas for the installation in your home. This section has not been detailed because the installation I did will likely be different from yours, therefore it simply provided you with insights into how this solution could also be implemented in your home.

We can finish this chapter with a few details about the installation of the LED strip controller project. I hope you enjoy it and it will serve as inspiration to create your own LED strip or LED string project. We will prepare to create a new hands-on project in the next chapter.

Summary

In this chapter, you learned how to create an LED strip controller project. You first learned how an LED strip works and we moved on to explaining and grouping the materials to build the project. In the sequence, it was explained how to easily interconnect the parts to create the project. The electronics part of the project was concluded and we continued with the software integration part.

The software of the WLED application was deployed to the project and you were guided on how to do it. Once the software was deployed, a couple of configurations were explained in detail so you could start putting the project to use. You learned how to create some configurations using the application software and later learned how to integrate and use the project in Home Assistant.

We reviewed some previous content, from *Chapter 5*, by creating a new automation where a new Home Assistant resource called a template was explored. You also briefly learned how to use them in the project.

Finally, I provided you with some general information on how I did the project installation in my home, to motivate you to create your own.

In the next chapter, we will continue to learn by doing another hands-on project. We will cover a complete application involving new hardware devices, and it could be useful to monitor different dependency temperatures in your house. I hope you enjoy the next project as much as you hopefully enjoyed the one covered in this chapter.

10

Hands-On Project 3 – Creating a Five-Zone Temperature Logger for Your Home

This hands-on project will guide you to create or integrate five commercial Bluetooth thermometers into an **ESP32 Bluetooth and Wi-Fi module**. It will show how to hack the thermometers to broadcast its data over Bluetooth, configure the ESP32 to get this data, and then share it with other applications, including **Home Assistant**. The project aims to expand your **home automation** capabilities, so the chapter will guide you to use some of the add-on tools installed in *Chapter 6*, such as **Node-RED**, **InFluxDB**, and **Grafana**, to create a temperature logger for your home.

This chapter will show you how to prepare and assemble material to build a **five-zone temperature logger**, set up a **data parser** in Node-RED, create and configure a database to store data using InfluxDB, and configure **charts** to be presented using Grafana. Also, there will be a section explaining how to configure and handle data in Home Assistant. This system will support you to monitor different temperatures inside and outside your home. You can use this temperature information to better control your **Heating, Ventilation, and Air Conditioning** (HVAC) system, improve energy efficiency, support preventive maintenance, optimize the system's schedule, and provide data insights and analysis.

The following topics will be discussed in this chapter:

- Understanding the five-zone temperature logger system architecture
- Creating and configuring the five-zone temperature sensors and the ESP32 module-based temperature hub
- Connecting the sensor data to a database using Node-RED
- Storing data in a database using InfluxDB
- Presenting InfluxDB data using Grafana
- Using the five-zone temperature sensor in Home Assistant

After completing this chapter, you will learn how you can create an application to monitor the temperature in different areas of your home and log this data for future reference, or to have fun with it. You will know how to use a sensor architecture, combined with a set of tools used for **IOT systems**, and use this data in Home Assistant to implement all the concepts learned in this book.

Technical requirements

Like *Chapter 7*, you will need to be familiar with databases, queries, and chart tools to better understand the concepts presented in this chapter. Also, I recommend you read *Chapters 3* and *4*, where I explained how to create and hack some devices used in my home. If you are familiar with **JSON** and **JavaScript**, you will understand the flow presented in Node-RED. Code and support material could be found at `https://github.com/PacktPublishing/Building-Smart-Home-Automation-Solutions-with-Home-Assistant/tree/main/Chapter%2010`. Check out the following video to view the Code in Action: `https://bit.ly/45aj7Ni`

Understanding the five-zone temperature logger system architecture

The temperature logger was born from two main needs I had. The first need was to try to keep the same temperature throughout the entire house, since it has two HVAC systems and the temperatures in the rooms are not the same. The second need (which came later) arose after some research on how to implement a temperature measurement in the rooms, where I saw the opportunity to learn and use different software tools and hardware devices in my projects. Unfortunately, I didn't succeed in implementing the feedback control performed by the HVAC controller, due to one of the two installed in my house being too old and a modern controller being incompatible. So, I decided to postpone the HVAC control when replacing the old HVAC. So, the project so far helps me verify and monitor the temperature in six locations in my home. The Kids1 and kids2 bedrooms, the kitchen, and the master bedroom temperatures are indoors. The garage and backyard temperatures are outdoors.

I will split the temperature logger system architecture into two parts for better understanding – *hardware* and *software*. These two parts will be explained in detail in the next two subsections.

Hardware system architecture

The five-zone temperature logger hardware system architecture is presented in the following figure:

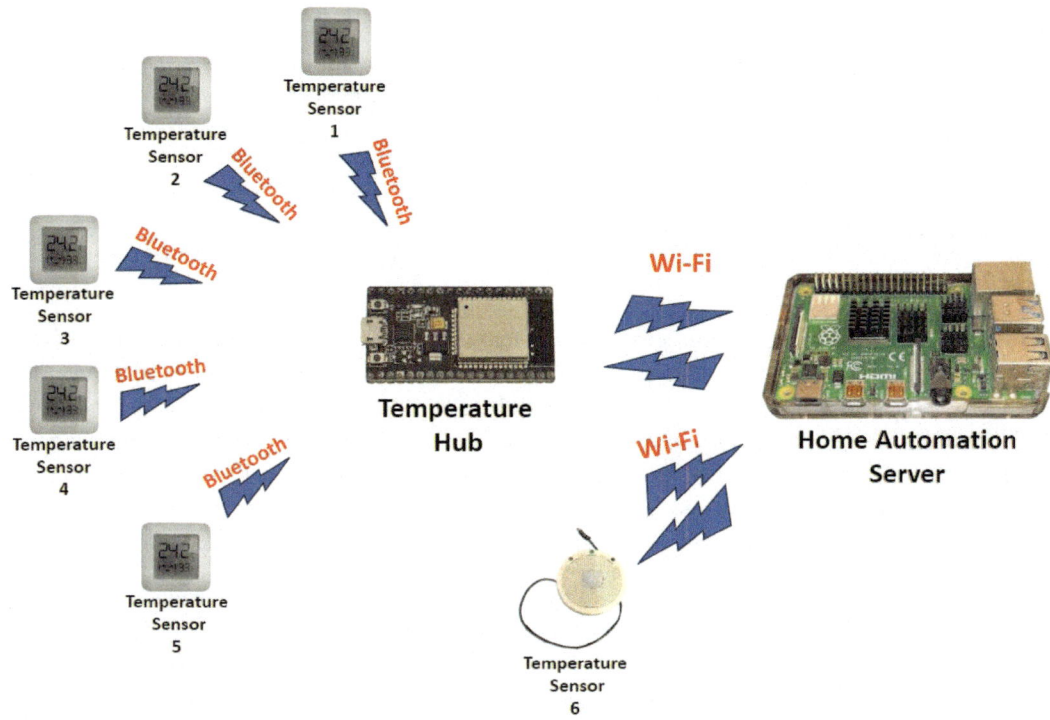

Figure 10.1 – Temperature logger hardware architecture

Reading *Figure 10.1* from left to right, you can see the **temperature sensors** from **1** to **5** sending temperature and humidity data to a **Temperature Hub** using Bluetooth communication. The temperature hub gets this data and sends the temperature and humidity of these five sensors to the **Home Automation Server**, implemented in the **Raspberry Pi**. This data is sent on one **MQTT package** every 5 minutes using Wi-Fi communication. I am also using, as part of the temperature logger system, the temperature sensor data from the **double measurement sensor** installed in my garage and created in *Chapter 3*.

The temperature sensors from *1* to *5* are **Bluetooth Low Energy** (**BLE**) sensors that can be bought at larger retail companies globally. The brand and model is a **Xiaomi Mijia Bluetooth - LYWSD03MMC** thermometer, as shown in *Figure 10.2*.

Figure 10.2 – The Bluetooth thermometer used in the project

These sensors have the following specifications:

- 28 mm x 28 mm LCD display

- DC2.5V – 3V battery power voltage

- Bluetooth 4.2 BLE wireless connection

- **Temperature range**: 0°C to +60°C (32°F to 140°F)

- **Humidity range**: 0% to 99% RH

As you can see from the specifications provided, the sensor can measure temperature and humidity, and it also includes the battery level as part of the data communication package. The Bluetooth temperature sensors have their original firmware hacked to be able to work and communicate to the temperature Hub firmware, using unencrypted messages. We will see in the following subsection more details about the firmware to be used and in the next section when we will create the system. Temperature sensor 6, as we mentioned, is the one created in *Chapter 3*. We will not need to change anything in its hardware; only the temperature data will be manipulated, which was not done previously.

The temperature hub is based on the **ESP32-WROOM-32** communication module made by **Expressif System**. Currently, this module is **Not Recommended for New Designs** (**NRND**), but any ESP32 communication module in mass production with Wi-Fi and Bluetooth communication capabilities can be used. Even though it is not recommended for new designs, you can still use this module in your project if you find it available for purchase. The ESP32 communication module we will use in this project is shown in *Figure 10.3*.

Figure 10.3 – The ESP32 communication module used in this project

The ESP32 chip is much more powerful and has plenty more features than the **ESP8266** used in the other projects in this book. The reason we will use it in this project is just because it has Bluetooth and Wi-Fi communication capabilities combined in a single module. Bluetooth communication is not available in the ESP8266. Bluetooth is required to get temperature and humidity data from the temperature sensors, and Wi-Fi is required to communicate with the home automation server. Nothing else is required beyond that, so the temperature hub's role is just to get temperature and humidity data from the sensors and pack to send to the Home Automation Server. The firmware required to run this module is a **Tasmota** variation built for ESP32, as we will see in the next subsection.

The home automation server is the same one we created in *Chapter 2*, and we will need to use some of the add-on software we installed in *Chapter 7*.

We will explore in the next subsection the software architecture used in this hands-on project.

Software system architecture

The software architecture used in this project is presented in *Figure 10.4*.

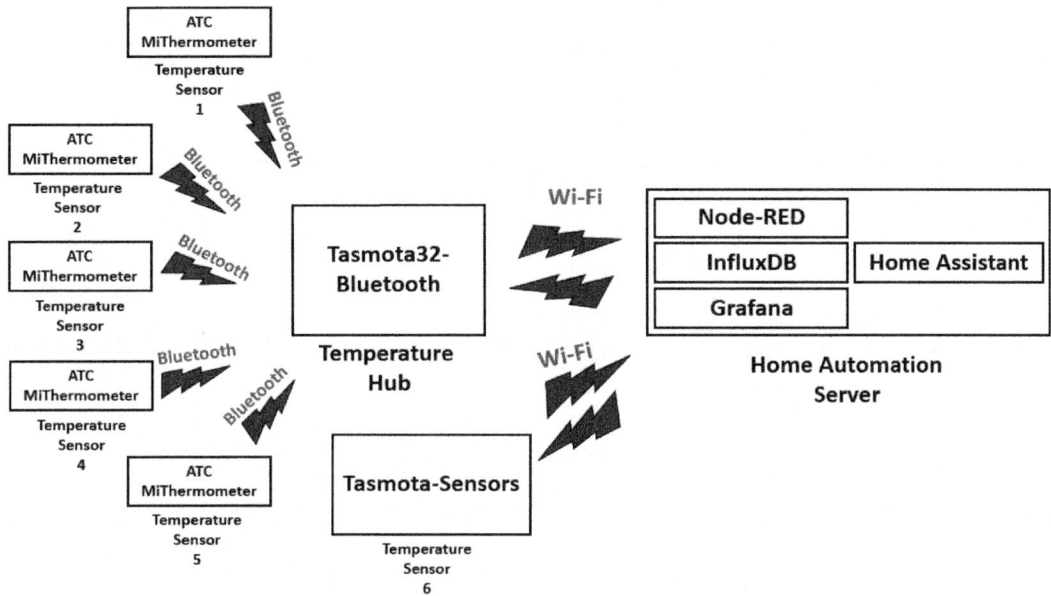

Figure 10.4 – Temperature logger software architecture

Reading *Figure 10.4* from left to right, the Temperature Sensors from **1** to **5** have software different from the original. I had to change the original software so that it can communicate with the upstream device or temperature hub without the need to decrypt messages. There is more than one firmware that can be uploaded to the **Mijia Thermometer**. I used the one provided at this link: https://github.com/atc1441/ATC_MiThermometer. It is called **ATC MiThermometer**, developed by Aaron Chrisophel. You can configure some parameters in the firmware, such as the *advertising time*, which is how often the display sends data to the temperature hub. I configured the sensors to send information every five minutes. You can also change how some information will be displayed – for example, whether the temperature is displayed in Celsius or Fahrenheit. We will see how to change the original firmware for this temperature sensor in the next section.

The next software block in *Figure 10.4* is the software for the temperature hub. This software is a Tasmota variation for the ESP32 communication module called **Tasmota32-Bluetooth**. It works like a gateway or bridge that automatically gets the Bluetooth temperature data packages and forwards them to the home automation server. We will see in the next section that the configurations to be made will follow the same approach we did before for devices in *Chapters 3* and *4*.

There is not much to comment about temperature sensor **6**. It is the same **Tasmota-Sensors** version we uploaded in *Chapter 3*.

The interesting aspect of this software architecture lies in the software used in the home automation server, which can be customized to suit your specific requirements. We will primarily use the add-on software Node-RED, InfluxDB, and Grafana to implement the logger, which we briefly covered in *Chapter 7*. Node-RED will be used to parse the data from the temperature sensors and format them for inclusion in the InfluxDB database. We will configure a dashboard in Grafana to get data from the InfluxDB database and populate some charts for temperature and humidity. We will be able to access this logged temperature data remotely using Grafana through our Home Assistant installation. We will also configure Home Assistant to read data from the sensors and display it in the dashboard, so you can check temperatures using the Home Assistant dashboard and create automations using this information.

Now that we have had an overview of the hardware and software architecture, we will now see how to set up software in Bluetooth thermometers and also how to upload the Tasmota variant firmware to the ESP32 communication module.

Creating and configuring the five-zone temperature sensors and the ESP32 module-based temperature hub

What we will need to do to create the hardware and software ecosystem presented in the last section, and *Figures 10.1* and *10.4*, is add the Bluetooth temperature sensors and the temperature hub hardware devices and set up the software on them. The Bluetooth thermometers are battery-powered and come with an adhesive sticker, so you can glue them to any room of your home. I have these sensors spread apart in distances varying from 5 to 13 meters. The ESP32 module will just be connected to the power supply, so you can connect it using a USB type A to micro USB type B cable, connected to a USB power adapter, or follow my approach by connecting it to Raspberry Pi, as shown in *Figure 1.8* in *Chapter 1*.

In the following subsections, I will guide you on how to upload and configure the software for the Mi thermometers and also how to install the Tasmota variant in the ESP32 communication module.

Changing the Mi Bluetooth thermometer firmware

If you want to flash the firmware of more than one thermometer and you have all of them with you, I recommend you remove the battery of all of them, except the one you want to update the firmware. After doing that, proceed through the following steps to change the thermometer firmware in each one:

> **Important note**
> Changing the original Mi thermometer improperly can make the device nonfunctional. When following these steps, you do so at your own risk.

1. Download the latest `ATC_Termometer.bin` file from `https://github.com/atc1441/ATC_MiThermometer/releases`. I will use *Release 78* from *July 2022*.

2. Open `https://atc1441.github.io/TelinkFlasher.html`. Refer to *Figure 10.6* for the buttons covered in the following steps.

3. Open the thermometer lid at the back, remove the battery for 10 seconds, and reconnect it to force a reboot in the thermometer. In the web page opened in *step 2*, click on the **Connect** button (refer to *Figure 10.6*). A window presented in *Figure 10.5* will scan for Bluetooth devices. Find the Bluetooth-supported device with the highest signal level; it might be the one you want to use. Click on the device indicator you want to connect to and click on the **Pair** button shown in *Figure 10.5*. If you could not find the Bluetooth device on the list, click on the **Cancel** button and restart the process by clicking on the **Connect** button (refer to *Figure 10.6*).

Figure 10.5 – The thermometer update when software scanning for Bluetooth devices

4. Click on the **Do Activation** button (refer to *Figure 10.6*). The **Device Know id**, **Mi Token**, and **Mi Bind Key** fields will be populated with some numbers. As a precaution, note the numbers presented in these fields and store them in a file. They will be helpful if, someday, you want to return to the original factory default firmware.

5. Click on the **Choose File** button and choose the file you downloaded in *step 1*. Click on the **Start Flashing** button. The firmware will start to flash in the Bluetooth thermometer, as presented in *Figure 10.6*. Do not touch or remove the thermometer battery at this time.

Figure 10.6 – The Mi thermometer firmware update in progress

6. In *Figure 10.6*, you can see at the bottom that the status is **60% done**. It took me around 29 seconds to get the firmware updated. You now can configure some parameters in the firmware by using the button options. The button options I configured are presented and highlighted in the following list and in *Figure 10.7*, which is part of the web page opened in *step 2*. Just click on the buttons to send the configuration commands directly to the thermometer:

-   **Sensor display**: In °C
-   **Sensor Advertising**: In °C
-   **Advertising interval**: 5 Minutes

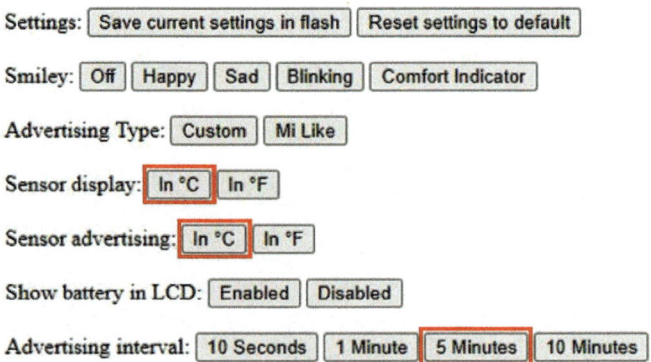

Figure 10.7 – The Mi thermometer firmware options to be configured

7. Replace the thermometer lid and repeat the steps from *step 3* onward if you want to flash the firmware for other thermometers.

You have to make sure you take note of the thermometer ID so that you can reference where it is located later. What I did to help with this task was to stick a label with the ID on the thermometer side. The thermometer ID will be in the *ATC-XXXXXX* format – for example, my backyard thermometer ID is *ATC-19F133*.

After you have uploaded the firmware to all thermometers and have all their IDs, identify where you will place them. Before you place them in their temperature measurement locations, I recommend you proceed to create the temperature hub by following the next section.

Uploading the ESP32 Tasmota firmware variant to the temperature hub

In *Chapter 3*, we used **Tasmotizer** to upload the Tasmota firmware code to the created **double measurement sensor**. Currently, Tasmotizer doesn't support the ESP32, only the ESP8266; therefore, in this chapter, we will use another tool to do the same task that Tasmotizer does.

We will use the **Tasmota web installer** to upload the Tasmota firmware to the ESP32 communication module. You need to follow these steps to do that, which are also explained in the video *Ch10-1*:

1. Open this web page on your computer: `https://tasmota.github.io/install/`. The page will look like the one presented in *Figure 10.8*.

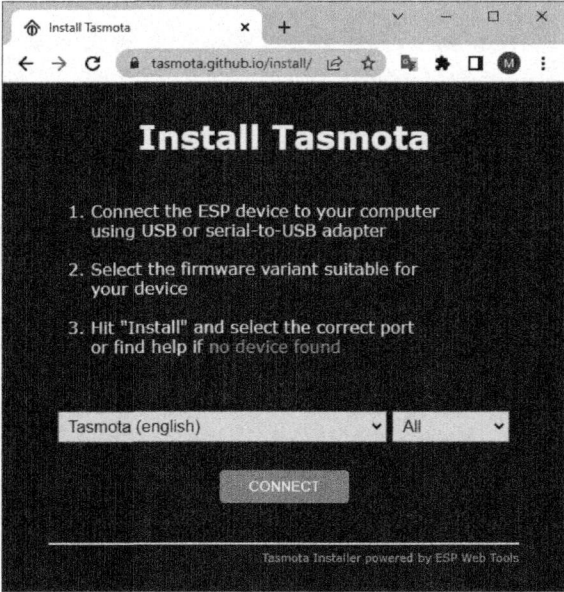

Figure 10.8 – Tasmota web installer

2. Follow the instructions from *1* to *3* on the website and shown in *Figure 10.8*, as follows:

   I. Get your ESP32 communication module and connect to the computer using a USB type A to microUSB type B cable. A red LED in the ESP32 module will be turned on.

   II. Click in the first drop-down box menu, as shown in *Figure 10.8*, to find and select the **Tasmota32 bluetooth (english)** option.

   III. Click in the second drop-down box menu, and select the option for your ESP32 module. In my case, I will use the **ESP32** option.

   IV. Click on the **CONNECT** button, and in the window that opens, select the serial port USB bridge that the ESP32 is connected to. Usually, it is the one indicated by the **CP2102 driver** (`https://www.silabs.com/developers/usb-to-uart-bridge-vcp-drivers?tab=downloads`). In my case, it is **CP2102 USB to UART Bridge Controller (COM9)**. Click on the **Connect** button.

3. In the **Tasmota** Screen, click on the **INSTALL TASMOTA32 BLUETOOTH (ENGLISH)** option, as shown in *Figure 10.9*.

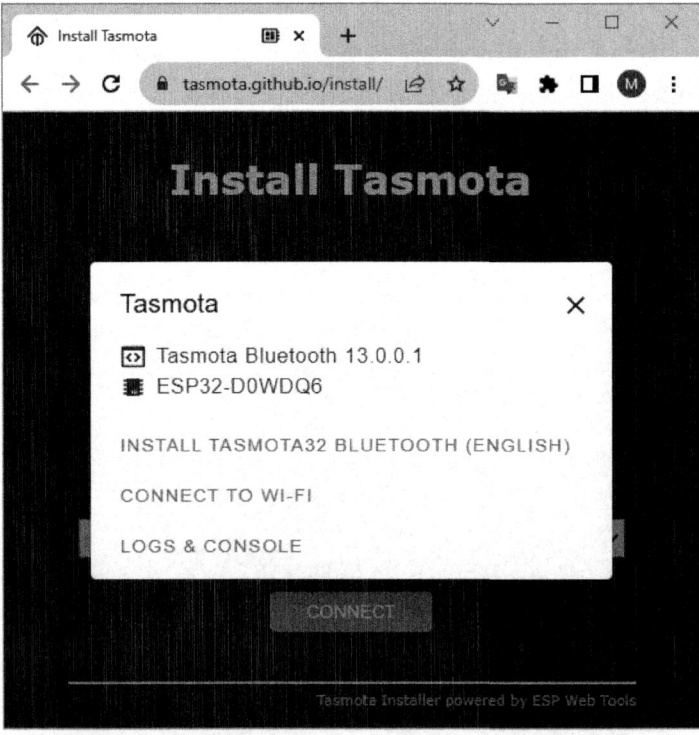

Figure 10.9 – The Tasmota web installer | the Tasmota screen

4. On the **Erase device** screen, mark the **Erase device** checkbox and click on the **NEXT** option, as shown in *Figure 10.10*.

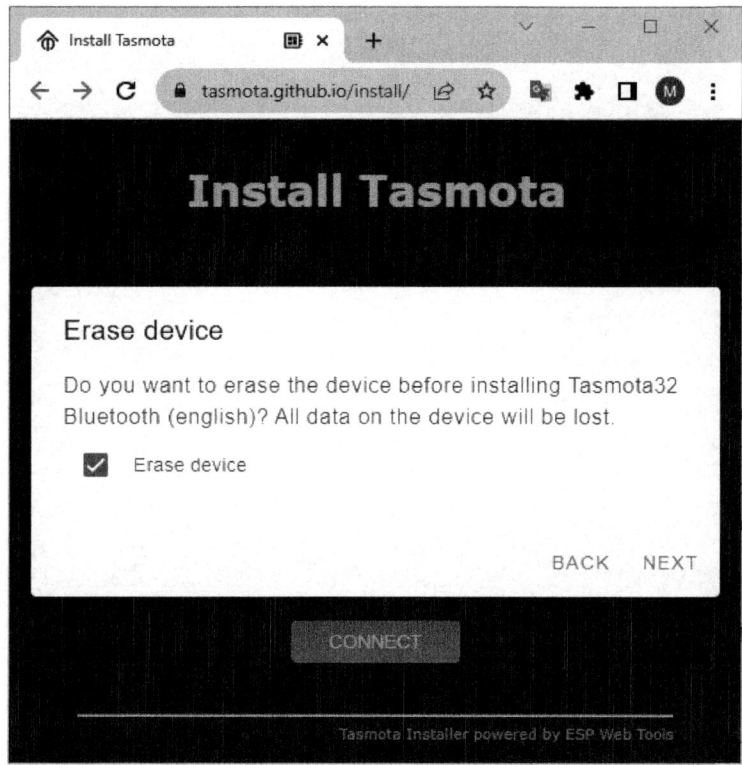

Figure 10.10 – The Tasmota web installer | the Erase device screen

5. On the **Confirm Installation** screen, click on the **INSTALL** option. If the communication fails, restart from *step 3* and press and hold the **BOOT** push button (as shown in *Figure 10.3*). If everything goes well, the device will be erased, and a progress circle will appear. After around two minutes, you will get the screen shown in *Figure 10.11*:

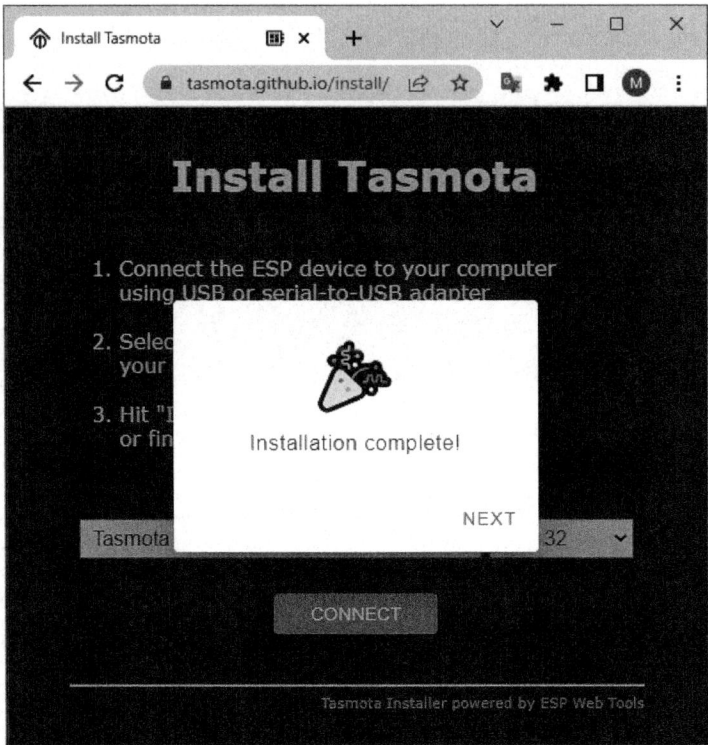

Figure 10.11 – The Tasmota web installer | Installation complete!

6. Click on the **NEXT** option, as shown in *Figure 10.11*. The **Configure Wi-Fi** screen will appear. Choose the SSID network and type the password in the **Password** field. Click on the **CONNECT** option. The device will be connected to the network, and if everything goes well, a screen will appear displaying **device connected to the network**. Click on the **VISIT DEVICE** option.

7. Another tab in your web browser should be open that points to the IP for your ESP32 or temperature hub. If the IP 0.0.0.0 is opened instead, try to reset your ESP32 module by pressing the **BOOT** push button.

After the installation, we will need to do some configuration as we did with the Tasmota sensors and actuators in *Chapters 3* and *4*. I will split these configurations into the following subsections.

Configuring the MQTT server

The **MQTT configuration** will be done as we did in *Chapter 3* in the *Configuring the MQTT information in the sensor* section. You will configure the temperature hub with the following steps:

1. Make sure you have the web browser pointed to the main Tasmota screen, presented for the ESP32 you just programmed in the previous section.

2. From the main menu, click on the **Configuration** button.

3. Click on the **Configure MQT** button; you will see the screen shown in *Figure 10.12*.

4. Type homeassistant.local in the **Host** field.

5. Type your_name in the **User** field.

6. Type your_password in the **Password** field.

7. Type ESP32_TEMPERATURE_HUB in the **Topic** field.

8. Click on the **Save** button.

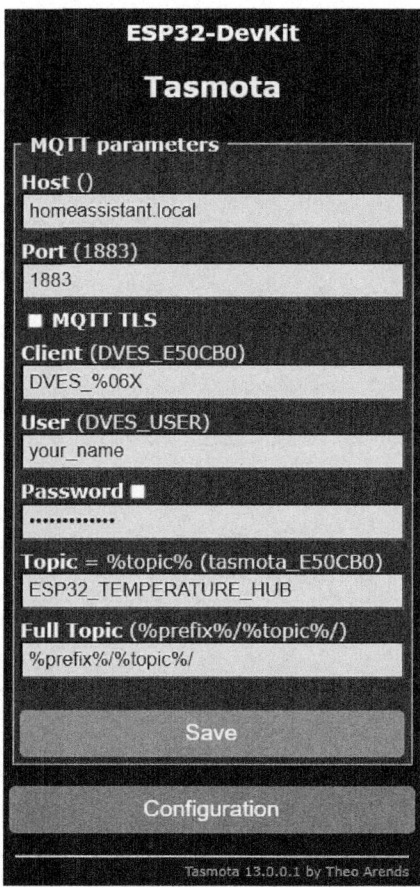

Figure 10.12 – ESP32 Tasmota MQTT configuration

After configuring the MQTT, we will need to configure the device name, which will be done in the next subsection.

Configuring the device name

The **device name** will be helpful to identify how the device will be named when found using the web page, or when listed by the **TasmotaAdmin** software. We will perform the following configuration to change the device name:

1. From the main menu, click on the **Configuration** button.
2. Click on the **Configure Other** button, and you will the screen shown in *Figure 10.13*.
3. Fill the **Device Name** field with ESP32_TEMPERATURE_HUB.
4. Fill the **Friendly Name 1** field with ESP32_TEMPERATURE_HUB.
5. Click on the **Save** button.

Figure 10.13 – ESP32 Tasmota device name configuration

After configuring the device name, we will enable Bluetooth in the ESP32 device so that we can start to receive data from the thermometers. We will do this in the next subsection.

Enabling Bluetooth on the device

The last step in the configuration is to enable Bluetooth communication so that we can start receiving information from the Bluetooth temperature sensors. We will do this by executing the following sequence:

1. From the main menu, click on the **Configuration** button.
2. Click on the **Configure BLE** button; you will see the screen shown in *Figure 10.14*.
3. In the **Bluetooth Settings** area, click on the **Enable Bluetooth** option.
4. Click on the **Save** button.
5. The unit will be restarted and show the data from the Bluetooth sensors in the main Tasmota configuration screen, as shown in *Figure 10.15*.

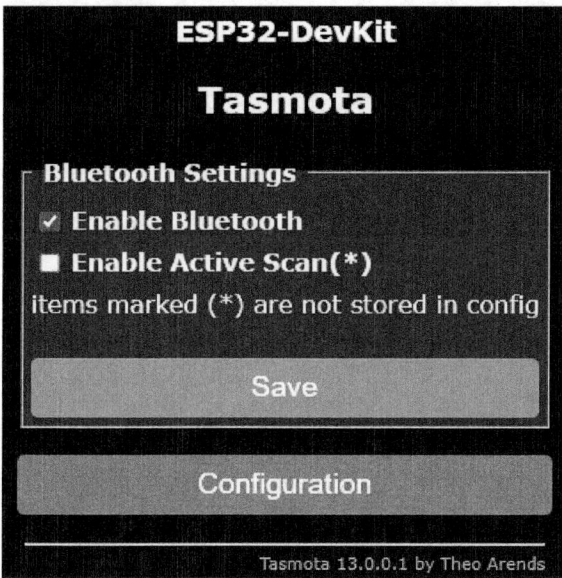

Figure 10.14 – The ESP32 Bluetooth Settings screen

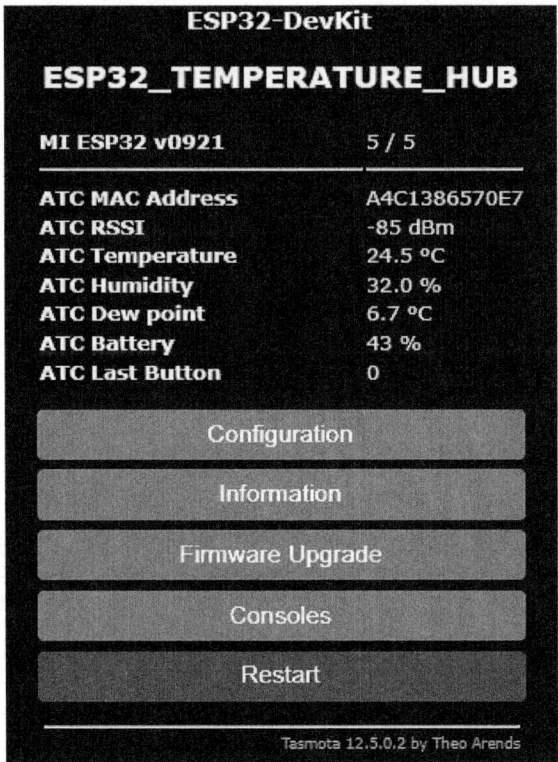

Figure 10.15 – The ESP32 temperature hub configured

The information presented in the preceding figure shows the data for one of the five sensors pre-configured. You can see all data from the sensors referring to the ATC firmware installed in the previous subsection.

For now, we are done with the temperature hub configuration. Now, we will move on to the home automation server and start to collect data from the sensors to be stored and presented.

Connecting the sensors data to a database using Node-RED

In *Chapter 7*, we briefly delved into Node-RED, where we created an automation flow. This flow involved capturing motion from the **double measurement sensor** introduced in *Chapter 3* and combining it with the sunset condition. As a result, an action was triggered to turn on the lights in my garage. In this section, we will use Node-RED to grab the temperature data from the double measurement sensor and the Bluetooth Mi temperature sensors via the temperature hub, format this data, and store it in the InfluxDB database.

The details about how to create the flow to manage the temperature data capture will be split into three parts:

- Double measurement sensor data capturing and formatting
- Temperature hub data capturing and formatting
- Configuring the data to be stored in the InfluxDB database

I will detail each one of these steps in the following three subsections.

Double measurement sensor data capturing and formatting

We will start with *step 1* by opening Node-RED from the Home Assistant sidebar, using the Home Assistant Operating System installation type done in *Chapter 2*, and following these steps:

1. We will click on the + symbol in the workspace area and rename the flow by clicking on the original name (for example, `Flow 1`) twice. In the **Edit flow** screen, we will add the name 5 `Temperature Logger` to the **Name** field. Click on the **Done** button.

2. Next, we will listen to the MQTT data from the double-measurement sensor. We will do that by clicking on the **MQTT in** node under the **Network** group. We will drag and drop the **MQTT in** node from the Node-RED palette into the workspace. Click on the **MQTT in** node twice and edit the information according to *Figure 10.16*.

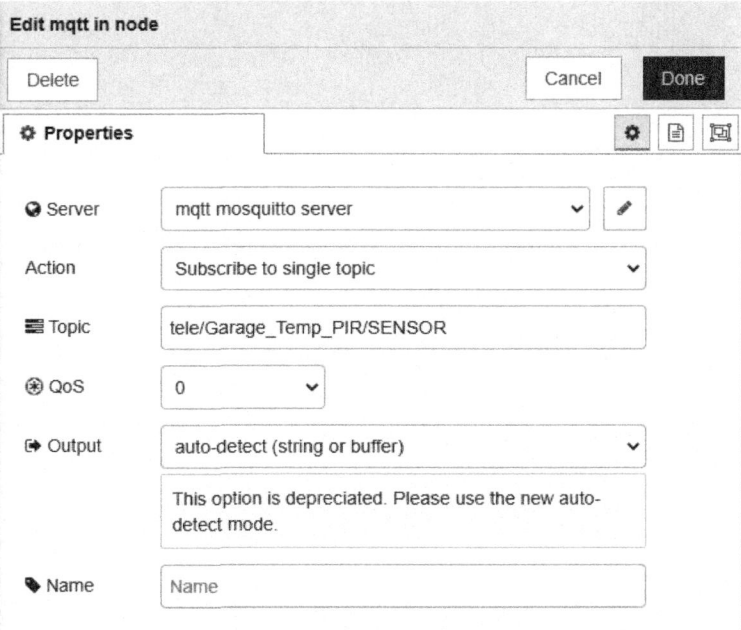

Figure 10.16 – The MQTT in node configuration | the double measurement sensor

3. We will include two configurations in the **MQTT in** node presented in *Figure 10.16* – **Server** and **Topic**. **Server** will be filled according to the configuration made in *Figure 7.3* in *Chapter 7*. We will add, in this case, `mqtt mosquitto server` to the **Server** field. The topic we will use is `tele/Garage_Temp_PIR/SENSOR`. Click on the **Done** button.

4. We will convert the data captured from the double measurement sensor from the JSON format to JavaScript format. This is required to better manipulate and format the data per our needs. We will do that by using the **json** node under the **parser** group. We will drag and drop the **json** node to the workspace and click it twice to configure it, according to the following options:

   - The **Action** field: `Convert between JSON String & Object`

   - The **Property** field: `msg.payload`

5. Click on the **Done** button once you have finished the preceding configurations. We will then connect the **MQTT in** node output to the **json** node input.

6. We will finish the configuration by adding a function to format the payload message with the contact we need, according to the data to be stored in the influxDB database table for the sensors. We will do that using the **function** node under the **function** group. We will drag and drop the **function** node from the palette and drop it into the workspace. Click twice on the **function** node and edit the properties according to *Figure 10.17*.

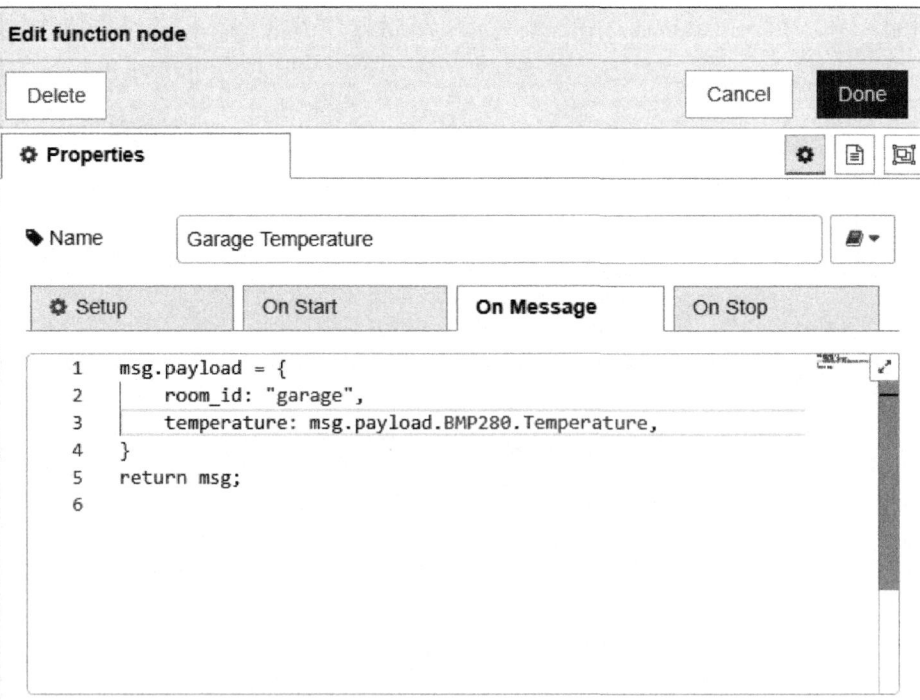

Figure 10.17 – The function node configuration | the double measurement sensor

7. We will add the name `Garage Temperature` to the **Name** field, as shown in *Figure 10.17*. We will fill the **On Message** tab with the code shown in the same figure. What we are doing here is just formatting the content of the `msg.payload` object, with the `room_id` value as `garage` and the `temperature` as the temperature read directly from the sensor via the **MQTT in** node or `msg.payload.BMP280.Temperature`. If we include a **debug** node from the **common** group, we will have the data shown in *Figure 10.18*:

```
tele/Garage_Temp_PIR/SENSOR : msg.payload : Object
▼object
   room_id: "garage"
   temperature: 29.2
```

Figure 10.18 – The debug output message | the double measurement sensor

The flow diagram we will have, as a result of interconnecting all wires of the nodes related to the double measurement sensor temperature data capture and format, will look like *Figure 10.19*.

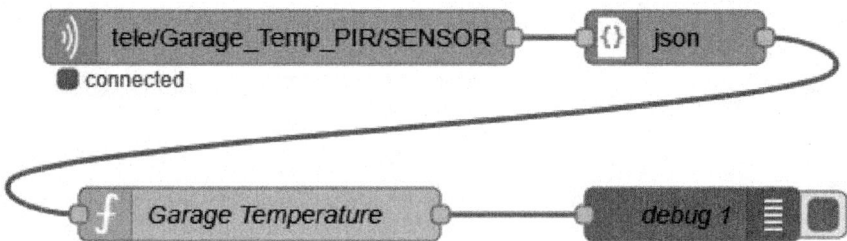

Figure 10.19 – The double measurement sensor data capture and format flow

Temperature hub data capturing and formatting

We will have to configure the same MQTT server as done in *step 2* of the *Double measurement sensor data capturing and formatting* subsection. We will follow the same process that we did for the double measurement sensor with another flow with the same node types, but we will manipulate the data differently. We will do this by following the these steps:

1. We will create another flow with the **MQTT in** and **json** nodes, interconnected one after the other, and will configure the parameters in each node as follows:

    • **MQTT in**:

        • The **Server** field: `mqtt mosquitto server`

        • The **Topic** field: `tele/ESP32_TEMPERATURE_HUB/SENSOR`

- **json**:

  - The **Action** field: `Convert between JSON String & Object`

  - The **Property** field: `msg.payload`

2. The data from the temperature hub combines five temperatures in one single message, but to populate the temperature database, they need to be sent one at a time. In this case, we will need to split the message and format it as we did for the double measurement sensor garage temperature. We will first split the data using the **Split** node in the **sequence** group. After dragging and dropping the **Split** node from the palette to the workspace, double-click on the node and configure the parameters according to *Figure 10.20*.

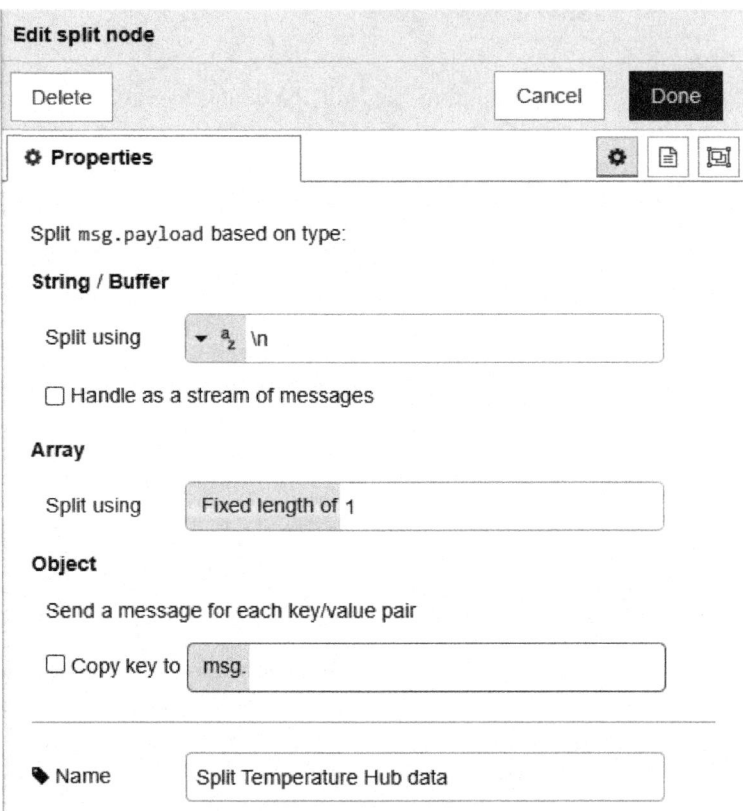

Figure 10.20 – The split node configuration | the temperature hub

3. We will configure the msg.payload data from the temperature hub to split the received message each time it has a **Line Feed** (\n) character type. We will configure each message fragment as an array of 1 message each. We will use the friendly name of Split Temperature Hub data to identify the node name. The next node to add is a **function** node from the **function** group. After including the node in the workspace, double-click on it and fill in the fields according to *Figure 10.21*:

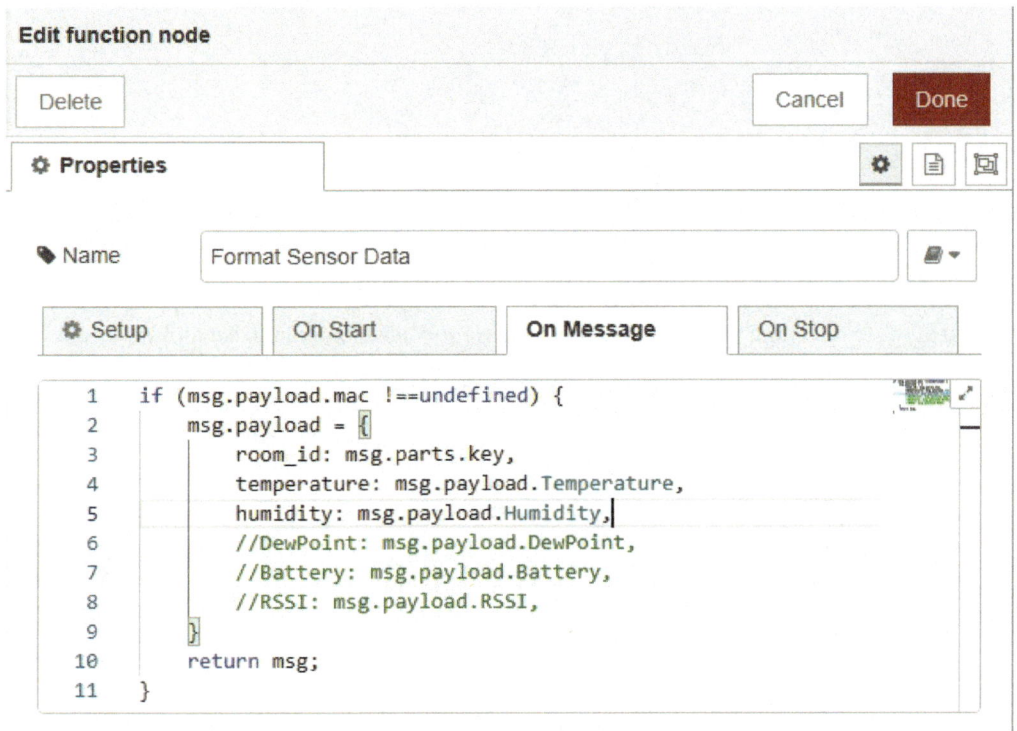

Figure 10.21 – Function node configuration | the temperature hub

4. We will name the node Format Sensor Data. We will check for messages with the msg.payload.mac defined or different from undefined (!==undefined). So, if we receive a message with a MAC defined, we will set up the temperature database information, with room_id as the msg.parts.key content, temperature as msg.payload.Temperature, and humidity as msg.payload.Humidity. We will return the formatted message (msg) content to the flow using the return msg command. Click on the **Done** button after finishing the configuration. By including a **debug** node after the **format Sensor data function** node, we will get a message such as the one shown in *Figure 10.22*.

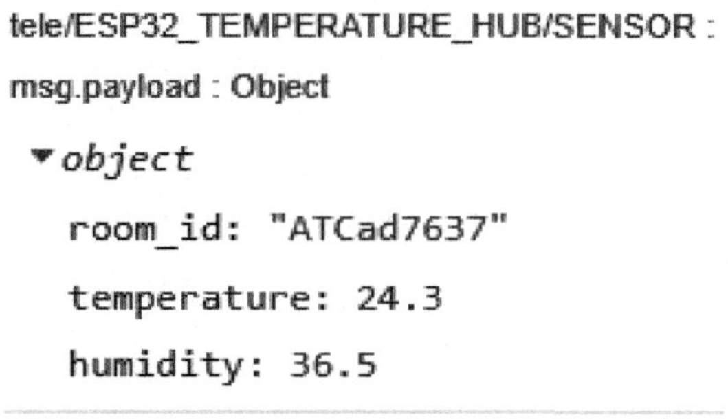

```
tele/ESP32_TEMPERATURE_HUB/SENSOR :
msg.payload : Object
  ▼object
    room_id: "ATCad7637"
    temperature: 24.3
    humidity: 36.5
```

Figure 10.22 – The function node configuration | the temperature hub

You can see in *Figure 10.22* that room_id is actually the sensor ID. We will have to map the sensor ID to the real room ID later in Grafana. You can also see that we now have the humidity information from the Bluetooth sensor, which we can get from the **BMP280 temperature** sensor installed in the garage.

At the end of the temperature hub node configuration, we will have something that looks like *Figure 10.23*.

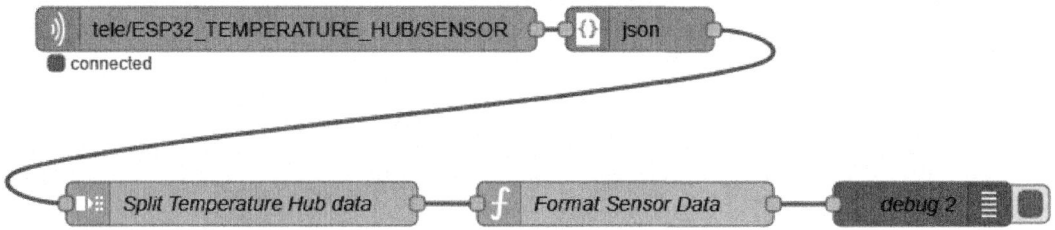

Figure 10.23 – The temperature hub data capture and format flow

Configuring the data to be stored in the InfluxDB database

The last configuration step is to connect the two flows created in the last two subsections to configure the data to be stored in the InfluxDB database. Fortunately, Node-RED has a single node that can do this for us. We will use the **influxdb out** node under the **storage** group and connect the outputs from the two flows previously created to the **influxdb out** node. We will double-click on this node and configure the parameters according to *Figure 10.24*:

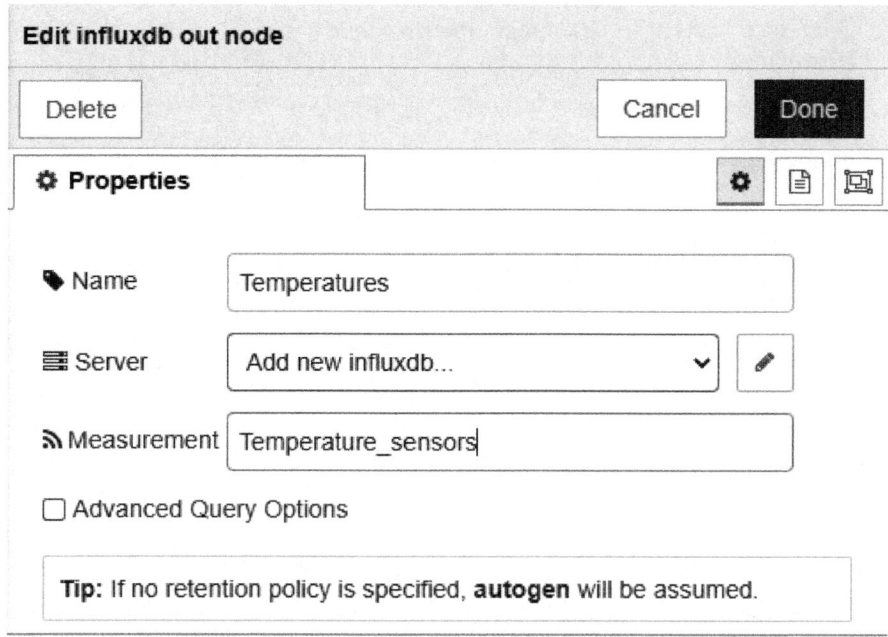

Figure 10.24 – The influxDB out node configuration | the temperature hub

We will fill out a friendly name for the node in the **Name** field, Temperatures. The **Measurement** field is the table in the InfluxDB database where we will store the data. We will see in the next section how this data will be stored. We will fill the **Measurement** field with the Temperature_sensors value. Next, we will have to add the InfluxDB server configuration. We will select **Add new influxdb** in the **Server** drop-down box and click on the **Pencil symbol** button. We will fill in the information according to *Figure 10.25*:

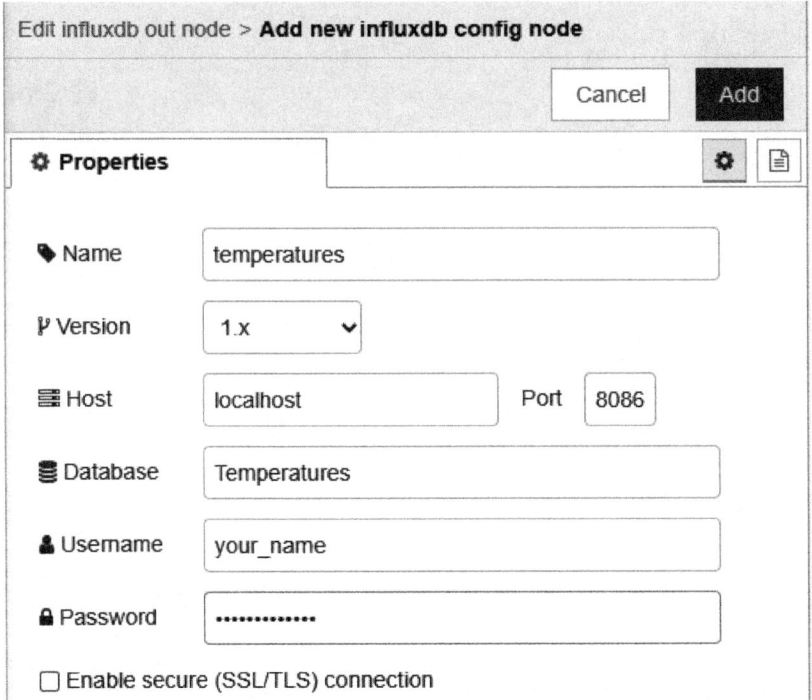

Figure 10.25 – The influxdb out node | the server configuration | the temperature hub

We will use the server connection name as temperatures. For the **Host** field, we will use the default InfluxDB server, localhost, and the default port, 8086. In the **Database** field, we will use Temperatures, which we created in *Chapter 7* during our InfluxDB overview. The username and password we will use is your_name and your_password. Click on the **Add** button after finishing with the configurations.

You will get an error message such as **Error: A 401 Unauthorized error occurred: {"error":"authorization failed"}**. This is because we did not configure the username and password on InfluxDB. This will be done in the next section.

Ultimately, our entire Node-RED flow will look like what is shown in *Figure 10.26*:

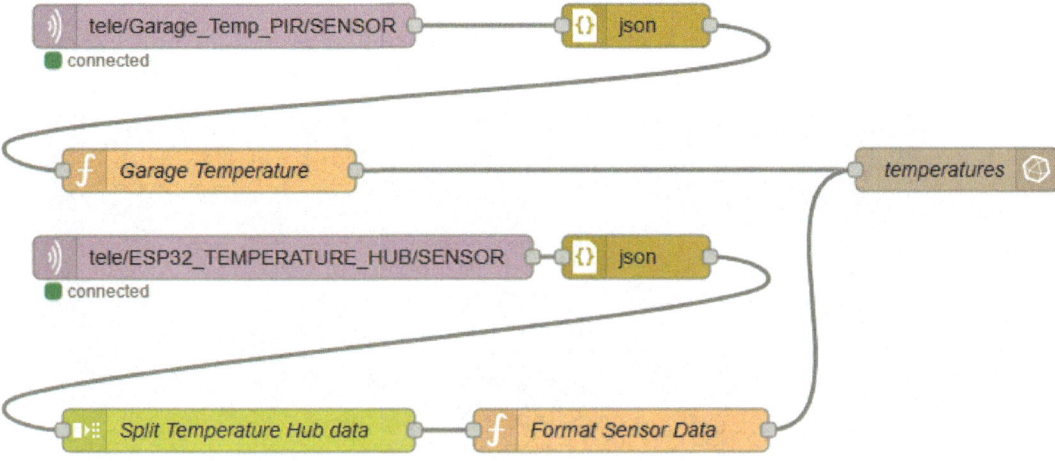

Figure 10.26 – The Node-RED complete flow | the five-temperature logger

We have finished the Node-RED configuration for the temperature logger, and we can now move on to the next section to configure the InfluxDB database to store data for the temperatures.

Storing data in a database using InfluxDB

We will have to configure two parameters to be able to start storing temperatures in the InfluxDB database:

- The InfluxDB database
- A user to access the database

We learned how the InfluxDB database works and how to create it in the *Installing and creating databases using InfluxDB* subsection in *Chapter 7*. I recommend you review that subsection, where I showed you how to create the *Temperatures* InfluxDB database we will use in this project.

Configuring a user to access the database is required to get credentials to store data in the InfluxDB database. We will do this by following these steps:

1. Open **Settings** | **Add-ons** | **InfluxDB** and click on the **OPEN WEB UI** button. The **Chronograf** interface will open.

2. Select the crown icon titled **InfluxDB Admin** in the Cronograf sidebar.

3. Click on the **Users** tab and then on the **+ Create User** button. In the **Create User** window, fill the **User Name** field with your_name, and in the **Password** field, add your_password. Click on the **Create** button. The your_name user will be created.

4. On the next screen, make sure to set permissions for writing and reading in the *Temperatures* database by clicking on the **WRITE** and **READ** buttons.

5. Click on the **Apply Changes** button in the top-right corner of the screen. Then, click on the **Exit** button in the top-right corner. The **Users** tab should look like *Figure 10.27*:

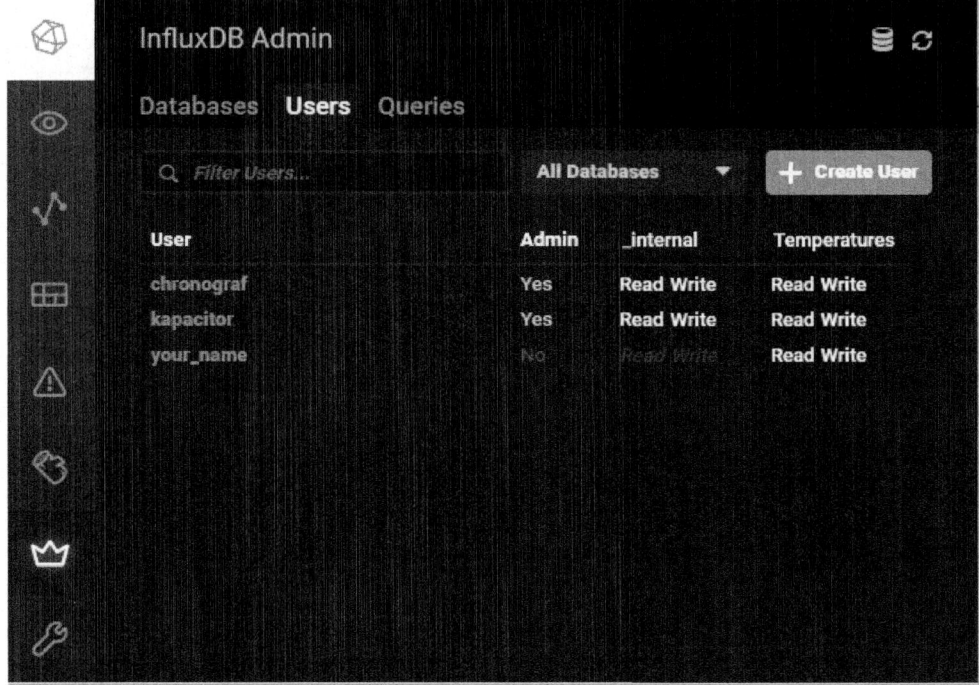

Figure 10.27 – The created your_name username

As you can see in *Figure 10.27*, the `your_name` user now has read and write access to the *Temperatures* database.

Surprisingly, there is nothing else to be configured in InfluxDB to store data in the *Temperatures* database. You should now return to Node-RED and verify that you will not continue to receive the `401` error type you got in the last section.

We can now manipulate the data in the database and present them in charts using Grafana. We will do this in the next section.

Presenting the InfluxDB data using Grafana

In this section, we will finalize the temperature logger setup by configuring Grafana, our chart manipulating tool, to get data from the InfluxDB database and present it in charts created in a

Dashboard environment. The first thing to do is to configure the database source where we will pull the data from. We will do that by following these steps:

1. Open Grafana by clicking on the link in the Home Assistant sidebar. Click on the Grafana **Configuration** menu (the gear icon) and then on **Data sources**. We will change the configuration we did in *Chapter 7* a little. Click on the **InFluxDB** data source. In the **Name** field, rename `InFluxDB` to `InFluxDB - Temperatures`. Make sure the **Database** field is filled with `Temperatures`. Fill in the **User** and **Password** fields with `your_name` and `your_password`, respectively. Click on the **Save & test** button. Now, as the database has data, you should get the message **datasource is working. 1 measurements found**.

2. Now comes the fun part of the chapter – data visualization. We will create a dashboard in Grafana that will present the temperature data for us. We will create a dashboard that will display four charts – **Inside Temperature**, **Outside Temperature**, **Inside Humidity**, and **Outside Humidity**. We can do that by clicking on **Dashboards** in the sidebar and then **New** | **New dashboard**. We will follow this sequence to create our first chart for **Inside Temperature**:

3. Click on the **+ Add visualization** button. In the **Query** tab, we will include the `InFluxDB - Temperatures` data source.

4. In the first query, we will assign the name `KID1`. I will populate the `KID1` query with this information in the fields:

   - **FROM**: `Temperature_sensors`
   - **WHERE**: `room_id = ATC6570e7`
   - **SELECT**: `field(temperature) mean()`
   - **GROUP BY**: `time(5m)`
   - **ORDER BY TIME**: `ascending`
   - **FORMAT AS**: `Time series`
   - **ALIAS**: `KID1_ROOM`

5. We will repeat *step 4*, creating three more queries by clicking in the **+ Query** button in the bottom of the screen, keeping the **FROM**, **SELECT**, **GROUP BY**, **ORDER BY TIME**, and **FORMAT AS** fields the same and populating the remaining ones according to *Table 10.1*:

Query name	WHERE	ALIAS
KID2	Room_id = ATC969ab4	KID2_ROOM
Kitchen	Room_id = ATCad7637	KITCHEN
Master Bedroom	Room_id = ATC5d22d1	MASTER BEDROOM

Table 10.1 – The values for different queries for the temperature and humidity charts

6. After creating these queries, we will name the **panel Title** as `Inside Temperature` and click on the **Save** button at the top right of the screen.

We will repeat the steps from 5 to 6 to create charts for **Inside Humidity** and include the same values as before, just changing the **SELECT** parameter to `field(humidity)`. We will fill the panel **Title** with `Inside Humidity` and click on the **Save** button to save the changes.

We will now create charts related to outside measurements. I consider the garage as outside because it is not part of my HVAC system. Also, my garage temperature sensor, based on the BMP280, does not have a humidity sensor, so the data in this chart will be just from my backyard. We will create new charts in the same dashboard by clicking on **Add | Visualization**. We will create the same queries as before by following *steps 5 to 6* but using the following parameters:

- **Outside temperature** and **Outside Humidity**:

  - **FROM**: `Temperature_sensors`
  - **WHERE**: `room_id = ATC19F133` for the backyard and `room_id = garage` for the garage
  - **SELECT**: `field(temperature) mean()` for the outside temperature chart and `field(humidity) mean()` for the outside humidity.
  - **GROUP BY**: `time(5m)`
  - **ORDER BY TIME**: `ascending`
  - **FORMAT AS**: `Time series`
  - **ALIAS**: `BACKYARD` for the backyard and `GARAGE` for the garage

We will name both created panels and charts `Outside temperature` and `Outside Humidity`, respectively, in the **Title** field. Save both panels by clicking on the **Save** button. By clicking on the **Apply** button after you click on **Save** button each time, you can see how your chart or panel is created and presents data. We will configure a name for the temperature dashboard created by clicking on the dashboard setting (the gear icon) and changing the **Name** parameter to `YourHome Temperature`. The dashboard, including the created four panels, is shown in *Figure 10.28*:

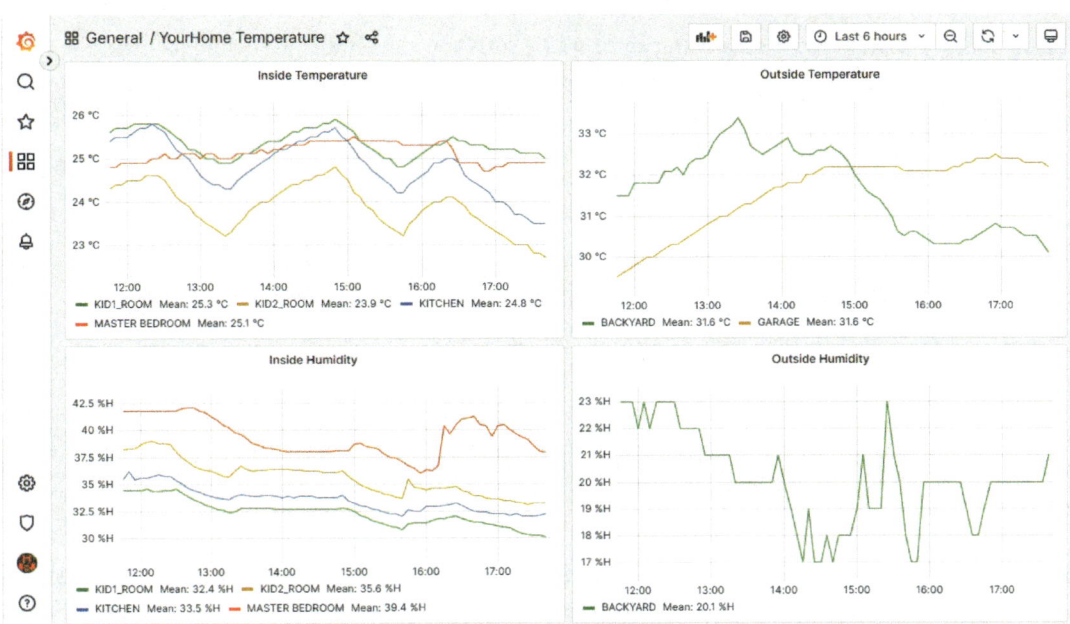

Figure 10.28 – The YourHome Temperature dashboard in Grafana

The charts in *Figure 10.28* display data from the last six hours, but you can adjust this time as you want. You can change the time interval to display the chart by clicking on the clock icon at the top-right of the screen and adjusting it. The time can range from 5 minutes to over a year or up to when you start to save data for your system. You can move the mouse cursor over the charts to see the values and time in more detail.

These temperature charts help me to make some decisions on how to adjust my HVAC system, based on inside and outside temperatures. The next step, as mentioned previously, is a plan to use these temperature values going forward to adjust the HVAC automatically and with a more uniform inside temperature for the entire house.

We can now finish this section and move on to the next, where we will add the Bluetooth temperature sensors to Home Assistant.

Using the five-zone temperature sensor in Home Assistant

When I first created this temperature logger application, I was able to use a configuration in Tasmota to automatically send data to Home Assistant independent of the **Tasmota integration**. This was done using the `setoption19 1` command in the **Tasmota console**. This option was deprecated, and it is not available in the new Tasmota installations anymore. The alternative solution for this issue is to add the temperature sensors manually in Home Assistant.

Tasmota reports the sensors data using an **MQTT JSON** message in the following format:

```
tele/ESP32_TEMPERATURE_HUB/SENSOR = {"Time":"2023-05-15T06:15:49","ATC
19f133":{"mac":"a4c13819f133","Temperature":25.7,"Humidity":30.0,"DewP
oint":6.8,"Battery":43,"RSSI":-82},"ATC969ab4":{"mac":"a4c138969ab4","
Temperature":24.6,"Humidity":41.1,"DewPoint":10.5,"Btn":0,"Battery":34
,"RSSI":-78},"TempUnit":"C"}
```

We will add the sensors manually by editing the `configuration.yaml` file and retrieving the data from the MQTT JSON message, using sentences in the following format:

```
mqtt:
    sensor:
      - name: "Backyard Temperature"
        state_topic: "tele/ESP32_TEMPERATURE_HUB/SENSOR"
        value_template: '{{ value_json.ATC19f133.Temperature }}'
        icon: mdi:thermometer-bluetooth
```

You will add this YAML code to `configuration.yaml` using the File editor add-on from the Home Assistant sidebar. The YAML code to add the sensors is basically so that Home Assistant can look for a `mqtt:` message and create and add information to `sensor:`, the name of which can vary according to where it is located (for example, `Backyard Temperature`). Also, Home Assistant should look for the MQTT message topic (`state_topic: "tele/ESP32_TEMPERATURE_HUB/SENSOR"`) and retrieve the temperature value from the `value_template:` sentence (`'{{ value_json. sensor_id.Temperature }}'`), where `sensor_id` is the sensor identification name. These sensors can be identified by `icon` using a `mdi:thermometer-bluetooth` type. We will have to create five instances of the same code to get all five temperature measurements from the Bluetooth sensors. The entire code for the `Configuration.yaml` file is available in the GitHub repository for *Chapter 10*.

The next step is to restart Home Assistant using **Developer tools | YAML**, and then click on the **RESTART** button. Click on the **CHECK CONFIGURATION** button first to see whether there is some problem with the `configuration.yaml` file.

We will now add these temperature sensors to the Home Assistant dashboard, creating two Entities cards, one for `Inside Temperature` and another for `Outside Temperature`. We will do that by following these steps:

1. Click on **Overview** from the Home Assistant sidebar. In the **Home** dashboard, click on the ellipsis (the three vertical dots at the top right of the screen) the **Edit Dashboard** option, and then the + **ADD CARD** button.

2. Select the **Entities** card, and fill in the fields according to the following:

   • **Title**: `Inside Temperature`

   • **Entity**: `Kid1_room Temperature`

- **Entity**: `Kid2_room Temperature`
- **Entity**: `kitchen Temperature`
- **Entity**: `Master Bedroom Temperature`

3. Click on the **SAVE** button to save the card and add it to the dashboard.

We will repeat *steps 1* to *3* to create another **Entities** card with the title `Outside Temperature` and entities `Backyard Temperature` and `GarageTempPIR BMP280 Temperature`. After these additions, we will click on the **DONE** button at the top-right of the screen. Ultimately, the **Inside Temperature** card will look like the one shown in *Figure 10.29*:

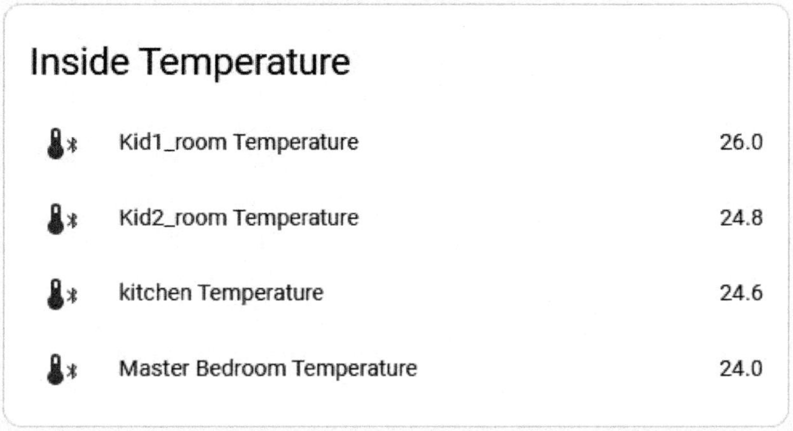

Figure 10.29 – The Inside Temperature card in Home Assistant

If you want to add the humidity data from the sensors, you just need to add five more sensor entities to the `configuration.yaml` file, changing the `value_template`: field to `value_json.sensor_id.Humidity`. I will leave this to you to practice or imagine how the code will look like.

That concludes this chapter, and I hope you have learned how to navigate through different applications by following this example.

Summary

In this chapter, we were exposed to different tools besides Home Assistant to create our second hands-on project, the five-zone temperature logger.

We started the chapter by understanding how the system architecture works. We configured the sensor hardware and software and then moved on to the home automation server, where we detailed how to parse the sensor data and send it to be stored in a database. Then, we did a proper configuration of the database so that the information could be stored correctly. Later, we learned how to configure a chart-based tool to create panels to display the temperature and humidity values from the sensors installed in different rooms at my home. We finished the chapter by showing you how to include the sensors information in Home Assistant by editing the configuration file. We had to do that as a workaround due to a deprecated feature in Home Assistant.

The next chapter will be the last of this book. It will introduce the latest trends and technologies in home automation to prepare us for what we expect to happen in the near future in this area. I hope you have enjoyed the book so far and will like our closing chapter.

11

The Road Ahead in Home Automation Technologies

We have explored **Home Assistant** in this book, which will open a lot of doors in the Home Automation world. **Home Automation** is much more than Home Assistant though. This last chapter is a wrap-up providing an overview of new technologies, trends, and other aspects that will contribute to the future of the Home Automation area. New concepts and information will help you be motivated, informed, and tuned into what is coming up in the area and how it might affect you.

I will review some of the common questions asked in forums and discussion lists related to Home Assistant and Home Automation. I will share how you can get new ideas for future projects to be implemented in your home.

I will compile a list of links you can follow for more information in the Home Automation area so you can extend your research and learn much more beyond this book. So, in summary, the following topics will be covered in this chapter:

- New technologies and trends in home automation
- Home automation and Home Assistant FAQs
- How to get ideas for projects to automate your home
- Additional resources

Technical requirements

For this chapter, you will not need any special type of knowledge unless you haven't read the previous chapters of the book. I will make many references to the previous chapters' contents and I recommend you return to the specified chapter to review what was learned.

New technologies and trends in home automation

I don't have a crystal ball to predict the future, but I used to follow the Home Automation market for quite some years and keep aware of the latest happenings in the area. I want to share with you my thoughts related to what is coming next in regard to trends and new technologies in the **Home Automation** area, and when it is the case, I will try to make links to Home Assistant. Let's split this subject into separate topics to be covered in the next subsections.

Using current and new technologies to interact with your home

The first topic I want to cover is related to how current and new technologies will affect the way you interact with your home. Devices and software technologies will support and improve the way you are interacting, and will interact, with your home. The next subsections will highlight some of them.

Using voice assistants

I didn't cover **voice assistants** such as **Amazon Alexa**, **Google Assistant**, and **Apple Siri** in this book, but they have already gained popularity in the home automation space. This trend is expected to continue with further advancements in natural language processing, allowing users to control and interact with their smart devices using voice commands more effectively. I use both Alexa and Google Assistant in my home not only to play music or answer questions but also to configure **routines**, which is what automations are called in Alexa. I also often use voice assistants to turn on and off plugs and lights.

Most sensors and actuators are compatible with these popular voice assistants and they will continue to be. In this book, we presented **Tasmota**, and even with this open source software, you can enable the use of voice assistants. You can do that by enabling the **Emulation** option by accessing **Configuration | Configure Other** from the Tasmota main menu and choosing the options according to *Figure 11.1*:

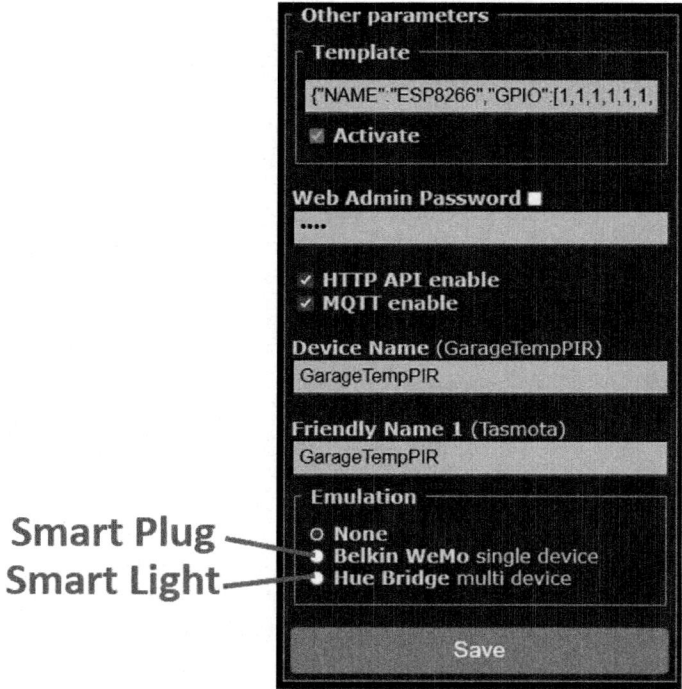

Figure 11.1 – Enabling the voice assistant interface on Tasmota

In *Figure 11.1*, depending on the option you selected, you will emulate a commercial **Smart Plug** or **Smart Light**, which can be detected and controlled by voice assistants.

Home Assistant supports voice assistants using an indirect feature called **Assist**. It was released in February 2023 and can be used on **Android** and **Apple** smartphones using the voice capture capabilities from these devices. Also, from **Home Assistant version 2023.5.2**, it is possible to manage voice assistants using an option from the sidebar menu and going to **Settings | Voice Assistants**. Using this option, it is possible to configure Assist; at the time of writing this book, a one-month free trial is being offered using a **Nabu Casa** subscription.

The next trend that is implemented in some Home Automation systems is the use of **Artificial Intelligence (AI)** and **machine learning**, which we will comment on in the next subsection.

Using AI and machine learning

AI and machine learning technologies are increasingly being integrated into home automation systems. These technologies enable devices to learn and adapt to user preferences, anticipate needs, and automate tasks accordingly. AI-powered voice assistants also improve natural language processing and provide more personalized interactions.

AI and machine learning can use the data information collected in your home and use it to optimize the household infrastructure, reduce utility bills, and improve services, making your day-to-day life easier and more efficient. It could be interesting to see, for example, how an AI model could be implemented in Home Assistant and suggest or even control the temperature in my house automatically based on the preferences in my setup over the years in summer and winter, and based on the data from the temperature sensors spread across my house.

I sometimes receive suggestions from the Alexa application on my cell phone like the one in *Figure 11.2*.

Create this Routine

Alexa can turn on master bedroom TV every day at 9:00 PM.

Figure 11.2 – Suggestion received by Alexa application

This routine is suggested by the Alexa application because I normally watch TV in my bedroom around 9:00 P.M. on the weekends and to do, that I ask Alexa in my master bedroom to turn on the smart plug, which we hacked with Tasmota in *Chapter 4*, that turns on the TV. I used to watch TV just on the weekends and sometimes on the weekdays. It will need some more data from Alexa to learn the days I watch TV to improve the suggestion in *Figure 11.2*, but it is a very good suggestion already.

Another way you get the benefit of AI is through chatbots. A popular example that is used widely is **ChatGPT** (`https://openai.com/chatgpt`). The way it works is simple: you ask and ChatGPT answers using a **Generative Pre-trained Transformer** (**GPT**) series of **Large Language Models** (**LLMs**); in other words, it can provide feedback for your question, providing a satisfactory answer that can be used in your Home Automation projects.

I recently got an idea about an automation I want to implement in my home, so I decided to test ChatGPT by asking it to create an automation in YAML for Home Assistant. It responded with code in YAML. The command prompt for ChatGPT was the following:

"Write a homeassistant automation in yaml that will use a motion sensor called master_bed to turn on a strip led light, but after midnight and up to 6:00AM. It has to be turned on for 1 minute and turned off after it. This automation should only run during the night time, unless it is disabled by a user button. This automation also should turn on a plug called coffeemachine if a motion sensor master_bed is detected and it is between 6:00 to 7:00AM."

It surprisingly provided me with code in YAML, as you can partially see in *Figure 11.3* and I have shared in the book's GitHub repository. I haven't implemented this automation at the time of writing this book, but I intend to do it soon.

MC write a homeassistant automation in yaml that will use a motion sensor called master_bed to turn on a strip led light, but after midnight and up to 6:00AM. It has to be turned on for 1 minute and turn off after it. This automation should only run during the night time, unless it is disabled by a user button. This automation also should turn on a plug called coffeemachine if a motion sensor master_bed is detected and it is between 6:00 to 7:00AM.

Sure! Here's a YAML configuration for the Home Assistant automation you described:

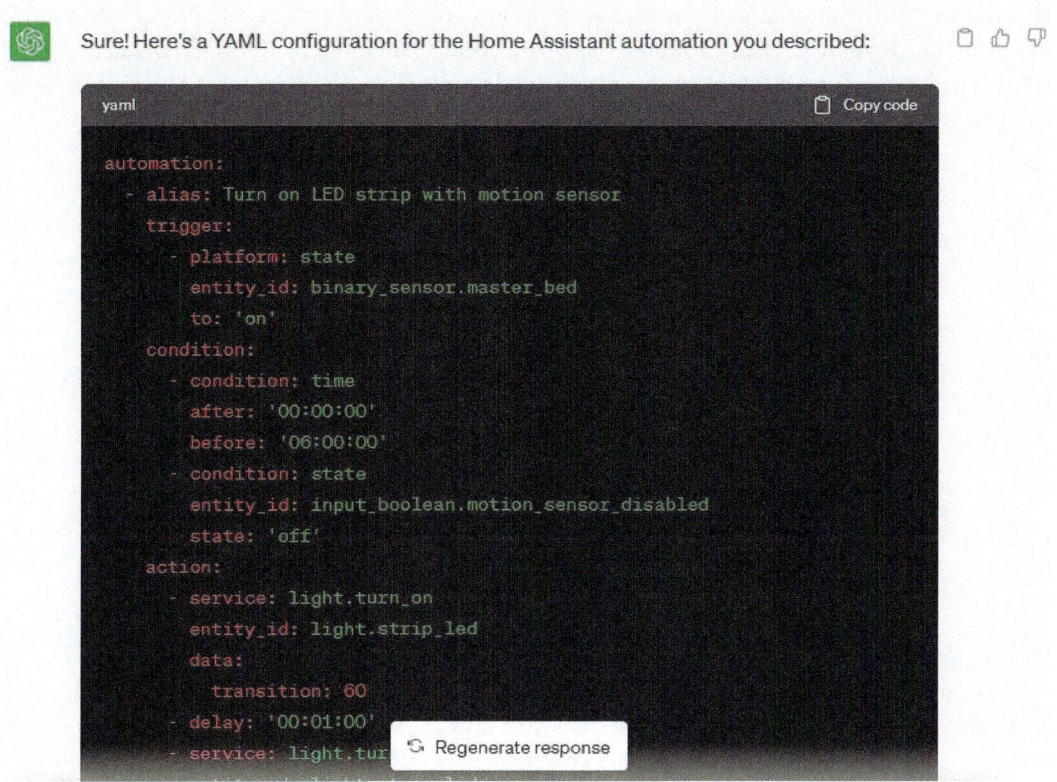

```yaml
automation:
  - alias: Turn on LED strip with motion sensor
    trigger:
      - platform: state
        entity_id: binary_sensor.master_bed
        to: 'on'
    condition:
      - condition: time
        after: '00:00:00'
        before: '06:00:00'
      - condition: state
        entity_id: input_boolean.motion_sensor_disabled
        state: 'off'
    action:
      - service: light.turn_on
        entity_id: light.strip_led
        data:
          transition: 60
      - delay: '00:01:00'
      - service: light.tur
```

⟳ Regenerate response

Figure 11.3 – ChatGPT creating YAML automation code based on my request

You can use your imagination and count on ChatGPT or any other AI tool to support you in the creation of your Home Automation system.

Unfortunately, Home Assistant does not officially implement AI and machine learning algorithms in its software distribution yet, but the data is collected and stored in the Home Assistant **Logbook**, which means it can be analyzed and automations can be proposed based on the day-to-day routines in your home in upcoming versions. We will follow closely until this moment happens.

The next subsection will discuss another trend, which is how you can interact with your home using **smartwatches**.

Using smartwatches within home automation

You can use Home Assistant to control your home using different types of devices—basically, any device that supports an internet browser connection. In 2022, I bought a smartwatch and was surprised that I can also access Home Assistant using it. This doesn't just apply to Home Assistant but also to other native applications related to smart sensors, plugs, and lights.

You can install the Home Assistant application on your smartwatch and configure it to receive notifications, or you can create **actions**, which are events generated by the smartwatch and can be attached to existing or new automations to control devices in your home. *Figure 11.4* shows the icon and two actions to control my home as an example:

 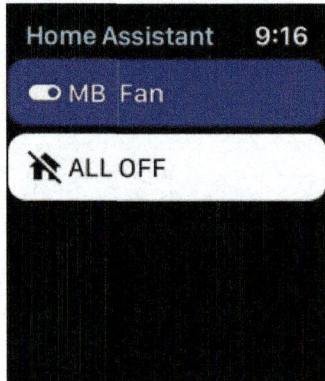

Figure 11.4 – Home Assistant accessed from an iOS smartwatch

You can see, on the left of *Figure 11.4*, the **Home Assistant** icon (the house symbol) and, on the right, two options, one referring to an event I created to toggle the fan in my bedroom and the other with the **ALL OFF** scene created in *Chapter 5*. You can see in Figure 11.4 right side that, in spite of the limited graphic resources and information you can configure to be managed by the smartwatch it still allows you to control devices from your home. It is worth mentioning that you can create **Complications**, which are any feature that is displayed on a watch face in addition to the time. These Complications can display, for example, the temperature of your backyard or one of your bedrooms on your watch face.

I believe the trend to add more resources or features to smartwatches to interact with your home will continue. The next subsection will cover what the new trends and technologies for devices to be used in your home might be.

Using different smart devices in your home

The popularity of **open hardware** started with **Arduino**, and lately the Wi-Fi modules **ESP8266** and **ESP32** have boosted the development of the **Internet of Things (IoT)** concept such that any device or appliance in your home can become *smart* and interconnected. This technology enables seamless automation and control through a centralized Home Automation server or smartphone app companion device. This system integration trend of adding more and more devices to your automated home will continue to grow.

The concept of IoT will evolve to different devices being incorporated into your home. Also, new features added to current **smart appliances** will lead to them becoming even more intelligent. It was released in 2023 an oven that has a smart camera capable of food recognition and burn detection and, using that, can recognize up to 80 different dishes and recommend cooking settings for each of them. This oven also can recommend meals based on your workout statistics, diet goals, and ingredients you have at home.

Consider a four-door Flex refrigerator recent released in 2023 that features a 32-inch vertical touchscreen that allows you to share photos, control your devices, make digital shopping lists, and watch TV. This is an example of an improved smart appliance device. Another example is an air conditioner with a 27-inch LCD screen that uses 70 percent less energy than the standard ones and can also operate at lower noise levels. This air conditioner exists.

Combined solutions have also started to be provided for Home Automation consumers. You can find, for instance, a front door that includes several devices embedded into it, such as power energy, LED lights, a smart lock, and a video doorbell. This convenient technology connected to your electrical and wireless home systems grants several applications to be created, such as motion-activated welcome lights or checking the door status, such as open, closed, locked, or unlocked.

Other appliances, including trash cans, washing machines, and even coffee makers, are being equipped with smart features. These appliances can be controlled remotely, have built-in sensors for improved efficiency, and can provide notifications and alerts. Integration of these devices to be compatible with voice assistants is also a trend.

Home automation systems are likely to integrate more features focused on health and wellness. This could include smart sleep systems, air quality monitoring, personalized lighting for circadian rhythm regulation, and integration with healthcare devices for remote health monitoring.

The use of robots in our homes is also something that we will continue to see more and more of. I have a vacuum cleaner robot at home that can be integrated with Home Assistant and I can build automations using it. Robots can be used for home or space navigation and robot companies manufacturers can use them to map your home to see whether you have room or enough furniture; it can eventually even make purchase suggestions. What I can also see is the increase of pet robots that can be used as voice assistants and also serve as smart toys, which can be useful for kids.

The list of new devices could be countless. Every year, new smart automation devices and innovations are launched, and this will never stop.

The next section will discuss an important and desirable aspect requested by Home Automation users: the use of a common communication protocol.

Using a single home automation communication protocol

One of the paradigms of this book is using an open source Home Automation ecosystem where you can use any type of device without any proprietary service. I should say that with the devices I use at home, I don't have any major issues with using them, but sometimes some device services will just work on the cloud, which means you will need to be connected to the internet to use them. So, the Home Automation market began to demand a way that this interoperability could be used seamlessly. In this context, **Matter** was created.

Matter (formerly known as **Project CHIP – Connected Home over IP**) is an emerging standard in the home automation industry that aims to improve interoperability and ease of use among smart home devices. Matter is backed by major industry players, including Apple, Google, and Amazon, which signifies its potential impact. It is maintained by the **Connectivity Standards Alliance (CSA)**. The first **Matter** specification(version 1.0) was released in October 2022, while version 1.1 was released in May 2023.

Matter's goal is to create a unified and secure connectivity standard for smart home devices, regardless of their brand or ecosystem. It aims to simplify device setup, enhance cross-compatibility, and ensure a more seamless user experience. By adopting a single communication protocol, Matter intends to overcome the issues of fragmentation and incompatibility that have been common in the smart home industry.

Figure 11.5 shows how Matter can fit in a network stack model we can use for Home Automation:

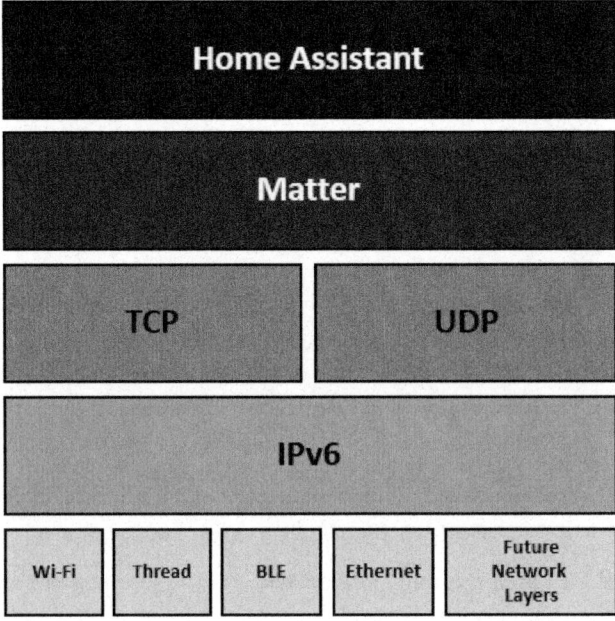

Figure 11.5 – Matter within the network stack model for home automation

In *Figure 11.5*, you can see **Home Assistant** sits on top of **Matter**. It has supported Matter through integration since release **2022.12**. **Matter** comes next and supports **TCP**, **UDP**, and **IPv6** as part of the **Transport and Internet layers**. The network access, which is the last line of blocks in *Figure 11.5*, is currently provided by four protocol types: **Wi-Fi**, **Thread**, **BLE**, and **Ethernet**. **Thread** is similar to **Zigbee** but runs over IP. **Bluetooth Low Energy** (**BLE**) is used with Matter just for commissioning or initial configuration to include the smart devices in the Matter network.

The introduction of Matter is generally seen as a positive development for home automation. Here's why:

- **Improved interoperability**: Matter's focus on interoperability means that consumers will have more freedom to choose smart home devices from different manufacturers, knowing they can work together seamlessly. This increased compatibility reduces consumer frustration and enhances the overall user experience.

- **Easier setup and control**: Matter aims to simplify the initial setup process for smart home devices, making it more user-friendly and intuitive. With Matter-certified devices, users can expect straightforward and consistent installation and control experiences, regardless of the specific ecosystem or platform they use.

- **Enhanced security**: Matter places a strong emphasis on security and privacy. The standard includes robust security measures, such as end-to-end encryption and secure device authentication, to protect user data and ensure secure communication between devices.

- **Industry collaboration**: The support and collaboration from major industry players, including Apple, Google, and Amazon, indicates a unified effort toward establishing a common standard. This collaboration increases the likelihood of widespread adoption and industry-wide compatibility.

While Matter shows great promise, it is still in the early stages of implementation. It will take time for Matter-certified devices to become widely available, and existing devices may require firmware updates or additional hardware to be compatible. However, with its potential to address interoperability challenges and improve the user experience, Matter has the potential to significantly advance the adoption and usability of home automation devices in the future.

In the next subsection, let's talk about the energy-efficient systems used for Home Automation.

Using energy-efficient systems

With a focus on energy conservation, home energy management systems allow homeowners to monitor and control their energy consumption. These systems provide real-time data on energy usage, enable the scheduling and automation of energy-intensive devices, and offer insights for optimizing energy efficiency.

LED lighting combined with smart controls is gaining traction. Smart lighting systems can be controlled remotely, programmed to adjust the brightness and color temperature, and integrated with other automation devices for energy efficiency and convenience.

With increasing environmental awareness, there is a growing emphasis on energy efficiency and sustainable living. Home automation systems will likely focus on optimizing energy consumption, using sensors and smart algorithms to automate lighting, heating, cooling, and other energy-intensive processes to reduce waste and lower utility bills.

We will see more and more homes integrated with solar panels and intelligent systems to manage them. You can make better use of energy by using it in your home, and if you have an electric vehicle, you can use this energy to charge it as well. Home Assistant can help you to manage your **grid system** by using the sidebar menu and the **Energy** option. *Figure 11.6* shows a bit about the first step of the **Electricity grid** configuration since I don't have it in my home yet:

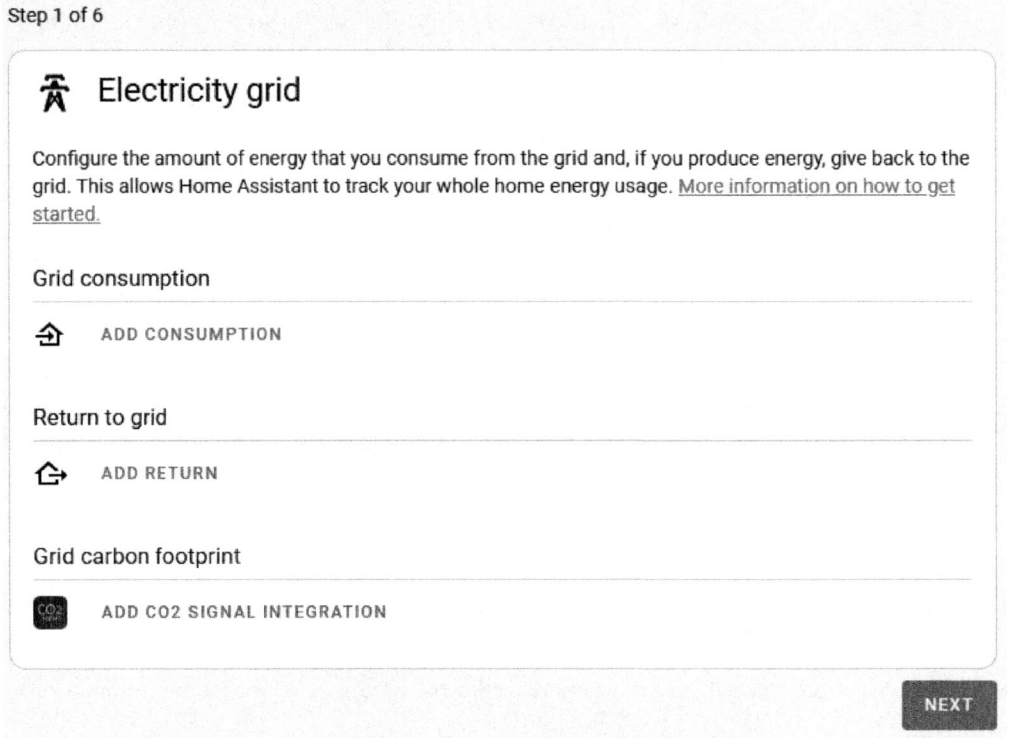

Figure 11.6 – Electricity grid configuration on Home Assistant

Using the **Energy** option partially presented in *Figure 11.6*, you will be able to track the energy flowing through your house. This is done in different ways; the most popular is to connect your energy meter to Home Assistant. This requires that your energy provider supports this feature. There are other ways to read the energy value directly from your meter using some projects available on the internet.

Another configuration that can be done using this menu is to configure and track the amount of energy you return to the energy provider company. This can be useful for people with solar panels installed in their homes. More information about the **Energy** menu can be found at `https://www.home-assistant.io/docs/energy/electricity-grid/`.

Another trend in the Home Automation area is the use of security. We will explore this subject in the next subsection.

Including security in home automation

The ability to control home automation systems remotely is becoming more important, as people become more mobile and spend less time at home. Home automation systems can be controlled using smartphones and other mobile devices, allowing users to adjust settings, receive alerts, and monitor their homes from anywhere in the world. **Remote systems control** is important but brings the concern of security and privacy if not handled properly. Expect advancements in technologies such as **biometric authentication**, **encrypted communication protocols**, and **robust security measures** to protect smart homes from cyber threats and unauthorized access.

A **Virtual Private Network** (**VPN**) is a handy tool to ensure the security of the data in your home. Home Assistant provides advanced VPN add-on tools such as **ZeroTier**. For more information about ZeroTier and how to install it, visit this link:

Talking about security-related subjects, home security systems have evolved with advanced technologies. Features such as facial recognition, motion detection, and remote monitoring through cameras and sensors provide enhanced security. Integration with smartphones enables users to receive alerts and control security systems remotely. I believe with technological advancement, more devices will be created to support this area.

These are the hot topics that I believe will be trending for the next few years in the Home Automation space. Next, let's answer some questions about the Home Automation world related to Home Assistant.

Home Automation and Home Assistant FAQs

In this section, let's review some common questions that could be asked by users who want to quickly learn about Home Automation systems and Home Assistant. I will refer to some chapters where we explored some specific questions related to each main subject.

Home automation FAQ

Let's first explore the Home Automation subject by answering some common questions related to it:

- **What is home automation?**

    Home automation refers to the use of smart technology and devices to control and automate various functions and tasks in your home. It allows you to remotely manage and monitor different aspects of your home, such as lighting, heating and cooling, security systems, appliances, and entertainment systems.

- **What are the benefits of home automation?**

  We explored this in more detail in the *Benefits of having an automated home* section in *Chapter 1*. Home automation offers several benefits, including increased convenience, energy efficiency, improved home security, and enhanced comfort. It allows you to control your home remotely, automate routine tasks, save energy by optimizing the use of appliances, and provide added security through smart locks, cameras, and alarms.

- **What devices can be controlled through home automation?**

  This question was explained and exemplified in *Chapters 1*, *3*, and *4*. **Home Automation systems** can control a wide range of devices, such as lights, thermostats, door locks, security cameras, smart appliances, speakers, entertainment systems, and even automated curtains or blinds. Many of these devices can be integrated into a single smart home platform for centralized control.

- **How do I control my home automation system?**

  Home automation systems can be controlled through various methods, including Smart Home software platforms such as Home Assistant, smartphone apps provided by device manufacturers, voice commands via virtual assistants such as Amazon Alexa or Google Assistant, dedicated control panels or touchscreens, remote controls, and even through your computer or smartwatch, as we saw earlier in this chapter, in the *Using smartwatches within home automation* subsection.

- **Is home automation secure?**

  Home automation systems have become more secure in recent years. However, it's important to take appropriate security measures, such as using strong and unique passwords for your devices, regularly updating firmware and software, and ensuring your network is protected with a strong password and firewall. Additionally, opt for devices and systems from reputable manufacturers that prioritize security. You can make your system more secure if you use a local network.

- **Can I integrate different brands of smart devices into my home automation system?**

  Yes, many home automation systems are designed to be compatible with a wide range of smart devices from different manufacturers. Look for systems that support common protocols such as **Zigbee**, **Z-Wave**, or Wi-Fi, as they provide greater interoperability and allow you to mix and match devices from various brands.

- **Do I need professional installation for a home automation system?**

  The complexity of the installation process depends on the specific home automation system you choose. Some systems are designed for DIY installation and offer user-friendly setup processes, while others may require professional assistance. Consider your comfort level with technology and the complexity of your desired automation setup to determine whether professional installation is necessary. Always keep in mind that electric installation could represent serious life-threatening hazards if not properly handled. Consult an electrician if you have never done this installation before.

- **Can I expand my home automation system over time?**

    Yes, one of the advantages of home automation is its scalability. You can start with a basic system and add more devices and features as your needs and budget allow. Most automation systems, such as Home Assistant, are designed to be expandable, allowing you to incorporate new devices and integrate additional functionalities seamlessly.

I hope these questions have clarified the vast subject of Home Automation a bit. The intent here is to give you a brief opportunity to make some connections with what was learned in previous chapters and to solidify the learned content.

Let's move on to the next subsection, which will cover some frequently asked questions related to Home Assistant.

Home Assistant FAQ

We will try here to answer common questions related to Home Assistant. This will be just the beginning to help you to connect the remaining dots after reading the previous chapters of this book. Let's get started:

1. **What is Home Assistant?**

    Home Assistant is an open source smart home platform that allows you to control and automate your smart devices and services. It acts as a central hub for your smart home, providing a unified interface to monitor, control, and integrate various devices and platforms. We cover Home Assistant basics in *Chapter 2*.

2. **How does Home Assistant work?**

    Home Assistant works by connecting to your smart home devices and services through different communication protocols, such as Wi-Fi, Zigbee, and Z-Wave. It gathers data from these devices and platforms and provides a user-friendly interface to control and automate them based on your preferences.

3. **Is Home Assistant compatible with different smart home devices?**

    Yes, Home Assistant supports a wide range of smart home devices and platforms. It has extensive compatibility with popular brands and protocols, allowing you to integrate devices from different manufacturers into a single ecosystem. You can check the official Home Assistant website (`https://www.home-assistant.io/`) or community forums for a list of supported devices.

4. **How do I install Home Assistant?**

    Home Assistant offers multiple installation methods, as we have covered in the book, including running it on Raspberry Pi, which was explored in *Chapter 2*, on a virtual machine, or as a containerized application explored in *Chapter 8*.

5. **Can I control or access Home Assistant remotely?**

Yes, you can control and access your Home Assistant installation remotely. It supports remote access through its companion mobile app or by securely accessing the platform using a web browser. You can manage your smart home, check its status, and perform actions from anywhere as long as you have an internet connection. We explored how to access Home Assistant remotely in *Chapter 7* using **Duck DNS** and this chapter, when we mentioned **ZeroTier** in the *Including security in home automation* subsection.

6. **Can I create automations and routines with Home Assistant?**

Yes, Home Assistant provides powerful automation capabilities, as we fully explored in *Chapter 5* and provided additional examples of in *Chapter 9*. You can create automations and routines using its automation editor or by writing YAML-based automation scripts. This allows you to define actions based on specific triggers, conditions, and time-based events to automate tasks and enhance your smart home experience.

7. **Is Home Assistant secure?**

We didn't comment on this much in this book, but Home Assistant takes security very seriously and provides several measures to protect your smart home data. It supports encryption for communication with devices and platforms, and you can secure your Home Assistant installation with **Hypertext Transfer Protocol Secure (HTTPS)** and **Secure Sockets Layer (SSL)/Transport Secure Layer (TLS)** certificates. Regular updates and community support ensure that security vulnerabilities are addressed promptly.

8. **Can I extend the functionality of Home Assistant?**

Yes, Home Assistant is highly extensible. It has a vast library of add-ons, as we saw in *Chapter 7*, integrations, as explored in *Chapter 6*, and community-developed custom components that allow you to integrate with additional devices, services, and platforms. You can also create your own custom integrations using the developer tools and APIs provided.

I hope these 16 questions support you in answering some last-minute questions or doubts about Home Automation or Home Assistant.

The next section will be helpful in inspiring you on how to get project ideas for automating your home.

How to get ideas for projects to automate your home

Think about your daily routine, what you do every day in the same way. Do an assessment of what you need and what could make your life easier. Try to identify areas where automation could improve convenience, efficiency, or security. Consider tasks you frequently perform and areas where you would like to have more control or automation. I used this idea to automate the front lights of my house. It is something I want to turn on every day but not at the same time, so it is triggered by the sunset.

Another approach is to research the available technologies. Explore the wide range of smart home devices and automation technologies available on the market. Look into smart lighting systems, thermostats, security cameras, door locks, voice assistants, and other devices that align with your needs and interests.

You can also browse online resources by visiting websites, blogs, and forums dedicated to smart home automation. Follow people and companies who talk about home automation products on social media. These platforms often feature project ideas, **Do It Yourself** (**DIY**) guides, and community discussions that can spark inspiration.

Seek inspiration from others by talking to friends, family, or neighbors who have already automated their homes. Learn from their experiences, challenges, and successes. They might have unique ideas or insights that could apply to your home.

Think about typical automation scenarios that can be useful for many homeowners, such as automated lighting based on occupancy, setting up routines for the morning or bedtime, integrating security cameras and motion sensors, or creating an entertainment system with voice control. This can bring clear and well-developed ideas for what you want to do.

As we have suggested in this book, start with a minimal system and prioritize your needs. Begin with smaller automation projects and basic tasks that align with your budget, skills, and immediate necessities. Prioritize projects that provide the most value or solve specific pain points in your daily life. As you gain experience and confidence, you will become more comfortable and be able to expand and tackle more complex technological projects.

Join Home Automation communities and engage with people and forums online dedicated to smart home automation. These communities are filled with enthusiasts and experts who can provide guidance, ideas, and troubleshooting assistance. Participating in these communities can lead to new ideas and insights and help you to develop your project.

Think of your house as a laboratory! Experiment and iterate! Home automation is a dynamic field with evolving technologies. Don't be afraid to experiment and try out different devices, setups, and automation rules. Learn from your experiences, make adjustments, and iterate to find what works best for your home and lifestyle. Enjoy the process of transforming your home into a smart, automated paradise!

These are my contributions to help you develop ideas for your next Home Automation project. Put them into practice so you will see the development and creation process begin.

In the next and last section of the book, I will provide a list of useful links for internet resources related to Home Automation and Home Assistant.

Additional resources

Everything I learned throughout the years related to Home Automation and Home Assistant is included in the next links. Other links and resources are spread throughout the book's chapters.

Websites

Websites are interesting resources for learning because their content is static, so you can work at your own pace to review information such as a tutorial. They are nice too because they can give written information about configuring and programming code, so you can follow and copy it if required.

In the next subsections, I have provided some website resources divided into three main subjects, so you can navigate and explore each of them further.

Home automation

These are websites that discuss various aspects of Home Automation. They are very generic and come in different formats, such as blogs, articles, and projects:

- `https://hometoys.com/category/smart-home/`: This website provides different articles related to Home Automation. It is good to get insights about Home Automation or about equipment and devices to be used to automate your home.
- `https://hometechhacker.com/category/smarthome/`: This website provides reviews of equipment and smart devices used to automate homes. You can join their community email to receive exclusive content and updates.
- `https://smarthomehobby.com/`: This website provides articles related to Home Automation, Alexa-compatible devices, and Home Assistant guides. It also has smart home device reviews.
- `https://smarthomescene.com/`: This site has sections dedicated to blogs, news, guides, Home Assistant, device reviews, and DIY. The DIY area has some projects you can try to automate your home.
- `https://blakadder.com/`: This site has Home Automation articles, written since 2020, exploring different subjects, such as Tasmota, smart device reviews, Zigbee, how-tos, and DIY. It also hosts a Tasmota device templates repository, `https://templates.blakadder.com/`, where you can find commercial devices compatible with Tasmota, as discussed in *Chapter 4*.
- `https://www.patrick-blom.de/diy-projects/`: This site provides generic DIY projects. You can try some of them in your home.

Home Assistant

I have provided just a few websites relating to Home Assistant, one being very technical and the other where you can find most of the resources you will need for Home Assistant:

- `https://developers.home-assistant.io/`: Dedicated website for Home Assistant developers. You can learn about how Home Assistant is structured, how to build new integrations to Home Assistant, and how to develop the user interface of Home Assistant.

- `https://www.awesome-ha.com/`: As the website defines, it is a curated list of awesome Home Assistant resources, including additional software, tutorials, custom integration, add-ons, custom dashboard cards and plugins, cookbooks, and example setups. It is worth visiting the **Online Resources** section, which contains plenty of other links to Home Automation, tech, DIY, IoT, and Home Assistant websites.

Smart device manufacturers

These websites are more for reference since most of them were mentioned in previous chapters. There are links to the main players in the Home Automation area at the time of writing, which are Google and Amazon:

- `https://itead.cc/smart-home/`: The website for the manufacturer of Sonoff BasicR2 – Itead. We hacked this smart device in *Chapter 4*.

- `https://www.espressif.com/`: The website for the manufacturer of ESP8266 and ESP32. These devices were used in all hands-on projects throughout the book.

- `https://www.raspberrypi.com/`: The website for Raspberry Pi, which was used as our Home Automation server in *Chapter 2*.

- `https://store.google.com/us/category/connected_home`: The website for all smart devices developed by Google.

- `https://www.amazon.com/b?ie=UTF8&node=9818047011`: The website for all smart devices developed by Amazon.

- `https://www.tuya.com/`: The website for a company that offers a cloud platform that connects devices via IoT. It is widely used among smart home devices.

YouTube channels

YouTube is, in my opinion, the best way to learn content online. This is because there are some very well-produced YouTube channels that summarize the content in a short period of time. For the most part, they are like classes where the YouTubers are teachers that provide information to the students or the public using real and live examples. They are very practical and, as said, a valuable resource that will help you to learn more about the subjects covered in this book.

As you will see, this is the most comprehensive list of resources I have provided. I have listed with each channel what I learned in general and how it helped me to author this book.

Home automation and Home Assistant

These YouTube channels mix home automation and Home Assistant content and were mostly where I learned significant content explained in this book:

- `https://www.youtube.com/@KPeyanski`: Kiril is one of the reviewers of this book and part of my knowledge of Home Assistant is thanks to him. He has more than 300 videos, most of them related to smart homes, Home Automation, and Home Assistant. He has a website too: `https://peyanski.com`.

- `https://www.youtube.com/@AndreasSpiess`: I have to say that I've learned a lot from Andreas tutorials and reviews related to sensors, ESP8266, Arduino, Raspberry Pi, and ESP32. He has more than 400 videos on his channel and I learned how to use the Home Automation IOTstack with one of them. He also inspired me to use the IoT software in *Chapter 10* when we created a five-zone temperature logger.

- `https://www.youtube.com/@TheHookUp`: This channel is very popular, which you can see by the number of subscribers. It has more than 150 videos related to smart home product reviews and tutorials

- `https://www.youtube.com/@digiblurDIY`: This channel has more than 300 videos focused on Home Automation in general.

- `https://www.youtube.com/@DrZzs`: This channel has an impressive number (almost 600!) of videos in the area of Home Automation area. Through this channel, I learned how to use the WLED software covered in *Chapter 9*.

- `https://www.youtube.com/@IntermitTech`: This is a channel with more than 400 videos that discuss LED lighting, custom (DIY) controllers, energy storage, Home Automation, home networking, and more. Through this channel, I learned about Bluetooth thermometers and how to change their firmware, which was covered in *Chapter 10*.

- `https://www.youtube.com/@mostlychris`: This channel has almost 200 videos, about technology, Home Automation, and simulation flights. Through this channel, I also learned about `https://www.youtube.com/@IntermitTech` Bluetooth thermometers and how to change their firmware.

- `https://www.youtube.com/@BeardedTinker`: This is a channel with more than 300 videos dedicated to home automation, DIY sensors, 3D printing, and so on.

- `https://www.youtube.com/@EverythingSmartHome`: This is an interesting channel I discovered recently. It has more than 180 videos and has general tech reviews, guides, and step-by-step DIY projects. Through some videos on this channel, I learned more about the dashboard customization covered in *Chapter 6*.

- `https://www.youtube.com/@JuanMTech`: This channel provides tips and guides related to smart home devices and home automation software. I also learned, in some videos on this channel, details about dashboard customization.

- `https://www.youtube.com/@SmartHomeMakers`: This YouTube channel has more than 200 videos related to home automation, internet security, and home multimedia streaming. Through this channel, I learned about templates in Home Assistant, which was briefly covered in *Chapter 9*.

- `https://www.youtube.com/@PatteTech`: This is a Brazilian Portuguese YouTube channel. It is one of the pioneer Home Automation YouTube channels, with more than 600 videos. It provides plenty of smart home tips and product reviews.

Home Assistant-specific

The YouTube channel in this section is for Home Assistant-sp:

- `https://www.youtube.com/@home_assistant`: This is the official YouTube channel for Home Assistant

Smart device manufacturers

The YouTube channels in this subsection are official channels for some device manufacturers used in this book:

- `https://www.youtube.com/@EspressifSystems`: This is the official YouTube channel for Espressif Systems, the manufacturers of ESP8266 and ESP32

- `https://www.youtube.com/raspberrypi`: This is the official YouTube channel for all Raspberry Pi resources

Online forums and communities

Online forums and communities are useful sources to exchange ideas, find solutions for problems in your system, seek information, and so on. They are organized and there are rules participants need to follow to better coordinate the discussion flow. I have provided a few of them based on their level of importance in each of the main relevant subjects of the book.

Home automation and Home Assistant

These forums and communities are where you will find more discussions around Home automation and Home Assistant:

- `https://www.reddit.com/r/homeautomation/`: Reddit is an online community where users can submit, discuss, and vote on various types of content. This specific link is for home automation discussion topics.

- `https://community.home-assistant.io/`: This is a dedicated online community for Home Assistant.

- `https://homeassistantbrasil.com.br/`: This is a specific online community for Home Assistant in Brazilian Portuguese.

Smart device manufacturers

This forum is specific for discussions around a device used in this book and it is maintained by the device manufacturer:

- `https://forums.raspberrypi.com/`: Official discussion forum for Raspberry Pi

Podcasts

Podcasts are resources you can listen to in various places, which is conducive to multitasking. As you cannot see the content, usually the information provided by them is mostly news, interviews, and generic product reviews. I recommend podcasts so you can be aware of what is happening in the Home Automation industry.

Home automation

These podcasts listed here are home automation related:

- `https://podcasters.spotify.com/pod/smarthome`: This podcast covers interviews and product reviews in the Home Automation area
- `https://smarthomesurgery.buzzsprout.com/`: This podcast covers interviews with industry leaders, peers, and influencers
- `https://player.fm/series/hometechfm`: This podcast has more than 440 episodes covering news, opinions, insights, and advice on the smart home subject

Home Assistant

This podcast listed is Home Assistant related:

- `https://player.fm/series/home-assistant-podcast`: This podcast features the newest Home Assistant releases and the latest Home Automation news. It also includes interviews with guests who use or contribute to Home Assistant.

Books

I have also found a few books related to Home Automation. I have listed them here:

- *Smart Home Hacks: Tips & Tools for Automating Your House* – `https://www.amazon.com/Smart-Home-Hacks-Tools-Automating/dp/0596007221`: I have a hard copy of this book. It was released in 2005 when we barely had Wi-Fi communication. The book is based on X10 devices and HomeSeer software. It was a good source of learning in my first Home Automation projects.

- *Advanced Home Automation Using Raspberry Pi* – `https://www.amazon.com/Advanced-Home-Automation-Using-Raspberry/dp/1484272730`: This book was released in 2021. I haven't read it but based on the title and the index, it seems the focus is exploring the Home Automation subject using Raspberry Pi. There is one chapter that discusses Home Assistant.

- *Home Automation with Raspberry Pi: Projects Using Google Home, Amazon Echo, and Other Intelligent Personal Assistants* – `https://www.amazon.in/Home-Automation-Raspberry-Intelligent-Assistants/dp/1260440354`: I haven't read this book, but based on the title and preface, it seems to be similar to the previous book where the focus is on Raspberry Pi and interfaces to voice assistants.

The internet is full of content; these links are just a small sample to start your research and learn more about Home Automation, Home Assistant, and device manufacturers.

We can now close this chapter and the content of this book. I believe this is not the end but just the beginning of your journey in the Home Automation world. I believe I shared most of my personal experience of automating my home with you. You now have the confidence to build or improve your own system.

Summary

In this chapter, we wrapped up the content of the book by discussing some trends and new technologies that are being developed or created that you will start to see in the next few years. Some of them already exist and they will continue to be improved over time. These insights will help you to follow the improvements and enjoy the evolution of Home Automation.

We also provided **Frequently Asked Questions (FAQ)** sections on Home Automation and Home Assistant, where we referenced where the topics were discussed in the book. This was a tentative way to solidify the knowledge learned throughout the chapters of the book. Please review the referenced chapters in the book to make sure you understand what was discussed in the answers for the questions.

Continuing the chapter, we provided a small section promoting the process to create your own home automation ideas. Following the advice in this section will help you to better define your needs and priorities when automating your home. This section will also help you to come up with the automations required in your home.

We concluded the chapter by providing a list of links to resources. I have used most of these resources and hope they can be used as a starting reference for you as well to grow your knowledge even more.

This paragraph marks the end of this book, but not the end of the possibilities that lie ahead of you for automating your home using Home Assistant and other software and hardware. You now have the knowledge, imagination, and motivation to create and evolve your system. So, this technical odyssey is just beginning. Good luck in your journey and thank you for following me on this amazing trajectory.

Index

Symbols

www.packtpub.com

Subscribe to our online digital library for full access to over 7,000 books and videos, as well as industry leading tools to help you plan your personal development and advance your career. For more information, please visit our website.

Why subscribe?

- Spend less time learning and more time coding with practical eBooks and Videos from over 4,000 industry professionals

- Improve your learning with Skill Plans built especially for you

- Get a free eBook or video every month

- Fully searchable for easy access to vital information

- Copy and paste, print, and bookmark content

Did you know that Packt offers eBook versions of every book published, with PDF and ePub files available? You can upgrade to the eBook version at packtpub.com and as a print book customer, you are entitled to a discount on the eBook copy. Get in touch with us at customercare@packtpub.com for more details.

At www.packtpub.com, you can also read a collection of free technical articles, sign up for a range of free newsletters, and receive exclusive discounts and offers on Packt books and eBooks.

Other Books You May Enjoy

If you enjoyed this book, you may be interested in these other books by Packt:

Architecting and Building High-Speed SoCs

Mounir Maaref

ISBN: 978-1-80181-099-9

- Understand SoC FPGAs' main features, advanced buses and interface protocols
- Develop and verify an SoC hardware platform targeting an FPGA-based SoC
- Explore and use the main tools for building the SoC hardware and software
- Build advanced SoCs using hardware acceleration with custom IPs
- Implement an OS-based software application targeting an FPGA-based SoC
- Understand the hardware and software integration techniques for SoC FPGAs
- Use tools to co-debug the SoC software and hardware
- Gain insights into communication and DSP principles in FPGA-based SoCs

Internet of Things for Smart Buildings

Harry G. Smeenk

ISBN: 978-1-80461-986-5

- Discover what's a smart building and how IoT enables smart solutions
- Uncover how IoT can make mechanical and electrical systems smart
- Understand how IoT improves workflow tasks, operations, and maintenance
- Explore the components and technology that make a smart building
- Recognize how to put together components to deploy smart applications
- Build your smart building stack to design and develop smart solutions

Packt is searching for authors like you

If you're interested in becoming an author for Packt, please visit `authors.packtpub.com` and apply today. We have worked with thousands of developers and tech professionals, just like you, to help them share their insight with the global tech community. You can make a general application, apply for a specific hot topic that we are recruiting an author for, or submit your own idea.

Share Your Thoughts

Now you've finished *Building Smart Home Automation Solutions with Home Assistant*, we'd love to hear your thoughts! Scan the QR code below to go straight to the Amazon review page for this book and share your feedback or leave a review on the site that you purchased it from.

`https://packt.link/r/1801815291`

Your review is important to us and the tech community and will help us make sure we're delivering excellent quality content.

Download a free PDF copy of this book

Thanks for purchasing this book!

Do you like to read on the go but are unable to carry your print books everywhere?

Is your eBook purchase not compatible with the device of your choice?

Don't worry, now with every Packt book you get a DRM-free PDF version of that book at no cost.

Read anywhere, any place, on any device. Search, copy, and paste code from your favorite technical books directly into your application.

The perks don't stop there, you can get exclusive access to discounts, newsletters, and great free content in your inbox daily

Follow these simple steps to get the benefits:

1. Scan the QR code or visit the link below

https://packt.link/free-ebook/9781801815291

2. Submit your proof of purchase
3. That's it! We'll send your free PDF and other benefits to your email directly

Printed in Great Britain
by Amazon

55893467R00198